Athanasius Kircher's
Theatre of the World

ANNO ÆTATIS LXII ⅭⅠↃ ⅠↃ Ⅽ LXIV. IHS P. ATHANASIUS KIRHERUS FULDENSIS E SOCIETATE IESU ANNO

Fruſtrà vel Pictor, vel Vates dixerit. HIC EST:
Et vultum, et nomen terra ſcit Antipodum.

Jacobus Albanus Ghibbeſius M.D.
in Rom: Sapientia Eloq: Prof.

Athanasius Kircher's Theatre of the World

Joscelyn Godwin

With 410 illustrations

Thames & Hudson

Page 1 Harpocrates, god of contemplation, from *Obeliscus Pamphilius* (see p. 261, Ill. 14.6).

Page 2 Portrait of Kircher, aged 62 (*China Illustrata*, opposite folio *5).

Page 6 The anatomy of the voice, from *Musurgia Universalis*, Volume 1 (see p. 158, Ill. 9.3).

First published in the United Kingdom in 2009 by Thames & Hudson Ltd, 181A High Holborn, London WC1V 7QX

thamesandhudson.com

British Library Cataloguing-in-Publication Data
A catalogue record for this book is available from the British Library

ISBN 978-0-500-25860-6

Printed and bound in China by SNP Leefung Printers Ltd

Table of Contents

Fig. IX

Fig. VIII

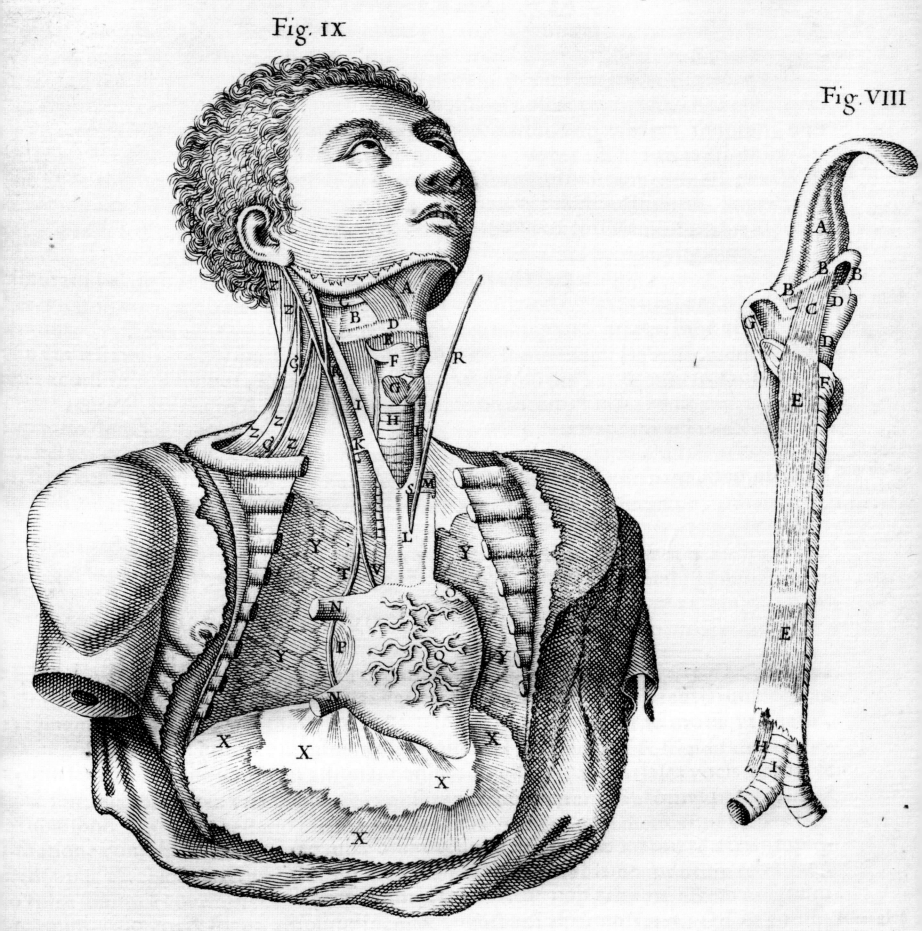

Preface

In May 2002, I was eating breakfast in a Chicago motel when a ribbon appeared on the television screen: 'Was Athanasius Kircher the coolest guy ever, or what?' It seemed for a moment that I had slipped into a parallel universe, in which it was not politicians and catastrophes that made the morning headlines, but subjects of real interest to me.

It turned out that Kircher's four-hundredth birthday was to be celebrated by a symposium at New York University,[1] organized by Professors Anthony Grafton of Princeton and Paula Findlen of Stanford, eminent scholars who had come to Kircher comparatively late in their careers. I had come to him early in mine, with a book in Thames & Hudson's 'Art and Imagination' series (*Athanasius Kircher: A Renaissance Man and the Quest for Lost Knowledge*, 1979), which, for all its shortcomings, was the first overview of Kircher for the majority of its readers in English, French, Spanish, German and Japanese. Gradually others discovered him, until with the new millennium the trickle of Kircheriana has become a flood. Moreover, most of these studies have all the freshness of their authors' venture into virgin territory, and are consequently a delight to read. This is the case with the splendid collective volumes edited by Eugenio Lo Sardo (*Athanasius Kircher: Il Museo del Mondo*); Horst Beinlich et al. (*Magie des Wissens* and *Spurensuche*); Daniel Stolzenberg (*The Great Art of Knowing*); and Paula Findlen (*Athanasius Kircher: The Last Man Who Knew Everything*).

Among the many monographs on Kircher, there is nothing to rival the dissertations of the late John Edward Fletcher, 'Athanasius Kircher, "Germanus Incredibilis": A Study of His Life and Works with a Report on His Unpublished Correspondence', and of Daniel Stolzenberg, 'The Egyptian Oedipus: Antiquarianism, Oriental Studies & Occult Philosophy in the Work of Athanasius Kircher'. Another monumental work is the two-volume *Athanasius Kircher: Itinerario del éxtasis o Las imágenes de un saber universal* by Ignacio Gómez de Liaño. Structured on the same lines as my earlier book, it offers hundreds more illustrations. On a smaller scale, Ingrid Rowland's *The Ecstatic Journey* is rich and entertaining out of all proportion to its modest size.

If one pushes this latter tendency a little further, Kircher lends himself to parodistic comedy, as in Umberto Eco's Kircherian (and Schottian) fantasy, *The Island of the Day Before*. The Museum of Jurassic Technology in Los Angeles, which was not invented by Eco but might have been, has a Kircher exhibit that most visitors have no idea whether to take seriously or not. Then there are the efforts, both real and promised, of the Internationale Athanasius Kircher Forschungsgesellschaft (International Athanasius Kircher Research Society), the creation of Commendatore Dr. phil. Olaf Hein. MA, Acc., and Cavaliere Rolf Mader, Acc., solemn experts in a bizarre kind of scholarly overkill. The Museum of Jurassic Technology is the subject of Lawrence Wechsler's *Mr. Wilson's Cabinet of Wonder*, and Commander Hein the unwilling hero of Anton Haakman's *Il Mondo Sotteraneo di Athanasius Kircher* (citing the Italian edition in preference to the Dutch; there is none in English).

Having mentioned my favourites among the long list of recent Kircher literature, I must justify adding another to them. My first principle is to let Kircher speak for himself, both in words and in pictures. Caterina Marrone writes: 'It has been said that Kircher could not think except in images, but in fact thinking in images was not a limitation for him, but rather the realization of a *forma mentis* which he constantly followed.'[2] However, in order for modern people to enjoy this kind of activity, most of them need a helping hand across the gulf of history, culture, religion and erudition that yawns between Kircher's age and ours.

This is why the present book supplies all of the important illustrations of Kircher's works with explanations based, whenever possible, on his own words. It may be a poor substitute for reading the books themselves, but few today have access to these rare volumes and time to read them. And, to be honest, who would want to? Kircher's writing abounds in superfluities, repetitions and sermonizing: that is why his books are so long, and why no one translates them. The illustrations, on the other hand, have a quality of ingenuity and strangeness that are particular to his century, and of singular appeal to ours. More eloquent to our sensibilities than his inflated prose, they cry out to be glossed and understood.

That applies especially to the great symbolic frontispieces and the didactic images. There is also a host of lesser illustrations that need little explanation. Some are purely decorative, but even these can open windows on Kircher's world and the attitudes of his contemporaries. What, for example, is one to make of a picture of a unicorn, or a dragon? (Kircher knew that the first no longer existed, but was sure that dragons did.) The serious consideration of his theories by bodies such as the Royal Society betrays a climate of attitudes far closer to Kircher's than to those of the scientists and philosophers who eventually turned out to be 'right', and who dominate a simplified historiography. Even now, not all of Kircher's errors have been rectified (experts still debate the chronologies of ancient empires, the makeup of the earth's interior, the causes of the tides). The biblical literalism that acted as a straitjacket on Kircher's brilliant mind is, astonishingly, still with us. Participation in Kircher's museum, or theatre, or ecstatic journey – whichever metaphor one prefers – is both an education and a surrealistic adventure, rather like the parallel universe in which he is deemed so 'cool'.

The plan of this book follows the categories of the *Kunst- und Wunderkammer*, the 'chamber of art and marvels' that was the precursor of museums: Artificialia (works of the human hand), here represented by Antiquities; Naturalia (wonders of nature); Scientifica (devices of human ingenuity); and Exotica (things from outside Europe). To these are added a chapter on the sciences of the ear, and one on the importance of maps and plans for Kircher's visualization of the world. These thirteen chapters complete the essential part of the book, Chapters 14 and 15 being more in the nature of appendices. Not every reader shares Kircher's fascination with pagan theology and didactic diagrams, but a few may be curious about the meaning of these often baffling images.

It is a pleasure to thank Colgate University's President, Dean of the Faculty, and Research Council for research and travel grants and a sabbatical term's leave; Elizabeth Fletcher for letting me see a pre-publication copy of the book by her late husband, John Fletcher; Robert Collis for letting me see an extract from his doctoral dissertation; my colleague John Gallucci for help with some Latin; the librarians of Cornell University's Special Collections, the Bodleian Library, the Biblioteca Nazionale Vittorio Emanuele II, and the Pontificia Università Gregoriana; and, as always, Thomas Neurath of Thames & Hudson for his encouragement.

Joscelyn Godwin
Hamilton, New York

Notes
1 See Bibliography under McLemee.
2 Marrone, 102.

Prologue   **Interesting Times**

Athanasius Kircher stands out against the background of his time like some rugged headland jutting into the sea – perhaps one of those formations in which the imaginative eye discerns a monstrous face. The tides swirl busily around it, but it stands aloof, proud, and oblivious of the erosion of its base. Then, one day, it collapses. A few rocks remain visible at low tide, but for the rest the seas wash over it as though it had never been.

That, with a little poetic exaggeration, has been Kircher's fate among the tides of history. Held in awe during his lifetime for his universal knowledge, he died an all but forgotten curiosity. His books were occasionally noticed, maybe for the wrong reasons but for ones to which we heartily subscribe. No longer were they repositories of ultimate wisdom: they became portals into a land in which truth is no longer the quarry. Wonderland has its own truths, one of which is the irony with which it helps us view our own.

There is a kind of tourism of the past that consists in visiting mental monuments, especially the ones most different from those at home. This book is an invitation to visit Kircher's mind, to whose quirks, dreams and inventions his illustrators gave memorable form. What did *he* think and feel as he leafed through his own books, hot off the press? To what inner world, what quality of soul, did these images serve as windows? And did his readers feel the same?

Up to a point, the answer must be yes. Kircher's books, if they did not achieve immortality, won the penultimate accolade of commercial success, as they poured by the cartload from the presses of Rome and Amsterdam. He had his legions of readers and, at need, defenders, especially in his own militant order, the Society of Jesus. What he was doing struck a certain chord, though one increasingly at variance with the predominant harmonies. Even after his time there were those who preferred his style, and tried to replay the tremendous concords of his certainty. For others, and they have had the last word, it was this certainty that, turning to hubris, ensured his eclipse.

René Descartes (1596–1650), raised like Kircher by the Jesuits and no less a Catholic, proposed that philosophy should make a fresh start on the basis, not of inherited certainties but of doubt. Although nearly all of Descartes' pet theories were discarded – for example, the existence of 'innate ideas', the mind–body connection at the pineal gland, the mechanistic biology that sees animals as machines, the arguments for the existence of God – his philosophical method was something so new, so stimulating, that it fathered an entire genealogy of philosophers, who now constitute the canon. Like him, they sought a philosophizing free from sacred authority, free from erudition and the wisdom of the ancients, in fact free from everything that Kircher revered.

While Descartes led a reclusive and shifting life, mostly outside France, his best friend and agent was Marin Mersenne (1588–1648), a friar of the Order of Minims. As firmly based in his Paris convent as Kircher would be in the Collegium Romanum, Mersenne's first mission was to purge the learned world of any taint of Hermetism and magic, using as his vehicle a stupendous commentary on Genesis. This task accomplished, his work lay on the borderline between philosophy and science. He found that experimental science was best advanced by assuming a mechanistic philosophy and employing a mathematical approach. These would become cornerstones of the scientific method, as would be the very idea that science advances, with its consequent future-centred attitude. Mersenne was also one of the century's great networkers, corresponding with the learned of Europe and coordinating their researches. It was he who introduced Galileo's work to France after the great scientist's condemnation, and with it the debate over the Copernican system and the shortcomings of Aristotelian physics.

Aristotle had few friends in this era, outside the schoolrooms. The new experimental scientists discredited one after another of his dogmas, whether concerning the disposition of the heavens, the laws of physics, or the physiology of animals. At the same time, adepts of the magical, alchemical and Hermetic philosophies reproved Aristotle for having rejected the higher wisdom, as they saw it, of his master Plato.

Mersenne's deathbed was attended by his friend and fellow priest Pierre Gassendi (1592–1655), another of the circle of mechanistic philosophers. To Aristotle's four elements, Gassendi opposed another classical system, the atomic theory of Epicurus, which would prove a lasting model for chemistry if not for physics. He also joined Mersenne in polemics against Robert Fludd (1574–1637), the Paracelsian doctor whose devotion to the World-Soul and the Hermetic doctrine of correspondences (which we will find in its ripest development in Kircher) seemed to them worse even than the stultified Aristotelianism of the schools.

These French philosophers helped to form an intellectual climate in which both philosophy and science could get on with their business without interference from religious dogmas on the one hand, or occult beliefs on the other. This business was what Francis Bacon (1561–1626) had defined as the 'Great Instauration', the restoration of humanity to its birthright of command over nature. Bacon's combination of commonsense philosophy with the experimental method, which he was the first to define, made him the godfather of the Scientific Revolution. From Bacon came the inductive principle of using experiments to discover the laws of nature, rather than taking the laws as already known; and also the assumption that progress in scientific knowledge is useful to mankind. His fictitious travelogue *The New Atlantis*, with its depiction of a utopia blessed with advanced technology, was an inspiration to the groups that would later coalesce to form the Royal Society.

These men all managed to avoid the collision of their philosophies with the religious authorities, unlike the two famous victims of the latter: Giordano Bruno (1548–1600) and Galileo Galilei (1564–1642). Although Bruno was originally a Dominican monk, he developed a mystic pantheism coloured by Hermeticism and magic, and a corresponding contempt for Judeo-Christian doctrines. Straying over into astronomy, he accepted the Copernican doctrine on metaphysical grounds (the sun being the proper centre of all), and went further to posit the infinity of the universe and the plurality of worlds. These notions threatened the biblical creation story and the scheme of Christian salvation, both of which presupposed a single world and a single Incarnation. For his obduracy in promoting his doctrines, he was burned at the stake.

Galileo escaped Bruno's fate but was condemned in 1633 to permanent house arrest. Strictly speaking, his offence was not his embrace of the heliocentric system, which had been given its latest and most persuasive form by Nicolaus Copernicus (1473–1543), a Polish churchman. It was Galileo's presumption, as a layman, to interpret the Bible so as to make it fit. This is what got him into trouble with the Church in 1616, from which he emerged with a mere caution, forbidden to 'hold, teach or defend' the theory. What caused much worse trouble was his disobedience when in 1632 he published his *Dialogue on the Two World Systems*. The accession to the papacy of his patron Maffeo Barberini (1568–1644; Pope from 1623) and the encouragement of his friends had emboldened him to believe the decree of 1616 past history. It was not. Galileo's mockery of the modern Aristotelians who dominated the universities had already made him enemies, and the ludicrous character in his book who defended the geocentric system seemed an outright insult to the Pope, who happened to hold that opinion.

Bruno and Galileo were minds of the very first order, self-confident, impatient with stupidity and ultimately foolhardy. This is not to excuse the religious establishment that made martyrs of them, far from it. But it does help one to appreciate the skill of Kircher and others similarly gifted, who steered through those perilous rapids unharmed. At what cost of personal integrity and the cohabitation of contrary beliefs, we shall never know, but we cannot blame them.

Galileo's achievement was twofold. First, he proved the power of technology to extend the reach of the senses and gather information from which natural laws could be induced. This he did by training his telescope on the sun, moon and planets, and noticing phenomena that could only be 'saved' (i.e. explained), by discarding the Aristotelian dogma of perfect and immutable heavens, and the Ptolemaic system that placed the earth motionless at the centre of the universe. Second, he showed that problems in physics and mechanics are best solved by mathematical methods.

None of this was of much importance to Kircher's type of science. Certainly it was experimental, but the end result of his experiments was not so much the advancement of knowledge as the making of some new machine to entertain a patron or adorn his Museum. He never paid much attention to the possibilities of the telescope or the microscope, preferring the more dramatic effects of magnetism and the magic lantern. When Christiaan Huygens (1629–1695) revolutionized the science of timekeeping in 1657 by inventing the pendulum clock, Kircher was still busy devising new sundials.

Galileo's condemnation and abjuration sent a shudder through the 'Republic of Letters', as Europe's relatively freethinking savants called themselves. Among his defenders, to the point of protesting to the Pope, was Nicolas-Claude Fabri de Peiresc (1580–1637). A member of the regional parliament of Aix-en-Provence, Peiresc was one of the Republic's chief nodes, somewhat as Mersenne was and as Kircher would become. In fact, it was Kircher who brought him the bad news about Galileo in August 1633.

With Peiresc, the emphasis moves from the natural sciences to the sciences of the past, such as chronology, philology, archaeology, palaeography and numismatics. The raw materials here are not simply knowledge, but the tangible remnants of antiquity, and in the place of the experimental scientist is the collector, which Peiresc was and, again, Kircher would be. With them came the transition from the cabinet of curiosities – the *Kunst- und Wunderkammer* – to the study collection that we know as a museum. Peiresc's most precious possessions were his manuscripts in oriental languages, and much of his correspondence and organizing skill went into acquiring them and finding experts to study them. Kircher was one such expert, whom Peiresc valued chiefly as a pioneer of Coptic studies. Yet the fact that Kircher was snatched from Peiresc's research team in order to become a professor of mathematics shows how irrelevant was the notion of specialization. All of the people mentioned so far were intellectual omnivores, collecting knowledge with no concept of today's disciplinary boundaries. As the telescope and microscope extended the sense of sight, the early museums were tools for the extension of the mind beyond its natural limits of time and space. A collection of coins might yield clues about ancient dynasties, and these in turn could be correlated with the Bible to arrive at a more accurate picture of the past. Artefacts from the Indies or the Americas, from Africa or the Ottoman Empire, bore witness to peoples formerly beyond the ken of Europeans, to their peculiar habits and beliefs; and these, too, could be used to supplement the skimpy account of the population of the globe as given in Genesis.

In the Republic of Letters, Catholics and Protestants alike agreed with Galileo that the Bible was not given to mankind in order to teach us science, but to show the way to salvation. However, while this attitude spelled freedom for physics, mechanics and even astronomy, it did not benefit the sciences of the past. The book of Genesis spoke unambiguously of the Creation in six days, the ages of the patriarchs, the universal deluge and the origin of languages. No interpretation that respected the numbers in that text could yield a creation date of more than six thousand years ago. Even Isaac Newton (1642–1727) accepted it, as he spent his old age poring over chronology and its counterpart, prophecy. Until this time barrier was broken, no progress was possible in understanding the processes of geology or astronomy, the taxonomy of animals and plants, the development of human capabilities and languages, the populating of the globe, the origin and extinction of species, to say nothing of evolution. Kircher's efforts were therefore doomed to obsolescence.

Newton, of course, was a heliocentrist. Living when and where he did, he did not fear the fate of Galileo or feel obliged, like Kircher and Gassendi, to sign on to the compromise system of Tycho Brahe (1546–1601), according to which the planets move around the sun while the sun moves around the static earth. More important to Newton were the discoveries and conclusions of Tycho's assistant Johann Kepler (1571–1630), who had broken the perfect circles that shaped all previous cosmologies (including Copernicus's). Through a dogged devotion to accuracy in observation and tabulation, Kepler had been led to the conclusion that the planets move in elliptical orbits, with the sun at one of their foci. His further conclusion, that God planned the proportions of their orbits on the basis of musical consonances, did not long survive, but it goes to show the continued relevance, to some scientists, of the classical as well as the biblical past. In this case, it was the Pythagorean doctrine of the Harmony of the Spheres, an important element of Kircher's cosmology and one which Newton, too, believed to conceal true physical principles.

The informal groups and corresponding circles of the earlier seventeenth century gave way in the latter part to more formal academies. The Accademia del Cimento, founded in Florence in 1657, continued in the tradition of its native son Galileo, and enjoyed the protection and participation of the Medici. It set the new style in which all religious issues were set aside, as was all reliance on Aristotelian or scholastic authority. The emphasis was solely on making experiments and evaluating the results (*cimento* means 'assaying'). England followed in 1665 with the Royal Academy, whose name indicates its level of patronage; France in 1666 with the Académie des Sciences, founded by Jean-Baptiste Colbert with royal assent. While they served a certain national pride, these academies were international in membership and scope. The first secretary of the Royal Academy was a German, Henry Oldenburg (1619–1677); Christiaan Huygens, who was brought to Paris as the new institution's chief research fellow, was a Dutch Protestant.

The academies instituted a new way of gathering and diffusing knowledge that has remained valid to the present day. Through collaborative research, peer review (instituted by Oldenburg) and periodical publication, findings could be shared, commented on and added to in a continuous self-correcting process. Kircher's method of compiling facts through erudition and correspondence and enshrining them in encyclopaedic works could not compete. While the motor of the new science was conversation, Kircher's was a monologue. At the same time, though, he had the advantage of the Society of Jesus, unequalled in its numbers, educational level and worldwide distribution.

The Society had many scientists and scholars in its ranks, but for all their brilliance, furthering science and scholarship was not their prime purpose. Their founder, Ignatius of Loyola (1491–1556), hoped to win the whole world for Christ. This first meant converting the heathens, notably Spain's nearest neighbours, the Muslims of North Africa. With the voyages of discovery, the field expanded commensurately, and the Society's missions were soon installed throughout the Old and New Worlds. But making Christians out of heathens was not enough. In Europe, the order lent its energies to the Counter-Reformation, whereby the Catholic Church tried by all means to suppress the rising tide of Protestantism.

Jesuit education had two levels. First, the colleges prepared the Society's members for a life of total devotion to the Christian cause. This included a thorough grounding in the arts and sciences, in theology, and in a system of self-discipline through Ignatius's 'Spiritual Exercises'. Second, there were the schools for laypeople, which were always of such a high quality that even Protestants would send their sons to them. The Jesuits valued learning; they regarded the world as potentially good, and worth knowing and enjoying, though they themselves, as soldiers of Christ, were indifferent to its pleasures. They also knew the appeal of the arts to the human mind and emotions. Drama, music, poetry and the visual arts all played a part in Jesuit education, though never lacking a moral or religious subtext.

Kircher was educated, worked and died in this spiritual hothouse. But in the world outside the Society he spent ten years as a refugee, and the rest of his adult life as an emigrant. His native Germany was devastated before his eyes in the series of conflicts known as the Thirty Years War.

Ever since 1555, with the Peace of Augsburg, the Catholic and Lutheran principalities of Germany had coexisted under the principle that each ruler should determine the form of Christianity to be followed by his or her subjects. (If Kircher had been born a few miles away, say in Calvinist Schmalkalden, his life would have taken a very different course.) The policy of conformity led to resentment among dissenters, especially the Calvinists who had not been included in the original settlement. Leagues were formed, nominally in self-defence against possible attack by the other side.

The Bohemian nobility set the spark to the tinder when in 1619 they elected Frederick Count Palatine, a Calvinist, as their king. This made possible a Protestant majority among the seven traditional Electors of the Holy Roman Emperor (the Count Palatine of the Rhine and the King of Bohemia; the Duke of Saxony and the Margrave of Brandenburg, already Protestants; and the

Catholic Archbishops of Cologne, Mainz and Trier). It was a situation that the fanatical Ferdinand of Styria, heir presumptive to the imperial throne, could not countenance. His suppression of the Bohemian rebels led to general war, with Denmark, Sweden and eventually France entering against the Empire and Spain. Much of the fighting was done by mercenary soldiers, who left unimaginable misery throughout much of present-day Germany.

What is most surprising, considering the wholesale slaughter, famine, disease and destruction of property, is the cultural achievement of those Germans who stayed behind. For instance, in 1617 Leopold von Anhalt-Köthen (1579–1650), who had been admitted to the Accademia della Crusca while in Italy, founded a society in emulation of that literary academy. This, the Fruchtbringende Gesellschaft ('Fruitful Society'), existed to further the German language as a proper vehicle for literature and scholarship. It met in Köthen with few interruptions for the duration of the war, counting among its members most of the century's important literary figures. Among the most eminent was Martin Opitz (1597–1639), who translated the ideals of Italian humanist poetry into his native tongue, and with the composer Heinrich Schütz (1585–1672) created the first German opera (*Dafne*, 1627). Schütz, the greatest German composer up to his time, served the Saxon electoral court in Dresden from 1615 until his death, except for a few years spent in Italy and Denmark. Andreas Gryphius (1616–1664) and Hans Jakob Christoffel von Grimmelshausen (1621–1676) grew up amid the turmoil to emerge, respectively, as the exemplary poet and dramatist, and the first novelist of the German baroque. The Lutheran pastor and mystical writer Johann Valentin Andreae (1586–1654), who in his youth helped to create the myth of the Rosicrucians, twice lost his home and his library. He fled to the independent city of Nuremberg, and returned to pass the last decade of the war as court preacher in Stuttgart. Thanks to these and many lesser lights, the postwar generation of Dietrich Buxtehude (1637–1707) and Gottfried Wilhelm von Leibniz (1646–1716) did not arise from a vacuum.

The Peace of Westphalia (1648) ended the war with a complicated transfer of territory, money and blame, and with Habsburg power, both Spanish and Austrian, much diminished. It was immediately followed by dire events in two of Europe's chief monarchies. In England, King Charles I was beheaded (1649) and the interregnum of the Commonwealth began. France witnessed the 'Fronde' (1648–1653), a sequence of skirmishes between the monarchy (represented, in the king's minority, by Cardinal Mazarin), certain nobles and the parliament. The English monarchy was restored with Charles II (ruled 1660–1685), and in 1661 Louis XIV (ruled 1643–1715) took over absolute power.

As for the Holy Roman Empire, its story was one of gradual decline. It did not exactly lose the Thirty Years War, but it had begun it with the high ambitions of Ferdinand II (ruled 1619–1637) to restore the entire empire to the Catholic faith; and it ended it with Ferdinand III (ruled 1637–1657) conceding to the German princes the right to conduct their own foreign and internal affairs. Conflicts with the France of Louis XIV and the assaults of the Ottoman Turks on its eastern borders blighted the reign of Leopold I (ruled 1657–1705),

though none of this prevented all three emperors from generously supporting artists, musicians and scholars.

For the second half of the war, Kircher was secure in his Roman home, and a spectator of one of the most grandiose periods of papal rule. The Papal States had grown ever since the popes returned from Avignon, and now they stretched from Terracina, south of Rome, to Bologna and Ferrara in the north, Rimini and Ancona on the Adriatic coast: an area larger than the Grand Duchy of Tuscany. The south of the peninsula, Sicily, Sardinia and the Duchy of Milan belonged to the Spanish Habsburgs and were ruled from Naples by a Viceroy. France dominated the northwest in an unhappy series of invasions. The Republics of Genoa and Venice maintained their independence, though their great days of controlling the trade routes were over.

The Pope was thus responsible not just for the Church but for a state, with all the headaches and expenses of raising armies, fortifying his cities and keeping the nobles in check. Whereas in most states, dynastic rule ensured continuity, the papacy lurched in succession around the great Roman families, each using the enormous papal income to further its wealth and status. That is why Rome boasts so many outsize palaces, notably (from our period) Palazzo Barberini, built by Urban VIII; Palazzo Pamphili on Piazza Navona, built by Innocent X; and Palazzo Chigi (now a seat of government), acquired by Alexander VII. Patronage of the arts and culture was part and parcel of this ambition, in which each Pope sought to make his reign more glorious than the last. The competition stopped, however, with the three last Popes of Kircher's lifetime: Clement IX, Clement X and Innocent XI. They were respectively too short-reigned, too old and too earnest to behave as their predecessors had done, and papal largesse was never the same again.

Outside Europe, the great voyages of discovery were over, the heyday of colonization not yet begun. The seventeenth century was the great era of the missionaries, who established themselves in the wake of the trade routes. The Jesuits rivalled the Franciscans in their global reach, and easily exceeded them in their curiosity and penetration of native cultures. There were Jesuit missions – and martyrs – all over the New World, from Tierra del Fuego to Canada. In Asia and Africa, their fortunes were affected by the rivalry of the Portuguese and Dutch, but wherever Portugal was installed, notably in Goa on the southeast coast of India, Jesuit churches rose in astonishing echoes of baroque Rome. For a while the Society's envoys were welcome at the court of the Mughal Emperor, ruler of most of India, and at that of the Emperor of China. Their monuments remain in Macao on the Chinese coast, and in the Philippines. In Japan they were at first tolerated, then cruelly put down.

Kircher, who lacked nothing in stamina or physical and moral courage, yearned to be a missionary but was denied his ambition. So for all his global vision, he never saw much of the world. Perhaps this is one reason that he was prone to believe every report that came in his mailbag. But it is this that makes him so fascinating, and, for all his apparent oddness, probably more representative of his times than any of the canonized saints of progress.

Chapter 1   Kircher's Life and Work: an Overview

Kircher has a fair claim to be the most learned savant of his age. His works on Egyptology, music, optics, magnetism, geology, linguistics and comparative religion were each definitive for their time. But history has not been kind to him, for several reasons. First, he wrote only in Latin, while other scholars were turning to the vernacular. Second, the breadth of his interests makes it almost impossible to appreciate his work as a whole. Third, his adherence to a Christian Hermetism rooted his thought in a set of assumptions that the world of science and learning was already discarding. Yet while his work was a tardy monument to the Renaissance ideal of universal knowledge, its celebration of the natural world opened new fields of study that heralded the age of secular science.

Kircher was born in Geisa, near the city of Fulda in that little-known region at the geographical centre of today's Germany. He writes in his autobiography[1] that he began life at three in the morning on the Feast of Saint Athanasius, 2 May 1602 – hence his name, which is Greek for 'immortal'.[2] His father, Johann Kircher, had worked until 1599 as an *Amstvogt* (bailiff) in Haselstein, administering affairs and justice for the local lord, the Prince-Abbot of Fulda. Then he moved to Geisa for a two-year period as *Stadtschultheiss* (mayor), before retiring into private life on his comfortable fortune.[3] Athanasius was the last of nine children from Johann's marriage with Anna Gansheck, daughter of a burgher from Fulda.

Two snapshots of Fulda history lend grim colour to these bland facts. From 1602 to 1606, under the rule of the witch-hunter Balthasar Nuss, no fewer than 260 witches were burned in that city.[4] During the same four years, the Prince-Abbot Balthasar von Dernbach expelled the Protestants (Lutherans and Calvinists) from Fulda, and the small town of Geisa, formerly of mixed religion, was formally 'recatholicized'.[5]

Kircher's autobiography takes no note of the atmosphere of sectarian hatred and paranoia that must have overshadowed his childhood. From his account, it was a time filled with adventure, in which his pride and curiosity repeatedly led to a fall, to prayer and then to a miraculous rescue. At least four times he escaped an early death: from being caught in a mill-race; from falling under the feet of racing horses; from getting lost in a forest; and from gangrene contracted while skating. Already in his youth he felt favoured by God and marked out for some special destiny – perhaps even sainthood, for

as Anton Haakman, most sly and perceptive of Kircherians, observes, 'Kircher wrote his very own hagiography, taking care to insert a number of miracles sufficient for canonization.'[6]

Kircher was first educated by his father, now retired and the possessor of a fine library. At the age of ten or eleven he was sent in the footsteps of his brothers to the Jesuits' Gymnasium in Fulda, a school of some 500 boys. Before he left at the age of 16, he had learned Latin, Greek and Hebrew, and presumably at some point had made the lifetime commitment to a monastic career. After failing in his first application, to the Jesuit College in Mainz, he was admitted as a novice to the college at Paderborn in 1618.[7]

By 1620 his novitiate was completed and his first vows taken, but the onset of the Thirty Years War interrupted his education. The advance of the fiercely anti-Jesuit Duke Christian of Brunswick prompted him, with two companions, to flee in January 1622. They struggled for three days through deep snow, penniless and begging their food, until a Catholic nobleman took them in. After a week at the Jesuit College at Münster they were advised to continue to Cologne. Passing through Düsseldorf they came to the frozen Rhine and proceeded to cross it. Halfway across, a piece of ice broke loose and Kircher was carried away on it. His companions expected never to see him again. But he succeeded in swimming through the freezing water to the bank, and walking for three hours until he reached the haven of the Jesuit College in Neuss.

Kircher duly completed his course in scholastic philosophy in Cologne, then in 1623 was transferred to Koblenz to study humanities and teach Greek at the Jesuit School. Up to now he had humbly concealed his true abilities, but when he gave up his pretence of mediocrity, he aroused so much jealousy that his superiors transferred him again, this time to the college at Heiligenstadt. The journey was a dangerous one through Protestant territory, but Kircher obstinately refused to wear a disguise, saying: 'I would rather die in the robes of my order than travel undisturbed in worldly dress...' This nearly transpired, as he was ambushed by Protestant soldiers. After stripping and beating him, they prepared to hang him from the nearest tree. But his calm demeanour so moved one of the men that he persuaded his comrades to spare the young Jesuit's life, and even to give him back his property.

Heiligenstadt was reached without further incident, and here the 23-year-old Kircher taught mathematics, Hebrew and Syrian.[8] When in 1625 delegates of the Archbishop-Elector of Mainz visited the college, Kircher arranged an astonishing entertainment of moving scenery and fireworks. Some onlookers feared that it was done by black magic, until he explained how it worked. As a result, he was summoned to the Archbishop's court at Aschaffenburg to make more such curiosities, and to draw up a survey of the principality, which he completed in only three months. Perhaps it was this commission, done with the help of the magnetic compass, that suggested the subject of Kircher's first book, *Ars Magnesia* ('The magnetic art', 1631).[9]

On the Archbishop-Elector's death, Kircher returned to Mainz for another four years. Although nominally studying theology, he managed to acquire a telescope, through which he observed the then unexplained phenomenon of sunspots. In 1628 he was ordained priest and entered his Tertianship (spiritual preparation for the ministry) at Gau um Speyer. A new world of humanistic learning opened there when he first saw pictures of Egyptian hieroglyphs, probably in Herwart von Hohenburg's *Thesaurus Hieroglyphicorum*, and longed to understand them.[10] But he could not yet pursue this interest, as he was next sent to teach at Würzburg. In 1630 he petitioned to go as a missionary to China, but was refused. The next year the Swedish army entered the region. In another miraculous episode, Kircher was granted the gift of prophecy and saw in a vision armed men drilling in the college courtyard; he was able to warn his fellows and the Würzburg College was hastily disbanded. Abandoning all his manuscripts, he took refuge in Mainz.

During his absence, one of his noble pupils, Johannes Jakob Schweigkard von Freihausen, took care of the publication of *Ars Magnesia* and obtained its dedication to the Prince-Bishop of Würzburg. The first part of the book describes magnetic phenomena and experiments, largely based on William Gilbert's *De Magnete* (1600). Kircher's explanation of magnetism, unlike Gilbert's more mechanistic one, is that things have an innate appetite or inclination towards their own good. In the second part, he discusses the deviations of compass needles and the use of magnets in medicine. He entertains the possibility of perpetual motion by using magnets, and describes magnetic tricks and toys. Thus his first work announces his characteristic blend of mathematics and experimental science with Hermetic philosophy and a delight in natural and artificial wonders.

Now that there was no future in Germany for a promising young Jesuit scholar, Kircher's superiors allowed him, with many others, to go to France. He passed through Lyon in 1632 on the way to Avignon, there to teach mathematics, philosophy and oriental languages. For the Avignon Jesuit College he designed an elaborate clock, described in his *Primitiae Gnomonicae Catoptricae* ('First fruits of the reflective sundial', 1635). Just as *Ars Magnesia* is a sketch for the large-scale *Magnes*, this short book on optics and sundials anticipates his later *Ars Magna Lucis*.

In France Kircher entered a new, cosmopolitan world of learning, thanks to Nicolas-Claude Fabri de Peiresc, member of the Parliament at Aix and a wealthy collector and patron of scholarship.[11] Through Peiresc, Kircher met Pierre Gassendi and started a correspondence with Marin Mersenne, both men of universal learning and wide connections. Peiresc was particularly interested in having Kircher work on deciphering his collection of Ethiopian, Arabic and Coptic manuscripts. This resulted in the foundational work of all Coptic studies, *Prodromus Coptus* ('Introduction to Coptic', 1636).[12] The book contains the first Coptic grammar, for which a special typeface was cast, and argues (correctly) that Coptic bears a relationship to the language of ancient Egypt. At the end of the book, Kircher published the projected table of contents of a much larger, three-part work, which he already knew would be titled *Œdipus Ægyptiacus*.

Kircher already saw himself as a new Oedipus, who would solve the Sphingian riddle of the hieroglyphs, but his linguistic research was again interrupted in 1633, when he was summoned by the Habsburg Emperor to be Professor of Mathematics in either Vienna or Trieste.[13] Peiresc and other patrons of Kircher's linguistic work lodged influential complaints, and consequently, when Kircher broke his long journey in Rome, he was ordered to stay there. He was appointed to the Roman College, the hub of the whole Jesuit order, as Professor of Mathematics, with a special commission from the Pope's nephew, Cardinal Francesco Barberini, to study hieroglyphs. This was to be his home until his death.[14]

When Kircher arrived in Rome, the scientific world was still reeling from the Galileo affair. The elderly scientist, once a friend of the Barberini Pope, had been hauled before the Inquisition in April 1633 and forced to desist from 'holding and teaching' the Copernican theory. In the previous year, Urban VIII had published a severe bull against astrologers, to counter the suspicion that had rested on him ever since he had summoned Tommaso Campanella to perform astrological magic for him.[15] By 1634 the atmosphere had turned sufficiently sour that Campanella, aided by Cardinal Barberini, slipped out of Rome and ended his days in France. Under these circumstances, a polymathic and enquiring mind like Kircher's had to be careful.

Kircher made only one further journey outside Italy.[16] In 1636, at least partly through his influence, Friedrich, Landgrave of Hesse-Darmstadt (1616–1682), was converted to Catholicism: a great catch for the Roman Church.[17] Wishing to travel in Italy, the young Landgrave chose two compatriots as companions: his confessor, Kircher, and his tutor, Lucas Holsten.[18] As the party moved south to Sicily, Kircher took every opportunity to explore new areas of natural science. He was keen to see Syracuse, to ascertain whether in 212 BC Archimedes could have used a burning-mirror to destroy the Roman fleet at anchor there. In a Messina monastery library he discovered a Greek musical manuscript,[19] and perhaps the legendary *Book of Enoch*, reputedly written by the deathless patriarch before the Flood.[20]

After Sicily, the party sailed to Malta, which the Landgrave, a Knight of the Order of Malta, had visited in the previous year. Kircher's presence was a welcome diversion to the Jesuits there, for whom he invented the rotating astronomical device described in *Specula Melitensis Encyclica* ('Circular Maltese mirror', 1638),[21] and he began a lasting friendship with the Apostolic Delegate, Fabio Chigi, the future Pope Alexander VII. Otherwise the island had little to offer Kircher and his ambitions, and after intervention in high places,[22] he was ordered back to Rome. The delay was timely, for in March 1638, on the homeward journey, he witnessed the eruptions of Etna and Stromboli and the destruction of the island of St Euphemia. When he reached Naples, Vesuvius was threatening to erupt, too. The insatiable Kircher climbed the volcano and had himself lowered into the crater to observe the process more closely. This experience would form the kernel of his great work on the Subterranean World.

Now Kircher began to publish his major works, creating an encyclopaedia on a different scientific or antiquarian subject every three or four years. First he returned to the subject of magnetism, with *Magnes* ('The magnet', 1641). One object of the work was to counter the magnetic argument for the Copernican theory, with which Kircher had flirted in his Avignon period but which now, after Galileo's condemnation, was anathema to the orthodox circles on which he depended for his career. Otherwise *Magnes* develops the same range of themes as the earlier work on the subject, especially the Hermetic idea of universal attraction and repulsion. This manifested itself as much in Kircher's 'sunflower clock', which turned to face the sun, as in the music of the Tarantella, which dislodged the poison of the tarantula spider from the bloodstream. At its highest level, it was the same magnetic force that attracted the human soul to God.

Lingua Ægyptiaca Restituta ('The Egyptian language restored', 1643) is another case of Kircher's expansion of an earlier work. He used the information from the traveller Pietro della Valle to compile a vocabulary of Coptic, Latin and Arabic in parallel columns. This was the book that helped Champollion decipher the Rosetta Stone nearly two hundred years later. It includes material on Egyptian chronology, weights and measures, fauna, flora, place names and philosophical terms. The book was dedicated to Emperor Ferdinand III, marking Kircher's breakthrough into the highest realms of patronage. Imitating the sobriquet of the mythical philosopher-king of Egypt, Hermes Trismegistus, Kircher addresses his patron as *Rex Trismegistus*, 'Thrice-Greatest King'.

Ars Magna Lucis et Umbrae ('The great art of light and shadow', 1646) was the first of Kircher's books to be organized along symbolic lines: its ten books are represented as the ten strings of the instrument with which the Psalmist declares he will praise God (Psalm 143:9). The work overlaps with *Magnes* in several places. It treats of eclipses, comets and astrological influences, also of phosphorescence, colour, optics, timekeeping and sundials. It includes the first printed picture of Saturn, flanked by two ellipses (which were how the rings appeared in Kircher's telescope), and devices for projecting images. The true magic lantern, however, would not appear until the second edition (1671).

In 1646 the Roman College relieved Kircher from teaching and in effect gave him a research fellowship for life. As his fame grew, so too did his correspondence. The Jesuit missionaries, for whom mathematics and technology were an important part of their training, sent back scientific reports from every corner of the globe. Receiving these from Chile, Peru, Brazil, Mexico, Tunisia, Aleppo, Isfahan, Agra, Surat, Goa, Manila, Guam and from most of Europe, Kircher was at the centre of the world's most efficient and best-educated network. He was the first to hear of any new discovery, and eager to share it with the world and with his swelling list of royal, aristocratic and ecclesiastical patrons.

Musurgia Universalis ('Universal music-making', 1650) does for sound what *Ars Magna Lucis* did for light.[23] Coming at the point where the newly expressive style of opera was superseding the earlier style of imitative counterpoint, it announces the 'doctrine of the affections' that underlies the former. However, unlike the Italian academies, whose studies of ancient Greek music had given birth to the new style, Kircher's ideal was the music of the ancient Hebrews; King David, rather than Orpheus or Pythagoras, was his model of the supreme musician. *Musurgia* begins with an exhaustive treatment of ancient music and mathematical tuning theory, ultimately based on the divine archetype of number. Kircher then describes all the musical genres and instruments current in his day. Natural magic is never far away, as he explains acoustical marvels, megaphones, eavesdropping devices, talking statues and Aeolian harps. Always practical, he gives directions for a composing machine, and offers samples of his own composition (see **Ill. 9.1**). About 1,500 copies of the book were printed, of which one was sent to every Jesuit college, 300 were given to Jesuits converging on Rome for the election of a new Superior-General, and 352 were distributed throughout Europe.[24]

Kircher was committed to the free exchange of information, irrespective of nationality or religion. Thus he sent a copy of *Musurgia* to August the Younger, Duke of Braunschweig-Lüneburg.[25] This led to a long correspondence and friendship with the Protestant ruler and bibliophile, to many gifts of money from the Duke, and to Kircher's reciprocal gift of his most precious manuscript, the fifth-century Syrian Gospels now in the Herzog-August Bibliothek in Wolfenbüttel. Kircher never succeeded in his gentle efforts to convert Duke August to Catholicism, but he did play a discreet role in the spectacular conversion and abdication of Queen Christina of Sweden (reigned 1632–1654), having been in correspondence with her for at least seven years before she abdicated. He dedicated *Itinerarium Exstaticum* to her, and entertained her in his museum.[26]

His growing reputation as a linguist made Kircher the obvious person to consult when Pope Innocent X decided to re-erect a fallen obelisk and to restore its inscription. In *Obeliscus Pamphilius* ('The Pamphilian obelisk', 1650), Kircher set out his principles for interpreting the Egyptian hieroglyphs as statements of Hermetic wisdom.[27] Although he already knew their language (Coptic), he read the hieroglyphs as a purely symbolic writing, rather than a verbal or alphabetical one, hence missing the path that eventually led Champollion, with the help of the Rosetta Stone, to their true decipherment.

This field of research came to fruition in Kircher's next and longest book, the long-awaited *Œdipus Ægyptiacus* ('The Egyptian Oedipus', 1652–1654)

PATRONS

By accepting the honour of a dedication, a patron was expected to contribute towards the cost of printing the book concerned. Kircher's publications would have been impossible without generous subsidies from popes, emperors, nobles and ecclesiastical dignitaries. A few of his patrons received the further honour of a portrait.

1.1 Pope Innocent X
Obeliscus Pamphilius, a1ʳ

Dedicated in the Jubilee Year of 1650, this unsigned tribute to the Pamphili Pope who helped to negotiate the end of the Thirty Years War reads: 'The dove binds together lilies, palm, and olive; she loves the flowering ages of victorious peace.' Innocent commissioned Kircher to decipher the inscription on the obelisk to be erected in front of his family's palace on Piazza Navona, and Bernini to supply it with its spectacular setting, the Fountain of the Four Rivers.

1.2 Archduke Leopold Wilhelm von Habsburg
Musurgia Universalis, Volume I, +1ᵛ

Leopold Wilhelm (1614–1662) was the Emperor Ferdinand's younger brother. At the time of the dedication, he was regent of the Spanish Netherlands. After Ferdinand's death in 1657 he was made regent of the Empire, but refused the offer of the imperial crown in favour of Leopold Ignatius, Ferdinand's second son.[28] In *Mundus Subterraneus* he is praised as having been very fond of Kircher's writings, and a loyal supporter for twenty years. It was through his mediation that the Emperor agreed to support *Œdipus Ægyptiacus*.

1.3 Emperor Ferdinand III
Œdipus Ægyptiacus, Volume I, +3ᵛ

The Emperor sits, or stands, with his hand on the globe and the Order of the Golden Fleece around his neck. On the table is the imperial crown made for Rudolf II, and a drawing of an obelisk. His financial support made possible the publication of *Œdipus Ægyptiacus*. Kircher thanked him in his letter of dedication, dated 1 January 1655, and paid him the compliment of a 'Polyglot Caesarean Triumph' consisting of 47 poems in praise of the Emperor, written by various specialists in 47 different languages or scripts, including one in hieroglyphics (see **Ill. 4.18**).

1.4 Pope Alexander VII
Mundus Subterraneus, Volume I, *2ᵛ

1.5 Pope Clement X
Latium, *2ᵛ

1.6 Emperor Leopold I
Phonurgia Nova, a2ʳ

1.7 Charles II, King of Spain
Arca Noë, *2ᵛ

When Kircher visited Malta in 1637, he made friends with Fabio Chigi, then Apostolic Delegate to the island. Rising through a series of political offices, Chigi became a trusted deputy of Innocent X, and was elected Pope on the latter's death in 1655. His twelve-year reign began triumphantly with the arrival of the newly converted Queen Christina of Sweden, a long-time correspondent of Kircher's. The dedication of *Mundus Subterraneus* was originally offered to her, but her chronic shortage of funds probably caused Kircher to turn elsewhere. The opening scenes of this magnificent volume recall his Maltese and Sicilian experiences.

The 80-year-old Cardinal Emilio Altieri (ruled 1670–1676) reluctantly accepted the papacy after the two-year rule of Clement IX. The two Clements, devout peacemakers, were in stark contrast to their three powerful predecessors whose patronage had so benefited Kircher. By the time *Latium* was published, Kircher's reputation was such that it is hard to say who was patronizing whom.

Emperor Leopold was a most cultured man, a musician of more than amateur quality, and a generous patron of Kircher. As a sign of these achievements he wears the laurels of Apollo, while above him are the crowns of the Holy Roman Empire and its subject kingdoms. Beneath are the symbols of his prowess in the arts of peace (geography, painting, literature) and of war, separated by the simple heraldic shield of the Empire. An olive branch encircles him, inscribed: 'Leopold Emperor, August, Just, Pious, Happy'.

In his dedication, Kircher reminds the king that his is a monarchy which stretches from east to west, from pole to pole, and that every season of the year is simultaneously present somewhere in it. 'Fresh violets, roses and lilies will never cease to waft their perfume to you; your table of dainties never lacks the fruits of heaven's wanderings. Thus *Arca Noë* contains as though in a *zootropheio* all the animal species that the sky's breadth contains. In very truth, what Noah had in a small space, you, High King, possess scattered throughout your realm' (*4ʳ). This is a specimen of the many pages of high-flown flattery with which Kircher prefaced his books.

where he assembled all that was known about the history and geography of Egypt, carrying out almost exactly his plan of twenty years earlier. His long-time patron Archduke Leopold Wilhelm negotiated a gift of 3,000 scudi from Emperor Ferdinand III, which covered more than half the cost of printing, and multiple dedications of the various sections ensured further gifts from those thus honoured. In seeking the meaning of the hieroglyphs, Kircher plumbed the sources of the 'ancient theology' as understood in the Renaissance: the Book of Enoch, the writings attributed to Zoroaster, Orpheus, Hermes Trismegistus, Pythagoras, Plato, Proclus, the Greek myths, the Chaldaean Oracles, and the Hebrew Kabbalah. He had no doubt that there was authentic sacred wisdom in the heathen nations, and especially in Egypt, as the cradle of arts and sciences after the universal Deluge and the place where both Moses and Jesus had been educated. Kircher paid no attention to the proof by the Protestant philologist Isaac Casaubon that the writings ascribed to Hermes Trismegistus dated from the early centuries AD. This made him almost the last in the chain of Christian Hermeticists that had begun with Marsilio Ficino and Giovanni Pico della Mirandola in fifteenth-century Florence. At the same time, through extending his study of ancient religion to include the new discoveries in India, China, Japan and the Americas, he was the first to take a global approach to the subject.[29]

Kircher's next work, *Itinerarium Exstaticum* ('Ecstatic journey', 1656) uses the fictional device of recounting a dream.[30] The author, called 'Theodidactus' (Taught by God), is led by the angel Cosmiel on a journey away from the earth, through the regions of the moon, sun and planets. While he does not hesitate to make use of Galileo's observations, Kircher's cosmology is geocentric.[31] Jesuit policy favoured the scheme of Tycho Brahe, who believed that the planets go round the sun, which in turn goes round the earth. Kircher says that the heavenly bodies are not, as in Aristotle's teaching, of a different substance from earth. The planets are uninhabited, but each one, and every star, has its Intelligence or angel. They send down influences in accordance with their traditional astrological characters, some of them seemingly evil but necessary to the general economy, for the universe was created for the sake of the earth, the earth for the sake of man, and man in order to love and know God.

The 'ecstatic journey' met with considerable criticism, though attempts to censor the work failed. Rather than reply to his enemies himself, Kircher allowed the loyal Kaspar Schott to prepare a second edition, greatly augmented with notes and detailed answers to the critical points, and publish it in Germany (*Iter Extaticum*, 1660), where the watchdogs of orthodoxy were less vigilant than in Rome.

The second volume of the work, *Iter Extaticum II* (1657) takes Theodidactus on a voyage in the opposite direction, beneath the surface of the earth. The book is advertised as the prelude to *Mundus Subterraneus*, a work that had been in preparation for many years. Here another angel, Hydriel, teaches his charge about the circulation of the seas, sucked in at the North Pole and spewed out at the South, and takes him on a terrifying journey from one pole to the other.

Cosmiel returns to teach him about the circulation of fire in the bowels of the earth and to lead him through the subterranean channels that link sea to sea. There is much discussion of how creatures are generated from the seeds enclosed in the earth, the growth of birds and fish, and the nature of whales. Kircher is here among the first to suggest that mountains rise and fall following natural movements in the earth's crust.

In 1656 the bubonic plague broke out in Rome, and the Jesuit College isolated itself behind locked doors.[32] While some fathers went out to tend the sick, Kircher used his microscope to seek the cause of the epidemic. In *Scrutinium Physico-Medicum* ('Physio-medical investigation', 1658), he summarizes the three types of explanation of the disease. One rests on the Hermetic medicine of Paracelsus and Cornelius Agrippa; the second on religious and moral causes; the third on official medicine. Kircher rejects the tendency to seek a scapegoat or to blame the epidemic on anyone but ourselves, whom God periodically visits, as in biblical times, with trials of our faith in Him. On a practical level, Kircher examined the blood of the victims under a microscope and saw 'animalcules'. While his instrument was not nearly powerful enough to have shown the actual plague bacillus, he may have seen the largest types of bacteria, and in any case was the first to suggest that disease may be caused by germs, rather than by imbalance of the humours, devilry and so on.[33] At the same time, he recommended wearing a dead toad around the neck, not out of any superstitious belief but as a scientifically proven 'magnet': as toads are notoriously poisonous and covered with unpleasant swellings, they naturally attract the poisonous vapours that cause such swellings in humans.[34]

Another phenomenon that the seemingly omniscient Kircher was invited to explain was the appearance of cross-shaped markings on the garments of those exposed to the fall of volcanic ash from Mount Vesuvius.[35] In *Diatribe de Prodigiosis Crucibus* ('Discourse on the prodigious crosses', 1661), he blames it merely on the effect of ashes staining the cross-woven fabrics, but does consider such natural events as divinely ordained. Kircher's linguistic interests next led to *Polygraphia Nova* ('New polygraphy', 1663).[36] In a typically Jesuit combination, it contains both material for a universal language, and a treatise on secret writing and cryptography. The noblest of his patrons were also given a special chest with movable slats that enabled them to encode secret political messages, but although everyone admired them, there is no evidence that they were ever used for this purpose.

Fabio Chigi, now Pope, was responsible for a new climate of reconciliation between the formerly warring sects within Christianity, and it was with his sanction that Kircher turned to a Protestant printer for his next works.[37] In August 1661 he signed an independent contract with the Amsterdam publisher Joannes Jansson van Waesberge, who offered 2,200 scudi for all of Kircher's stock of books published in Rome, along with their copperplates, woodblocks, characters and punches.[38] It took another four years for the first fruits of this relationship to appear in print: this was *Mundus Subterraneus* ('The

KASPAR SCHOTT, THE FAITHFUL FRIEND[39]

Kaspar Schott, of whom no portrait or family history exists, was born on 5 February 1608, in Königshofen, Franconia. In 1627 he entered the Jesuit College in nearby Würzburg, where Kircher arrived as a teacher in 1630. After a year, during which Schott was Kircher's pupil in mathematics, they went their separate ways. Schott was evacuated to the Low Countries, then sent to Sicily where he spent eighteen years in various Jesuit colleges, first as trainee, then as teacher. In the meantime, he read every word that Kircher wrote, and started a correspondence with him.

Schott's golden years were 1652–1655, when he was sent to Rome and was able to satisfy his long-held ambition to work with Kircher again. Beside proof-reading *Œdipus Ægyptiacus*, Schott edited the revised (third) edition of *Magnes,* in which he discovered innumerable errors which he managed not to blame on his master.[40] He read Kircher's correspondence and other manuscripts in the Roman College's library, and paid particular attention to the machines in Kircher's museum (see p. 45). In his own writings he gives us occasional glimpses of idyllic ramblings in the environs of Rome, and visits to the villas with their sundials, gardens and water-works.[41] After three years his superiors, never keen on fostering friendships between their charges, dispatched Schott back to Würzburg. However, this separation opened up a brief and meteoric career for him in the exciting world where prelates and secular rulers sated their boredom with mechanical toys, and the upcoming class of serious scientists finally shook off the burdens of Aristotelian and biblical dogma.

In 1655, Schott made contact with Johann Philipp von Schönborn, the Bishop of Würzburg who was also Archbishop-Elector of Mainz and one of the most powerful men in the waning Holy Roman Empire. Schönborn had just been at Regensburg for the Imperial Diet and had there witnessed a demonstration of Otto von Guericke's air-pump. The Elector accepted the dedication of Schott's first book, *Mechanica Hydraulicopneumatica* ('Mechanics of water and air'), which was mostly based on Kircher's machines but also contained the first published account of Guericke's 'Magdeburg Experiment', which had demonstrated the power of the vacuum.[42] This was an epochal event in the history of science, for it led to the acceptance of the vacuum and, soon after, to the understanding of air pressure. But it challenged Aristotle's physics, still dogma in the Jesuit world, which denied the possibility of a vacuum. Schott carefully negotiated his way between the two incompatible world views.

Schott continued as Kircher's best publicist in the German-speaking regions. In 1657–1659 he published, in four volumes, the great work on natural magic that Kircher had never had time for, *Magia Universalis Naturae et Artis* ('Universal magic of nature and art'). Next he wrote an account of Kircher's latest mathematical instrument, the Pantometer (*Pantometrum Kircherianum,* 1660), defended the popular *Itinerarium Exstaticum* against its Roman critics and produced a second edition, with much additional material, under his own name (*Iter Extaticum,* 1660). In *Physica Curiosa* ('Physical curiosities', 1662) he filled 1,500 pages with accounts of strange phenomena, anomalies of nature and monsters. The next year, 1663, saw his *Anatomia Physico-Hydrostatica Fontium ac Fluminum* ('Physical and hydrostatic anatomy of springs and rivers') and *Arithmetica Practica* ('Practical arithmetic').

Only two years remained to Schott. If Kircher's productivity is impressive, that of his pupil is well-nigh miraculous, for Schott managed to issue the thousand-page *Technica Curiosa* ('Technical curiosities', 1664), *Schola Steganographica* ('School of cryptography', 1665) and *Joco Seria Naturae et Artis* ('Serious amusements of nature and art', 1666), and to leave behind a manuscript on Kircher's mathematical machine, *Organum Mathematicum* (published 1668). He died on 22 May 1666; his few epitaphs unsurprisingly attribute his death to overwork.

Schott never had the advantages of Kircher's Amsterdam publisher. His books are just as long, but they are smaller in format and printed on inferior paper. The illustrations are numerous, but it is not unfair to call them 'quaint'. However, they brought Kircher's work and ways of thinking into the hands of those who could never have afforded the Jansson folios. Schott's logomania, writing a Latin as prolix and redundant as his master's, must have been less tiresome to his readers than it is to our more hurried age. He deserves to be remembered as the person who, in the most chaste sense, fell in love with Kircher and remained true to him until death.

subterranean world', 1664–1665),[43] which Kircher had mostly finished a decade earlier under the title of *Geocosmus*. It expands the themes of *Iter Extaticum II*, appealing to a wider public through lavish illustrations, and develops his earlier theories of vulcanism and the generation of animals and plants. Convinced that even frogs and mice can arise through spontaneous generation, Kircher explains that the Creator has infused in the *massa chaotica* (chaotic mass) of the earth a *panspermia rerum* or *semen universale* (universal seed of things) endowed with *vis radiativa* (radiating energy). This is the source of all bodily existence, growing as circumstances allow into all manner of creatures. Other themes in *Mundus Subterraneus* on which Kircher's opinions are of historical interest are the tides, alchemy, petrefaction and palingenesis (the resurrection of dead matter, e.g. of a plant from its ashes). The whole work is less a scientific treatise than a pageant of the wonders of creation, intended to induce love and respect for the Creator. At the same time, it opened up many new areas to popular and scientific discussion.

By now Kircher was a celebrity. His portrait, engraved in 1655 by Cornelius Bloemaert, was published as the frontispiece to *Mundus Subterraneus*. Visitors to Rome sought interviews with him, or at least entry to the museum that he was assembling in the Jesuit College. Holding an important place in the history of museums, this collection had begun with the donation of Peiresc's Egyptian objects. It grew as objects arrived from the various Jesuit missions, including natural freaks and enigmas such as stones with designs imprinted on them (another result, Kircher thought, of the 'universal seeds'). Kircher added ingenious machines of his own design, based on tricks of magnetism, acoustics and optics. The museum was raided for souvenirs after his death, and fell into decay. After the confiscation of Jesuit property in 1870 the remaining contents were dispersed to various Italian museums, and little remains of it today, while the building now houses a *liceo* (secondary school).

Kircher's recreation was exploring the countryside surrounding Rome. In 1661, while searching for antiquities south of Tivoli, he found the ruins of an old sanctuary built by the Emperor Constantine at Mentorella, the legendary site of St Eustace's vision of Christ between the horns of a stag. Kircher arranged for the restoration of its church, dedicated to the Virgin Mary, and of the chapel of St Eustace, begging donations from the Emperor and his other influential friends. It became a place of pilgrimage and his favourite retreat. He described the place and its history in his first topographical work, *Historia Eustachio-Mariana* ('Eustachian and Marian history', 1665).

Arithmologia ('Arithmology', 1665) is, in John Fletcher's words, 'a dull and lengthy treatise written in strict conformity with the mathematical trends of the seventeenth century, and containing little of interest'.[44] It does, however, include a treatment of the Kabbalistic and magical uses of number. Kircher did not approve of magic, in the sense of supernatural operations. But his Hermetic world view, based on the correspondence of all levels of being, did allow for influences to travel from higher to lower levels – for example, from the planets to plants and the human body. To exploit these correspondences and to harness the occult or hidden forces in matter was *natural* magic, shading imperceptibly into what we call technology. At the summit of the Hermetic chain of being is the mind of God, which seems to contain number as the archetype of archetypes. This is the 'true and licit mystery' mentioned in the subtitle of the work.

The unearthing of a broken obelisk near the former Temple of Isis, and the decision of Pope Alexander VII to re-erect it, led to *Obeliscus Ægyptiacus* (1666). The side facing the ground was not visible, but Kircher, after studying and translating the other three sides, successfully predicted the hieroglyphs that would be found on it. This convinced any further doubters that he had correctly solved the mystery of the hieroglyphs.

The reports of Jesuit missionaries to the Far East enabled Kircher to compile *China Monumentis … Illustrata* ('China illustrated with monuments', 1667), one of his least original works but in many ways the most important historically, as it was the foundation of oriental studies.[45] It contained new documents on oriental geography, geology, botany, zoology, religion and language, including the first picture of the Potala in Lhasa, Tibet, the first Chinese vocabulary, and the first reproduction of the Sanskrit alphabet and grammar. Kircher attributed all oriental religions to the deviation of Noah's son Cham, who had polluted the original true religion with polytheism, idolatry, and demonic magic. Alone among Kircher's books, *China* was translated during his lifetime into French, Dutch and German, and partially into English.

A short third book on magnetism, *Magneticum Naturae Regnum* ('The magnetic kingdom of nature', 1667), contains Kircher's last thoughts on sympathies and antipathies in the animal, vegetable and mineral realms. It was probably the new phenomena from the East, such as the reputed snake-stone from India that cured snakebite, that prompted him to write on the subject once again.[46] His main efforts during the mid-1660s went into the composition of *Ars Magna Sciendi* ('The great art of knowledge', 1669), his most ambitious attempt to lay a foundation for all possible knowledge. He appears to have known nothing of Francis Bacon's *Novum Organum* (1620), in which the experimental method is suggested as a way of finding out things unknown; not, as Kircher used it, as a way of confirming a world view already fixed. He ignored René Descartes' *Discourse on Method* (1636), which approached the problem of knowledge from a standpoint of ignorance. There was no scepticism or nominalism about Kircher, who assumed that since everything in the universe was connected, it was all knowable if only one had a framework into which to fit it. The framework in this case was a blend of Aristotelian and Thomistic logic with the categories of Ramon Llull, the fourteenth-century Mallorcan mystic. Kircher developed a symbolic language for syllogistic and other statements, based on his own expansion of Lull's categories.

Kircher's wanderings in the countryside now gave birth to *Latium* (1671), a topography of the region around Rome, illustrated with imaginative reconstructions of the ancient Roman villas, as well as the modern ones.[47] A companion work treating the region around Florence, *Iter Hetruscum*

('Tuscan journey') remained unpublished and appears to be lost.[48] *Splendor et Gloria Domus Joanniæ* ('The splendour and glory of the house of Juan'), otherwise titled *Principis Christiani Archetypon Politicum* ('Political archetype of a Christian prince', 1672), is a study of the ideal ruler, illustrated with emblems. It is an atypical and sycophantic work, made for a Spanish patron.[49]

Although *Phonurgia Nova* ('New phonurgy [acoustics]', 1673) is largely taken verbatim from *Musurgia Universalis*, it has the distinction of being the first book ever dedicated entirely to the science of acoustics. It describes the propagation and amplification of sound through devices such as the speaking trumpet.

Arca Noë ('Noah's Ark', 1675) and *Turris Babel* ('The Tower of Babel', 1679) form a pair, expensively designed by the publisher Jansson as an illustrated compendium of prehistory.[50] To combat the growing scepticism about the Bible, Kircher proves that the Ark could have contained all the necessary animals, and that all of mankind descends from Noah. He strives to reconcile the Bible with other sources of ancient history, holding firmly to 3984 BC as the date of Creation. In *Turris Babel* he continues the story to show how the world was repopulated after the Flood, and how the original language of mankind (Hebrew) split into today's 72 or more tongues. His treatment of the Tower of Babel and the Seven Wonders of the ancient world belongs within the Jesuit tradition of mystical architecture and the Art of Memory.[51]

Kircher returned once more to Egyptology in *Sphinx Mystagoga* ('The Sphinx, teacher of the mysteries', 1676), to interpret the hieroglyphs on some mummy cases recently brought to Europe. It includes a lengthy discourse on ancient beliefs in metempsychosis and reincarnation, which he vigorously refutes. Kircher's last work, befitting one whose career had begun as a professor of mathematics, was *Tariffa Kircheriana* ('Kircherian table', 1679), treating the squaring of the circle, trigonometry, and musical proportion.[52] It was issued with a comprehensive set of multiplication tables (as was necessary in pre-logarithmic days), furnished by Benedetto Benedetti.

In Kircher's last year, Jansson published a digest of experiments drawn from his many works: *Physiologia Kircheriana Experimentalis* ('Kircher's experimental physiology', 1680), compiled by J.S. Kestler. As Brian Merrill says,[53] it shows what a good editor could have made of Kircher's own work. Kircher himself had by now withdrawn from public life. Suffering his share of the ailments of old age, he gave himself increasingly to spiritual exercises, and died on the same day as his friend the sculptor Bernini: 27 November 1680.

Notes

1 Kircher's autobiography was published in 1684 as a supplement to Hieronymus Langenmantel's selection of his letters (see Langenmantel in the Bibliography). There is a complete English translation in Fletcher 1966. Where the following brief biography differs from Kircher's and other standard accounts, it is indebted to Berthold Jäger's study of Kircher's roots and early years (see Jäger). For present purposes, I have not distinguished between verifiable events and those for which we have only Kircher's word.

2 He was never quite certain about the year. On the last page of *Magnes*, he notes that he finished it on 2 May 1641, the same day as he was born in 1601, with the sun in the 10th degree of Taurus. That birthdate often appears in earlier biographical and bibliographical sources.

3 Athanasius loyally credited his father with a doctorate in theology from the University of Mainz, then as Professor of Theology, teaching the Benedictine monks in Seligenstadt. But none of this can be documented, and Johann's degree was at most an MA. See Jäger, 9, 11.

4 Jäger, 12.

5 Jäger, 14, 19.

6 Haakman, 51.

7 See Smith, 123, fig. 109, for a photograph of the portal of the Jesuit College in Paderborn, finished three years before Kircher's arrival. Smith's book is invaluable for understanding and imagining the German Jesuit world in which Kircher grew up.

8 Syrian or Syriac was the script and language now generally known as Aramaic.

9 On Kircher and magnetism, see Hine.

10 See Stolzenberg, 'Kircher's Egypt'.

11 On Kircher and Peiresc, see Miller.

12 See Miller; Marrone, 40–54.

13 Not, as often said, to be court mathematician; see Stolzenberg 2004, 30; see also ibid., 38, where Kircher's romantic story of his surprise landing in Rome is shown to be false.

14 See Lucas, 37–43, on the foundation of the Roman College and its associated churches, and on the political advantages of their location.

15 The Pope was afraid of eclipses, and had Campanella released from his thirty-year captivity as the only man who could still do the Ficinian magic necessary to avert their effects. See Walker, 205–210.

16 See Fletcher 2006, [468], for a list of Kircher's excursions around Rome and visits to Tuscany.

17 Friedrich proceeded to a vigorous career in sea warfare against the Turks, and was later made a Cardinal. See Hein and Mader, 23–24, 74–75.

18 On Holsten, who later became the Vatican Librarian, see Hein and Mader 1997, 69–70.

19 Transcribed in *Musurgia Universalis*, I, 542.

20 See Pastine, 94.

21 The author is given as Salvatore Imbroll, long thought to be a pseudonym for Kircher himself but now independently identified; see Hein and Mader 1997, 122–128. Further on the Maltese machine, see Arecco, 53.

22 See the exchange of letters in Hein and Mader 1997, 36–49.

23 On Kircher and music, see Beck; Gouk; Scharlau 1969 and 1988; Zarpellon.

24 See Findlen, 'A Jesuit's Books', 330.

25 See Fletcher, 'Athanasius Kircher and Duke August', 101–102.

26 On 11 November 1651 Kircher wrote to Queen Christina that he was worried about having had no reply from her for three years. He apologizes that the dedication of *Obeliscus Pamphilius* is already bespoken by the Pope, but that *Mundus Subterraneus*, no less large, could be dedicated to her (APUG Ms. 561, f.50). On Kircher's role in Christina's conversion, see Åkerman.

27 On Kircher and the hieroglyphs, among many other studies, see David, 43–56; Marrone.

28 Merrill, 15.

29 On Kircher's attitude to non-Christian religions, see Pastine.

30 On Kircher's ecstatic journey and its reissue by Schott, see Siebert, 'Vom römischen *Itinerarium*'.

31 On Kircher's astronomy, see Monaco.

32 On this episode and the resulting book, see Baldwin, 'Reverie in Time of Plague'.

33 For an important treatment of issues raised by Kircher's microscopy, see Strasser, 'Science and Pseudoscience', 229–235.

34 See Baldwin, 'Matters Medical', 89.

35 For a thorough treatment of the *Diatribe*, see Pastine, 168–184. See also Stolzenberg, 'The Connoisseur of Magic', 55–56.

36 On the *Polygraphia*, see Wilding.

37 Rowland, 22, states that before he became Pope, Chigi had been facilitating Kircher's access to Protestant publishers.

38 The *scudo* was a gold coin weighing about 1/9 ounce (3.5 grams), equivalent to the Venetian *zecchino*, the Netherlandish and Austrian *ducat*, and the French *écu d'or*. Kircher followed the advice of his more worldly friends in accepting Jansson's proposal to pay the contracted amount of 2,200 less six per cent (i.e. 2,068 scudi) immediately on signature of contract, rather than the entire sum in five annual payments. See his very businesslike letter of 25 August 1661 (APUG Ms. 563, f.265).

39 This account is mainly based on the most thorough treatment so far of Schott's life and work: Gorman and Wilding's 'Technica Curiosa: The Mechanical Marvels of Kaspar Schott (1608–1666)', in Schott 2000, 253–279, and 'Kaspar Schott (1608–1666): A Chronology', in ibid., 280–283.

40 Schott 2000, 256, 258.

41 See, for example, the account of a visit to a French nobleman's villa in Schott 1658, 219.

42 The experiment consisted of fitting together two iron hemispheres, pumping out the air, harnessing eight horses to each one, and trying to pull them apart. Schott's illustration in *Technica Curiosa* was widely copied and disseminated.

43 On Kircher's geology, see Kelber and Okrusch; Morello.

44 Fletcher 2006 [149].

45 Among the many studies of *China*, see Leibold; Rivosecchi, 77–98; Saussy. The translation by Charles D. Van Tuyl (see Bibliography) is the only complete English translation of any of Kircher's works.

46 See Baldwin, 'The Snakestone experiments'; Fletcher, 'Athanasius Kircher and Duke August', 113.

47 On *Latium*, see Schürmann.

48 The work was rejected by the censors on the grounds of inaccuracy. See Siebert, 'Kircher and His Critics', 84–86.

49 John Fletcher writes on this and other instances in which Kircher's knowledge, energy and obedience were exploited by others in 'Athanasius Kircher, a Man under Pressure'.

50 On both books, see Taylor, 81–91; Thomsen; on Kircher's conception of history, see Stolzenberg, 'Kircher Among the Ruins'; on Kircher's zoology in *Arca Noë*, see Capanna; on *Turris Babel*, see Pastine, 101–135.

51 See the article by Taylor.

52 On Kircher's mathematics, see Vollrath, 'Das Organum mathematicum'.

53 Merrill, 71.

Chapter 2   **Frontispieces**

On opening Kircher's major books, the first thing to greet the reader is a symbolic image encapsulating the whole work.[1] In the previous century, this had usually been combined with the title page and simulated a triumphal gateway or theatrical proscenium, which would frame essential information such as the title, subtitle, author, dedicatee, place, publisher, printer, bookseller and date. Once Kircher was famous, his publishers gave his books the full baroque treatment of a two-part prelude. On the verso (left-hand) page was a symbolic engraving properly called the frontispiece, while facing it on the right was the title page, set in type alone except for the printer's own insignia. There were variations, such as putting both frontispiece and title on the recto (right-hand) page, but the commonest usage was to address eye and mind in a single spread: the image on the left, the words on the right. Together they gave the reader an epitome of the work to come.

This chapter introduces Kircher's cosmology and some of his habits of thought by way of his emblematic frontispieces. The first of them appeared in *Magnes* (1641) (**Ill. 2.1**). A double-headed eagle, heraldic bird of the Habsburg dynasty, dominates the scene, with a magnet or lodestone on its breast containing the dedication to Emperor Ferdinand III (1608–1657). Kircher had no qualms about the propriety of absolute monarchy, and was probably sincere in his conviction that the so-called Holy Roman Empire was indeed 'holy'.[2] Here it receives its theological sanction at the top of the page, where God's eye directly adjoins the symbols of earthly rule, orb and imperial crown. Everything from there downwards is similarly linked, but here the topic of the book enters in, for all the links are due to the power of magnetism: the chain, the three crowns and the three sceptres all hold together by mere contact.[3] Fascinated as he was by the magnetism of iron and lodestones, in Kircher's cosmology they were the material aspect of the attraction and, ultimately, the divine Love that suffuses and binds the universe.

The many arrows on the eagle's wings refer to the magnetic compass and its varying declinations, which at the time seemed to hold the clue to the vexing problem of finding longitude at sea (see p. 193). The three crowns in the eagle's right claw are those that were bestowed on Ferdinand before he became Emperor: King of Hungary in 1625, King of Bohemia in 1627 and King of the Romans in 1636. The motto reads: 'He has added kingdoms to kingdoms and new sceptres to crowns. [He is] the needle of both north and south.'

The Latin contains a pun, for *Austri acus*, 'needle of the south', is also *Austriacus*, 'Austrian'. In the third edition of the work (1654), the inscribed lodestone was replaced by a miniature portrait of Ferdinand wearing the Order of the Golden Fleece.

Usually one such frontispiece would suffice for the whole work, but the third book of *Magnes* also opened with an elaborate symbolic title page (**Ill. 2.2**). In the foreground, an arrangement of discs is joined by magnetic chains. The motto on the ribbon reads 'All things are at rest, connected by secret knots.' In particular, what was connected in Kircher's view were the three principal worlds that constitute reality, and it is these that provide the key not only to many of his frontispieces but to his spiritual philosophy.

The four discs that form a triangle at the centre of the design symbolize these three worlds: the Archetypal world which is beyond reach of the senses, indicated by the eye of the threefold God; the Sidereal world of the heavenly bodies (sun, moon and stars), including those stars that make up the belt of the zodiac; and the Sublunary world beneath the moon's sphere with its four elements (earth, water, air, fire). The fourth of these inner discs pictures Man as Microcosm, shown as a figure with arms outstretched to encompass the spheres of his own little world, for in Hermetic philosophy, all that is in the universe is reflected in Man, and vice versa.

The outer discs, from the top clockwise, show with their appropriate symbols the human arts and sciences: Theology, Philosophy, Physics, Poetry, Rhetoric, Cosmography, Mechanics, Perspective, Astronomy, Music, Geography, Arithmetic, Natural Magic and Medicine (with the name of its patron goddess Hygeia). In the background is a woodland scene, partly to lend the discs the additional symbolism of fruits on the Tree of Life, and partly because nature, and particularly trees, are shown in the book to be magnetic.

This frontispiece seems to have been omitted when the entire book was reset, with all the illustrations newly engraved or woodcut, for the second edition (Cologne, 1643). In the third edition (Rome, 1654) it reappeared in larger format (**Ill. 2.3**), surrounded by a decorative border which contained further symbols of an eagle, scales and attributes of royalty.

Nothing so far in Kircher's works anticipates the splendid frontispiece of *Ars Magna Lucis et Umbrae* (1646) (**Ill. 2.4**). Here the three worlds are laid out in their full symbolic meaning. The name of God in Hebrew letters (IHVH)

2.1 Frontispiece of Book I of *Magnes*, as re-engraved for the second edition of 1643. The design combines a tribute to the Holy Roman Empire (the double-headed eagle, orb and crown beneath the eye of God) and the subject of the book, magnetism (chain, three crowns, three sceptres). The town below is imaginary.

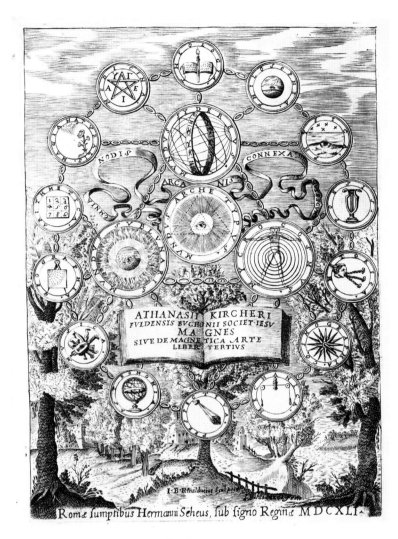

2.2 Title page of Volume III of *Magnes* (1641). The motto on the ribbon reads, 'All things are at rest, connected by secret knots.' The discs, joined by magnetism, are symbolic at many levels, from the three worlds to the arts and sciences.

2.3 Title page of the third edition of *Magnes* (1654). A decorative border has been added with attributes of royalty and at the top a royal eagle holding scales.

occupies the summit, just as it did in countless books, prints, coins and medals of Kircher's century – both Catholic and Protestant. Gazing directly at God are representatives of the Nine Orders of Angels. Beneath the clouds is a visual treatise on the ways by which humans can know what God chooses to reveal to them. The best way of all is 'Sacred Authority', or the Bible, for that comes via books written directly by God, as we can tell from the rays that, here alone, penetrate the cloud barrier. Second is Reason, which is a God-given gift that casts its own light on its ratiocinations.

Now we descend from the divine to the Sidereal world, marked (as in the same artist's design for *Musurgia Universalis* – see below) by the sphere with the zodiacal belt. Preeminent in this world are the sun and moon.

The flaming sun god has the zodiac signs marked on his body at the places ruled by those signs (heart–Leo; knees–Capricorn, etc. – compare **Ill. 15.5**), and holds the caduceus of Hermes, its windings marked by the signs of the five other planets and crowned by another eye, perhaps denoting the Hermetic wisdom that reveals the secrets of the lower worlds. In homage to the heraldic eagle of the imperial Habsburgs, that of the sun god has two heads, and so does the peacock that supports the moon goddess opposite. Her staff bears the owl, symbol of Athena the goddess of wisdom and complement to Hermes. But she gives off no rays of her own, shining only with the reflection from the sun. The best her light can do is to illuminate the moondial in the lower left corner.

2.4 Frontispiece of *Ars Magna Lucis et Umbrae* (1646). The symbolism focuses on the three worlds – divine, Sidereal and earthly, and the various levels of authority that they represent. The portrait in the centre is the dedicatee Ferdinand von Habsburg, son of the Emperor.

2.5 Frontispiece of *Obeliscus Pamphilius* (1650), a sort of self-advertisement. The ancient Egyptian obelisk has been thrown down by Father Time, but Kircher's muse, resting one foot on a masonic cube, is on hand to translate and explain the hieroglyphics.

Whilst Sol sits above a formal garden with its sundial and elegant casino, the very image of Apollonian order on earth, Luna sits above a dark and rough cavern. Beneath their clouds are two further sources of human knowledge. Sense relies on the natural light of the sun, and can be improved by technological aids such as the telescope pictured here. Profane Authority, on the other hand, is no better than a candle casting its faltering rays through a dark lantern. The frontispiece is a manifesto of the ways of knowledge as defined by Catholic tradition.

The miniature portrait in the centre is of the dedicatee, Archduke Ferdinand von Habsburg (1633–1654). He was the eldest son and heir of Emperor Ferdinand III, but predeceased his father.

In the frontispiece to *Obeliscus Pamphilius* (1650) (**Ill. 2.5**), Old Father Time has toppled the obelisk. It lies among the undergrowth near the Appian Way, and its Fame stands sadly chained to it. But there is hope! Hermes, messenger of the gods and patron of 'hermeneutics' as well as of Hermetism, flies down and interprets the hieroglyphs to the attentive Muse of Athanasius Kircher, who is backed by books of Egyptian wisdom, Pythagorean mathematics, Greek philology and Chaldaean astrology. Harpocrates, the infant god of secrecy, is keeping half the scroll in shadow and urging silence, for we must await the great *Œdipus Ægyptiacus* to garner the full fruits of Kircher's research into the languages inscribed on the pedestal: Hebrew, Samaritan, Coptic, Arabic and Ethiopian. With one foot he subdues the crocodile, symbol of the evil Typhon. Kircher's Muse rests her foot on a cubic stone bearing three symbols: a mason's square, a staff with the head of the hoopoe bird and a lituus or curved trumpet. The square and trumpet were in fact misreadings of the common pharaonic attributes of the flail and crook, with disastrous consequences for Kircher's understanding of Egyptian symbolism. Their significance is given in the commentary on the 'Symbol of Horus' (see **Ill. 15.20**). This is not a treatise in miniature, like the frontispiece to *Ars Magna Lucis,* but an example of the self-advertisement at which Kircher was adept.

In the same year, *Musurgia Universalis* appeared, with a frontispiece (**Ill. 2.6**) again structured around the Archetypal, Sidereal and Elemental worlds. At the summit the eye of God radiates from a triangle, marked by three signs that might be intended as the Hebrew letter Yod (the initial of IHVH), or the number 9 (that of the angelic choirs). I do not know whether the 34 stars of the triangle, or the 21 rays, are numerologically significant. The nine groups of winged infant heads are the nine angelic orders or 'choirs': Seraphim, Cherubim, Thrones, Dominations, Principalities, Powers, Virtues, Archangels and Angels. Two larger figures with six wings are the Seraphs described in the vision of the prophet Isaiah (Isaiah 6:2–3), who call to one another 'Holy, holy, holy is the Lord of hosts; the whole earth is full of his glory.' Here they hold a scroll containing the notation of a 36-voice canon on these words, which Christian liturgy adopted as the *Sanctus* of the Mass.

Next, in the cosmic realm, we find Apollo sprawled on the celestial sphere with its signs of the zodiac. He is crowned with the laurel of his beloved Daphne, and holds in his right hand a seven-stringed lyre (symbol of the seven planetary spheres and their harmony), while with his left he thrusts aside the sevenfold panpipe of his rival Marsyas. The sphere is inscribed with a quotation from the Book of Job (38:37): 'Who shall make the concert of heaven to sleep?'

In the elemental realm, Pythagoras points with one hand to his famous theorem, and with the other to the blacksmiths (working with the element of Fire), the clang of whose hammers gave him the vital clue to the mathematical basis of harmony. Ancient instruments are piled at his feet. Opposite him, on a much larger heap of modern instruments, is a Muse. The bird (inhabitant of Air) perching on her head is probably one of the Pierides, who in retribution for competing with the Muses in song were turned into magpies. Behind her, a stair leads up Mount Helicon to where Pegasus strikes the rock and brings forth Hippocrene, the spring of inspiration. At the foot of the mountain, one shepherd quotes Virgil's second Eclogue: 'pascite ut ante boves' (feed your cattle, as before) while another hears only the echo, 'oves' (sheep). To complete the musicality of the elements, a triton with a trident swims in Water in a round dance with mermaids, while on Earth, Pan pipes to a ring of satyrs.

Like *Magnes*, *Musurgia* has a second frontispiece (**Ill. 2.7**). The inscription on the pedestal reads: 'Apollo's right hand holds the world-lyre; his left fits high to low; thus good things are mingled with ill.' The figure, however, is not Apollo (it lacks his solar rays and arrows), but his devotee, Orpheus. With his god-inspired music, the Thracian singer has tamed the three-headed dog Cerberus, entered Hades, retrieved Eurydice, and now is unwisely looking back over his shoulder. His subsequent career illustrates the warning motto.

Towards the end of the book, when he turns from earthly music to celestial and divine harmony, Kircher uses this principle to explain the presence of malefic planets, and, by extension, the existence of natural evil in the world.

> To this end, God has placed in heaven by his natural act two dissonant bodies, Mars and Saturn, from whose pestiferous vapour all ills in the Sublunary world have their origin. But lest their evil should bring disaster to the undefended economy of the whole lower world, he placed in between them the benign planet Jupiter.... So there is nothing evil in the nature of things which does not eventually contribute to the good of all and the conservation of the universe. What else are Mars and Saturn but dissonances? Tied and syncopated by Jupiter in perfect consonance, they give to music not sweetness, exactly, but a great embellishment.[4]

These three large early works form a metaphysical trio. *Magnes* contained the doctrine of the secret coherence of the universe; *Ars Magna Lucis,* that of the ways of knowledge and illumination; *Musurgia Universalis,* a justification of the existence of evil. All the pieces of Kircher's world view were now in place, firmly anchored at the top end in dogmatic theology, and at the bottom by an exhaustive knowledge of the phenomenal world, both seen and unseen.

2.7 Frontispiece of Volume II of *Musurgia Universalis* (1650). Orpheus, having tamed Cerberus, has entered Hades to rescue Eurydice, but unwisely looks back at her.

2.6 Frontispiece of Volume I of *Musurgia Universalis* (1650). Once more the theme is the three worlds – at the top the eye of God in a triangle, in the middle the cosmic realm governed by Apollo and at the bottom the earthly world represented by the arts and sciences.

2.8 Frontispiece of *Œdipus Ægyptiacus* (1652–1654): an Egyptian landscape with palms, obelisks, temple and pyramid. The book held by the angels lists all the languages mastered by Kircher, who was fond of referring to himself as the riddle-solving Oedipus.

Œdipus Ægyptiacus (1652–1654) opens inevitably in a landscape of palms, obelisks, a temple and a step-pyramid (**Ill. 2.8**). Oedipus declares to the Sphinx that he has solved her riddle with the help of Sense, Experience and Reason. These last two are personified by angels whose open book lists the languages of the authorities on whom Kircher has called: Latin, Greek, Hebrew, Chaldaean, Syriac, Arabic, Samaritan, Armenian, Coptic, Persian, Ethiopian, Italian, German, Spanish, French and Portuguese. Nine seals dangle from the book, being the tools or disciplines involved in the decipherment: Wisdom of the Egyptians, Theology of the Phoenicians, Astrology of the Chaldaeans, Kabbalah of the Hebrews, Magic of the Persians, Mathemat-

ics of the Pythagoreans, Theosophy of the Greeks, Mythology, Alchemy of the Arabs and Philology of the Latins.

This frontispiece continues the theme of *Obeliscus Pamphilius*, celebrating Kircher's own achievement. Not only did he liken his solution of the Sphingian riddle of the hieroglyphs to the triumph of Oedipus, but he commonly referred to himself by that name. The Sphinx, he later reveals, 'was the symbol of arcane Wisdom, and of virtues detached from matter.'[5] This is probably why she looks so demure. In Kircher's mythology she is no man-eater, but the wisdom that is only accessible to the intellect when it is liberated from the senses. The connection with his decipherment of the Egyptian hieroglyphs is that, in his reading, they are always statements of 'supersensible wisdom'.

Kircher's *Itinerarium Exstaticum* appeared in 1656 with a plain title page. Only with the second edition, brought out and amplified by Kaspar Schott in 1660, was there any illustration at all. The frontispiece pictures Kircher not allegorically but as himself in his Jesuit robes, setting out with his handsome angel guide Cosmiel to measure the heavens with the geometer's tools of ruler and compass (**Ill. 2.9**). This image was almost certainly concocted by Schott, with the overt intention of defending Kircher from suspicion of astronomical heresy. The diagram of the planetary orbits demonstrates his allegiance to the Tychonian cosmology – that is, the system devised by Tycho Brahe – rather than to the perilous heliocentrism of Galileo. By 1660, the learned world had largely accepted Galileo's arguments for a static sun in the centre of the universe, and a moving earth, but the Jesuit order would long give lip service, at least, to the contrary. As it appears from this diagram, the starry sphere and the planets Saturn, Jupiter (with its four moons), Mars, Venus and Mercury revolve around the sun, but the sun, with the moon, revolves around the earth, which is the only unmoving body in the universe.

But what if this image were intended to be ironic? No one doubts that Kircher believed in the God whose Hebrew name blazes from the clouds, but the absurd smallness of the earth, and the feeble dotted line of the sun's orbit that sustains his orthodoxy, seem almost calculated to arouse suspicion.[6]

One of Kircher's greatest frontispieces is the one his friend Johann Paul Schor created for *Mundus Subterraneus* (1664–1665) (**Ill. 2.10**). From the blaze of uncreated light the hand of God emerges, holding the end of a chain. Threaded on it is the Egyptian symbol of a winged globe with a serpent, which Kircher interpreted as the Anima Mundi or 'soul of the world'. The serpent holds in its jaws a ribbon with a quotation from Virgil: 'The spirit sustains it from within: infused through its every member, Mind sets the mass in motion.'[7] The chain passes through the Sidereal realm, in which are seen the sun and moon, to the globe of the earth at the centre of the universe.

Close to the earth, whose arrangement of land and sea answers to no known map, is the meteorological realm of wind and weather. Here are the twelve winds, each blowing with a different quality: we see mist, hail and bunches of flowers. On the ground, two Muses contemplate the earth (on the left) and the heavens (on the right). The right-hand Muse has a telescope and also a pair of

ARE PROTESTANTS ALL DAMNED?

Kircher was a Catholic Christian, an ordained priest, and a lifetime member of the Society of Jesus. This defines both the rock on which his work was founded and the limits within which his mind was free to operate. For a religious living in the heart of the Catholic theocracy, there was no question of outward dissent, nor is there reason to think that he was a secret rebel. It would be anachronistic to project modern attitudes onto a man of his time, in his position.

The conversation with the angel Cosmiel at the end of *Itinerarium Exstaticum* brings one as close as one is likely to get to Kircher's religious convictions. The scene is as follows. At the end of his journey, Theodidactus (representing Kircher himself) asks Cosmiel about the future prospects for earth and mankind. The angel replies that the earth as we know it will be destroyed; there will be a new heaven and a new earth. The blessed will go to heaven, and the heretics and heathens will be damned for all eternity.[8]

THEO: If all the heavenly bodies will be renewed, where will the prison of the damned be?

COS: Inside the terrestrial globe, eternally crusted over so that no light or anything else can enter: a place of eternal horror and confusion.

THEO: How can the multitude of the damned all fit in?

COS: Just as the blessed will have glorious bodies, so the damned will have bodies consisting of punishment. Packed together in eternal hatred, they will gnaw each other's viscera.

THEO: What about the demons?

COS: The damned will have them for company. But the elect will see none of this.

[This is not enough comfort for Theodidactus, for he numbers many 'heretics' – that is, Protestants – among his correspondents, patrons and publishers.]

THEO: I can see how none can be saved without implicit or explicit faith in Christ. But I see all these heretics believing in Christ, and certainly they are far on the road to salvation.

COS: God doesn't like faith that comes only from pride in one's own intelligence. He only approves the faith of the Church which He has founded for the interpretation of His mind. Thus heretics are like putrid members separated from the Church, and are reckoned to have no faith.

THEO: But they believe everything revealed in the Holy Scriptures.

COS: Yes, they study it and interpret it with their own intelligence, but they're doing nothing more than you do when you study Plato or Aristotle. They get nothing out of it but their own opinions: hence their confusion and perplexity. Look at how many different sects have arisen among the Calvinists and Lutherans, how many different opinions they hold. How could this be real faith? Faith must be one, holy and Catholic, conforming to the Church which is the firmament of truth. Anyone who goes the slightest bit astray from it walks in darkness, destitute of any hope of salvation.

THEO: The heretics say the Apostles' Creed every day; they believe in the Communion of Saints and the Catholic Church. Isn't that a sort of faith?

COS: If they don't want to be members of the Catholic Church, they are reciting things that they don't mean. Do you think the Lutheran or Calvinist churches are Catholic?

THEO: They believe that they are.

COS: Where do you see the Lutheran or Calvinistic faith disseminated through the whole world? Where's its sanctity, its mystery, its head, priesthood, jurisdiction? It has hardly managed to spread beyond Germany, whereas we're in India, Japan, China, America – all over the globe. Where are their saints, their martyrs, their miracles?

THEO: I see Lutherans even celebrating the Mass, absolving sin, and similar things that they wouldn't do if they lacked authority.

COS: But in separating from truth, they've lost the divine influx that gives the Church perpetual celestial gifts. Who gave them the keys of power? Secular princes? No one can give something that he doesn't have. Theirs is a pseudo-church. When they think that they're consecrating the Body of the Lord, they do no more than any peasant pronouncing the same words.

THEO: Then can heretics hope for no salvation?

COS: As long as they persist in error, none at all. Moreover, since they reject salvation by works, their 'faith' can't possibly please God. As Saint James writes, 'Faith apart from works is barren'. The heretics corrupt the Holy Scriptures; they do nothing but pervert and mutilate the words of Christ.

THEO: How you have dispelled my doubts and opened the way of truth! You've really proved that the heretics are perfidious. I've always suspected non-Catholic religion, and now I know for certain that it's not from God, but from man, just as Platonism comes only from Plato.

But how can God, who has the good of humanity at heart, save so few? It grieves my heart to think of America, which had no prophets or apostles until it was discovered 200 years ago, and all the other nations sunk in idolatry.

COS: Neither men nor angels can know the divine decrees. God made man for His own glory, and to know the ineffable vision of Himself. But He always converts everything to good, which means to the manifestation of His glory.

THEO: But wouldn't it have been better not to leave so many without help, and to have made it possible for the whole human race to be saved?

COS: God always desires the salvation of a sinner, but He won't drag a man to heaven by force, or compel the unwilling.

[With this, the matter is dropped, and Theodidactus ends the book with a paean of praises to his God.]

The two-part *Itinerarium* is Kircher's only piece of fiction, his only work written in dialogue form, and the one that most riled the censors.[9] Reading the dialogue that I have paraphrased above, I recall the accusation against Galileo's *Dialogue on the Two World Systems*: that although he claimed that it presented fairly both the sun-centred and the earth-centred systems, it cast the latter in a poor light and placed the arguments for it in the mouth of a fool. In Kircher's scenario, where the burning issue is whether Protestants will be saved or damned, Theodidactus argues passionately in their favour, while the angel, though no fool, can only retail the party line of the Counter-Reformation. More than that, Theodidactus even calls God's justice into question with his suggestion that things could have been better arranged for the salvation of all mankind.[10] No wonder that Cosmiel ducks that question.

▲ **2.9** Frontispiece of *Iter Exstaticum Kircherianum* (third edition, 1671), probably invented by Schott, showing Kircher in his Jesuit robes. The cosmology is that of Tycho Brahe, not that of Galileo, though it is not impossible that he privately subscribed to the latter.

▶ **2.10** Frontispiece of Volume I of *Mundus Subterraneus* (1664–1665). The winged globe with a serpent is the Soul of the World, which a chain, held by the hand of God, joins to the sidereal and earthly realms. The globe, which corresponds to no known geography, is surrounded by the winds.

scales, for measuring the equilibrium in which the whole system is held.

The frontispiece appears in copies dated 1665 and 1668, and in the third edition of 1678.[11] The title page, exceptionally, also carries a symbolic engraving (**Ill. 2.11**). It pictures Wisdom with the motto around her head: *Sapiens dominabitur astris* (The wise man will dominate the stars).[12] She sits at the border of earth, air and sea, filled with the natural phenomena of which

she is writing in her book: the sun and moon, volcanoes, the interior of the earth, strange creatures, fossils and experimental science. Her book symbolizes Kircher's own.

The same inspirational figure – let us again call her Kircher's Muse – appears on the title page of the second volume of *Mundus Subterraneus* (**Ill. 2.12**). She has set her geometrical instruments on the ground and is busy

ATHANASII KIRCHERI
E SOC. JESU

MUNDUS SUBTERRANEUS,

in XII Libros digestus;

QUO

Divinum Subterrestris Mundi Opificium, mira
Ergasteriorum Naturæ in eo distributio, verbo παυλάμορφον
Protei Regnum,

Universæ denique Naturæ majestas & divitiæ summa
rerum varietate exponuntur , Abditorum effectuum Causæ acri indagine
inquisitæ demonstrantur , cognitæ per Artis & Naturæ conjugium ad
Humanæ vitæ necessarium usum vario Experimentorum apparatu,
necnon novo modo & ratione applicantur.

AD

ALEXANDRUM VII.
PONT. OPT. MAX.

EDITIO TERTIA,

Ad fidem scripti exemplaris recognita, & prioribus emendatior : tum ab Auctore Româ
submissis variis Observationibus novisque Figuris auctior.

TOMUS I.

AMSTELODAMI,

Apud JOANNEM JANSSONIUM à WAESBERGE & FILIOS,
ANNO cIɔ Iɔc LXXVIII. *Cum Privilegiis.*

▲ **2.11** Title page of Volume I of *Mundus Subterraneus* (1665, 1668 and 1678), featuring the figure of Wisdom sitting at the border of earth, sea and air.

▶ **2.12** Title page of Volume II of *Mundus Subterraneus*. The same figure, 'Kircher's Muse', is studying hieroglyphics and drawing obelisks. She is visited by Mercury and Apollo. A putto holds a medallion of Leopold I. In the background is a statue of Diana of Ephesus and a painting of an alchemist; through the doorway miners investigate the interior of the earth.

drawing obelisks and studying the Egyptian hieroglyphs. Three messengers interrupt her. One is a putto, carrying a medallion of Emperor Leopold I. The work was dedicated to Pope Alexander VII, but this seems to have been a secondary homage, in recognition of the Emperor's support. The eagles holding up the title banner are a version of the double-headed eagle of the Habsburgs, each with an imperial orb.

The Muse's other visitors are Mercury and Apollo, who are urging her to turn her attention elsewhere. They point to the statue of Diana of Ephesus (whose complicated symbolism is explained in connection with **Ill. 14.5**). Here, the emphasis is on her rulership of the terrestrial globe. The background shows two ways of investigating the latter. On the wall is a painting of an alchemist seated at his furnace with alembics behind him on the floor. This is in shadow and barely discernible, which may suggest that it is not the best way to understand how the earth is constituted. Outside, in contrast, miners are at work at the mouth of a cave. By exploring the cavities of the globe, at first in person during his study of volcanoes, and later with logical reasoning and imagination, Kircher arrived at what he considered its true workings.

The scroll below quotes two lines from the Orphic Hymn to Kronos: 'You who, as progenitor, dwell in every part of the world; you consume all things and replenish them, too.'[13]

Arithmologia (1665) is one of Kircher's most difficult books and I do not pretend to explain it here, beyond the frontispiece (**Ill. 2.13**), which again uses a three-worlds structure. The eye of God in the centre of a flaming triangle denotes the Trinity. The letters in the corners, Iod and He, are the shortest

2.13 Frontispiece of *Arithmologia* (1665), which again represents the three worlds, incorporating the eye of God, the nine orders of angels, the cosmic spheres and (on the earthly plane) two sources of arithmetic – the Bible and Greek philosophy.

of the Hebrew names of God, found in Psalm 68:4 (King James version: 'extol him that rideth upon the heavens by his name JAH, and rejoice before him'). The Nine Orders of Angels form an ingenious geometrical arrangement of three intersecting triangles, together making a nine-pointed star. The flying angel on the left carries a ruler and a plumb line; the angel on the right, a tablet with the magic square of three. They allude to a famous passage in the apocryphal Wisdom of Solomon, 11:20: 'But thou hast ordered all things in measure, and number and weight.'

The visible cosmos is bounded by the fixed stars and contains the orbits of the seven planets around an unmoving earth. It is represented here as a winged sphere, an Egyptian symbol that Kircher interpreted as the Anima Mundi or Soul of the World. Outside it, two fine dotted circles denote the Crystalline sphere and the Primum Mobile: two invisible spheres sanctified by geocentric tradition, one to circumscribe the Sidereal world, and the other to keep it spinning round the earth once a day.

On the mundane plane are two philosophers, one a learned Jew with an open book showing the stars of Solomon and David, and the other a pagan philosopher with Pythagoras's theorem. They represent the twin sources of arithmological tradition in the Bible and the pagan classics. I cannot explain the presence of the cat.

The publication of *Obeliscus Ægyptiacus* (1666), also called *Obeliscus Alexandrinus* and *Interpretatio Hieroglyphica*, added little to Kircher's exposition of Egyptian mysteries, but put them into an abridged and readable form. In the frontispiece (**Ill. 2.14**), a portrait of Pope Alexander VII with attendant angels occupies the place usually assigned to God. Above an idealized Egyptian landscape, two other putti are erecting the Minervan obelisk, discovered in the gardens of Santa Maria sopra Minerva and restored by Bernini under the Pope's patronage (see **Ill. 4.17**). Kircher's prediction of what would be found on the hidden side marked the apogee of his reputation as an infallible oracle, yet on closer scrutiny this was not such an extraordinary achievement.[14] The inscriptions on two opposite sides are virtually identical, and after his experience with other obelisks, Kircher could be almost certain that the unseen side would match the upper one.

Magneticum Naturae Regnum (1667) was a small book with much less illustration than Kircher's audience had come to expect. The decorative title page (**Ill. 2.15**) reads: 'The magnetic realm of nature, arranged in a triple magnet: inanimate, animate and sensitive'. The large circles hanging on the magnetic chain show the inanimate magnetic needle, with the motto 'Indeclinably'; the cock and stag for animate beings, with the motto 'Nature rejoices in nature'; and the sensitive palm tree, with the motto 'When pressed down, it rises again.' The ribbon above them carries a paraphrase of the epigram used in *Magnes*: 'The world is bound by secret knots,' which might well serve as the motto for all of Kircher's work.[15]

The magnetic chain depends from the hand of God and passes through the sidereal world of sun and moon. These have their correspondences on earth in the shape of the sunflower (on the left), which follows the course of the sun as though magnetically drawn to it, and a lesser-known flower (on the right) that supposedly follows the moon. The cock and stag, too, are respectively solar and lunar creatures; so 'nature rejoices in nature' by joining all things in chains of correspondence and magnetic attraction.

The two snakes at the bottom of the frontispiece are the main reason that Kircher published this atypically pocket-sized book, years after exhausting the subject in his great treatise *Magnes*: he wanted to write about the newly discovered phenomenon of the 'snake stone'. Missionaries from India had reported that a stone found in the head of a certain snake had the power to cure snake bite through simply being applied to the affected part. They sent a sample to Kircher, who arranged an experiment with a dog and a large viper, and found that the stone worked just as it should: the dog, though bitten, survived. The rest of the book is filled with a concise account of the magnetic philosophy, with examples mostly taken from his earlier work.

Unlike the frontispieces formed around the three worlds of Kircher's cosmology, that of *China Illustrata* (**Ill. 2.16**), from 1667, shows only two, and with good reason. The Jesuits standing on earth – recognizable as the missionaries Adam Schall and Matteo Ricci – are fellows with the Jesuits kneeling in heaven – Sts Ignatius Loyola and Francis Xavier. The missionaries receive God's illuminating rays directly, and have no need for the intermediate world of the stars and planets. An angel is showing them a map of the territory in need of conversion to the Catholic faith, and they in turn are unveiling it for us. All this takes place on a stage, before a portico of Corinthian columns, which might equally well be in one of Rome's more theatrical churches.

Instead of the Hebrew name of Yahweh or the eye, the most usual symbols for God, there is the Jesuit monogram 'IHS', which has been interpreted in various ways. It was originally the Greek abbreviation for *Iēsous* (the capital letters Iota, Eta, Sigma). When read as Latin, it could mean *Iesus Hominum Salvator* (Jesus, saviour of men); *In Hac Salus* (in this [cross is] salvation); or the revelation to Emperor Constantine, as he beheld a cross in the sky: *In Hoc Signum Vinces* (in this sign you will conquer), the fourth word being suggested by the three nails beneath the letters. In any case, it denotes the particular dedication of the Society of Jesus to the Second Person of the Trinity.

Two complex frontispieces decorate *Ars Magna Sciendi* (1669). The first (**Ill. 2.17**) is a prime example of Kircher's self-image as an inspired mediator between heaven and earth.[16] Beneath the eye of God, angels unfurl a banner with fifteen seals representing the chief domains of knowledge: Theology, Metaphysics, Physics, Logic, Medicine, Mathematics, Moral Ethics, Ascetics, Jurisprudence, Politics, Scriptural Interpretation, Controversy, Moral Theology, Rhetoric and the Combinatorial (i.e. Lullian) Art. These are known through the eye of Reason on the left, and the ear of Use and Experience on the right.

Wisdom, in the Hebrew writings, is always represented as female, and she sits here on a throne decorated with the heads of wise elders and cherubim,

▲ **2.14** Frontispiece of *Obeliscus Ægyptiacus* (1666), featuring the obelisk restored by Bernini under the patronage of Pope Alexander VII.

▶ **2.15** Frontispiece of *Magneticum Naturae Regnum* (1667), which divides the 'magnetic realm' into 'inanimate, animate and sensitive' – the inanimate magnetic needle, the animate cock and stag, and the sensitive palm tree. The two snakes at the bottom relate to the phenomenon of the 'snake stone' which 'magnetically' cured snake bites.

▲ **2.16** Frontispiece of *China Illustrata* (1667), dedicated to the Jesuit missionaries who went to that country in Kircher's time. Two of them, Adam Schall and Matteo Ricci, stand on earth, while the Jesuit founders kneel in heaven. The Jesuit monogram IHS takes the place of God.

▶ **2.17** Frontispiece of Volume I of *Ars Magna Sciendi* (1669). A banner unfurled by angels carries fifteen seals symbolizing the different disciplines of knowledge. The female figure on a throne is Wisdom, who rejects the eye of Reason in favour of the Holy Scriptures.

the reader with the result of her findings, or Kircher's: the 'Alphabet of the Art' with its twenty-seven (3^3) 'letters' in three columns: Goodness, Magnitude, Duration, Power, Wisdom, Will, Virtue, Truth, Glory; Difference, Concordance, Contrariety, Beginning, Middle, End, Majority, Equality, Minority; God, Angel, Heaven, Elements, Man, Beast, Vegetable, Mineral, Predicament. It states that 'In these is contained the sum of human knowledge'. The base of her throne is inscribed with a Greek sentence that, again, could serve as Kircher's motto: 'Nothing is more beautiful than to know the All.'

Several of Kircher's frontispieces suggest an underlying geometry based on the Kabbalistic tree of the Sephiroth (see also **Ill. 2.15**). In this one it is the middle pillar that seems best to correspond, with Wisdom's head as Kether (crown), the sun as Tiphereth (beauty), the base of the throne as Yesod (foundation), and the world below as Malkuth (kingdom). With some ingenuity, one might find correspondences between the flanking elements of the picture and the other six Sephiroth, but I am reluctant to force an interpretation for which there is no corroborating evidence.

her human and angelic preceptors. In her right hand she holds a sceptre with the eye of Reason, but she neglects it: her glance is directed to the two cherubs to her right, who are guiding her through the open book of the Holy Scriptures. On her breast is the sun of the Intellect, valued in Neoplatonic and Scholastic philosophy as a higher faculty than Reason. Her left hand presents

2.18 Frontispiece of Volume II of *Ars Magna Sciendi*, where Wisdom displays the sun of the Intellect on her bosom and holds the Holy Scriptures in her right hand. Below, the Muses contemplate their respective arts.

2.19 Frontispiece of *Latium* (1671). Here the enthroned genius is the nymph Latia. To her right and left are Mount Atlas with a giant supporting the heavens and a volcano – Vesuvius or Etna. Neither is in Latium but they symbolize the power of Rome. In the lower register are the river gods Tiber and Aniene.

The second volume of *Ars Magna Sciendi* opens with a most remarkable tripartite image (**Ill. 2.18**). Wisdom bursts through the dome of the heavens to reveal the fact, written around the eye of God, that 'All things [are] in One.' Her twin sources of inspiration are now closely allied: the sun of the Intellect on her bosom and the Holy Scriptures clutched in her right hand. The building is a circular temple, or maybe just an apse, whose dome is an image of the heavenly bowl. In this intermediate realm, once again, is Kircher's own contribution, the Alphabet of the Art. Its first ennead is written on shields held by cherubs perching on the cornice; its second and third are engraved on the capitals and entablature. At ground level, nine pensive Muses contemplate their respective arts, and the caduceus of Hermes is conspicuous beneath their feet. While this might be simply the attribute of Rhetoric (Mercury being the giver of eloquence), its humble position could hint that Hermetic philosophy has been superseded by Kircher's new and improved way of wisdom.

The opening page of *Latium* (1671) carries a rich symbolic image (**Ill. 2.19**) engraved by one of Kircher's most distinguished illustrators, Romeyn de Hooghe (see chapter 3). The personified *genius loci*, Latia, sits enthroned in a nymphaeum, its balustrade, benches and waterworks redolent of the Renaissance villas of the region. In the background we glimpse Mount Atlas, with the giant supporting the heavens on his shoulders, and an erupting volcano, perhaps Vesuvius or Etna. None of these are in Latium, but according to Gómez de Liaño they symbolize respectively the spiritual and temporal power of Rome. Atlas is a metaphor for the Roman Catholic Church and Vesuvius stands for the city's 'volcanic' past.[17]

On our right, which is Latia's left, is a trophy of ancient arms and armour, with quiver, lorica, swords and standards. Opposite is a corresponding modern trophy with a cuirass, powder flask, musket rest and barrel. Latia turns her back on the past, on Romulus and Remus with their wolf foster-mother. She herself wears a mural crown (symbol of the protective deity of a city) with the heraldic star of the Chigi (for Pope Alexander VII), and an ecclesiastical cope. A fold of it protects the imperial eagle; her left foot rests on the orb, putting the Holy Roman Empire firmly in its place. Instead of a sword, she holds a sceptre with the Hand of Justice. She faces to her right, towards the mitre, cardinal's hat, sword, book and vessels of Catholic ritual. A putto offers her the papal tiara and St Peter's keys. The message is clear: in the modern age, Latia's power and glory are vested in the Church of Rome.

At the lower level are two river gods with their symbols of a steering-oar. The stream from the one on the left is marked 'Tibrus', the river Tiber that flows through Rome; that on the right 'Anius', the tributary that comes from Tivoli, now the Aniene. His companion with butterfly wings is the goddess of the Aniene who was assimilated to Ino, a figure who appears in the *Odyssey* to succour Odysseus. She herself was set adrift by her husband, Athamas (hence the broken mast and sail behind her), but rescued by Venus, who turned her into the water deity Leucothea.

2.20 Frontispiece of *Splendor et Gloria Domus Joanniæ* (1669, 1672) depicts St John the Evangelist and St John the Baptist with Minerva, goddess of Wisdom.

The inscription states: 'Latium, to which none is equal, and second to none.' It applies to Latium, of course, but might also apply to the author.

No one has explained satisfactorily why Kircher set his vast mind to work on the almost trivial subject of his next book. Scholars refer to it confusingly in three different ways: by the title on the frontispiece, *Splendor et Gloria Domus Joanniæ*, by the first words of the title page, *Principis Christiani* (Of a Christian Prince), and by the following words that are the subject of the phrase, *Archetypon Politicum* (Political Model). Gómez de Liaño writes of its frontispiece (**Ill. 2.20**):

The sun dominates the scene from the clouds, with the inscription IHS, the cross and three nails. On either side St John the Evangelist and St John the Baptist watch over the destinies of the house of Juan. A robust Minerva or Providence stands out in the centre, supporting a column with each arm. Next to the attributes of wisdom, the one on the right

SPLENDOR ET GLORIA DOMUS JOANNIÆ: A KIRCHERIAN ANOMALY

2.21 Medal of Honorato Juan. The medal was sent to Kircher by Antonio Juan de Centellas, who asked him to decipher its meaning. Kircher published his interpretation in *Splendor et Gloria* (1672, 12).

The impetus for this curious book came in 1667, when the Spanish king's counsellor, Marqués Antonio Juan de Centellas, sent Kircher a large medal designed by Pompeio Leoni, commemorating his ancestor Honorato Juan (**Ill. 2.21**), asking him to explain its meaning.[18] Kircher obliged with an interpretation based on his Egyptian hieroglyphic studies that is almost a self-parody. For example, he praises Honorato's physiognomy, and especially his aquiline nose because it resembles the beak of the falcon-headed god Osiris (actually Horus).[19] Honorato had been a favourite of the previous century's Spanish kings, Charles I and Philip II, and tutor to the latter's demented son Don Carlos (died 1568). His portrait (**Ill. 2.22**) includes what might be symbols of his ardous task in supporting the heir to the throne: Atlas holding up a sundial, and, glimpsed through the window, Mercury, the patron of eloquence, flying into a city.

Kircher must have had some obligation to Antonio Juan, who is also pictured in the book (**Ill. 2.23**). His table holds the equipment of a senior bureaucrat (writing implements and clock), and on his cloak is the insignia of the Order of Calatrava. Much of the book is given over to the history and genealogy of this hidalgo family, which Kircher surely did not research for himself but transcribed from documents supplied by Antonio. (He had already done something of the kind in compiling the genealogy of the Dukes of Polana for his book on the sanctuary of Mentorella.) The rest is platitudinous moralizing about the duties and virtues of Christian kings and princes. Near the end, Kircher adds a more personal signature by writing lines in praise of Honorato in the languages of the nations that the latter had visited during his lifetime: Latin, Greek, Hebrew, Spanish, Italian, French, Arabic, Syriac, Chaldaean, Samaritan and Coptic. Lastly, he composes an encomium in Egyptian hieroglyphs (**Ill. 2.24**), which the artist depicts on an obelisk, planted in the lonely Pyrenean landscape.

2.22 Portrait of Honorato Juan, tutor to Don Carlos, the son of Philip II of Spain. Atlas supporting the world symbolizes Honorato's task. Mercury is the patron of eloquence (*Splendor et Gloria*, 122–123).

2.23 Portrait of Antonio Juan de Centellas, the man who commissioned *Splendor et Gloria* (before title page). He is shown as a royal counsellor and Knight of the Order of Calatrava.

2.24 Imaginary obelisk of Honorato Juan, with an inscription in Kircher's 'hieroglyphs' praising him (*Splendor et Gloria*, 235).

2.25 Frontispiece of *Phonurgia Nova* (1673),
celebrating the phenomenon of sound.
An angelic orchestra proclaims the Emperor
Leopold I's patronage. On the left
are Apollo with the nine Muses and Pan.

2.26 Frontispiece of *Arca Noë* (1675), showing God ordering the Flood to begin. In the foreground are Noah and his wife, and their three sons and their wives.

carries the inscription: 'Wisdom is the support of great enterprises.' The one on the left, dedicated to 'Martial valour, origin and glory of the great houses', has the attributes of fortitude and valour. The views and objects on either side correspond to the symbolic meanings of the two columns of Hercules, associated with the Spanish monarchy.[20]

The German artists responsible for the frontispiece of *Phonurgia Nova* (1673) (**Ill. 2.25**) composed a variation on that of *Musurgia Universalis*, celebrating the universality and ubiquity of music. At the top, once again, is the threefold God and his angelic choir, but now they are playing instruments as though in some baroque church ceiling. Fame flies across the sky with her trumpets, whose banners bear the double-headed eagle of the Habsburgs and the motto 'She proclaims the Emperor's illustrious arms.' The musical Emperor Leopold I (see portrait, **Ill. 1.6**) was the patron and dedicatee of the work.

Down below on the right, the horns of tritons escort Neptune across the sea; trumpets and kettledrums encourage a cavalry charge; a huntsman winds his horn; one man speaks through a tube, bouncing the sound off a flat surface to communicate with another whom he cannot see.[21] On the left are the two contrasting and rival musics: that of Apollo and the nine Muses on Mount Parnassus, from which the Pierian Spring pours down its inspiring waters, and that of goat-footed Pan with Silenus and the Bacchic rout. The central figure on the pedestal again seems to be Fame, crowned with laurel and blowing an antique trumpet.

The frontispieces of Kircher's late biblical works are more pictorial than symbolic, though there is plenty of meaning to be read out of them. In that of *Arca Noë* (1675) (**Ill. 2.26**), God gives his orders to putti bearing the symbols of the Flaming Sword that guarded the Garden of Eden, Alpha and Omega denoting the Beginning and the End, and the Oroboros Serpent of Eternity. Beneath him is the dove of the Holy Spirit, and beneath that the Ship of the Church with its cross-like mast and spar, and Jesus sitting in the crow's nest. On the sail is inscribed 'Outside which there is no salvation.' Aspiring souls half arise out of the sea, hoping to get on board. This theological background states in symbolic terms that God punishes mankind's disobedience, that he sees all things and knows all of time, and determines the beginning and the end of things; and that only the Church (Roman Catholic, of course) can save mankind, as the Ark saved Noah and his family.

The eight people in the foreground are Noah with his three sons Ham (Cham), Shem and Japheth on the left, and their wives on the right. It is probably Noah's bad son Ham and his wife who turn their backs on us, and wear frivolous brocaded garments. Ham's trousers and shaven head suggest an Oriental potentate, perhaps a Turk, at a time when the Turkish invasion of Europe was an ever-present threat. God is saying to Noah 'Make yourself an ark.' Noah is holding the plan of the vessel; on the steps are the names of the author and the title: 'Noah's Ark, explicated with a great variety of things.'

In the frontispiece of *Turris Babel* (1679) (**Ill. 2.27**) Nimrod stands with his bodyguard. Although Kircher gives his dates as 2236–1980 BC, this 'first on earth to be a mighty man' (Genesis 10:8) wears the costume of a Roman general. The standard-bearer, whose gaze meets our own, is displaying not Nimrod's banner but the triumphal name of Kircher. The architect's apprentice kneels to display a sketch of the tower as it will be when it is completed, with its spiral ramp culminating in a domed and finialed tip. Meanwhile – and we must imagine this to be happening later – the architect himself addresses us and proudly points to his work, now far advanced amid furnaces and stoneyards. But there is trouble in the air. God's impassive, all-seeing eye has spied this threat to his authority, and he is angry: lightning flashes from the clouds. However, the tower will not be destroyed by lightning, but left to slow decay after the workmen cease to speak Hebrew, chattering instead in a myriad of other languages. It is a lesson in the impermanence of all human efforts, as Kircher muses in the opening pages: 'Where once was a retreat for the delight of emperors and kings, today you will find among thorns and thistles the lairs of wild beasts, snakes and toads; and you will see with admiration buildings that were built to last for all eternity, fallen in a few centuries into vast ruins.'[22]

Near the end of Kircher's life, his Amsterdam publisher, Johann Jansson van Waesberge (see p. 55), published three more books drawn from Kircher's own material, though they bear the names of other authors. The first to be finished,[23] though it was not published until five years later, was *Physiologia Kircheriana Experimentalis* (1680), edited by Kircher's assistant Johann Stephan Kestler. It contains 337 experiments in magnetism, optics, medicine, physics, mathematics, mechanics and chemistry, some of them simple kitchen-table experiments, others demanding much expense and equipment. Among the latter are the magic lanterns that were the most spectacular addition to the second edition of *Mundus Subterraneus*.[24] It was an easy job for Jansson to produce, for he simply re-used the plates and woodblocks from Kircher's other books, especially *Ars Magna Lucis* and *Mundus Subterraneus*, not even erasing their original (and now incorrect) page numbers; but he did commission a worthy frontispiece (**Ill. 2.28**). God has been left out of this one, but his light pierces the clouds with the words 'Reverberating from here' and strikes the portrait of Kircher hanging in the tree, from which 'thus it shines' to enlighten the voluptuous Muse of Physiology. She has a magic wand with ears and an eye, which in turn inspires her sisters, busy in the background with weighing, measuring the globe, cultivating heliotropic flowers, playing the harp, using the magnetic compass and contemplating the intersecting triangles with their traditional Hermetic meaning of 'as above, so below'. In contrast to this bright and happy scene, two philosophers and two monks sit in a drab enclosure, reading and writing books and dropping them on the barren earth. One of them half raises his head, as if he has heard something going on above. He should learn that experimentation trumps book-learning.

The second compilation of Kircher's twilight years was Giosefo Petrucci's *Prodromo Apologetico alli Studi Chircheriani* ('Apologetic vestibule to Kircherian

2.27 Frontispiece of *Turris Babel* (1679). Nimrod is dressed as a Roman general, but his banner bears Kircher's name. The architect of the tower proudly indicates his work, while God's all-seeing eye threatens punishment for his arrogance.

2.28 Frontispiece of *Physiologia Kircheriana Experimentalis* (1680), published in Amsterdam by his assistant Johann Stephan Kestler. Most of its illustrations are taken from Kircher's originals, but this frontispiece is new. Kircher's portrait hangs from a tree reflecting divine light, while the Muse of Physiology indicates the many spheres of knowledge that he had mastered.

2.29 Frontispiece of *Prodromo Apologetico* (1677), another tribute compiled by a disciple, Giosefo Petrucci. The seated author is writing with two pens at once, producing works on all conceivable subjects, which are piled up on the right.

studies', 1677), an introduction to his oeuvre together with a defence against his critics and some new material on the Orient. On first sight, the frontispiece (**Ill. 2.29**) seems to be an imitation of Giovanni Canini's (Caninius) design for *Obeliscus Pamphilius* (see **Ill. 2.5**). There is a flying figure holding a scroll, a child hiding beneath it, a seated figure and a crocodile. But there is a big difference here: it is the seated figure, scribbling with two pens at once, who is producing the scroll with elements of astronomy, music, chemistry and geometry. The works he has already written are piled up in the corner.

Above the writer's head are two winds and the arctic constellation of the Little Bear, signifying his origin in the North (at least relative to Italy). The woman is crowned with the imperial crown – an allegory of the patronage of the Holy Roman Emperors which so contributed to Kircher's success. She has a laurel wreath ready for his bare head, as the traditional crown for artistic and academic achievement, and the palm of victory over his critics. The upper end of the scroll is inscribed: 'He has unrolled that which has been rolled up' – in other words, he has revealed the secrets of nature and history. But no one

2.30 Frontispiece of *Musaeum Celeberrimum* (1678), the famous view of Kircher's museum in Rome, published by another disciple, Georgius de Sepibus. In the foreground Kircher is welcoming two visitors. The scale of the museum is hugely magnified in the engraving, but it accurately reflects its contents.

has yet revealed to us why the serpent eating its tail, signifying Eternity, is coiled around the sun in the sign of Leo; nor the meaning of the basilisk that spreads its wings on a rock by the seashore; nor that of the white and black birds perching on the books.

Lastly, not long before Kircher's death, Georgio de Sepi published an anthology of extracts from Kircher's later works as *Musaeum Celeberrimum* – 'The famous Museum of the Roman College of the Society of Jesus' (1678). The frontispiece (**Ill. 2.30**) is the only recorded view of Kircher's museum, described in the distich below as: 'The house of Kircher, theatre of nature and art, whose equal is scarcely to be seen anywhere.' Here, too, there is a suggestion of the three worlds, with angels at the top of the plate, the heavenly bodies painted on the ceiling, and the collection of earthly marvels below. These include three of the traditional categories of the Kunst- und Wunderkammer: natural wonders like the crocodile and the skeleton, antiquities represented by the obelisks and Roman busts, and scientific machines in the window to the right.

In the foreground, Kircher in black robe and beretta welcomes two gentlemen visitors. The human figures are dwarfed by the magnificent models of obelisks on baroque pedestals, which dominate the central space beneath a vaulted ceiling of imposing height. But something is awry. These people are so small that they could hardly reach the second shelf of the display on the left, and could easily shelter under the table before the window. One should never accept uncritically what Kircher, or his artists, want us to believe. A photograph of the gallery in question, taken before the dissolution of the museum, shows it to have been quite modest in size.[25] As for the four model obelisks, they were happily discovered by Valerio Rivosecchi in 1988, stored in the attics of the building (now occupied by the Liceo Visconti).[26] One of them, with a hieroglyphic inscription invented by Kircher in honour of Pope Clement IX, corresponds exactly to the one on the left of the illustration. Excluding its base, it stands at a little over three feet tall.[27]

Notes

1 See Rhodes and Sawday (especially the essays by Stephen Orgel and Claire Preston), which shows how late Renaissance frontispieces, diagrams such as Kircher's Ark, collections and museums were all part of a complex enterprise for which today's tool, or at least metaphor, is the computer. Corbett and Lightbown's study of English frontispieces is a model for exegesis in a 'pre-postmodern' mode.

2 See *Œdipus Ægyptiacus*, I, 133–135, for Kircher's panegyric of the monarchical system as 'image of the universe', and warning of the dangers of democracy.

3 The chain of rings hanging by magnetic force alone was chosen as its emblem by the 'Parthenia et Academica Congregatio' of Kircher's own Jesuit College, because 'the growth of this Parthenian Congregation first occurred through a certain occult divine inspiration'. *Œdipus Ægyptiacus*, II, i, 12.

4 *Musurgia Universalis*, II, 383.

5 *Œdipus Ægyptiacus*, III, 454.

6 See Rowland, 77, 100, for the doubts of his superiors. Yet in his manuscript report approving Jansson's *Atlas Coelestis* (4 July 1660; APUG Ms. 563, f.102), Kircher states that 'to teach that the earth really goes round the sun with the other planets is rightly prohibited and condemned by the Catholic Church and the Sacred Congregation as an audacious dogma, contrary to the Holy Scriptures'.

7 *Aeneid*, VI, 726–727.

8 To spare the reader the extreme wordiness of Kircher's writing, I have reduced the following conversation to its essentials. It occupies pages 405–440 of the 1656 edition.

9 See the thorough analysis of the censorship issue in Siebert's 'Kircher and His Critics' and 'Kircher und die Astronomie'.

10 The reader may recall the argument of Abraham and Yahweh in Genesis 18:23–33.

11 In the first issue of *Mundus Subterraneus*, the first volume was dated 1665, but the title page of the second volume carried the date 1664 (for an example, see Merrill, 39). In most copies of the first edition, both volumes are dated 1665 (see the list in Fletcher 1988, 185), but this explains why '1664–1665' is given as the date of publication.

12 This post-medieval Latin tag is sometimes translated in the contrary sense, as 'The wise man will be ruled by the stars', which would be correct were *dominor* not a deponent verb, passive in form but active in meaning.

13 Hymn no. 13, 'To Kronos', lines 8 and 3, trans. Apostolos N. Athanassakis.

14 Explained in Marrone, 13–21.

15 And so it does in the Kircherian exhibit of the Museum of Jurassic Technology, Los Angeles. See *Das Museum Kircherianum*.

16 See Daxenmüller, 'Die Welt als Einheit', for a study of this work and its context.

17 Gómez de Liaño, I, 127.

18 *Splendor et Gloria*, 1.

19 *Splendor et Gloria*, 13.

20 Gómez de Liaño, II, 261; my translation.

21 Kircher explains this on page 120 of the work.

22 *Turris Babel*, **3.

23 The dedication to Cardinal Nithardo is dated 15 October 1675.

24 *Physiologia Kircheriana*, 125, 126, 127.

25 Reproduced in Daxenmüller, 'Ein Gang durch Zeit und Raum', 50.

26 Hein and Mader 1991, 18. This booklet illustrates the four models in colour, as does Donadoni's article 'I geroglifici'.

27 To be precise, 102.5 cm.; see Donadoni, 106, ill. 30. The correct ascriptions of the other models are as follows: the Sallustian (Donadoni, ill. 26; Hein and Mader, ill. 7), the Lateran (Donadoni, ill. 27; Hein and Mader, ill. 6) and the Medicean (Donadoni, ill. 29; Hein and Mader, ill. 4).

Chapter 3   The Illustration of Kircher's Works

Though not a gifted draughtsman, Kircher was well aware of the advantages of illustrations, whether explanatory or decorative. His book on sundials, *Primitiae Gnomonicae Catoptricae*, published in Avignon in 1635, had only one engraved plate (**Ill. 3.1**), besides the frontispiece, but it heralded several aspects of his later and grander images, and the idea of it would later expand to the limits of the medium (see **Ill. 11.17**). In principle, it depicts the complicated vertical sundial which is the subject of the book, but the presence of a kneeling Jesuit points to its purpose – to know the time of day everywhere that the Jesuits had their missions – and consecrates the invention to a higher purpose. Meanwhile, the inscriptions in several Oriental scripts proclaim Kircher's expertise in a field of learning reserved for the very few. The engraving is simultaneously technical information, religious propaganda and self-advertisement: the three pillars of Kircher's scientific writings.

Illustrations played an essential role in Kircher's promotion of his hieroglyphic interpretations. In *Prodromus Coptus* (1636) they showed the missing link (as he thought) between Egyptian hieroglyphs and the Greek alphabet, confirming his theory of the evolution of writing. Here the beetle-man of the Bembine Table (see **Ill. 4.2**) made his first and crucial appearance, and the tiny tablet in his claws was touched up to proclaim the doctrine of universal love, proving that Hermes' religion was a forerunner of Christ's. Here, too, in an ungainly woodcut (see **Ill. 4.4**), Kircher invented his first didactic image to explain the 'Egyptian world system'. Its jumble of geometric figures, letters and beetle perfectly answered to the Art of Memory, in which the more grotesque the image, the easier it is to remember. Faced with these unfamiliar ideas in graphic form, Kircher's readers would have had no reason to doubt that they were genuinely Egyptian.

We have no drawings by Kircher from this early period, but the notebook of a student contains a most revealing copy of one of them. It is in one of the two surviving manuscripts that record Kircher's activity as a professor of mathematics.[1] The frontispiece to the Roman manuscript of *Mathematica Curiosa* (**Ill. 3.2**) takes the form of a family tree of the mathematical sciences, with the sciences themselves as its fruits. Some of them are hung with their emblems, such as a number table for Arithmetic, a weight-lifting pulley for Statics, a pipe and viol for Music, and a sundial for 'Gnomics'. At the bottom are two ibises in significant postures. One has its beak crossing its legs, which

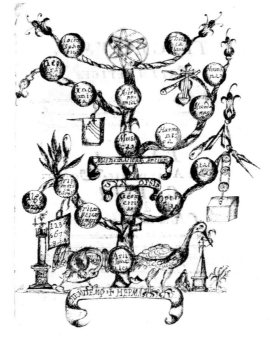

3.1 Kircher clearly prepared schematic drawings for the illustrations in his work which could then be realized by professional draughtsmen. This engraving of a catoptric clock depicts the mechanism of the vertical sundial that is the subject of his *Primitiae Gnomonicae Catoptricae* (1635), but it is the kneeling Jesuit who conveys the purpose and function of the book – to tell the time wherever the Jesuits had their missions.

3.2 The frontispiece of *Mathematica Curiosa* consists of a family tree of the mathematical sciences, with each science shown as a fruit.

KIRCHER'S SKETCHES

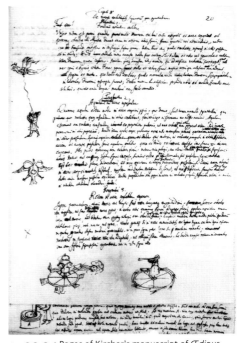

▲▼ 3.3, 3.4 Pages of Kircher's manuscript of *Œdipus Ægyptiacus*.

Kircher's partial manuscript for *Œdipus Ægyptiacus* gives an idea of how he directed his artists in the minor illustrations of his works. On one page (**Ill. 3.3**) he has sketched in the margins a dragon-shaped kite announcing 'Ira Dei fugite' (flee God's wrath!) and several other mechanical toys (compare the printed version of the kite in **Ill. 10.21**). These might have been sufficient for the artists. However, the sketch of the scarab-man in the same manuscript (**Ill. 3.4**) was not so used, for the eventual woodblock that appears in several of Kircher's works (see **Ill. 4.2**) is much closer to the original reproductions of the Bembine Table by Eneo Vico or Herwart von Hohenburg. In this case, then, Kircher's sketch was merely indicative of the image to be placed, which must have been supplied to the artist separately.

The sketches here (**Ills. 3.5–3.12**) are found in a draft manuscript of *Mundus Subterraneus*, dated 1656 and entitled *Geocosmus*.[2] While there is no proof that they are by Kircher's hand, it is definitely his handwriting on them.

3.5 Section through the earth, showing subterranean water and fire (compare **Ills. 7.5, 7.11**).

3.6 'Hydrophylacium': a cave fed by underground springs (compare **Ill. 7.14**).

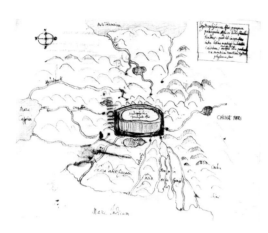

▸ 3.7 The Asian reservoir (compare **Ill. 12.3**).

▾ 3.8 Mount Etna (compare **Ill. 7.6**).

▾▾ 3.9 Africa, with the source of the Nile (compare **Ill. 12.2**).

▲ 3.10 The eruption of Vesuvius (compare **Ill. 7.7**), enhanced by a professional artist, perhaps Johann Paul Schor (see below).[3]

◂ 3.11 The Alpine reservoir (compare **Ill. 12.4**).

▾ 3.12 The South American reservoir (compare **Ill. 12.5**).

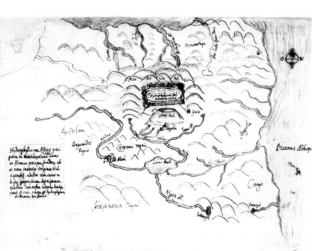

Kircher interpreted as the hieroglyphic origin of the letter A. The other holds a snake in its beak, recalling its service to the snake-infested land of Egypt (see p. 62). These and the obelisk on the right show that Kircher was already Egyptianizing his scientific teachings.

This sketch is the sort of design that puts its point across even in the most childlike rendering, and which anyone could copy according to his artistic ability. The originality lies in its invention, which we presume was Kircher's own. A similar drawing probably served the artist who drew the beautiful frontispiece to the third book of *Magnes* (see **Ill. 2.2**).

The illustration of Kircher's books grew steadily in both quantity and quality as his fame increased, and publishers like Jansson became anxious to make the most of it, knowing that the investment would be worthwhile. The seventeenth century was a golden age of the illustrated book, and Kircher's works were carried along on a wave of enthusiasm for them on the part of the buyers, and by advances in printing technology. Since the birth of printing (and even before) books had been illustrated with woodcuts, but this method was now joined by the more detailed and versatile medium of copper engraving, producing the 'plates' – a term still in use, though methods have changed. There was a distinct hierarchy among illustrations, with copperplate engravings being comparable in function, status and expense to colour plates in modern books.

One might think that it was more trouble to carve a negative image into a block of hardwood, leaving only the lines raised, than to draw it with a burin on a polished copper plate, but the evidence is otherwise. In a major work like *Ars Magna Lucis* or *Mundus Subterraneus*, woodcuts occur by the hundreds, engravings only by dozens. One reason is that a woodcut block can be fastened into the same form as the type, so that the image is printed along with the text. Printing an engraving requires a different technique, especially of inking the plate, and must be done in a separate press which not every printer possessed. If the image is to be combined on the same page with type, the paper must pass through the presses in two separate processes, with all the expenditure of time and waste that this may cause. Consequently, the general rule was to keep the engravings on separate sheets, and when illustrations occurred in the text, to use woodcuts.

It was *Magnes* (1641) that inaugurated Kircher's series of books illustrated with both woodcuts and engravings. The financer was Hermann Scheus, who collaborated with several Roman publishers and had already underwritten the Jesuit G. B. Ferrari's *De Florum Cultura* (1633), a botanical work with forty splendid illustrations. Besides its woodcut diagrams, *Magnes* contained two engraved frontispieces (discussed in Chapter 2) and thirty-two full-page copper plates. More than half of these depict a circular dial surrounded by inscriptions; they are presented as blueprints for sundials, moondials, magnetic compasses, astrolabes, zodiacs and planispheres, but the medium of engraving allows for a virtuoso display of curly ribbons and exotic scripts. These illustrations are not just informative, but also arouse wonder, like

a museum of scientific instruments whose use most visitors can only vaguely comprehend.

The other engravings in *Magnes* are mostly designs for machines that exploit the power of magnets to act at a distance. Although a few of them were built and exhibited in Kircher's museum, some of them strain one's confidence in the range and power of magnets, at a time before the electrical induction of magnetism was possible. Whether they were ever made or not, their illustrations carry all the conviction of an engineer's plans, extending the imaginary museum from the dimensions of a glass case to that of entire rooms and fogging the boundaries between reality and science fiction. Kircher repeated this successful scheme of seeding full-page plates among the cheaper woodcuts in his next books, *Ars Magna Lucis et Umbrae* (1646), which contains thirty-four numbered plates, the shortish *Obeliscus Pamphilius* (1650), with six, and *Musurgia Universalis* (1650), with twenty-three.

Only two years after the first edition of *Magnes*, a second edition appeared in Cologne, 'much more correct than the Roman one'. Not only was the entire text reset, reducing it from about 900 to a mere 800 pages, but every illustration was redrawn. Comparing the two versions, one finds that the engravings in the German edition are superior in quality, being slightly smaller and more detailed, whilst the woodcuts show less care than those of the Roman edition. None of the illustrations is signed. It is a sobering thought to contemplate the labour involved in reprinting a book of this size, and the ill-paid skills of the anonymous craftsmen who cut the woodblocks and engraved the plates, all within a couple of years at the most.

Most illustrators in the seventeenth century were not regarded as artists, but as craftsmen, just like the typographers, printers and binders of books. It was a rare thing for them to sign their work.[4] However, Kircher's books contain so many illustrations that these scattered signatures yield over thirty different artists' names, most of which can be traced in the reference literature. They constitute a most varied and interesting assembly of nationalities, styles and competences.

Of the two types of book illustration, the woodcuts are almost never signed. The engravings, when they are, typically bear the name of the artist, specified with the words *fecit* (made), *delineavit* (drew), *invenit* (invented), or their abbreviations and that of the engraver who cut it (*sculpsit*, or again *fecit*) on copper. From well-researched cases such as the book illustrations of Peter Paul Rubens,[5] we can judge the relative contributions of artist and engraver, often to the benefit of the latter. The artist would sometimes provide only a pencil or pen and wash drawing, and it was the engraver's job to interpret vague lines and shadings in the crisp, unforgiving medium of the copper plate. He might also use a mirror to reverse the image, so that the plate would print the same way round as the original. Sometimes artist and engraver were one and the same person (as in the case of Coenraet Decker), but the two techniques were quite different and more often assigned to specialists.

There follows a list of the signed illustrations in Kircher's works:

Magnes, 1641, Frontispiece
Signed *Cl. Dagli sculp*

Magnes, 1641, Book III, Frontispiece
Signed *I.B. Rinalducius Sculpsit. I.B. Ficavazza fecit*

Ars Magna Lucis et Umbrae, 1646, Frontispiece
Signed *Petrus Miotte Burgundus sculp:*

Sundial of celestial medicine (*Ars Magna Lucis*, 1646, 533)
Signed *Petrus Miotte Bur. Sculp.*

Moondial (*Ars Magna Lucis*, 1646, 557; 1671, 419)
Signed *P. Miotte Sculp.*

Obeliscus Pamphilius, 1650, Frontispiece
Signed *Io: Ang: Caninius Rom: inuentor et del. C. Bloemaert sculp.*

The Pamphilian, or Piazza Navona obelisk (*Obeliscus Pamphilius*, d2)
Signed *P. Miotte Fecit*

How the ancients transported obelisks (*Obeliscus Pamphilius*, 90)
Signed *Petrus Miotte Burgundus Fecit.*

The ancient gods interpreted (*Obeliscus Pamphilius*, 226)
Signed *Petrus Miotte Burgundus sculp:*

Musurgia Universalis, 1650, Volume I, Frontispiece
Signed *Io. Paulus Schor, delin. Baronius F. Romae.*

Portrait of Leopold Wilhelm, Archduke of Austria (*Musurgia Universalis*, Volume I, +1ᵛ)
Signed *Io: Paulus Schor delin. Roma. Paulus Pontius sculpsit: Antverpiae. Anno 1649.*

Musurgia Universalis, 1650, Volume II, Frontispiece
Signed *Petrus Miotte Bur Sculp.*

Œdipus Ægyptiacus, 1652–1654, Frontispiece, Volume I
Signed *Io: Ang: Caninius Rom: del. C. Bloemaert sculp.*

Portrait of Emperor Ferdinand III
(*Œdipus Ægyptiacus*, Volume I, before title page)
Signed *Iacobus Bichi delin. C. Bloemaert sculp: Romae*

Isis, Great Mother of the Gods (*Œdipus Ægyptiacus*, Volume I, 189)
Signed *Rosello F.*

The seventy-two names of God (*Œdipus Ægyptiacus*, Volume II, i, 286)
Signed *Petrus Miotte Fecit*

The Tree of the Sephiroth (*Œdipus Ægyptiacus*, Volume II, i, 288–289)
Signed *Petrus Miotte fecit*

The Flaminian, or Piazza del Popolo obelisk (*Œdipus Ægyptiacus*, Volume III, 212)
Signed *Domˢ Barriere fecit*

The Sallustian, Ludovisi, or Trinità dei Monti obelisk (*Œdipus Ægyptiacus*, Volume III, 256)
Signed *Petrus Miotte Burgundus sculpsit*

The mummy-crypt (*Œdipus Ægyptiacus*, Volume III, 400)
Signed *Titus Livius Burrattinus*

Pyramids and the mummy crypt (*Œdipus Ægyptiacus*, Volume III, 403)
Signed *G.Bᵃ. Balatri F*

Magnes, 1654, Book III, Frontispiece
Signed *P. Valentini sclr*

Iter Extaticum, 1660, Frontispiece
Signed *F. Sc.*

Arms of Joachim von Gravenegg (*Iter Extaticum*, f.)(1ᵛ)
Signed *Fleischb. Sc.*

Mundus Subterraneus, 1665, Volume I, Frontispiece
Signed *Jo. Paul: Schor delin. Romae. Theod Matham sculpsit.*

Mundus Subterraneus, 1664, Volume II, Title page
Signed *C. vande Pas delineavit. A. Siourtsma sculpsit.*

Bucket pump (*Mundus Subterraneus*, Volume II, 228)
Signed *H. Bonzon delineavit*

Elements of Sanskrit (*China Illustrata*, 154–158)
Signed *W. vander Laegh*

Sanskrit letters (*China Illustrata*, 5 plates following 162)
Each plate signed *W. vander Laegh scripsit et sculp.*

Latium, 1671, Frontispiece
Signed *R. de Hooge fecit*

The apotheosis of Homer (*Latium*, 82–83)
Signed *Io. Bapt. Galostruccius pict. Florentinus del. et Scul. Romae. 1658*

The Nile mosaic from the Temple of Fortune in Praeneste (*Latium*, 100–101)
Signed *Agapitus de Bernardinis Civis et Pictor Praenestinus 1668*

The town of Palestrina (*Latium*, 112–113)
Signed *Auth. Agapito Bernardini pictore.*

The Jesuits' horoscope (*Ars Magna Lucis*, 1671, f. (*)3)
Signed *Athanasio Kirchero S.I. Inventore*

Phonurgia Nova, 1673, Frontispiece
Signed *Felix Cheurier del. G. And. Wolfgang s.*

Portrait of Emperor Leopold I (*Phonurgia Nova*, a2)
Signed *Franz Herman, del. G. And. Wolfgang sculp.*

Portait of Charles II, King of Spain (*Arca Noë*, *2ᵛ)
Signed *C. Decker fec.*

Noah and his progeny (*Arca Noë*, 226)
Signed *C. Decker jn. et f.*

Submerged mountains (*Arca Noë*, 154–155)
Signed *C. Decker jn et f.*

Pyramids and the mummy-crypt (*Sphinx Mystagoga*, 42–43)
Signed *C. Decker jn et fe –*

Turris Babel, 1679, Frontispiece
Signed *G. Laires. delin. I.V. Munnichuysen Schul.*

The Tower of Babel (*Turris Babel*, 40–41)
Signed *Cᴱᵀ DECKER. F. L. Cruyl euditer delin: 1670*

Babylon (*Turris Babel*, 52–53)
Signed *C. decker in et fec.*

Semiramis's citadel (*Turris Babel*, 59)
Signed *C. Decker f.*

The Hanging Gardens of Babylon (*Turris Babel*, 58–59)
Signed *C. Decker fec. Ex mente R.P. Athan: Kirchery. Liv. Creyl delin: 1670.*

The earliest of these is 'Dagli', apparently Claudio Aglio, who signed the frontispiece of the 1641 *Magnes* with its ferocious magnetic eagle (see **Ill. 2.1**). His paper-thin reputation hangs on this and one other engraving.[6] I can discover nothing of the artists whose collaboration produced the extraordinary sylvan frontispiece to Volume III of the same work (see **Ill. 2.2**), Giovanni Battista Rinalducci and Giovanni Battista Ficavazza. Pietro Valentini,[7] who enlarged the image for the third edition (1654) by adding a frame of imperial symbols (see **Ill. 2.3**), was a Capuchin monk, active in Rome and Bamberg as an engraver and painter. A copy by him of Guido Reni's *Saint Michael* was recently sold in Munich.[8]

The most teasing 'unknown' is Pierre Miotte,[9] who identified himself as Burgundian and was active in the 1640s and 1650s. Putting his signed works together reveals no common style between them. He could reproduce a classically proportioned figure like the Orpheus in the second volume of *Musurgia* (see **Ill. 2.7**), but when he copied an amateurish zodiac figure, as in *Ars Magna Lucis* (see **Ill. 11.16**), he made no effort to bring to it any elegance. His engravings for *Obeliscus Pamphilius* are so quaint that one can only assume that he

copied exactly what he had in front of him. Since Miotte's name is never coupled with that of an artist, it is possible that he worked directly from Kircher's sketches or from pre-existent materials, while the frequency of his signature suggests that he probably did many of the other engravings in the books to which he contributed: *Ars Magna Lucis*, *Obeliscus Pamphilius*, *Musurgia Universalis* and *Œdipus Ægyptiacus*. He may, for instance, have copied the illustrations of musical instruments from Mersenne's *Harmonie Universelle* that Kircher used in *Musurgia*. As for the frontispiece to *Ars Magna Lucis* (see **Ill. 2.4**), though it is a brilliant concept (surely thanks to Kircher himself), the form is cluttered and the execution wooden. One only has to compare it with the first frontispiece of *Musurgia* (see **Ill. 2.6**) to see the gulf between Miotte's work and that of J. P. Schor, to whom the latter is attributed.

The Innsbruck-born Johann Paul Schor (1615–1674) was one of the highest-paid foreign artists in papal Rome. His range included decorative painting in Castel Gandolfo and Palazzo Colonna, the decorations and carriages for the entry into Rome of Queen Christina of Sweden, theatre sets, designs for rich objects, portraits, a cycle of paintings of Noah's Flood for the Quirinal Palace and assisting Bernini on the Cathedra Petri in St Peter's.[10] In his last year he took on the modest commission to paint frescoes at the monastery church and chapel of Mentorella,[11] which suggests more than just a professional relationship with Kircher (see box opposite).

It was probably Schor who improved Kircher's drawing of Mount Vesuvius in eruption, already shown (**Ill. 3.10**). The author's uncertain lines are visible at the top of the volcano, and he has done his best to show the chaos within, while at the bottom of the picture the artist's sure hand has added a city by the sea with boats, waves and reflections.

The Roman publishers of *Musurgia* employed Schor's talents for the frontispiece and the portrait of the dedicatee, Archduke Leopold Wilhelm (see **Ill. 1.2**). As engravers of these drawings we find two prolific specialists. 'Baronius' is assumed to be Jean Baron (probably born 1616–1620), known as 'Il Tolosano' from his home town Toulouse.[12] He moved to Rome and lodged in the house of Cornelis Bloemaert (see below), where he died shortly after 1650. Among over a hundred known works are many portraits of Italian artists and renderings of Poussin's paintings. Paulus Pontius (1603–1658), who engraved the portrait, was an Antwerp native and lodged in Rubens's house, where he was one of the principal engravers after that master's paintings. He also had an independent career as a portrait engraver.[13] Even famous painters relied for publicity on such experts in the ever-improving craft of reproductive engraving. This was true until well into the era of photography.

Returning to the Egyptological works, we find the same practice of using a superior artist to ring up the curtain, and leaving the subsequent performance to lesser talents. The frontispieces of *Obeliscus Pamphilius* and *Œdipus Ægyptiacus* (see **Ills. 2.5, 2.8**) were both drawn by the Roman painter Giovanni Angelo Canini (1617–1666), a pupil of Domenichino.[14] As a painter he specialized in altarpieces, but he also collected and dealt in antiquities and made

THE MENTORELLA FRESCOES

3.13, 3.14, 3.15 The tiny chapel of St Eustace, perched above the monastery of Mentorella, was decorated by Johann Paul Schor with a figure of Christ, two scenes from the saint's life, and ceiling paintings of angels.

The panel on the (ecclesiastical) south wall shows the conversion of St Eustace, in a format very similar to that of a tiny painting above the piscina in the monastery church. This may have been part of the earlier decorations, imitated both by Schor and in the frontispiece to Kircher's *Historia Eustachio-Mariana* (reused in *Latium*; see **Ill. 6.31**). The chapel's north panel shows St Eustace and his wife being punished for their conversion to Christianity by the attentions of a very tame lion. Both panels have been defaced by graffiti and probably spoiled by inept repainting of the faces, but the Christ above the altar appears to be intact, and may profitably be compared with Pythagoras, Apollo and the Muse in Schor's frontispiece of *Musurgia Universalis* (see **Ill. 2.6**).

drawings of them, many of which were engraved by Cornelis Bloemaert or his assistants. In the process, Canini assembled the kind of 'paper museum' that was popular at the time, picturing ancient cameos, coins and reliefs. He accompanied Cardinal Flavio Chigi (the Pope's nephew) on a mission to Paris, where he offered the collection to Louis XIV. Its publication was completed by his brother Marcantonio, as *Iconografia Cioè Disegno d'Imagini dei Famosi Principi, regi* [etc.], 1669.

Of the other contributors to Kircher's Egyptology, Giovanni Battista Balatri (circa 1627–after 1669) was a Florentine sculptor and architect.[15] His major work was the reconstruction of San Paolino, the church of the Theresian Fathers in Florence, but as a young man he had engraved the first, if not all nine, of the plates of Giovanni Nardi's Lucretius edition.[16] These in turn found their way into *Obeliscus Pamphilius*. How reliable Balatri was may be judged by

the way he adapted a factual drawing by Burrattini (see below) into an Egyptomaniac fantasy (see **Ill. 5.24**).

Tito Livio Burrattini (1617–1681) was an atypical member of Kircher's illustrators, though not of his correspondents. A traveller and polymath, he actually visited Egypt, where he drew the mummy crypt near Dashur (see **Ill. 5.23**) that has given rise to much speculation.[17] He later abandoned Italy to live comfortably under the patronage of the King of Poland as a natural philosopher and man of letters. His principal claim to fame rests on his proposal for a *metro catholico*, a universal unit of measure derived from the length of a pendulum that swings in exactly one second.

The last identifiable contributor to the hundreds of illustrations of *Œdipus Ægyptiacus*, Dominique Barrière (1618/1622–1678),[18] was probably in Rome by 1640, where he enjoyed the patronage of Prince Camillo Pamphili. Even so, according to Préaud, he relied on the charity of his compatriots at the church of St Louis des Français to support his family of eight children. Barrière produced some splendid collections of plates illustrating Villa Aldobrandini, Villa Borghese, Villa Pamphili and many engravings of Claude Lorraine's paintings.[19]

As a curiosity, *Œdipus* contains the one instance in Kircher's works of a signed woodcut, as opposed to an engraving. It is the image of Isis (**Ill. 14.2**), signed 'Rosello F.' (presumably *fecit*). But none of the artists similarly named or spelled fits the time and place. This and many of the other woodcuts in the work bear a symmetrical monogram made from the letters M and A superimposed – or is it an M with an inverted V, for the publisher Vitale Mascardi, who was also a draughtsman?[20]

Kircher's posterity owes a particular debt to Cornelis Bloemaert (circa 1603–1692).[21] The son of a famous Utrecht engraver, Abraham Bloemaert, Cornelis studied with Gerrit van Honthorst and Crispijn van de Passe the Elder. After a spell in Paris, he was brought to Rome by Joachim von Sandrart to engrave Sandrart's drawings from the Giustiniani collection. Bloemaert lived in the Giustiniani Palace until 1644, when he was able to buy his own house. This became a haven for foreign artists and the site of a flourishing printmaking business, in which Bloemaert eventually employed twelve Dutch assistants.[22] He has already been mentioned as the engraver of Canini's work. He contributed to the *Tableaux du Temple des Muses* (picturing antiquities from the Favereau collection), but his main appeal to collectors today is in his splendid illustrations of apples and pears in *Hesperides sive de Malorum* (1646).

On Kircher's 53rd birthday, 2 May 1655, Bloemaert sketched a portrait, now in the Smithsonian Institution, which is the one and only authentic likeness of its subject. All the other portraits of Kircher, engraved or painted, have imitated it to one degree or another (see Frontispiece).[23] In 1664, Bloemaert worked his drawing into a finely detailed etching: the classic Kircher portrait, published in *Mundus Subterraneus* and widely distributed as a single sheet. No substantial change was made to reflect the subject's age, now given as 62, though this was not for want of trying. Jansson wrote to Kircher on 18 June 1664:

> All the figures that belong to the first volume have now been engraved. We are currently correcting them and putting in what is missing. For the portrait of Your Reverence, we have the one that Bloemaert engraved, but it was not done at the present time, and the difference of ten or twelve years greatly changes a person. Would Your Reverence be pleased to give us advice, and we will follow the one of Bloemaert, making it larger, or else Your Reverence will send us another made at the present time.[24]

Kircher's public image, like that of certain monarchs, remained ageless. The portrait even reappeared in 1678, with the age updated to 76.[25] It also served as the model for the full-length portrait of Kircher (see **Ill. 2.9**) on the frontispiece to Schott's augmented edition of *Itinerarium Exstaticum* (1660, 1671), which is

simply signed 'F. Sc.'. Fortunately the splendid arms of the work's dedicatee are signed 'Fleischb. Sc.', enabling both plates to be attributed to Johann Friedrich Fleischberger, a Nuremberg engraver specializing in portraits and active at the time in question.[26] The fact that this edition was printed in Würzburg under Schott's direction explains why a local illustrator was used.[27]

Probably many of Kircher's unnamed illustrators belonged to the circle of foreigners working in Rome that included Bloemaert and Schor. The only other identifiable one is the Haarlem-born Theodor Matham (1605/6–1676),[28] who engraved many designs of Schor's, including the frontispiece for *Mundus Subterraneus* (see **Ill. 2.10**) and worked with Bloemaert on the *Temple des Muses* and the Giustiniani project.

After Kircher's books were taken on by Jansson (see box opposite), a much greater proportion of illustrations was rendered by engraving, as opposed to woodcut. Whereas in earlier works the engraved pages were separate folios, printed on one side with keys to tell the printer where to insert them in the text, Jansson frequently included a smaller engraving on a typeset page.

Along with the greater investment in time and craftsmanship, Kircher's later works benefited from other distinguished artists. The Dutch painter Romeyn de Hooghe (1645–1708),[29] who signs the frontispiece for *Latium* (see **Ill. 2.19**) was an admirer of Rembrandt, who did him the honour of painting his portrait. De Hooghe became an important figure in his native Holland as artist, historian and political and cultural leader. Michele Rak writes of him:

> He was one of the greatest illustrators of all times, and comprehends within himself all the various faculties of the universal mind of the Baroque. He was etcher, painter, sculptor, engraver of coins, designer of all kinds of crafts, scholar and doctor of law. His work is the last apotheosis of the grand Baroque spirit before its dissolution.[30]

Seen in the Roman context, de Hooghe's allegory of Latium is in a very different style from the typical frontispiece; it is deliberately casual and almost untidy, like some of Rembrandt's etchings. This and the sensuous figures, one entirely nude, must have raised some eyebrows when the book reached the Collegio Romano.

The other known illustrator of *Latium* is Giovanni Battista Galestruzzi (between 1611 and 1620–after 1669).[31] Alone among these artists, he took care to proclaim his native city (Florence), the fact that he both drew and engraved the plate, the place (Rome) and the date (1658, thirteen years before *Latium* was published). Galestruzzi is recorded as an imitator of Stefano della Bella and a prolific illustrator of classical gems. His best-known work was the engraving of Polidoro da Caravaggio's friezes and reliefs in the Palazzo Milesi, Rome, and his delineation of the 'Apotheosis of Homer' (see **Ill. 5.21**) is in the same vein.

Kircher's works of the 1670s saw the debut of another young Amsterdam artist, Coenraet Decker (1651–1685).[32] A pupil of Romeyn de Hooghe, Decker

KIRCHER'S DUTCH PUBLISHER

Kircher's contract with the Protestant publisher Jansson was an extraordinary step to take for a religious based in Rome. Ingrid Rowland attributes it to Kircher's friend Fabio Chigi, who became Pope Alexander VII in 1655, and had long worked for reconciliation and collaboration between Protestant and Catholic Europe, while being well aware of the stifling censorship and declining publishing standards in his own realm.[33] The founder of the Dutch house was Jan or Johann Jansson[34] [I] of Arnhem (died 1629), a partner of Jodocus Hondius (1563–1612), who early in the century had bought the engraved copperplates of the world atlas from the heirs of the great cartographer Gerardus Mercator (inventor of 'Mercator's Projection', still used today). Hondius integrated them with new plates drawn and engraved by himself, and he and Jansson published the collection as *Atlas Minor* (1607–1621).

Shortly after Hondius's death in 1612, the two families were joined through the marriage of Johann I's son, Johann Jansson [II] (1588–1664), to Hondius's daughter Elisabeth (born 1588/1589). The young couple set up business in Amsterdam, where Jan II collaborated with his brother Jodocus (1613/1614–1655) and his brother-in-law Hendrik Hondius (1596/1597–1651) on the ever-expanding project. By 1641 the Mercator-Hondius *Atlas* had enjoyed thirty editions in various languages. It continued its career as *Atlas Novus* (1650), then as the eleven-volume, multilingual *Atlas Maior* (1658–). And just as globes came in sets of two (terrestrial and celestial), so Jansson also published an atlas of the heavens with the resounding title of *Atlas Coelestis seu Harmonia Macrocosmica* (1660–1661).[35]

Jansson and Hondius's only competitor in the field of global mapping was the house of Blaeu, and the rivalry between them was fierce. During the 1630s, Blaeu accused the Amsterdam publishers of stealing material from him and then abusing him in print. (Schilder, 20–24, 286). Meanwhile, the Jansson brothers were also publishing books, sometimes under their separate names, sometimes together. The earliest I have seen is P. Bertius, *Commentarium Rerum Germanicum* (1616), a history and topography of the German-speaking nations, which used the firm's graphic resources to enhance the text with many engraved portraits, maps, itineraries and town views. For the most part, the Janssons seem to have published whatever came their way, usually in pocket-book format. Among their more ambitious productions were two illustrated botanical works: Emanuel Swert, *Florilegium Amplissimum* (1633) and Giovanni Battista Ferrari, *Flora* (1646). Their typographical flair can be seen in two pioneering works of Scandinavian history: Ole Worm, *Runir* (1636), which uses fonts of Gothic and runic letters, and Johann Isacius Pontanus, *Rerum Danicarum Historia* (1631), a folio with huge folding maps by Mercator and others, and the Lord's Prayer in seven languages. The firm's Protestant allegiance was evident in their publishing the two-volume commemoration of Henry, Prince of Orange: Isaac Commelin, *Histoire de la Vie et Actes Memorables de Frederic Henry de Nassau* (1656). In the arcane field, they published many alchemical treatises by Johann Rudolf Glauber. From the firm's point of view, Kircher was a great asset, but their major project during and after the publication of *Mundus Subterraneus* was a polyglot bible, which was to be called *Biblia Alexandrina* in honour of Pope Alexander VII. It was imperative for the firm to obtain the Pope's approval, and Jansson's letters to Kircher in 1666 show his anxiety over the matter and reliance on Kircher as a go-between.

The Jansson in question, who wrote to Kircher first in French, then in Dutch ('because as you are born High-German, you can read it'[36]), was the third of that name. When Johann Jansson II died in 1664, his estate was divided three ways between the children of his late brother Jodocus and his own two daughters. One of them, Elisabeth, had in 1642 married another Johann Jansson [III] of Rotterdam (circa 1616/1617–1681), also related to the Hondius family (see Briels, 529), who upon his marriage had adopted the name 'van Waesberge'. It was he who now took over management of the business on behalf of the heirs, together with his partner and son-in-law Elizaeus Weyerstraet (died 1666).[37]

Thus *Mundus Subterraneus* was published in 1664–1665 'Apud Joannem Janssonium & Elizeum Weyerstraten,' that is, by the two partners, and reprinted in 1668 'Apud Joannem Janssonium à Waesberge, & Viduam Elizaei Weyerstraet,' that is, 'published by Johann Jansson van Waesberge and the Widow of Elizaeus Weyerstraet.' The 1678 edition was published 'Apud Joannem Janssonium à Waesberge & Filios', that is, by Johann Jansson van Waesberge & Sons – the widow having presumably died or sold her interest; and the 1682 Dutch edition 'By d'Erfgenamen van wylen Joannes Janssonius van Waasberge', that is, by the heirs of the late Johann Jansson van Waesberge.

These heirs, Johann [IV] and his brother Gillis Jansson van Waesberge, carried the firm over into the eighteenth century, collaborating for large-scale publications with the old rival families of Elsevir and Blaeu.[38]

was not yet twenty when he signed and dated (1670) the great vision of the Tower of Babel (**Ill. 6.13**) and the Hanging Gardens of Babylon (**Ill. 6.21**). He must have worked simultaneously on *Arca Noë* and *Turris Babel,* though the latter would not be published for nine more years. The frontispiece to *Arca Noë* (**Ill. 2.26**) has the informal quality of de Hooghe's work, and whoever did that might have also have done the picture of Adam and Eve (**Ill. 6.1**). However, the plate of Noah (**Ill. 6.2**), which Decker signs as both artist and engraver, is so superior in landscape, gesture and facial expression that one wonders whether two different pupils of de Hooghe were involved. In any case, another hand altogether was responsible for the series of large plates depicting the events before, during and after Noah's Flood (see **Ills. 6.4–6.7, 6.10**). Charming as these are, they show an almost mediaeval approach to perspective and human proportion.

By the time Kircher's books appeared in print, Decker's career was well advanced. In 1672, he was contracted by Jansson to do the plates for *Asiographia,* including maps, city views, allegories and military scenes, and he continued with a long stream of topographical and travel books. His work for Kircher's publisher was partly shared, as the signatures show, with Lievin Cruyl (1634–after 1690), a far better documented artist.[39] Cruyl was born in Ghent, matriculated at the University of Louvain, was ordained as a priest and served both in church posts and as an architect. In 1662 he submitted a design for the completion of the St Michielskerk in Ghent with a tower in late Brabantine Gothic style, 440 feet (134 metres) high. It was never built for lack of funds, but as J.-P. Esther remarks, 'although unoriginal and of an outdated style, the design had elegance and grandeur'.[40] It seems fitting that Cruyl should have been the engraver of the Tower of Babel.

By 1664 Cruyl was working as an architect in Rome. Barbara Jatta, who assumes that he did the other illustrations for *Turris Babel,* credits Kircher for revealing to him the knowledge of optics and the camera obscura that were essential to Cruyl's later work.[41] She writes of how the buildings in *Turris Babel* unite antique with modern elements, such as motifs from the Pantheon or the Temple of the Sibyl at Tivoli with ones from Bernini, Borromini or Cortona.[42] Once set on this path, Cruyl continued in the same vein, his rigorous perspective lending power to his fantastic battle scenes, seascapes and architectural caprices.

Given that the collaboration of Decker and Cruyl, such as it was, spanned nearly a decade and the distance between Rome and Amsterdam, one can see the futility of trying to reconstruct and attribute the illustration of any of Kircher's later works. Did the misprinted *erudite* in the plate of the Tower of Babel signify that Decker only produced a sketch which sat on Kircher's shelf (or Jansson's) for years, while Cruyl, when at last the book saw the prospect of publication, put his erudition to work in stocking the Babylonian landscape with classical buildings? Did Decker design and engrave the scene of Babylon (**Ill. 6.15**) years later, drawing on his own interim experience in illustrating works of oriental travel? If only Kircher's correspondence

included any letters to or from his artists, one might be able to answer such questions. But it does not.

The two frontispieces of Jansson's first Kircher production, the 1664–1665 *Mundus Subterraneus,* involved four different artists. We have already mentioned Schor and Matham, who created the first. The designer of the second was Crispin van de Passe the Younger (1597/8–1670 or after),[43] the son of Bloemaert's teacher. Van de Passe was born in Cologne, worked in Paris, then settled in Amsterdam. He specialized in 'Arcadian' book illustrations (Ovid, Daphnis, etc.) and in mildly erotic picture-books with titles such as 'The mirror of the most beautiful courtesans of these times' (*Le Miroir des Plus Belles Courtisanes de ce Temps,* Amsterdam, 1630) or 'The true portraits of some of the greatest ladies, disguised as shepherdesses' (*Les Vraies Pourtraits de Quelques-unes des Plus Grandes Dames Desguisées en Bergères,* Amsterdam, 1640).[44] His design for Kircher's second volume, in comparison with the awe-inspiring illustrations of the first, has no flavour of the subterranean world, but instead brings a courtly note to the relations between the classical deities (see **Ill. 2.12**). It was engraved by Anthonie Heeres Siourtsma (or Sioertsma, born 1626/1627),[45] who is only known for being one of Van de Passe the Younger's pupils.

The difficult task of reproducing the Sanskrit lettering in *China Illustrata* (see **Ills 13.1, 13.4**) fell to Willem van der Laegh (1614–1674), who signs several of the calligraphic plates, and may, for all we know, have been the engraver of the illustrations. Van der Laegh was a Haarlem-born engraver, chiefly known for portraits, who worked in Amsterdam and in Copenhagen.[46] The even more challenging plate of the Sino-Syriac stele, with its more than one thousand Chinese characters, was 'written by his own hand from the autograph by Mattheus Sina Oriundus ex Siganfu in the year 1664', that is, by a Chinese convert from Siganfu.

Among the other artists identified by signature, Gérard de Lairesse (1641–1711) commands attention for his frontispiece to *Turris Babel* (see **Ill. 2.27**).[47] It shows a third tendency in later seventeenth-century book illustration, equally remote from Romeyn de Hooghe on the one hand, and from Crispin van de Passe on the other. This example bears out Thieme-Becker's description of Lairesse as the chief academic classicist of the Rembrandt era. Working mainly in Germany and the Netherlands, he was a successful painter and an engraver of architecture, anatomies and the title pages to the luxurious scores of Lully's operas. Here the eye in the sky and the tumbling putti pay homage to the symbolic tradition, but the scene below is like any history painting of the era. The characters are enlivened and given character by indicating the different directions of their glances: a sophistication to which Kircher's other illustrators seldom aspired. The engraver, Jean van Munnichuysen (1654/1655–after 1701) also engraved other title pages by Lairesse.[48]

Another small cluster of foreign artists came together in the opening plates of *Phonurgia Nova,* which was published in Kempten, equally distant from Kircher's home in Rome and his publisher's in Amsterdam. Consequently there are no ties with the Roman emigrant artists who had made such a contribution to Kircher's earlier works. The frontispiece of *Phonurgia* (see **Ill. 2.25**) is signed by Felix Cheurier, whose name appears nowhere in the reference literature. This is a pity, for it is an ingenious and memorable design, with its multiple fields of interest being more like a ceiling painting than a single-focused view. The imposing portrait of Emperor Leopold (see **Ill. 1.7**) is by Franz Herman, probably to be identified as Franz Georg Hermann (1640–1689),[49] the first of that name and of an artistic dynasty in Kempten. Most of his known work was for churches in that region. The engraver for both of the signed *Phonurgia* prints was Georg Andreas Wolfgang the Elder (1631–1716), a native of Chemnitz and pupil of Melchior Küsel.[50] The whole team was highly competent, which cannot be said of those who hacked out the rest of the illustrations, mostly imitated from *Musurgia Universalis*.

This leaves a few loose ends, such as the identity of Ficavazza and Rinalducci (see above), or that of two artists whom I suspect to have been local amateurs: H. Bonzon and the 'Prenestine citizen and artist' Agapito Bernardini.[51] Giacomo (or Jacopo) Bichi appears in the reference literature[52] solely as author of the portrait of Emperor Ferdinand III that prefaces *Œdipus Ægyptiacus*.

This short overview of Kircher's known illustrators reveals a strong contribution from German- or Dutch-speaking artists resident in Rome, linked to each other by ties of apprenticeship or dependency, and earning the greater part of their living from work for the great Roman families. This involved assisting artists like Pietro da Cortona and Bernini in massive decorative schemes for palaces and churches, and supplying the voracious demand for paper reproductions, whether of portraits, collections, antiquities, paintings or topographical subjects. Jacques Kuhnmünch writes of how after the 1620s the tendency towards brighter paintings, with Cortona, Sacchi and Lanfranco, gave a new impulse to the print trade.[53] He names Bloemaert and Jean Blondeau as the chief suppliers of engraved reproductions, which now stretched back in time to the canonized 'old masters' Michelangelo and Titian. Beside these decorative items, there was a parallel business in religious prints, which were sold to give as gifts to the sick and even to apply to diseased parts of the body.[54] This helps to restore perspective to the illustration of Kircher's works, which may loom large in the Kircherian microcosm but was only a tiny part of a larger and more variegated economy.

At the other end of Europe, Johann Jansson was able to call on the resources of Amsterdam, Utrecht, Antwerp and other rich artistic centres. This resulted in the contributions of Gérard de Lairesse, Romeyn de Hooghe and Hooghe's pupil Coenraet Decker, again supplemented by a host of apprentices and wood-engravers. One artist had connections with the two networks: Crispin van de Passe the Younger, whose father had trained Bloemaert but who remained in the north. But here, too, things should be kept in perspective. Just as the illustration of Kircher's works was a very minor commission for all these busy artists, so their names emerge like icebergs from a far greater number of anonymous draughtsmen, engravers and, at the bottom of the hierarchy, the woodblock cutters.

Notes

1 Biblioteca Nazionale Vittorio Emanuele II, Ms. S. Fr. Paola 4: *Mathematica Curiosa Authore Pr. Athanasio Kircher, Anno Domini MDCXXXX*, frontispiece. The date of 1638 appears in the text. The other manuscript is Kircher's *Institutiones Mathematicae* in the handwriting of Andreas Weick, 1630, in the Badische Landesbibliothek Karlsruhe, Ms. St. Blasien 67. On this, see Beinlich 2002a, 163–164; Beinlich 2002b. 126–131.

2 Rome, Biblioteca Nazionale, Ms. Gesuiti 562, ff. 101, 160–166. For a reproduction of the professionally drawn frontispiece (f. 170), see Beinlich 2002b, 139 and back cover. This manuscript is part of an early version of *Mundus Subterraneus* in ten books, titled *Geocosmus*, as also announced and summarized in *Iter Extaticum* II (1657), 228. Another manuscript in the same library, Ms. Gesuiti 546, is part of the later version in twelve books dated May 11, 1663. On these manuscripts, see Strasser 1982.

3 For a coloured reproduction, see Lo Sardo, 178 and back cover.

4 An informal survey of 70 books published by Johannes Jansson held in Cornell University Library's Special Collections revealed only six signed engravings, three of them by Coenraet Decker (in Christoph Adolph Balduin, *Aurum Superius et Inferius*, 1675, and Paolo Boccone, *Recherches et Observations... Touchant le Corail*, 1674).

5 See *Rubens and the Book*, 185–198; Judson and Van de Velde, with numerous examples of the drawings and subsequent engravings.

6 On Aglio, see Thieme-Becker, I, 119; *Allgemeine Kunst-Lexikon* (hereafter *AKL*), I, 521. Many of the illustrators mentioned in this chapter are so obscure that a few unsigned lines in Thieme-Becker's encyclopedia are the fullest record of them.

7 There is a minimal reference to Valentini in Thieme-Becker, XXXIV, 66.

8 Auction records of Ketterer Kunst, 26 Nov. 1997, via Internet.

9 Thieme-Becker, XXIV, 584, has three lines on Miotte, without noticing his work for Kircher.

10 On Schor, see Thieme-Becker, XXX, 263–264.

11 Called in Thieme-Becker, as often elsewhere, 'Vulturella'.

12 The identity of 'Baronius' is suggested in Merrill, 15. On Baron, see Thieme-Becker II, 515; M. Préau in *AKL*, 7, 125.

13 On Pontius, see Thieme-Becker, XXVII, 249; *Grove Dictionary of* Art (hereafter Grove), 25, 221.

14 On Canini, see Thieme-Becker, V, 504–505; A. Pampalone in *AKL*, 16, 150–151.

15 On Balatri or Balatrio, see Thieme-Becker, II, 385; 'S.P.' in *AKL*, 6, 388.

16 Lucretius, *De Rerum Naturae Libri Sex, cum Paraphrasistica Explanatione, & Animadversionibus, D. Ioannis Nardii Florentini.* Florence: Amato Massa, 1647.

17 See Beinlich, 'Kircher und Ägypten'.

18 On Barrière, see Thieme-Becker, II, 533; M. Préaud in *AKL*, 7, 174.

19 Information from sales catalogue of Martayan Lan, Paris, 2006, via Internet.

20 On Mascardi, see Thieme-Becker, XXIV, 199.

21 On Bloemaert, called 'the Younger' to distinguish him from his grandfather, see Thieme-Becker, IV, 127; G. Seelig in *AKL*, 11, 549–550.

22 For this and other details, see Mayer-Deutsch, 110.

23 See examples in Mayer-Deutsch; Beinlich 2002a; Beinlich 2003.

24 APUG Ms. 562, f. 167ʳ; original in French.

25 See Rowland 2000, 32.

26 On Fleischberger, see Thieme-Becker, XII, 84.

27 Fleischberger also signed the heraldic decoration in Schott's *Technica Curiosa* (1664); see Schott 2000, frontispiece.

28 On Matham, see Thieme-Becker, XXIV, 238–239.

29 On Romeyn de Hooghe, see M. D. Henkel in Thieme-Becker, XVII, 458–461; M. J. C. Otten in Grove, 14, 736–737.

30 Rak, 48.

31 On Galestruzzi, see Thieme-Becker, XIII, 94; 'S.P.' in *AKL*, 47, 445–446; A. N. Spina in Grove, 12, 4.

32 On Coenraet or Conraet Decker, see Berkhout in Thieme-Becker, VIII, 520–521; R. Feurer in *AKL*, 25, 124–125, who establishes the artist's date of death as 1685, not 'before 1709' as in earlier references. He is not to be confused with Cornelis Decker (1643–1678), a Haarlem landscape painter.

33 Rowland, 22–23.

34 Jan is the plain Dutch name (=John). In Latin works, the publisher's byline reads 'Apud Joannem Janssonium' (=accusative case of Joannes Janssonius); in French ones, as 'Chez Jean Jansson', and in German ones, as 'Bei Johan(n) Jansson'. An English contemporary referred to him as 'Johnson the printer at Amsterdam' (Fletcher 2006, 467, n.73).

35 On the history and genealogy of the Hondius and Jansson families, see *Tooley's Dictionary of Mapmakers*, II, 429–430; Battini, 218; Briels, 322–325. Shirley, 636, gives their combined family tree.

36 APUG Ms. 562, f.173, letter of Dec. 29, 1666 informing Kircher of Weyerstraet's death.

37 Elizaeus Weyerstraet is identified as Johann III's son-in-law in Fletcher 2006, 467, n.73.

38 E.g. in *Corpus Juris Civilis* (1681) published together with the widow of Daniel Elsevir and others; Isaac Vossius, *Opera* in 6 vols (1695–1701), with W. Blaeu and others.

39 On Cruyl or Creyl, see P. Bergmans in Thieme-Becker, VIII, 179–180; B. Jatta in *AKL*, 22, 483–484; Jatta 1992.

40 J.-P. Esther, 'Cruyl, Lievin', in Grove, 8, 220.

41 Jatta, 10.

42 Jatta, 82–83.

43 On Van de Passe, see M. D. Henkel in Thieme-Becker, XXVI, 281–282; I. M. Veldman in Grove, 236–237.

44 On the courtly illustrations of the two Van de Passes, see Verwey, 58.

45 On Siourtsma, see Thieme-Becker, XXXI, 96.

46 On Van der Laegh, see M. D. H[enkel] in Thieme-Becker, XXII, 193.

47 On De Lairesse, see M. D. Henkel in Thieme-Becker, XXII, 233–237.

48 E.g. those of Theodor Zwinger, *Theatrum Botanicum* (Basel, 1696); Jean le Clerc, *Geschiednissen der Vereenigde Nederlanden* (1730). On Munnichuysen, see Thieme-Becker, XXV, 272.

49 On Hermann, see M. Feulner in Grove, 14, 456, updating the entry by 'J. M.' in Thieme-Becker, XVI, 485.

50 On Wolfgang, see Thieme-Becker, XXXVI, 221.

51 On Bernardini, see Thieme-Becker, III, 437.

52 On Bichi, see Thieme-Becker, III, 607.

53 Kuhnmünch, 8.

54 Kuhnmünch, 15.

Chapter 4   Antiquity Misread

When Kircher first set his mind to deciphering the Egyptian hieroglyphs, he already had a profound knowledge of the esoteric philosophies of the ancient world, and an evident sympathy for them.[1] He had absorbed the canon of the *prisca theologia*, the 'earliest theology' that was supposedly the common inheritance of all peoples. It was the Florentine Platonists of the fifteenth century who had promoted this idea, especially Marsilio Ficino with his translations of the *Corpus Hermeticum*, the Platonic dialogues and the Neoplatonists, and Pico della Mirandola, with his addition of a Christianized Kabbalah to the mixture. Three other important elements were the Hymns of Orpheus, which Ficino used for the magical invocation of planetary influences, the gnomic sayings known as the Golden Verses of Pythagoras, and the Chaldaean Oracles ascribed to Zoroaster. The fact that several of these sources, which the Florentines believed to be as old as Moses or older, dated from late antiquity was neither here nor there. What was important, both to them and to Kircher, was the theology and cosmology that seemed to be common to all of them.

Theologically it was a kind of monotheism, with an impersonal One that was ultimately responsible for emanating all that is. It was also a polytheism, for among the first emanations from the One were powers that the ancients knew, and worshipped, as gods and goddesses. Cosmologically it was a hierarchy, a ladder or chain of beings descending from the One, through the gods, to lower spiritual beings like daemons and the souls of heroes, to mankind, then further downwards to animals, vegetables and the four elements of the earth itself. An important corollary, never quite spelled out in antiquity, was the 'doctrine of correspondences': that each level of being corresponded to, or reflected, the adjacent ones. This doctrine supplied a rationale for magic, in which something on a lower level, such as a metal or a herb, could be used in order to pull on the chain of being and cause a reaction from the corresponding entity on a higher level, such as a planet or a god.

Since the only known writing from Egypt was the *Corpus Hermeticum*, a collection of Greek treatises and dialogues filled with these ideas, Kircher was convinced that if the hieroglyphs could be read, one would find the same ideas there. He never swerved from this conviction. It was there in his earliest efforts at decipherment, published in *Prodromus Coptus* (1636), in the two central Egyptological works, *Obeliscus Pamphilius* (1650) and *Œdipus Ægyptiacus* (1652–1654), in *Obeliscus Ægyptiacus* (1666) and the late *Sphinx Mystagoga* (1676).

Kircher's interest in the hieroglyphs was probably kindled by a chance encounter[2] with Herwart von Hohenburg's *Thesaurus Hieroglyphicorum*, an exceedingly scarce book that is nothing more than a folio of twenty-nine engraved plates.[3] Its compiler, Johann Georg Herwart von Hohenburg zu Perg und Planegg (1553–1622) is best known as a friend and correspondent of Johann Kepler, whom he helped to obtain the post of Court Mathematician and Astronomer at the court of Emperor Rudolf II.[4] Born to a prominent Augsburg family, Herwart became a privy councillor of Elector Maximilian I of Bavaria, who commissioned him to catalogue and arrange the electoral library.[5] He was also an historian and a collector of antiquities, with a particular fascination for Egypt. The *Thesaurus Hieroglyphicorum* was a 'paper museum' containing illustrations of all the relevant objects he had been able to locate.

Nearly half of Herwart's illustrations are of the Bembine Table of Isis, a bronze table-top or tablet inlaid with silver and niello and depicting mysterious Egyptian figures (**Ill. 4.1**).[6] Kircher's account of its origins is as follows: it was discovered in the shop of a Bologna metal-smith and bought by the great humanist Cardinal Bembo. After his death it passed from his collection to that of the Dukes of Mantua, where it disappeared after the sack of their city in 1630. Since then, all efforts to find it were in vain, but fortunately it had been faithfully copied: in 1559 Aeneas Vico of Parma was commissioned by the Cardinal's nephew, Torquatus Bembo, to make a copper engraving the exact size of the original (50 by 30 inches or 127 by 76 cm), which he dedicated to Emperor Ferdinand I. After all the prints made from this were exhausted, new engravings were made for the *Thesaurus Hieroglyphicorum* of Herwart von Hohenburg, Chancellor of the Duke of Bavaria. Kircher concludes: 'From this, with all possible diligence, we have reproduced it in smaller proportion.'[7]

It is surprising that Kircher should have discovered the Bembine Table through this route, rather than through the more accessible book of Lorenzo Pignoria, *Vetustissmae Tabulae Aeneae* (1605).[8] Pignoria, a distinguished Paduan antiquarian, not only reproduced Enea Vico's life-size engravings of the Table, but supplied a commentary on it.[9] However, if Kircher had only seen Pignoria's version, he would not have discovered the man-headed scarab beetle (see below) which gave him such a stroke of inspiration.[10] As for the famous Table, it was not lost. Kircher did not know it, but in about 1628 the Duke of Mantua sold it, with other pieces from his collection, to Carlo Emanuele of Savoy. The Savoy

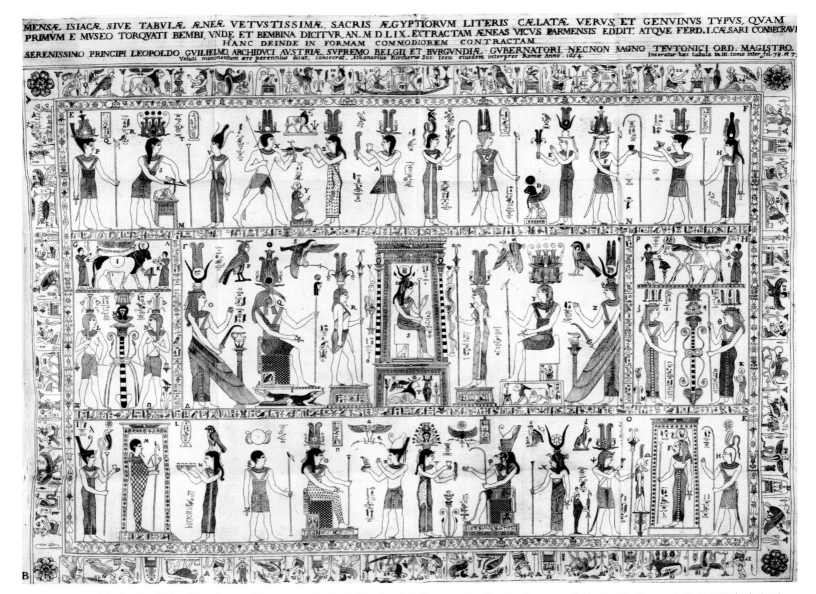

MENSÆ ISIACÆ, SIVE TABVLÆ ÆNEÆ VETVSTISSIMÆ, SACRIS ÆGYPTIORVM LITERIS CÆLATÆ VERVS, ET GENVINVS TYPVS, QVAM PRIMVM E MVSEO TORQVATI BEMBI, VNDE ET BEMBINA DICITVR, AN. M D LIX. EXTRACTAM ÆNEAS VICVS PARMENSIS EDDIT, ATQVE FERD. I. CÆSARI CONSECRAVI HANC DEINDE IN FORMAM COMMODIOREM CONTRACTAM SERENISSIMO PRINCIPI LEOPOLDO GVILIELMO ARCHIDVCI AVSTRIÆ, SVPREMO BELGII ET BVRGVNDIÆ GVBERNATORI NECNON MAGNO TEVTONICI ORD. MAGISTRO. Veluti monimentum ære perennius dicat, consecrat, Athanarius Kircherus Soc. Iesu eiusdem interpres Romæ Anno. 1654. Inseratur hæc tabula in III. tomo inter fol. 78. et 79.

4.1 An engraving of the Bembine Table of Isis, a bronze table-top owned by Cardinal Bembo, depicting mysterious Egyptian figures, now in the Egyptian Museum in Turin. In Kircher's time it was believed lost and he knew it only from engravings. He interpreted it enthusiastically as 'the epitome of the whole Egyptian theology'. (*Œdipus Ægyptiacus*, Volume III, fp. 78/79)

family donated it to the museum of the University of Turin, where it remained during the second half of the eighteenth century. It was among the Italian treasures looted by Napoleon, then returned to Turin, where Champollion saw it in 1824. Since 1832 it has been on display in the Egyptian Museum there.[11]

Herwart annotated his facsimile with the names of the winds, the ecliptics, the poles and the centre of the world, apparently thinking that it was about navigation by means of the magnetic compass.[12] Beyond that, he made no pretence at explaining the hieroglyphs. Kircher, on the other hand, regarded the Table with awe. He was certain that it was 'no less than the epitome and

anacephalaeosin of the whole Egyptian theology, both practical and theoretical, as will appear from the following interpretation. And before I begin', he added disarmingly, 'I declare that nothing will derive from my own opinion or notion.' At the same time, he was afraid that there was a lot of unhealthy pagan magic tied in with it, so he hedged his admiration with a warning: 'Therefore I trust the Christian reader to discern clearly the thousand tricks that the Devil has devised for the ruin of souls, hidden beneath the mask of some religion or divine worship, so that once these are known, he may steer clear of them with oars and sails, to his soul's great fruit and benefit.'[13]

In *Œdipus Ægyptiacus*, the Bembine Table served as a grandiloquent portal to the third volume, which finally came around to translating the hieroglyphs. Kircher analysed every detail of it, treating each figure from eight viewpoints: its shape, place, gesture, operations, costume, headdress, staff and the smaller symbols around it. But in the 1630s, at the foundational stage of his work, these were not nearly so important as a tiny figure in the margin which I have already mentioned: a scarab beetle with a human head (**Ill. 4.2**).

This beetle was to Kircher what the Rosetta Stone was to Champollion. He reproduced it from the same woodblock six times over a span of thirty years, and never went back on his original interpretation of it. In *Prodromus Coptus* (1636), he announces that he is going to treat it like an anatomist, and dissect it to show the separate parts and their interrelations. The winged orb with a serpent represents the 'soul of the world' infusing life into things. The body of the hybrid creature symbolizes the moderator or motive power of the whole world. The Egyptians chose this symbol because of the scarab's habit of rolling around a ball of dung containing its egg: it symbolized the 'moderator' of the universe propelling the heavenly bodies. The concentric ovals are the planetary orbits, nested inside each other. The youthful human head is that of the god Horus, who in Egyptian religion represented the sun. The moon is simply the moon. The cross has nothing to do with Christianity, but stands for the four elements earth, water, air and fire, hence for the elementary or physical world. The creature's various parts thus cover the entire created universe.

In a later work, Kircher will add that the beetle's hard shell represents the heavens; its diaphanous wings, the airy and fiery spaces above the earth; the rest of its body, the earth, aptly marked by five lines representing its five zones (two arctic, two temperate, one tropical). The thirty claws on its six legs correspond to the thirty-day months of the sun's journey through the zodiac. Its rolling ball imitates the sun's course through the sky, and the hatching of its egg correlates closely with the lunar cycle.[14]

More important still is the tablet with its four scarcely discernable signs. Kircher reads them as four Coptic letters, ΦΥΛΟ, equivalent to the Greek word φιλο, *philo,* meaning Love. In Herwart's enlarged detail, the only letter that looks similar to Kircher's reading is the O, but Kircher says that it is much plainer on Aeneas Vico's original copy.[15] It certainly is in the version Kircher drew in the margin of his manuscript of *Œdipus Ægyptiacus* (see **Ill. 3.4**). Whatever the accuracy of the various transcriptions, the crux of the matter was that Coptic letters appeared in a context of hieroglyphs.[16]

Kircher linked this to a statement of Clement of Alexandria that the Egyptians used three sorts of characters.[17] The first became the letters of Coptic; the second were symbols used by priests to write about sacred things; the third were images of animals and objects. Kircher could now demonstrate that the three types were not separate, but all of a piece. He goes on to illustrate some more examples of Coptic letters mixed with hieroglyphs. He had

4.2 A detail from the Bembine Table showing a scarab beetle with a human head. To Kircher this was the clue to the whole symbolism of ancient Egypt: its body stood for the motive power of the world, the concentric ovals for the orbits of the planets, and so on. (*Œdipus Ægyptiacus*, Volume II, 415)

already noticed in several hieroglyphic inscriptions a symbol that resembled the letter A; now he feels justified in reading it as exactly that.

The presence of archaic letters among the hieroglyphs might have led Kircher to assume that the hieroglyphs themselves were phonetic or alphabetical (as indeed they turned out to be when correctly read), but he takes the opposite view: that all the signs, alphabetic or pictorial, were symbolic. Needing to find a meaning for this letter A, he makes a leap in the dark which few of his readers can have caught. Without the slightest explanation, he writes that the A means *Agathos Daemon*, the 'good genius' of the Nile Delta or of Egypt in general. He had come across the two words in his study of Coptic: they are Greek, as are many Coptic words, but he had already made up his mind that Coptic was an older language and script than Greek. He now promises to clarify his interpretation with an example, but this is just as much of a leap: he simply illustrates two specimens of the A beside a hawk-headed figure, translating the result as 'Osiris, that is, the sun, source of light and heat, the *Agathos Daemon* or good genius of Egypt'. A more flagrant jumping to conclusions would be hard to find.

As further proof, Kircher calls to witness Herwart's illustration of a dog-headed figure surrounded by various symbols.[18] At this early stage he could not command the resources of engraving to reproduce the entire plate (see **Ill. 14.7**), but only two of the smaller symbols flanking the main figure (**Ill. 4.3**). One is the horned head of the god Amon; the other, a capital M in a triangle, of this latter Kircher writes: 'It signifies none other than these Coptic words: *Agathos Daemon*, since all the letters of the word AMON can be seen expressed in it.'

◀ 4.3 Kircher's first demonstration that the Egyptian hieroglyphs and the Coptic alphabet had a common origin and purpose. (*Obeliscus Pamphilius*, 273)

▼ 4.4 The Egyptian world system, a composite pseudo-hieroglyph invented by Kircher from material in the Bembine Table. (*Œdipus Ægyptiacus*, Volume II, 418)

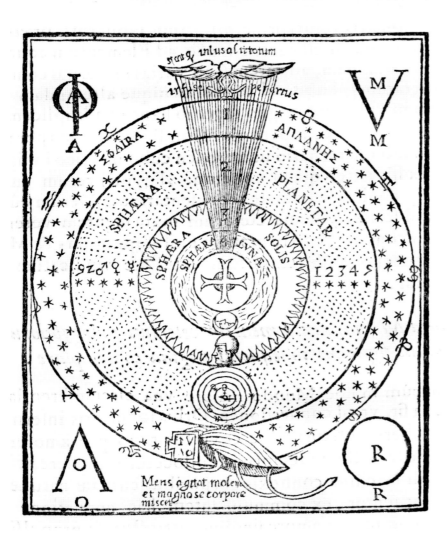

Having now shown that there are Coptic letters mixed in among the hieroglyphs, Kircher took it upon himself to reveal their origins. He assumed that the Coptic alphabet was an interim stage between the pictorial hieroglyphs and fully alphabetic scripts such as Greek or Latin. As such, every letter must have had a prior, pictorial meaning, and it only remained to find, or invent, this meaning.

He began by seeking the image behind this conspicuous letter A, and found it in the ibis, a wading bird with a long curved beak, sacred to the Egyptians. Why was it sacred? Kircher found the reason told by 'old writers', as follows: once part of Egypt was under the sea. Osiris, the first king, diverted the Nile and new land appeared, but huge serpents spawned from the putrid mud. Every day someone was bitten by them and died, including Osiris's own general, Canopus. Osiris then imported the ibis, which quickly devoured the serpents and made the area habitable. The Egyptians pictured this bird with just its legs and its beak thrust across them, forming a letter A. The same stance also gave them the letter Δ, which happened to be the shape of the Nile Delta. Thus they attributed many other benefits to the ibis, and took it to be the Agathos Daemon, the good genius of Egypt. Hermes Trismegistus, who invented hieroglyphs, made it the first letter, and when Cadmus created the Greek alphabet, he did likewise.[19]

It is typical of Kircher's style that before analysing the man-headed scarab that holds the ΦVΛO tablet, he tells a 'funny story' (*historia iucunda*) that he found in an Arabic source. A Persian pilgrim in Egypt accidentally trod on one of these beetles, as it was rolling its ball of dung. The Egyptians around him threw up their hands in horror and beseeched the god not to be angry, assuring him that they weren't guilty of the crime. Turning to the Persian, they said: 'How dare you insult the form of our god Osiris?' After that, the Persian watched his step, 'so as not to bring down the indignation of the Divinity by hurting this muddy godling'.[20]

As we have seen, Kircher interpreted the scarab man as a cosmography in miniature. Now, in a further logical leap, Kircher explains why the word on the tablet means Love. As Plato, Dionysus the Areopagite, Porphyry and many others tell us, it is love that moves higher things to benefit lower ones, and brings equals together. So not only does the scarab-man contain the cosmos, but he also tells us what makes it work. This little hieroglyph, tucked away in the frame of the Bembine Table, turns out to carry the combined weight of Egyptian cosmology and Neoplatonism.

There is more. When Kircher takes the letters of the word ΦΥΛΟ one by one to penetrate their symbolism, the middle two letters suggest two pyramids pointing in opposite directions. This recalls the symbol of intersecting pyramids that he probably owed to Robert Fludd[21] (see Ill. 15.1). Beside explaining the symbolism of the tablet, this suggests to him a reason why the Egyptians were so given to erecting pyramids and obelisks: it was to express the same symbolism as contained in the hieroglyph.

Kircher interprets the letter Φ as a symbol of the world, with its two poles. He then devises a composite 'hieroglyph' of his own, combining the four letters of the tablet with the winged sphere, the scarab and the cosmos (Ill. 4.4).[22] Its meaning, with obvious Christian undertones, is that the 'soul of the world' enters the world and stirs up its contents, filling them with love. Later, when he reprints this image at the beginning of *Œdipus Ægyptiacus*, he adds Virgil's phrase: 'Sic agitat molem, & magno se corpore miscet' – 'Thus it shakes the heap, and mingles itself with the great body'.[23] The readers of *Prodromus Coptus* may not all have understood that this image was his own invention, presented as it is alongside authentic hieroglyphs. To complete the circular argument, he then projects his invention backwards in time, suggesting that a diagram resembling his own was the original hieroglyph from which the Coptic letter Φ derived.

Kircher takes many more words to come to this point, but I have extracted the crucial steps of his argument. With a text of fearsome erudition, full of Coptic, Greek, Hebrew and Arabic quotations and lightened with anecdotes, he creates a smokescreen concealing a series of leaps in the dark and preconceived notions, passed off as logical deductions.

It is no wonder that Peiresc, Kircher's early patron, was troubled by his attitude. In 1633 he wrote to his friend Cassiano dal Pozzo about Kircher's first draft of a book purporting to explain the hieroglyphs. Beside his use of Herwart von Hohenburg's collection, Kircher had relied heavily on an Arabic manuscript by a Babylonian rabbi, Barachias Nephi or Abenephius, which he had probably acquired or copied before he left Germany.[24] Kircher was cagey about this manuscript, giving Peiresc only a glimpse of it, but its Neoplatonic interpretations became the foundation of his own. Here is shown his undated transcription of an obelisk with its hieroglyphs, Barachias's Arabic text and a Latin translation (Ill. 4.5),[25] which runs thus:

4.5 Barachias's obelisk, copied in Kircher's hand from an Arabic manuscript by a Babylonian rabbi. This started Kircher on his mistaken 'translation' of hieroglyphs.

Here the sun, the moderator of all things, the fertile divinity of the Nile, on account of the benefits conferred on mortals, is to be celebrated with divine service. Here the inventor of agriculture, planting, seeding, the preserver of Egypt, the Genius of the universe, the repeller of evils, the fertile divinity of the Nile, the vigilant guardian of things, on account of the benefits conferred on mortals, is to be celebrated with divine honours and service.

Peiresc was second to none in his enthusiasm for deciphering the long-lost script, but his experience with the ambitious young linguist was disillusioning (see box on p. 64).

'He had inserted the interpretation of an Egyptian obelisk which the said Barachias claims to have seen on the shore of the Red Sea, and which he attributes to Oziris. And he had also inserted an interpretation of his own of an obelisk, found in a copper engraving among those of Rome in the edition of Hervartius, as if it was that of St John Lateran; but I soon discovered that the figures were all made up after the artist's fancy, like grotesques, which had nothing of the ancient style of Egypt and could have no relation with the real hieroglyphic figures of the Lateran obelisk itself, which are repeated three times in Herwart's very work.

'I made [Kircher] see this and, in the end, admit it, though with difficulty, because he had found some fine interpretations, and, as it seemed to him, well authorized by all the figures contained in it, or by most of them. There was something admirable in this, since the human mind is easy to trick, and imposture is sometimes powerful, of which he was quite ashamed in the end.

'He was very regretful at being forced to confess the deceit by which he had been taken in, because he had abandoned the interpretation of the true obelisk of St John Lateran without daring to attempt it, to amuse himself with one which had nothing true but the dimensions and form of the stone and its ornaments, all the figures having been supplied at pleasure, like grotesques, by some artist who didn't have the patience to draw them, one by one, on the site, and who was content to record the shape of the stone and its enrichments, thinking it praiseworthy to put on it such figures and caprices as seemed good to him, since in any case they were unknown.

'I sent [Kircher] in Avignon the Ammianus Marcellinus, to let him see what was reported there on the interpretation of the obelisk transported by Constantius, and to show him that from that time onwards the most ancient Greek authors related the writing to particular actions and praises of a king: far removed from those first origins about which his Barachias amuses himself, and where he had got stuck in his *Prothéories*. But he gave no sign of having seen it, and when I spoke to him of it, he never gave in, to the point of showing surprise at the misunderstanding of the depictions, of which he had put aside the most legitimate and faithful one in order to follow one that was all made up, and incompatible with the manner and antiquity that this work should display, at a time when the rayed crowns hadn't yet been introduced, as well as an infinitude of other things of very recent origin, only seen in modern grotesques made for amusement in these last centuries.'[26]

The Obelisks of Rome

Herwart's *Thesaurus Hieroglyphicorum* was more to Kircher than just a stimulus for research. Once his principles were established, much of his hieroglyphic translation could have been done from that book alone, with no other resource than his own imagination. In his own works he reproduced (i.e. had re-engraved) several of Herwart's illustrations less impressive than the Bembine Table but no less packed with meaning: the dog-headed Mercury already mentioned, a truncated statue of Isis (**Ill. 5.9**), a statue of Harpocrates (**Ill. 14.6**), one of Mithras slaying the bull (**Ill. 14.14**) and two supposed images of Horus (**Ills. 15.20, 15.21**), as well as two lions with hieroglyphs on their bases.[27]

Herwart's *Thesaurus*, as Peiresc's letter indicates, also shows some of the Roman obelisks. Some are dated 1589 and signed by Nicolaus van Aelst.[28] Presumably Herwart took them from van Aelst's engravings in his own collection. Others, with all their four sides carefully reproduced, are dated 1607; I suppose that Herwart had them specially done for his book.

Apart from the Bembine Table, it was the obelisks that most excited Kircher's ambition to decipher the hieroglyphs, and were the very reason that he was summoned to Rome (see below). Once there, Kircher paid no attention to Peiresc's criticism and set out to translate every surviving specimen with utter self-confidence. He also took pains to have them all illustrated.[29]

In Kircher's historical scheme (as in actual fact) obelisks were a later development than the pyramids. According to his Arabic sources, the latter had existed even before Noah's Flood:

> Some of the Arabs cited above tell that after the Flood, Cham and his posterity rebuilt on their old foundations the pyramids that had been destroyed in the inundation, which he himself had known before the Flood, and others standing to this day in Egypt, that they might prolong the memory of his ancestors among his descendants. Then came the second Hermes, who is said to be the first to have changed pyramids to obelisks, thinking them more suitable for containing the monuments of his wisdom.[30]

Kircher's first published translation of an obelisk was in *Obeliscus Pamphilius* (1650), which treated the one that now stands in Piazza Navona (**Ill. 4.6**). It is in fact a Roman imitation of Egyptian models, possibly made for the Isis temple at Campo Marzio; its inscription includes the name of Emperor Domitian. In the fourth century AD it was moved to the Circus of Romulus, near the Appian Way, then fell and remained in pieces, where it was noticed by travellers but otherwise neglected. In 1651, Innocent X ordered it to be transported to Piazza Navona, originally the site of Domitian's Circus, and re-erected in front of the Palazzo Pamphili, his family's palace. He also commanded Kircher to translate its inscription, which gave Kircher the opportunity to reveal part of his long-prepared Egyptological theories; their full publication in *Œdipus Ægyptiacus* had to wait a few more years.

▲ 4.6 The Pamphilian, or Piazza Navona obelisk, found broken in pieces, was restored and re-erected in the Piazza Navona in Rome by Pope Innocent X and given the setting of the Four Rivers by Bernini. Thought by everyone, including Bernini, to be an ancient Egyptian obelisk, it is in fact a Roman imitation. (*Obeliscus Pamphilius*, opposite 2)

▶ 4.7 The Lateran obelisk, the oldest and largest of all Rome's Egyptian obelisks. (*Œdipus Ægyptiacus*, Volume III, fp. 160/161)

In this illustration, the putto flying above the obelisk displays the two sides of a commemorative medal, with the Pope's portrait on the obverse and a tiny scene of the Piazza Navona on the reverse. This is the only place in the book given to what later generations mainly admire: the Fountain of the Four Rivers, created by Gian Lorenzo Bernini as a pedestal for the obelisk. Bernini's design, moreover, is based on Kircherian geological theory, for it has the four rivers emerge from a cavern beneath a stylized mountain (see Chapter 7).

In Œdipus Ægyptiacus, thanks to the generous patronage of Emperor Ferdinand III, Kircher was able to show the major obelisks in six folding plates. The first is of the Lateran obelisk (Ill. 4.7), Rome's oldest, largest (106 feet or 32 metres high), and heaviest (455 tonnes). It bears the names of the XVIIIth dynasty pharaohs Thothmes III and IV, enabling it to be dated to the fifteenth century BC.[31] In the illustration, two putti carry the monument up to the Emperor's portrait, above the square in front of the Lateran Palace where the obelisk stands. The lower inscription tells its history, saying: 'This greatest of all the Egyptian obelisks was erected by Ramses, son of Sothis, in Thebes in 1297 BC. Constantine the Great destined it for his capital, Constantinople, but his death in AD 315 intervened and the obelisk was left in Alexandria. In AD 341, Constantius brought it to Rome and erected it in the Circus Maximus. Here it was buried, until Pope Sixtus V erected it in 1587. Silent from time immemorial, Ferdinand now restores its voice, with Kircher as interpreter.'

This is the obelisk to which Peiresc refers (see box, p. 64), and is the only one of which an ancient author provides a translation. The fourth-century chronicler Ammianus Marcellinus, in his Rerum Gestarum, Book xvi, quotes the Greek translation made by an Egyptian priest called Hermapion. One section of it runs thus:

> Dedicated to King Ramses, whom Sol and mighty Apollo, ruling the whole earthly globe, love; lover of truth, son of Heron born from God, ruler of the earthly globe, chosen by the Sun, King Ramses of strong Mars; to whom with fortitude and bravery the earthly globe is subject, King Ramses immortal son of the Sun.[32]

It is impossible to say which of the twelve columns of hieroglyphs (three per side) Hermapion's text is meant to correspond to; also this is, at best, a translation from Egyptian to Greek to Latin to English. But it is probably not a translation at all. The modern scholar Abdel-Kader Selim writes that 'here and there, a few phrases of the translation correspond to those appearing frequently on the Lateran and Flaminian obelisks, but there the resemblance ends; and one may conclude that the priest, eager to oblige his superiors, either faked a knowledge that he did not possess, or else ordered the phraseology of the text in a way that would fit their prejudices.'[33] Here is a sampling of Selim's translation (north face, left-hand column): 'Horus, mighty bull, son of Seth; Horus of gold, rich in years, great in victories; king of Upper and Lower

Egypt: son of Rê, who fills the castle of the ba with his splendid acts, lord of the two lands: the son of Rê, blessed in life, for ever!'

The second large folding plate in this section of Œdipus Ægyptiacus shows the Flaminian, or Piazza del Popolo obelisk (Ill. 4.8). It is Rome's second oldest, bearing the names of the XIXth dynasty pharaohs Seti I and Ramses II (thirteenth–twelfth centuries BC). According to the caption, Psammirtaeus, King of Egypt, erected it at Heliopolis in 807 BC. Caesar Augustus brought it to Rome and placed it in the Circus Maximus in 22 BC. Pope Sixtus V had it excavated and erected at the Porta Flaminia, consecrating it to the Holy Cross, in AD 1589. Finally, in 1652, Emperor Ferdinand III had its meaning brought to light by Athanasius Kircher. The plate is dedicated to the Emperor's ill-fated son Ferdinand IV, King of Rome, who was expected to succeed to the imperial throne but died before his father.[34] The obelisk, guarded by four Egyptian-style lions, now anchors that remarkable architectural and sculptural complex, the Piazza del Popolo.

Next comes the obelisk variously known as Sallustian, Ludovisi or Trinità dei Monti (Ill. 4.9). According to modern scholars, it may have come from Egypt, but its inscriptions were done in Rome, in servile and inaccurate imitation of those on the Flaminian obelisk. The third in Kircher's series of large folding plates shows it in its broken state in the Sallustian Gardens, and as it would hopefully be restored and erected. On its peak it bears the imperial double-headed eagle, and its dedication is to Leopold, Archduke of Austria, the younger son (and eventual heir) of Emperor Ferdinand III. It was not re-erected in Kircher's time. In 1789 it found its home at the top of the Spanish Steps before the church of Trinità dei Monti.

Most important to Kircher's career was the Pincian or Barberini obelisk (Ill. 4.10) found in 1633 in the vineyard property of one Curtius Saccoccia near the site of Emperor Aurelian's circus. Cardinal Francesco Barberini, nephew of Pope Urban VIII, persuaded the owner to sell it, and its three fragments were brought to the Barberini Palace. Kircher was at that time in the south of France, and it was then that Peiresc, knowing his facility in deciphering obscure languages and his possession of the Barachias manuscript, suggested to his Roman contacts that they summon him to interpret the hieroglyphics on the obelisk.

In this fourth great obelisk plate, the fragments are shown lying on the ground in front of the Palazzo Barberini, flanked by the two Egyptian telamones which are now in the Vatican Museum. Fame and her putti perform a triple homage: the infants raise the Barberini shield with its heraldic bees, while Fame sounds her trumpet to proclaim the honour of the Emperor Ferdinand, and also, implicitly, that of Kircher. This obelisk is in fact entirely Roman work of Hadrian's time, and may have served as part of an Egyptian-style funerary temple for the emperor's favourite, Antinous, who appears in the act of worship at the top of each side. It had to wait until 1822 before being erected in the Pincian Gardens, where it stands today among the busts of Italy's forgotten immortals.

4.9 The Sallustian obelisk, a Roman copy of the Flaminian obelisk, now at the top of the Spanish Steps. The background shows it in its broken state in the Sallustian Gardens. (*Œdipus Ægyptiacus*, Volume III, fp. 256/257)

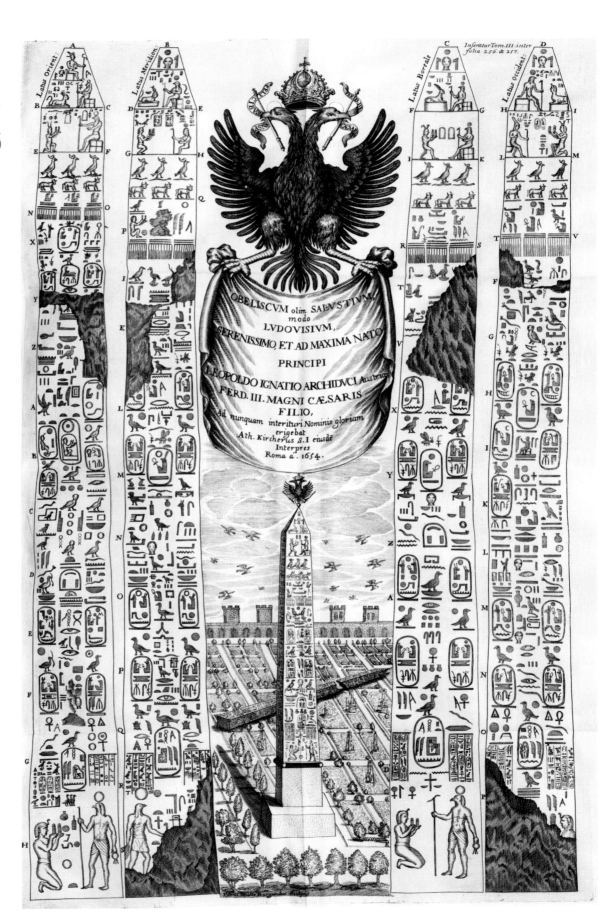

4.10 The Barberini obelisk, shown lying in fragments in front of the Palazzo Barberini. This, too, is a Roman imitation from Hadrian's time, whose lover Antinous is shown worshipping in the upper part of each side. (*Œdipus Ægyptiacus*, Volume III, fp. 270/271)

4.11 The Constantinople obelisk, which stood, and still stands, in the former Hippodrome. Kircher had to depend on helpers at the Ottoman court for a copy of the inscription. (*Œdipus Ægyptiacus*, Volume III, fp. 304/305)

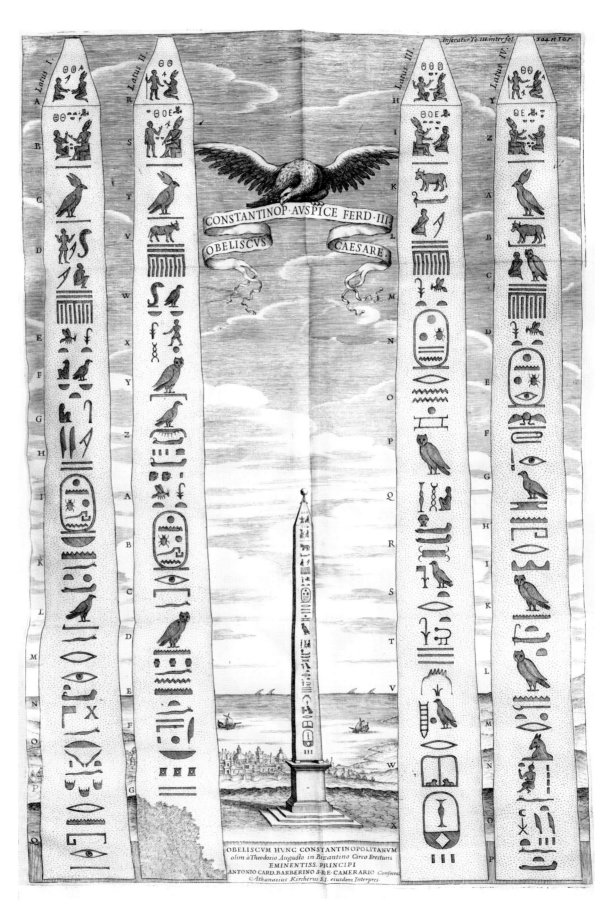

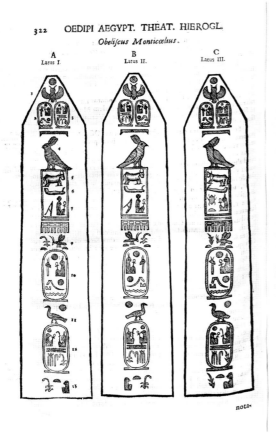

322 OEDIPI AEGYPT. THEAT. HIEROGL.

Obeliscus Monticœlius.

A
Latus I.

B
Latus II.

C
Latus III.

SYNT. VII. OBEL. MONT. MEDIC. MAHVT. 323   CAP. III.

4.12 The Celian obelisk, from Heliopolis, now on Monte Celio in Rome. Kircher gives it a fantastic Neoplatonic interpretation. (*Œdipus Ægyptiacus*, Volume III, 322, 323)

A fifth folding plate shows the obelisk that the Emperor Theodosius erected at the Hippodrome of Constantinople (**Ill. 4.11**). Beyond it are the domes of the Byzantine capital (now Istanbul) and the Sea of Marmara. As it was the only known obelisk outside Rome and Egypt, Kircher was eager to obtain drawings of the hieroglyphs on its faces. We can appreciate the difficulty of the task when he writes that he contacted a fellow Jesuit in Constantinople, Francisco Martino, who in turn applied to Simon Reiniger, a German employed as orator by the Ottoman Emperor. Reiniger passed on the commission to a Greek, Panaiotis Nicusio, who worked as interpreter for the imperial legate to the Ottoman court. As Kircher relates the story, all these people took the utmost trouble, out of kindness and 'zeal for the republic of letters', to supply him with an accurate drawing, sending it to him on 15 June 1654, just in time to be included in the last volume of *Œdipus Ægyptiacus*.

Before Kircher's time, the obelisk had frequently appeared in drawings and engravings of Constantinople. It has never left its site in the former Hippodrome, now At-meidan Square. Abdel-Kader Selim points out that its inscription is almost identical to that of the obelisk of Thutmosis III at Karnak, on the left-hand side of the entrance to the Temple of Amon, and concludes that it must have been the right-hand one of the pair.[35]

After treating the major obelisks of Rome and the one of Constantinople, Kircher goes on to what he calls the minor obelisks. The first of these has been known as the Celian, Capitoline, Villa Mattei or Villa Celimontana obelisk (**Ill. 4.12**). Like the Flaminian and Macutean obelisks, it comes from the Egyptian city of Heliopolis, where it was dedicated by Ramses II. The bottom part of it is lost, leaving only an inscribed section nine feet (three metres) high, mounted on a later plain extension. For a long time it was on the Campidoglio, until in 1582 the city authorities gave it to Duke Ciriaco Mattei, who erected it in front of his villa on Monte Celio, south of the Coliseum. It is now in the park there.

The Celian obelisk is small enough that we can use Kircher's translation of one side as a concise example of his method. He always reads an obelisk, as I have read his frontispieces, from the top down, beginning with the supreme deity, passing through the intermediate worlds and ending with earthly concerns.

Supramundane Osiris, concealed in the centre of eternity [1], flows down into the world of the genii that is most near, similar, and immediately subject to him [2]. This into the Osirian spirit of the sensible world, and its soul, which is the sun [3]. This [4] into Osiris Apis, the benefic

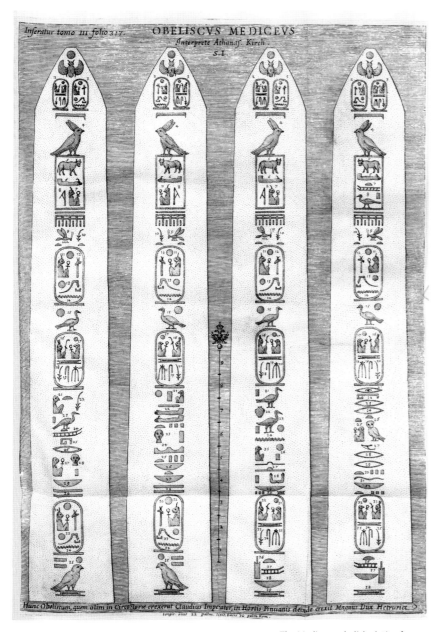

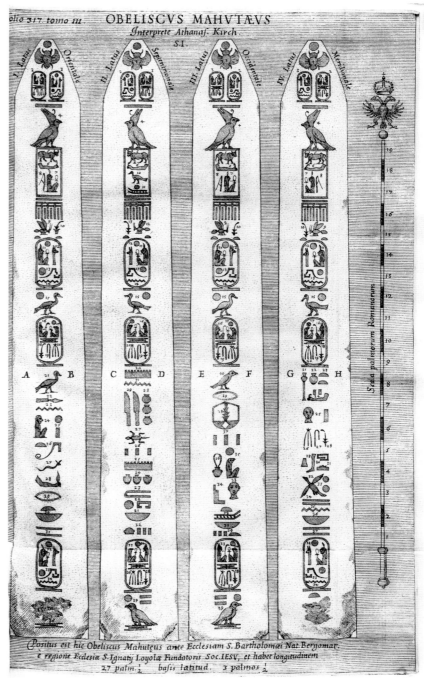

▲ **4.13** The Medicean obelisk, dating from the time of Ramses II, and now in the Boboli Gardens in Florence. (*Œdipus Ægyptiacus*, Volume III, fp. 316/317)

▶ **4.14** The Macutean obelisk. In Kircher's time it stood near the church of San Macuto, and now on a fountain in front of the Pantheon. (*Œdipus Ægyptiacus*, Volume III, fp. 316/317)

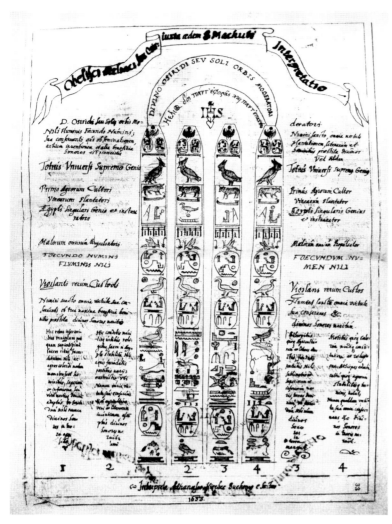

▲ 4.15 Kircher's transcription and interpretation of the previous obelisk, in his own hand.

▶ 4.16 The Vatican obelisk was in 1586 moved by Pope Sixtus V from its original position to the centre of Piazza San Pietro, where it remains. It has no inscription. (*Œdipus Ægyptiacus*, Volume III, 371)

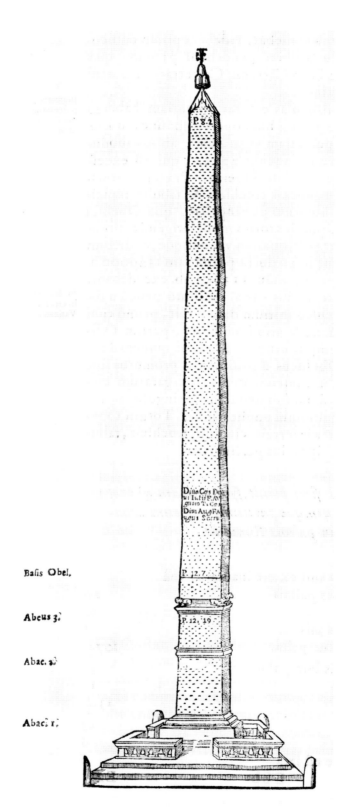

Agathodaemon of the elementary world [5–6], who distributes the participated virtue of Osiris into all the members of the lower world. His minister and faithful assistant, the polymorphous daemon [7], shows by the variety which he causes and controls an abundance and plenty of all necessary things [9]. But the benefic energy of the polymorphic daemon can be variously impeded by adverse virtues; hence the sacred tablet of Mophta and Mendes [10] must be employed, through whom it acquires the humid strength and fertility of the Nile, so that it can

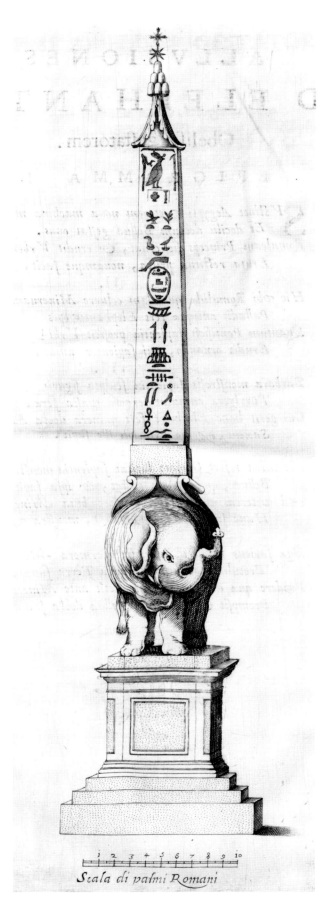

4.17 The Minervan obelisk, sixth century BC. This is the obelisk that Bernini placed on the back of an elephant, following a woodcut in the *Hypnerotomachia Poliphili*. (*Obeliscus Ægyptiacus*, 1)

Scala di palmi Romani

make the good influences flow unimpeded. Because the polymorphous daemon is unable to complete this unaided, the cooperation of Isis is needed [11], whose humidity tempers Mendes's dryness; for obtaining which the following sacred Osirian tablet is ordained, by which sacrifices may be conducted as prescribed in the Comasian rites. Through this tablet, then, and through the sight of it [12], supramundane Osiris shows the wished-for bounty of necessary things.[36]

After such eloquence, the readings of modern scholars such as Selim and Marucchi seem rather flat. They agree that it says something like this: 'Horus, powerful bull, beloved of Maat, king of Upper and Lower Egypt, son of the Sun, Ramses II.'[37]

Next among the minor examples in Kircher's collection is the Medicean obelisk (**Ill. 4.13**). The inscription at the bottom of the plate says 'This obelisk, which the Emperor Claudius once erected in the Circus of Flora, the Grand Duke of Tuscany has erected in the Pincian gardens.' This too dates from the time of Ramses II. It stood in the gardens of the Villa Medici until 1790, when it was moved to the Boboli Gardens in Florence and replaced by a copy.[38]

A third minor obelisk, now called Macutean, Pantheon, or della Rotonda (**Ill. 4.14**), was discovered in 1374 during the building of the church of Santa Maria sopra Minerva. It has been identified as a pair to the fragmentary Celian obelisk, likewise dedicated to Ramses II and originating from Heliopolis.[39] In Kircher's day it lay near the tiny church of San Macuto (or Machutus), a few steps away from his home in the Collegio Romano. He transcribed and translated it as early as 1633, shortly after his arrival in Rome, as can be seen from his elegant manuscript (**Ill. 4.15**).[40] To his disappointment, the obelisk was not erected in his lifetime. In 1711 it was placed on a fountain in front of the Pantheon.

The Vatican obelisk, at 82 feet (25 metres), is the second largest in Rome. (**Ill. 4.16**), and was the first to be moved in modern times. Alone among the Roman obelisks, it had remained standing where the Romans had placed it, marking the spina of the vanished Circus of Caligula and Nero. The building of St Peter's had shouldered it into an inconspicuous corner beside the sacristy, from which Sixtus V wanted it brought to form the focal point of the new piazza. Kircher gives statistics and details of how the obelisk was moved in 1586 under the direction of Domenico Fontana (see **Ill. 10.16**). The process was so successful that the same equipment was used to move three more obelisks: the Esquiline (1587), Lateran (1588) and Flaminian (1589). For Kircher, though, the Vatican obelisk was of little interest, for it bore no hieroglyphic inscriptions.

The Elephant obelisk, officially called Minervan, or Piazza della Minerva, (**Ill. 4.17**) was dedicated at Sais in the XXVIth dynasty (sixth century BC) by the pharaoh Uahabra or Apries, son of Psammeticus II. It is not known when it was brought to Rome, but it may have belonged to the Isis temple of Campo Marzio. It was discovered there in 1665 and submitted to Kircher

HIEROGLYPHS FOR THE EMPEROR

As a prelude to *Œedipus Ægyptiacus*, Kircher presents a 'polyglot triumph of Caesar': a collection of poetic and prose addresses to the Emperor Ferdinand III in forty-seven different languages, mostly written by Kircher himself and ending with this one (**Ill. 4.18**). Having misread the hieroglyphs, he drew on the vocabulary thus gained in order to miswrite them, but there is something noble in the attempt.

THE ANCIENT WISDOM OF EGYPT

EMPEROR FERDINAND III, the instrument of divine providence, the eye of the political Universe, the Austrian Osiris, his intellect penetrates all things with a royal eye, so as to establish them all with providence as guide; bountiful benefactor of all, conspicuous for wisdom in both heart and tongue, supporter of the Mercurial arts, author himself of various creations, HORUS, Imperial Legislator, especially concerned to take care of essential matters; the Austrian Momphta in fortitude and strength, furrowing all things, directing the operations of his mind in conformity with the intellectual Archetype; divine Legislator of the political World, earthly Osiris making the Imperial Vessel fruitful with a vital influx; tireless sentinel to the peoples of the Three Kingdoms, providing with careful vigilance for the peoples of the three Kingdoms and their needs; extremely zealous defender of Religion and the Ecclesiastical power; the Good Genius striving for the preservation of the twelve cities; extirpator, destroyer and expeller of all evils.

By erecting this obelisk, Athanasius Kircher, S.J. has dedicated an everlasting hieroglyphic inscription to the immortality of Emperor Ferdinand III.

4.18 Obelisk dedicated to Emperor Ferdinand III, invented by Kircher using his own fanciful version of hieroglyphics, here given in 'translation'. (*Œdipus Ægyptiacus*, Volume I, +++++++++ [3ʳ]⁴¹

for interpretation, which he provided in *Obeliscus Ægyptiacus* (1666). No doubt in collusion with Kircher, and to the delight of future tourists, Gian Lorenzo Bernini put it on top of an elephant. The notion came from an illustration in the *Hypnerotomachia Poliphili* (1499), an epic novel by Francesco Colonna; it may have been the Pope's own idea, since he owned and annotated a copy of the work.[42] Kircher justified it by the following inscription on the plinth: 'You who see here the figures of Egyptian wisdom carved on an obelisk, carried by an elephant, strongest of beasts, understand its message: you must be strong-minded in order to sustain solid wisdom.'[43]

Kircher paid no attention to the Esquiline obelisk (in Piazza del Esquilino behind Santa Maria Maggiore) or its pair, the Quirinal obelisk in front of the Quirinal Palace. Like the Vatican obelisk, they have no hieroglyphs. Nor did he treat the Montecitorio obelisk, formerly the gnomon of Augustus's giant sundial, erected in 1792 in front of the Parliament building. Kircher was aware of its discovery and recommended restoring it, but owing to its fragmented state the idea was not taken up, and it was reburied.[44] But his preoccupations helped to fortify the tradition, founded by Augustus and revived by Sixtus V, that has endowed Rome with the richest collection of obelisks in the world.

Notes

1   On the role of esotericism and Hermeticism in the European vision of Egypt, see Curl, 68–70; also ibid., 12–24, on the intriguingly parallel absorption of Egyptian religion in the Roman era.

2   'During this time the task was given me to locate a book – I forget the title – in the college library. Whilst examining the books one by one, I stumbled, be it by chance or through divine providence, upon a book which depicted, with illustrations, all the obelisks with hieroglyphic characters re-erected by Pope Sixtus V in Rome.' Kircher's Autobiography, in Fletcher 1966 [432]. No book perfectly fills the description, but since Kircher mined Herwart's work (see next note) for illustrations, it is the best candidate.

3   It appeared without place, publisher, or date, possibly in 1607, though some bibliographers date it 1610, and both Munich and Augsburg are given for its place of publication. Here is its complete title: *THESAVRVS HIEROGLYPHICORVM è museo Ioannis Georgij Hervvart ab Hohenburg, vtrivsque Iuris Doctoris, & ex Assesore summi Tribunalis Imperatorij, atq; ex Cancellario supremo Serenissimi vtriusq; Bauariae Principis, suae Seren.ᵐᵃᵉ Celsitudini à consiliis intimis, Praesidis Svvabiae, & inclytorum Statuum Bauaricorum Cancellarij*. I consulted the copy in the library of the Victoria and Albert Museum, London.

4   Janssen, 333–334.

5   Vehse, 156–157, who gives his titles as 'Geheimer Raths-Präsident, Landschaftskanzler, und Pfleger zu Schwaben'.

6   The definitive study of the Bembine Table is Leospo.

7   *Œdipus Ægyptiacus*, III, 80–81. Herwart's book shows the Bembine Table twice in its entirety: once as Plate 2, with the central figure of Isis facing left, and again as Plate 3 in reverse, with Isis facing right. I suspect that Herwart's engraver first copied Vico's version onto his copperplate, causing it to be printed in reverse, and that Herwart decided that it was important to have the Bembine Table reproduced the right way round, so had it done again. The next eleven plates are enlarged details of the second version.

8   Pignoria was the source for a remarkable use of 'hieroglyphs' in the frontispiece to Sir Walter Raleigh's *History of the World* (1617); see Corbett and Lightbown, 130–132.

9   Herwart copied several illustrations from Pignoria, including the broken statue of Isis with a harpy on her breast (see Ills. 5.9, 15.19), to which Kircher paid great attention.

10   The hieroglyph in question (in fact, all of the Bembine Table's 'hieroglyphs' are sheer invention) is in the lower frame or margin of the table. Pignoria's book of 1605 omitted the two plates in which Enea Vico had condensed this frame; Herwart's book included them. Posthumous editions of Pignoria, such as the 1669 Amsterdam edition entitled *Mensa Isiaca*, included the frame and also some of Kircher's interpretations, followed by Chiflet's refutations of them.

11   *Egyptian Civilization: Religious Beliefs*, 237. A remarkable modern facsimile of the Bembine Table, printed in silver on black to resemble the original, is in Manly Palmer Hall, *The Secret Teachings of All Ages*, Los Angeles: The Philosophical Research Society, 1928 and reissues, pp. LVI–LVII.

12   Kircher records and dismisses this idea in *Obeliscus Pamphilius*, 153. It derives not from Herwart's own book (which has no text), but from that of his son, Johann Friedrich Herwart von Hohenberg, based on his father's theories. I have not seen this book, which is referred to in Leospo, 3, and Baltrušaitis 1967, 255. The full title is: *Admiranda ethniae theologiae mysteria propalata, ubi lapidem magnetem antiquissimis passim nationibus pro Deo cultum et artem qua navigationes magneticae per universum orbem instituerentur, a veterum sacerdotibus, sub involucris deorum, dearumque et aliarum perinde fabularum cortice, summo studio occultam esse, noviter commonstratur* (Ingolstadt, 1623), which translates as 'The remarkable mystery of pagan theology revealed, wherein it is newly shown that in all the most ancient nations, the magnetic stone was worshipped as a god, and the art by which magnetic navigations were undertaken throughout the globe was carefully concealed by the priests of the ancients in the guise of gods and goddesses, and under the husk of other fables'.

13   *Œdipus Ægyptiacus*, III, 86.

14   *Obeliscus Pamphilius*, 337–339.

15   *Prodromus Coptus*, 225.

16   This is true, but Rachewiltz and Partini, 156, offer the more plausible suggestion that the tablet reads NVΛO, Nilo, and is simply the artist's signature.

17   What follows is paraphrased from *Prodromus Coptus*, 225–233.

18   Herwart copied this from Vincenzo Cartari's *Gli Immagini degli Dei degli Antichi* (1st ed. Venice, 1556).

19   *Prodromus Coptus*, 234.

20   *Prodromus Coptus*, 240–243.

21   Several of these are illustrated and explained in Godwin 1979a, 42–50.

22   For further explanation of this hieroglyph, see Ill. 15.2.

23   *Aeneid*, VI, 727.

24   On Peiresc, Kircher and the Barachias manuscript, see Miller, 134–140; for a detailed evaluation of the manuscript (which no one has seen), see Stolzenberg 2004, 23–69.

25   From the Archive of the Pontificia Università Gregoriana, Rome, published in facsimile on the University's 2006 Calendar.

26   Peiresc 1989, 133–134n; my translation. Despite this, Peiresc continued to give Kircher moral support and encouragement in his linguistic studies, as is evident from Peiresc's letters of 1633–1635 in *APUG* Ms. 568.

27   These are not illustrated here. The originals are in the Vatican Museum, and copies of them decorate the Fountain of Moses on the Quirinal Hill in Rome.

28   Nicolaus van Aelst (1526–1613) was a native of Brussels who worked in Rome. He received many privileges from the Pope for prints of Roman churches and architectural monuments.

29   See Rachewiltz and Partini, 102–124 and unnumbered plates, for histories and illustrations of all the Roman obelisks. For translations of the hieroglyphs on modern principles, see Selim and Marucchi.

30   *Obeliscus Pamphilius*, 45. *Œdipus Ægyptiacus*, I, 81 gives this 'Hermes,' or Tautis Mercurius, as the twelfth king of Egypt after the Flood, dated *anno mundi* 1810 or 180 *post diluvium*.

31   Selim, 200.

32   *Obeliscus Pamphilius*, 149–150.

33   Selim, 221; my translation.

34   The young Ferdinand's death was commemorated in a famous composition by Kircher's correspondent Johann Jakob Froberger: *Lamento sopra la Dolorosa Perdita della Real Maestà di Ferdinando IV Rè de Romani*, included in his *Libro Quarto*, 1656.

35   Selim, 118.

36   *Œdipus Ægyptiacus*, III, 325.

37   Selim, 247; Marucchi, 101.

38   Rachewiltz and Partini, 124, misprinting '1970' for 1790.

39   Selim, 245.

40   From the Archive of the Pontificia Università Gregoriana, Rome, published in facsimile on the University's 2006 Calendar.

41   The front matter of *Œdipus Ægyptiacus* is unpaginated. The signatures are not numbered, but marked with from one to nine crosses, to which I have added the foliation with *recto* and *verso* indications.

42   The suggestion is made in Rachewiltz and Partini, 115.

43   Sapientis Aegypti/inscvlptas obelisco figvras/ab elephanto/bellvarvm fortissima/gestari qvisqvis hic vides/docvmentvm intellige/robvstae mentis esse/solidam sapientiam svstinere.

44   See Rachewiltz and Partini, 119–120.

Chapter 5   **Antiquity Preserved**

Mummies

After the obelisks, which displayed Egyptian imagery in the most public places, it was the mummies that gave Kircher's generation its best impression of Egyptian style. Mummies were not imported to Europe out of pure archaeological curiosity, but because they were believed to have medicinal properties; ground-up *mumia* was a stock item in the early modern pharmacopoeia. Only antiquaries were sensitive to the painted sarcophagi with their peculiar proportions, enigmatic decorations, and haunting faces.

Kircher borrowed his first illustrations of mummies from a book by his main contact in Florence, Giovanni Nardi, court physician to the Grand Duke and the owner of a museum of antiquities in his own right. In 1647 Nardi published a commentary on Lucretius's *De Natura Rerum,* with an appendix of nine engraved plates depicting ancient objects from Florentine collections.[1] He probably lent his copper plates to Kircher for use in *Œdipus,* for the prints from them are quite worn in comparison to the engravings made specially for that book.

Nardi made an early attempt – perhaps the first ever – at a scientific unwrapping and recording of an Egyptian mummy, using a specimen in his patron's collection. The engravings show successively the outer case, the inner case with the mummy visible inside, the outer wrappings, and the inner wrappings of the body (**Ills. 5.1, 5.2**).

From the latter illustration (**Ill. 5.2**) one can appreciate the care with which Nardi copied the hieroglyphs on the various items that emerged when the mummy was unwrapped. Here, for once, Kircher's interpretation of the hieroglyphs was in principle correct, for he read them as prayers averting evil spirits from the soul of the deceased. **Ill. 5.3** shows some other small objects from Florentine collections: the pottery *ushabti* figures that Egypt has produced in countless numbers, and, more interestingly, a funerary collar depicting the process of mummification. At the end of this series of figures from Nardi, Kircher adds some woodcut illustrations (not reproduced here) that show the hieroglyphs written on the linen wrappings of the mummy. That seems to be as far as the investigation went. An eminent doctor like Nardi would not demean himself to perform surgery.

Nardi also had some mummies of his own. He sent drawings and descriptions to Kircher (**Ill. 5.6**), who interpreted them according to his own lights.

On the right-hand mummy case, anyone will recognize the hieroglyph on its shoulders as the stylized Egyptian eye, but Kircher, incredibly, thought it was a *phallus oculatus* (phallus with an eye).[2] Consequently he read it as a symbol of Osiris, the supreme deity:[3] first because he sees all things and provides for them; second because Osiris's own phallus, thrown into the Nile after his murder by Typhon, indicates 'the fecundating power of humidity'. The arms depending from these particular eyes denote Osiris's generosity. In the compartments beneath are symbols of various kinds of genii or spirits: lunar (the apes), mercurial (dogs), and winged Iynges (see below) representing the *spiritus mundi.* The purpose of picturing all these on the coffin was the protection of the soul of the deceased, as it passed through the spheres of the genii to its union with Osiris.[4]

Kircher scoured Europe for Egyptian relics. In 1652, when the first volume of *Œdipus Ægyptiacus* was already in print, his assistant Bartholdus Nihusius provided precise drawings of an Egyptian mummy in the private museum of an Amsterdam merchant, Hieronymus van Werle (**Ill. 5.5**). Figures G, H, I and K show the four sides of the case; Figure D shows the mummy inside it, with a detail of the pectoral ornament. Figures A, B, E and F show three further mummy cases in the collection of the Grand Duke of Tuscany, again thanks to Nardi.

While Kircher was still in southern France, in 1632, there came a report that a pair of giant 'effigies of tutelary spirits', seven feet tall and weighing 800 pounds each, had recently been imported by a merchant of Marseille (**Ill. 5.4**). He decided then and there that they must figure in his *Œdipus* and commissioned a fellow Jesuit, Ludovico Brusetto, to research their origin and obtain drawings of them. The merchant told Brusetto how the statues had been found inside a great pyramid in the province of Said, not far from the Red Sea. With great difficulty they had been brought to Cairo, 60 days' journey away, through deserted lands haunted by Turkish bandits. Prince Doria offered a huge sum of money for them, but the merchant declined to sell them, and shipped them to his native city.[5]

When, twenty years later, Kircher came to publish these drawings, he interpreted the eight winged figures on the left-hand statue as Iynges.[6] The Iynx, he explains, is the symbol of the primal mind, hidden in the uttermost recesses of the deity and comprehensible only to the intellect. The statue represents

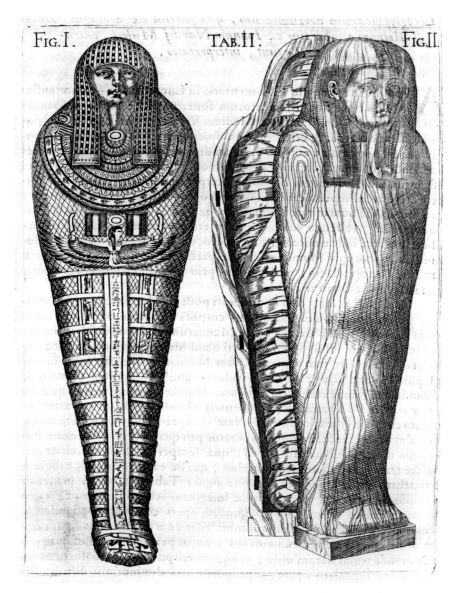

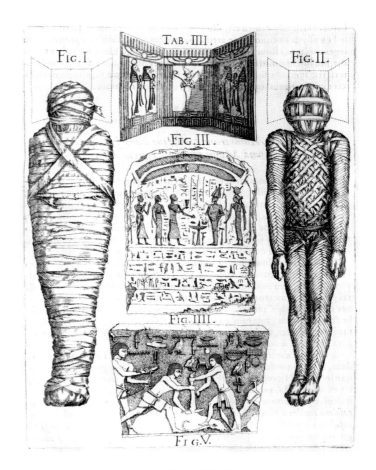

5.1, 5.2, 5.3 The opening of a mummy case, and apotropaic figures and amulets from the wrapping of a mummy. These engravings are borrowed by Kircher from an account recorded by Giovanni Nardi of Florence. (*Œdipus Ægyptiacus*, Volume III, 412, 413, 512)

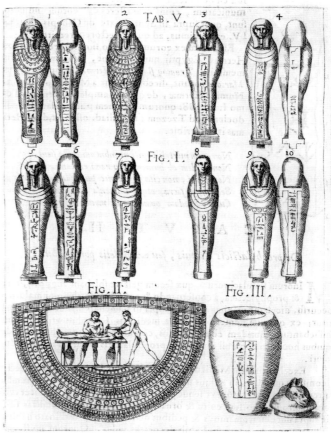

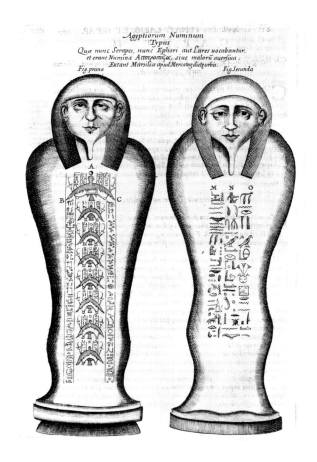

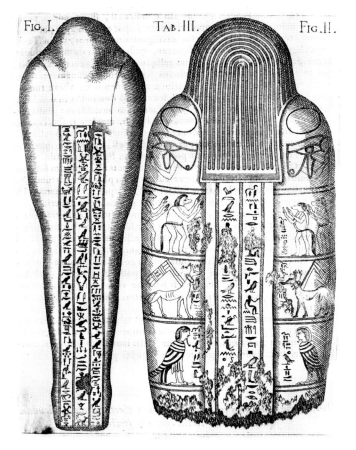

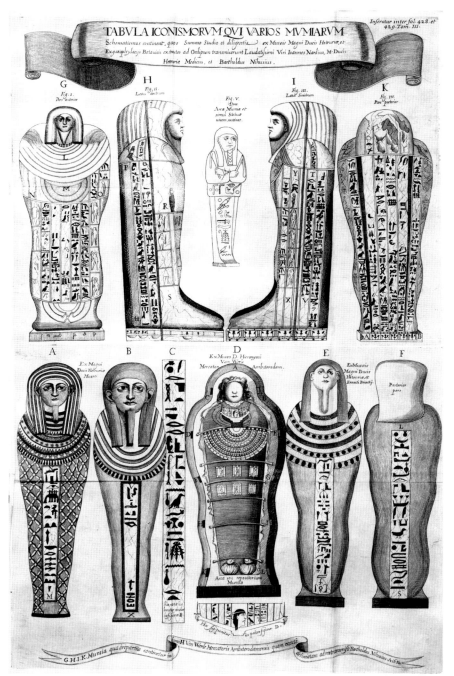

◄▲ 5.4 Two statues from a Marseille collection discovered during Kircher's lifetime near the Red Sea. Kircher produced a detailed Hermetic explanation of what they meant. (*Œdipus Ægyptiacus*, Volume III, 478)

◄ 5.6 Two mummy cases from Nardi's collection showing the symbol that Kircher read as an 'eyed phallus'. (*Œdipus Ægyptiacus*, Volume III, 414)

▲ 5.5 Drawing of mummies from Florence and Amsterdam collections, provided for Kircher by his assistant Bartholdus Nihusius and Giovanni Nardi. (*Œdipus Ægyptiacus*, Volume III, fp. 428/429)

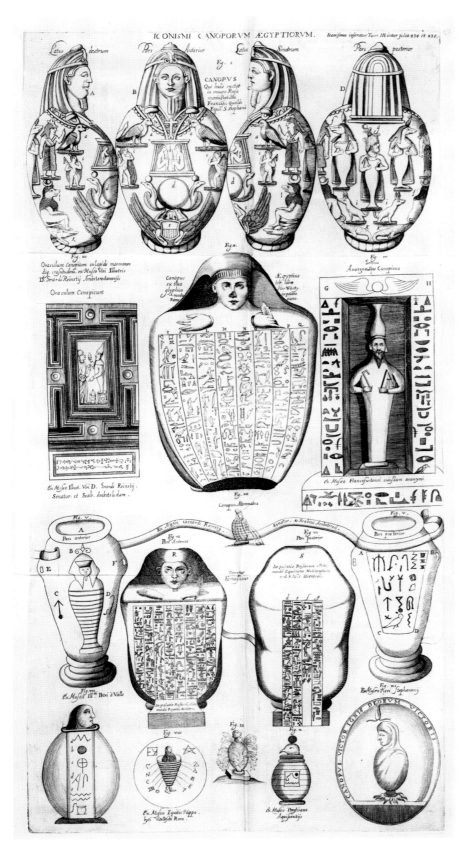

◄ 5.7 Canopic jars from various collections. Kircher was fascinated by these jars, and read their hieroglyphs as cosmographical statements. The shrine, two serpents and frog are on the jar in the top row, second from the left. The god Canopus is left and right in the line below, and bottom row, second from left, surrounded by Coptic letters. (*Œdipus Ægyptiacus*, fp. 434/435)

▲▲ 5.8 A gem from a Roman collection. Kircher interpreted the symbolism as an allegory of the annual Nile flood. (*Œdipus Ægyptiacus*, Volume III, 461)

▲ 5.9 Statue of Isis with a harpy, surrounded by a collection of late Egyptian gems. (*Œdipus Ægyptiacus*, Volume II, 467)

it by its veiled head, its black marble, and its cone-shaped body, which refers to its remoteness from 'any corporeal or material contagion'. The bird-like symbols engraved on the front represent the energy of the intellect, rising to knowledge of this first mind. The eight birds form a 'chain' corresponding to the starry sphere and the seven planetary spheres, meaning that the influence of the Iynx propagates in each of the worlds. And why, Kircher asks, should a statue of such profound significance be placed in a tomb? His reply is pure Hermetism: it was to protect the soul from evil, and to express the belief that the soul, after many transmigrations, finally returns to the sphere from whence it came.

As for the second statue, it is of white stone, and represents the tutelary deity in charge of the sensible world. According to Egyptian theology, this world, too, is ordered according to the Ideas of the Iynx. Kircher reads the column marked 'O' as a concise statement of this philosophy: 'The provider of the vital humid intelligence tempers all things by a marvellous reason, through the symmetry and love that it infuses into the various things in this world.'

The more one reads Kircher's hieroglyphic translations, the more they take on a certain sameness. He was, in truth, not very imaginative in his interpretations. Always expecting to find a portentous statement in the style of the Hermetica, the Chaldaean Oracles, or the Neoplatonists, that is what he found.

Moving to smaller items, it was the canopic jars that most fascinated and challenged Kircher's powers of interpretation. A large folding plate (**Ill. 5.7**) shows some of these, with small Egyptian artefacts from various collections in Rome (those of Francesco Qualdi, Pietro Stephanoni, Palazzo Farnese, Ippolito Vitelleschi, and the Order of St John of Jerusalem), Amsterdam (Gerard Reinstius), Frankfurt (collection unknown), and Aix-en-Provence (Nicolas Peiresc). Kircher did not know that canopic jars were used to preserve the extracted viscera of mummified bodies. As in the case of Barachias, his command of rare Arabic sources misled him. When he read in one of these[7] about such jars being equipped with many breasts, like Diana of Ephesus, he leapt to the conclusion that they were for offering Nile water to the divinities. Thus armed, he was able to connect them to other symbols of nurturing, vivification, and the effects of the higher powers on the lower worlds, and to interpret the hieroglyphs on the jars in the same spirit. In Figure I, side B, he discovers symbols of the many-world system that frames all of his interpretations. The frog at the bottom symbolizes matter (the Elementary world), which receives the divine influx from the globe with two serpents that represents the starry spheres (the Sidereal world). Higher up is a shrine with two Horuses, between two figures of Harpocrates: these are the world of the genii. Finally the veiled head represents the Archetypal world.

Kircher saw all the objects in this plate in the light of a half-Hermetic, half-Chaldaean theosophy. Moreover, in Graeco-Roman mythology Canopus was a personified divinity after whom a star was named, and Kircher's further interpretations took this as their starting-point. The objects then illustrated

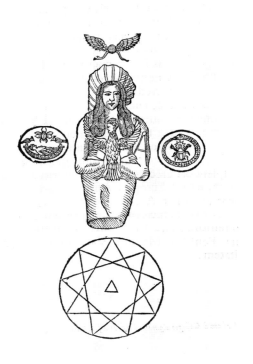

Schema hieroglyphicum Libri ideam exhibens .

5.10 Hieroglyphic scheme of a book. Kircher reuses the Isis statue as the central symbol of his work of decipherment. (*Obeliscus Ægyptiacus*, +4ᵛ)

the ancient belief that the god Canopus gives oracles (as he is shown doing in Figure III), repels evil influences (in the form he takes in Figure IV), and spreads his influence among the ten kingdoms of nature (represented by ten Coptic letters surrounding Canopus in Figure VIII).

Magical and Enigmatic Objects

When he interpreted symbols, rather than trying to translate hieroglyphs, Kircher's range was much greater, for he could call on his wide knowledge of the ancient world. For instance, the gem from the Roman collector Petrus Stephanonus (**Ill. 5.8**), which Kircher admits is more of Greek than Egyptian workmanship, becomes a statement about agriculture. The sphinx is the genius of the Nile flood; the lions stand for the sign of Leo, the house of the sun when the flood starts; and the bull represents the earth, or the work of agriculture, which is 'devoured' by the rising of the waters.

In the illustration of a group of gems or seals (**Ill. 5.9**), Kircher identifies the subjects as follows: 23, Isis with the asp, lituus and staff; 24, Typhon, with a fish on his head, standing on a crocodile; 25, Isis with mural crown, the Egyptian Cybele, with two hawks (solar symbols) and the 'marine absinthe' plant sacred to her; 26, Isis, Serapis, and the Genius of the Nile; 27, Anubis, with astrological motifs; 28, Anubis or Mercury; 29, Canopus; 30, Memphitic Isis; 31, Ibis amulet against diseases of the head.

The central figure is far more important. Kircher had it copied, either from Pignoria or Herwart von Hohenburg,[8] and reused it in a significant position in his later work, *Obeliscus Ægyptiacus*, as the centre of a 'hieroglyphic scheme, exhibiting the idea of the book' (**Ill. 5.10**; see **Ill. 15.19** for the other symbols). His interpretation, while lacking any archaeological validity, once again blends the Hermetic teachings with those of the Chaldaean Oracles:

> A nude figure, the lower part truncated and the arms crossed, with a beautiful veil, in whose breast is a bird with a virgin's face, and, in place of wings, branches spreading on both sides, holding an A in her right hand. This refers directly to what the Zoroastrians call Iynges: Agathodaemons of the superior order. She is nude because she is only comprehensible with the mind, as Zoroaster teaches; she is truncated below for the same reason, because there are no vestiges of her in the lower world. She wears a variegated veil because her variety manifests only in the higher world; her crossed arms designate the intricacy of all nature, over which she rules. She holds in one hand what was shown to be the Agathodaemon: it is pressed to her breast, with a human face and branched wings extending from it, indicating the supreme Intelligence, fertile with ideas which it communicates to the lower worlds.[9]

While Kircher liked to sanctify with a philosophical interpretation the ancient objects that were brought to him, or which he sought out, he was often uneasy about them. Gems and intaglios, in particular, were suspicious things: they reeked of the superstitious practices of the later Egyptians, Gnostics and Ephesians, among whom hieroglyphs became a support for planetary and angelic (or, in his opinion, demonic) magic. The section of *Œdipus Ægyptiacus* that treats 'Hieroglyphic Magic' illustrates many such gems, of which **Ill. 5.11** is a sample. In his commentary, Kircher associates the ones numbered 17 and 19 with a 'horned serpent' that appears frequently in the Bembine Table. The letters LIS stand for *Libertatem saluam* or *Liberorum salutem*. No. 18 is the figure of Osiris with the hoopoe-headed staff, familiar to Kircher's readers, and Nos 20 and 5 represent the same deity. Nos 21 and 22 are Egyptian amulets of Harpocrates and Arueris, and No. 7 is the Three Graces, as they were placed before the portal of the Temple of Ephesus.

Kircher's approach to hieroglyphs was not exclusively Egyptian. On the contrary, he justified his symbolic interpretation of them by showing that other peoples and eras had used comparable images. Therefore he mixed in with the ancient magical gems some examples of later 'hieroglyphs' from the common fund of Renaissance magic. These sigils, associated with Cornelius Agrippa, John Dee, and others, combined astrology, arithmology and Kabbalah, with the intention of attracting the good influences of the planetary angels. In this same plate is a medal consecrated to the sun (in Greek *helios*), bearing the zodiac sign ruled by the sun, Leo; the sun's archangel, Raphael; the igneous trigon (i.e. the three fiery signs of the zodiac) of Leo, Aries and Sagittarius; and the sixfold magic square of the sun. The medal beneath it is another modern concoction which shows Jupiter; the Kabbalistic angel of

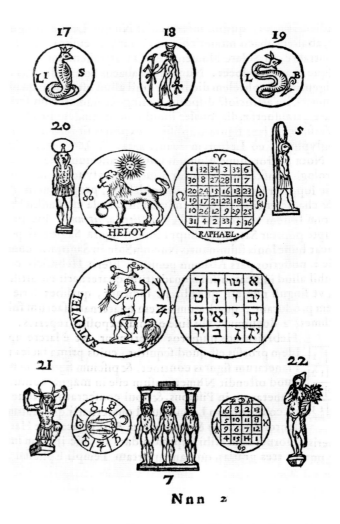

▲ **5.11** Magical gems, which to Kircher seemed dangerously suggestive of demonic influences. (*Œdipus Ægyptiacus*, Volume II, 465)

▶ **5.12** Amulet of Venus and Mars. A well-known sigil from Christian Kabbalist circles. (*Œdipus Ægyptiacus*, Volume II, 480)

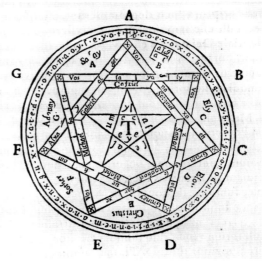

CENSORING DANGEROUS IDEAS

The illustrations shown here demonstrate that Kircher's enthusiasm could sometimes carry him too far – either for his own better judgment or for the censors of his books. For instance, in the manuscript of *Œdipus Ægyptiacus*, he transcribes forty of Psellus's commentaries on the *Chaldaean Oracles of Zoroaster*, but only thirty-five of them made it into the printed version, and many of these were doctored.

In the upper pair of pages (**Ills 5.13a, b**) one can see that a passage has been crossed out. Below (**5.13c**) is the corresponding page of the book as published, with the passage omitted and the numbering adjusted. The censored commentary reads:

'The Furies are the constrainers of mankind. For the conveying Angels draw souls to themselves from their first origin, whereas the avenging furies and tormentors of human souls, surely [envious] of the nature granted to us, entangle them in material passions and as it were strangle them. Nor do they harm only those possessed by the host of passions, but also those who turn to the immaterial essence. For even these need purification, since they are also begotten and joined to matter. Thus one sees many who live a holy and blameless life afflicted by unforeseen calamities.'[10]

More obviously dangerous was a magical spell addressed to the angels, included in the same manuscript and then crossed out (**Ill. 5.13d**). It reads:

'I adjure you, holy, blissful and blessed Angels, both fiery, airy, watery, earthy, higher, and lower, that what this telesma requests should come to pass; and this through the concurrence of the stars and the spheres, and by command of created things; that they may be enriched in the light of the Sun and the Moon, and that whatsoever is created, both animals beneath the earth, and birds in the sky, even reptiles and unclean creatures, should serve you for the purposes invoked.'[11]

While Kircher could safely expose himself to such things, protected by the certainty that to practise such magic would only attract demons, his more naïve readers might be tempted to try it. Consequently none of this appears in *Œdipus Ægyptiacus*. In its place there is the succinct remark *adiurationem consultò omitto*: 'I deliberately omit the conjuration.'[12]

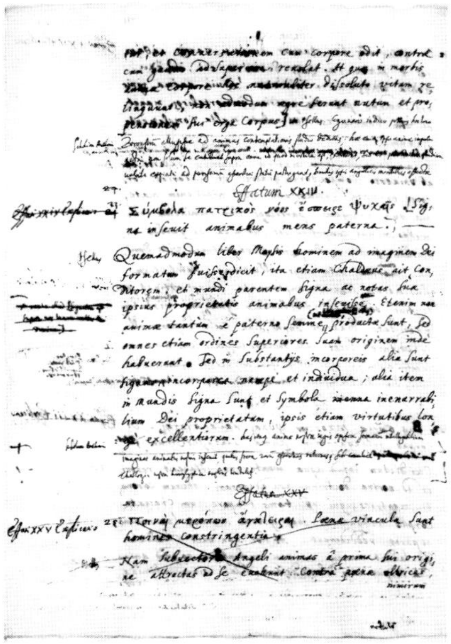

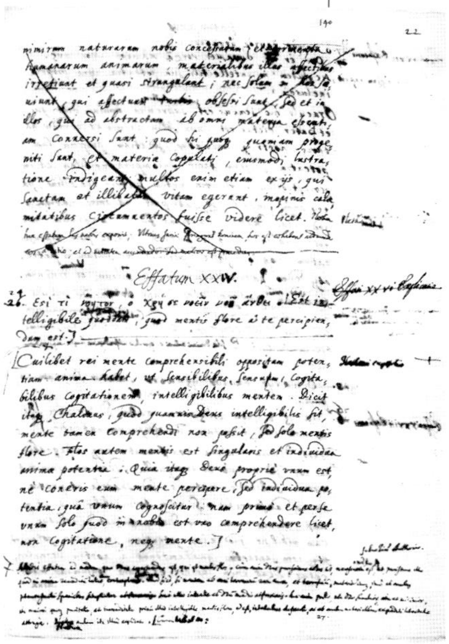

▲▲ **5.13 a, b** Manuscript of *Œdipus Ægyptiacus*, with censored passage.

CAP.III. 146 OEDIPI ÆGYPTIACI GYMNAS. HIEROGL.

Effatum XXII. [illegible]

Psellus. *Vi corpus relinquentium animæ sunt purißimæ.* Psellus ita explicat. *Qui dictum istud æquâ mente auscultauerit, reperiet id nostræ doctrinæ non aduersari. etenim coronati martyres, qui afflictionis tempore cum cruciatu corpus reliquerunt, suas ipsorum animas lustrarunt & puras reddiderunt. At hoc non vult Chaldæus, sed laudat omnem mortem violentam, eò quòd anima, quæ corpus cum dolore deserit, hanc vitam abominatur, & conuersationem cum corpore odit, contrà cum gaudio ad superiora reuolat. At quæ in morbis animæ corpore hoc naturaliter dissoluto vitam relinquunt, non admodum ægrè ferunt nutum & propensionem sui erga corpus.* Ita Psellus. Ego verò iudico potiùs hoc loco Zoroa-

Scholion Authoris. strum allusisse ad animas contemplationis studio deditas; hæ enim ipso animæ impetu actæ non solùm se supra omne id quod mortale est, extollunt, sed & per dictum studium veluti expiatæ ad purissimum essentiæ statum pertingunt, similes ipsis Angelicis mentibus effectæ.

Effatum XXIII. [illegible]

Psellus. *Signa inseuit animabus mens paterna.* Quemadmodum liber Moysis hominem ad imaginem Dei formatum fuisse dicit, ita etiam Chaldæus ait, conditorem & mundi parentem signa ac notas suæ ipsius proprietatis animabus inseuisse. Etenim non animæ tantùm è paterno semine (vt loquitur Psellus) productæ sunt, sed omnes etiam ordines superiores suam originem inde habuerunt. Sed in substantijs incorporeis alia sunt signa, incorporea nempe & indiuidua; alia item in mundis signa sunt & symbola inenarrabilium Dei proprietatum, ipsis etiam virtutibus longè

Scholion Authoris. excellentiorum. Has itaque animæ nostræ iugis opifex formarum intelligibilium imagines animabus nostris inseuit, quibus freta rerum essentias rationesque sibi conciliet, de quibus in Theologia nostra hieroglyphica ampliùs tractabitur.

Effatum XXIV. [illegible]

Est intelligibile quoddam, quod mentis flore à te percipiendum est. Alludit

Scholion Authoris. effatum ad modum quo Deus cognoscendus est, qui est mentis flos; cùm enim Deus purissimus actus sit, necessarium est, vt purissimo illo quod in anima reconditum latet, eum contemplando attingas. Quod fiet, si mentem ab omni terrenarum rerum cura, & terrestrium, materialiumq; imò ab omnibus phantasmatum speciebus simpliciter sine vllo inter te & Deum medio abstraxeris: hoc enim pacto, vti Deo similior, & vicinior, ita maiori quoq; puritate, & iucunditate primum illud intelligibile mentis flore, id est, intellectus defæcati, & ab omnibus materialibus expe-

Plethonis expositio. diti libertate attinges. Plethon autem ita illud explicat. *Cuilibet rei mente comprehensibili oppositam potentiam anima habet, vt sensibilibus sensum, cogitabilibus, cogitationem, intelligibilibus mentem. Dicit itaq; Chaldæus, quòd quamuis Deus intelligibilis sit, mente tamen comprehendi non possit, sed solo mentis flore. Flos autem mentis est singularis & indiuidua animæ potentia. Quia itaque Deus propriè vnum est, ne coneris eum mente percipere, sed indiuidua potentia, qua vnum cognoscitur. nam primò & per se vnum solo quod in nobis est vno comprehendere licet, non cogitatione, neque mente.*

Effa-

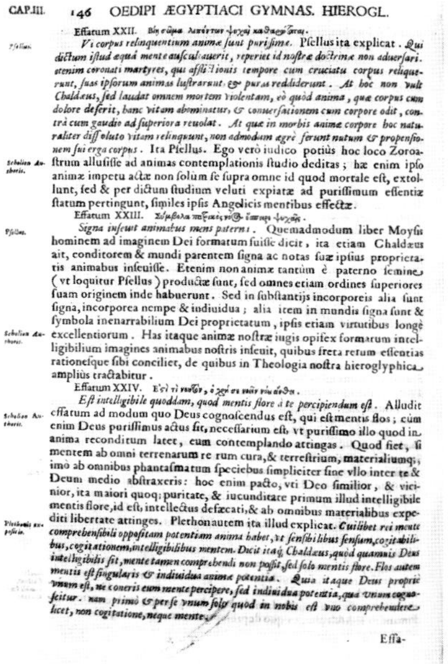

◄▲ **5.13c** The corresponding page in the printed version.

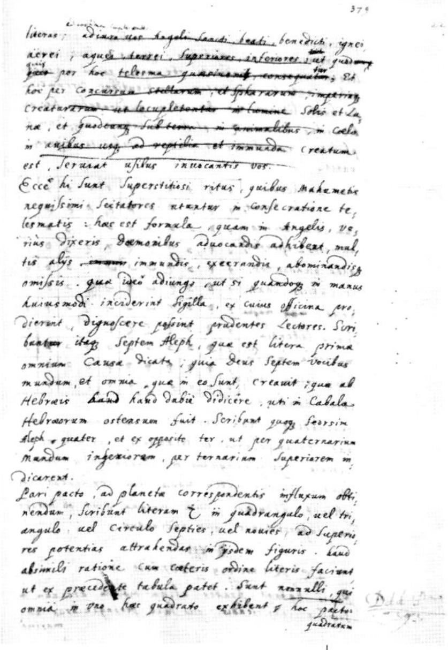

▲ **5.13d** A magical spell, cut out of the same manuscript.

Jupiter, Zadkiel; and the fourfold magic square of the planet, in which the numbers corresponding to the Hebrew letters add up to the same total in each direction. The third medal of this set, Kircher says, was consecrated in the sign of Pisces during a great conjunction of the planets, whose seven signs are shown on the obverse. On the reverse is another magic square of four.

Kircher was leading his readers to the brink of the abyss by including another modern (or rather, mediaeval) amulet (**Ill. 5.12**). He says that it contains the 72 letters of Kabbalah, 'very badly translated into Latin letters', seven names of God, attributes of Christ, and Kabbalistic words that, in general, show 'angels of darkness appearing in the form of light'.[13] Its object, like its dedication, is twofold: 'to obtain full fruition of carnal desires, and victory against all one's adversaries'. Kircher declines to print the words that have to be spoken when using it, 'lest they wound Christian ears'.[14]

Was this decision always his own, or was it the censor's? One Kircher scholar, Daniel Stolzenberg, writes: 'Indeed, Kircher enjoyed demonic magic in much the same way that he enjoyed its licit variety. Both were fascinating intellectual diversions and opportunities to display his learning and ingenuity...'[15] The partial manuscript of *Œdipus Ægyptiacus*, Book II, in the National Library of Italy suggests that it was the censors who thought otherwise (see box on p. 83).

When he comes to comment on Nardi's plate (**Ill. 5.14**) showing small statuettes of animal, semi-animal, and grotesque creatures, Kircher cannot conceal his disgust. He explains that they were phylacteries, carried to repel the influences of evil demons. No. 13 is what he calls the *phallus oculatus* (see above). Nos 11, 19 and 23 show demons pressed under large stones, 'for according to Psellus's *Book of Demons*, no verbal threats affect demons as much as those of imprisonment and destruction; not that they can be destroyed or imprisoned, but a perpetual condemnation to one place is contrary to the order prescribed for them by the Author of Nature. They are so terrified by threats of this kind, as they think, that they cannot bear them, nor stand any such images.'[16]

As *Œdipus Ægyptiacus* nears its close, Kircher seems anxious to leave nothing unsaid or unexplained, and none of his contributors uncredited. It is as though having completed a tour of a museum with its grand exhibits, he takes his readers down to the storeroom. The remnant in **Ill. 5.15** required some archaeological detective-work, but when Kircher the geometer calculated that there must originally have been 365 stars around its band, the meaning leaped out: the stars, corresponding to the days of the year, must refer to the ruling genii which the ancients believed to influence earthly events, and to whom their rites were consecrated. He reads the hieroglyphic text of column I–K as follows: 'Agathodaemon, the ruler of universal life, pours the liquid of the great crater from the higher crater, enriched with the immense variety of things, into the lower craters, for the fertile propagation of the living.'[17]

In speaking of the gods of Egypt, Kircher was hampered by a fundamental misunderstanding: he thought that the hawk-headed god Horus was Osiris. This is how he interpreted a fairly common representation of Horus (**Ill. 5.16**).

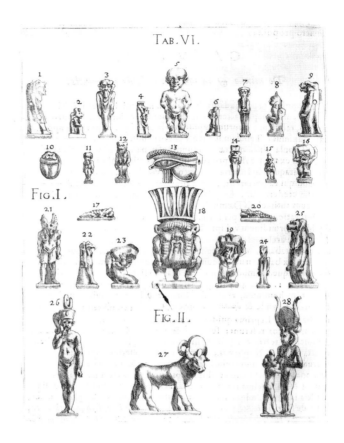

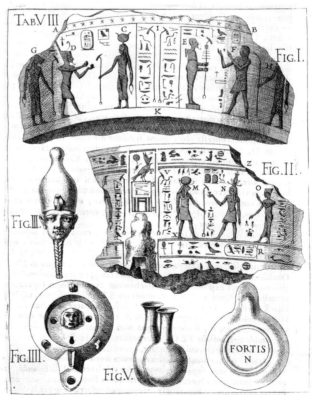

◄ **5.14** Grotesque statuettes, reproduced from Nardi but condemned by Kircher as diabolical. (*Œdipus Ægyptiacus*, Volume III, 522)

◄▼ **5.15** Fragments from the Museo Gaddiano, Florence, parts (according to Kircher) of a diagram showing the ruling demons for each day of the year. (*Œdipus Ægyptiacus*, Volume III, 385)

► **5.16** Statue of Horus, found on the site of the former Isis temple in Rome, believed by Kircher to be a 'polymorphic' image of Osiris. (*Œdipus Ægyptiacus*, Volume III, 501)

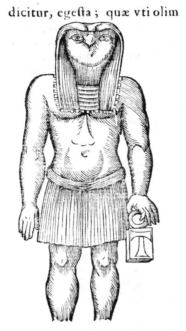

dicitur, egesta ; quæ vti olim

De Polymorphi

◄ **5.17** 'Polymorphic daemon, or the mind of the supreme Numen, executor of everything'. (*Œdipus Ægyptiacus*, Volume III, 502)

▼ **5.18** The Cult of Isis, explained by Kircher by reference to Apuleius's account of her rites in *The Golden Ass*. (*Œdipus Ægyptiacus*, Volume III, 426)

Kircher writes that it was excavated from the paving of Santa Maria sopra Minerva, a church built on the site of the former temple of Isis, and that no other site in the city has furnished so many Egyptian remains. He calls it a 'polymorphic statue', in which a human form is transformed by various animal heads. As for its meaning, he explains it on the next page when he treats a stele in the collection of the Grand Duke of Tuscany (**Ill. 5.17**). He writes that he has seen the same type in several Roman collections. In his interpretation, it is an amulet that features the 'polymorphic daemon, or the mind of the supreme Numen, executor of everything as it descends into the breadth of nature'. The androgynous figure is crowned with symbols of the sun (lion head) and moon (horns); energy and fecundity are shown by the plait twisted into the shape of a horn; the benefits of the daemon's reign by the full breasts; the snakes and scorpions in its grasp show its domination of life and death, good and evil, generation and corruption; the lion and dog held in the hands are the energies of Momphta and Anubis, which must only be applied in conformity with divine law; the male genitals beneath, with the female breasts above, indicate that the daemon is active with regard to inferior things, but passive in its reception of higher influences. The two crocodiles are the Typhonian energy, which it totally dominates and exterminates.[18]

No such arcane interpretations arise with the figures on a column discovered among the ancient sculptures of the Villa Medici in Rome (**Ill. 5.18**). An explanation was readily at hand in Apuleius's description of the rites of the goddess Isis in his *Metamorphoses, or, The Golden Ass*. Three of the figures play

Pompa Isiaca iuxta Apuleij descriptionem, ex hortis Mediceis.
Pars Prior.

Pars Posterior.

Odo-

◀ **5.19** Lamp fragment in the form of a sphinx: on one level a symbol of the Nile, on another the light of the divine mind. (*Œdipus Ægyptiacus*, Volume III, 541)

▶ **5.20** Typhonian lamp, a dwarf perched on an ass's head – that is, according to Kircher. Silenus (the dwarf) masters the evils that beset Egypt (Typhon). (*Œdipus Ægyptiacus*, Volume III, 343)

musical instruments (tambourine, sistrum and triangular harp), while the other three carry images of the gods and of Isis's sacred cow.

Lastly, there are some illustrations of ancient lamps in the Grand Duke of Tuscany's collection. Terracotta lamps have survived from antiquity in vast numbers, and their variety of decoration has always been a source of fascination to antiquarians. One is in the form of a sphinx (**Ill. 5.19**), which Kircher interpreted earlier on as a divinized form of the Nile. His reasoning was that the Nile flood occurs each year when the sun is in the signs of Leo and Virgo, hence the double form of the sphinx as woman and lion; and because of the river's hidden source and its life-giving power, the Egyptians gave it divine attributes.[19] But that is only a lowly interpretation. Now, at the end of the book, he reveals the mystical meaning: that the sphinx signifies the hidden wisdom that prepares the soul for the company of God. When she is pictured on lamps, she represents the light of the divine mind that illuminates everything in the world.[20] This shows how closely his idea of the ancient theology approximated to Christian mysticism.

One wonders whether Dr Nardi smiled when he sent the illustration of a lamp showing a dwarf perched on an ass's head (**Ill. 5.20**). Kircher, anyway, had no trouble explaining it. He writes that the Egyptians did not make lamps with figures of benevolent gods alone, but also with those of malefic ones. The ass is a symbol of Typhon, who stands for every evil that besets Egypt: sterility, contagious disease, drought, corruption and destruction. These qualities are mollified by the flowing Nile water, and so the dwarf is a

Silenus (one of the followers of Dionysus), who also stands for the fertility of the Nile: he masters the contrary tendencies symbolized by the ass-headed Typhon. The eagle or hawk claw beneath does not rightly belong to the same object, but it is appropriate since its meaning is similar: the bird of prey represents the harmful influence latent in the sun.[21]

After the publication of *Œdipus Ægyptiacus*, Kircher continued to receive news and pictures of antiquities and requests for explanations of them, and occasionally included them in his later books. One such was a splendid sculptured relief (**Ill. 5.21**) discovered by peasants working the soil near Marino, on the Alban Lake. It was brought to Rome and an engraving made, of which Abbot Marcello Severolo gave Kircher a copy. He immediately recognized it as an apotheosis of Homer.[22] The upper part shows Mount Parnassus, where Zeus is being petitioned by the Muses for Homer's elevation to divinity. Here too appears the sculptor's signature: Archelaus Apollonii of Priene. In the middle part, 'Poetry holds the lyre in her left hand, the plectrum in her right, as though in the act of playing. On the table there is a globe, to which the second figure points, signifying nothing other than the merit of Homer, who in his poetry describes the making of the world and all that is in it through a certain divine afflatus.'

This seems to echo the cosmogonic interpretations of *Œdipus Ægyptiacus*. Moreover, behind the right-hand figure Kircher discerned the Egyptian *ankh* or *crux ansata*, and refers the reader to four of his own works in which its symbolism is explained.

The lower part is backed by the curtain of a temple, because only Homer could see beyond it and discern the nature of the gods. On the left, Homer enthroned holds his *Iliad* and a sceptre with a lotus finial, and receives the laurel crown from a winged victory. Approaching him are allegorical figures of History, Poetry, Tragedy, Comedy and Physics. At the right, Virtue, Memory, Faith and Wisdom cluster together. All of these Kircher interprets with irrelevant reference to Egyptian customs, gestures and symbols. As for its provenance, he guesses that it came from a nearby villa of the Emperor Caligula, who for all his faults was a great lover of Homer, and knew the poet's works by memory.

Another Roman object had genuine Egyptian associations, which Kircher unaccountably missed. This was the Nile mosaic from the Temple of Fortuna Primigenia in Praeneste (**Ill. 5.22**), which was illustrated on a grand scale in *Latium*. It was discovered around 1600 and a detailed drawing made for the Museo Cartaceo (paper museum) of Cassiano dal Pozzo. By the time Kircher was in Rome, the property belonged to his patron Cardinal Francesco Barberini, who restored the mosaic and displayed it in his palace, built on the former Temple of Fortune, where it is still to be seen.

The left-hand cartouche reads: 'Interpretation of the most ancient monument now surviving in the ruins of the Temple of Firstborn Fortuna at Praeneste, in which are depicted in mosaic work the various chances of unstable Fortune, and the rites and ceremonies for venerating and placating the goddess. Solemn games are being festively celebrated, for obtaining a happy lot from Fortuna in campaigns.' The right-hand cartouche pays tribute to Cardinal Francesco Barberini for restoring the monument, and for enabling it to be drawn once again from the original for insertion into the present work. The artist identifies himself as a citizen and painter of Praeneste, which by this time was called by its modern name of Palestrina.

Kircher interprets the upper portion of the mosaic as depicting the dangerous and malefic aspect of fortune under the guise of wild beasts. He reminds us that the inhabitants of Praeneste were also devotees of Hercules, whose famous temple in Tyburtinus was not far away; and that Hercules, with his slaying of monsters and other labours, is the type of the man who overcomes adverse fortune.[23]

The next level down shows the ways of placating Fortuna through worship and of obtaining oracles from her. On the left (A) is the temple either of Fortuna herself or of Neptune, outside which two priestesses are delivering a lot to a trident-bearing sailor. The middle temple, marked B, is dedicated to Diana; Kircher has nothing to say about this. The one on the right (D) is the temple of Serapis, 'chief god of Egypt', whose worship, Kircher tells his reader, was widespread in the Roman Empire. It is identifiable by the figures of Egyptian deities outside its walls. The devotees who are approaching it are presumably going to elicit the goddess's judgment through the sacred sleep and dreams that constituted the oracle of Serapis.[24]

At the bottom level are scenes of processions and festivals intended to

5.21 Apotheosis of Homer. On Mount Parnassus, Zeus is petitioned by the Muses to make Homer a deity. The relief itself is now in the British Museum. (*Latium*, opposite 82)

gain Fortuna's favour. Kircher's descriptions here lack precision and conviction, but he hurries on to declare his own disbelief in the whole concept of fortune. Only God, he says, dispenses good and bad fate to mankind; and if we ask why God sends us evils, surely it is in order that the good may increase by comparison.[25]

Nowadays the Praeneste mosaic is interpreted as a stylized representation of the Nile from source to mouth at the time of its inundation, and dated to the end of the second century BC.[26]

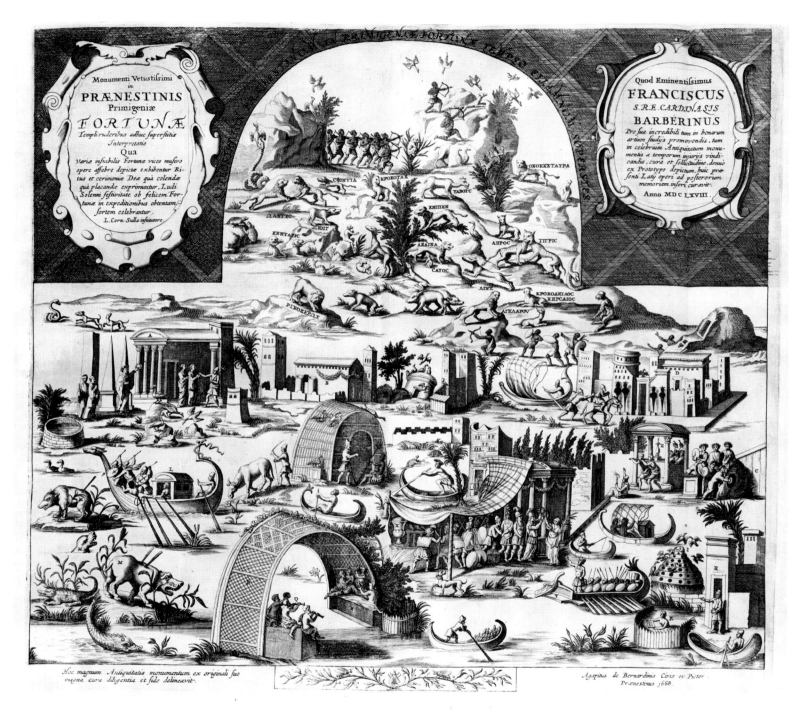

5.22 Nile mosaic from the Temple of Fortune at Praeneste. This was discovered about 1600 and restored by Cardinal Francesco Barberini. The modern view is that it represents the course down the Nile from source to mouth. For Kircher it was an allegory of Fortune. (*Latium*, opposite 100)

Topography

As a topographer, Kircher was torn between the responsibility of recording places in their present state, and the wish to admire them as they might have been. Usually the second motive won out, as we will see in the strange case of the mummy crypts, brilliantly investigated by Horst Beinlich.[27]

While Kircher was well advanced with his work on *Œdipus Ægyptiacus*, he had a brief correspondence with a wealthy and adventurous antiquarian, Tito Livio Burrattini (1617–1681/2).[28] Burrattini had travelled in Egypt from 1637 to 1641, making drawings and maps and collaborating with the English explorer John Greaves. On his return to Europe, he moved to Poland and remained there as royal architect, administrator and ambassador.

No one is quite sure where Burrattini found the mummy crypt (**Ill. 5.23**), though it was probably near the Red Pyramid of Dashur, and may yet be rediscovered there.[29] Burrattini lost all his Egyptian drawings in 1645, so he must have reconstructed it from memory. He copied the oval cartouches on the walls well enough for them now to be identified as those of Ramses II and Sesostris I. But since the style of the crypt is much later than those pharaohs,

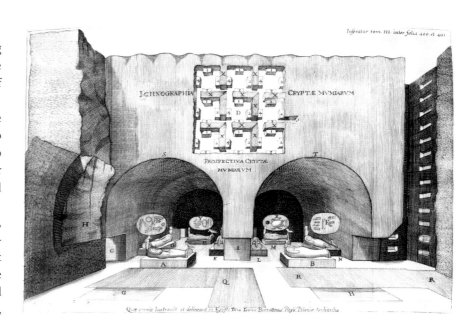

▲ 5.23 The mummy crypt had been discovered in Egypt around 1640 by Tito Livio Burrattini, who sent a drawing, made from memory, to Kircher. (*Prodromo Apologetico*, opposite 189)

◄◄ 5.24 Pyramids and the mummy crypt, a fanciful re-drawing of Burrattini's sketch by Giovanni Battista Balatri. (*Œdipus Ægyptiacus*, Volume III, 403)

◄ 5.25 Frontispiece of Kircher's *Sphinx Mystagoga*. Here Coenraet Decker improves on Balatri's version of Burrattini's drawing.

5.26 The Great Pyramid and the Sphinx
of Giza, imagined after travellers' reports
from the time when sand covered all but
the sphinx's head and shoulders. (*Turris
Babel*, 67)

Burrattini must have filled in their names from another source: probably his own drawing of the Flaminian obelisk (**Ill. 4.8**), though without knowing, any more than Kircher did, that cartouches signify the names of kings.

Later artists took Burrattini's factual drawing as a starting point for richer and more improbable scenes, such as the one that Giovanni Battista Balatri invented for *Œdipus Ægyptiacus* (**Ill. 5.24**). Beinlich points out that: 1. Burrattini's architectural drawing has been transformed into a landscape picture; 2. the tomb has been given a much enlarged ground plan; 3. the number of vaults has been reduced, and a modern staircase added; 4. the coffin is different in shape; 5. the hieroglyphs are left out.[30] Coenraet Decker used Balatri's schema as the frontispiece to Kircher's *Sphinx Mystagoga* (**Ill. 5.25**). His superior artistry is evident in the grouping of the pyramids and the sense of perspective, with the Nile vanishing in a Merianesque landscape.

James Stevens Curl remarks that this illustration 'shows an array of pyramids of the excessively spiky variety owing more to the Cestius model and to obelisks than to the Gizeh type'.[31] In fact, Kircher himself did not make a strong distinction between pyramid and obelisk, because he approached them from the point of view of symbolism, rather than aesthetics or architecture. Italian artists' conception of pyramids was overshadowed by their very own pyramid, the tomb of Gaius Cestius in Rome (circa 12 BC), which has a much steeper angle than those of the pharaohs. However, the large pyramid on the left of Balatri's drawing perhaps owes something to eyewitness reports of the Great Pyramid of Giza. Kircher devotes another illustration to this pyramid and the nearby sphinx (**Ill. 5.26**), calling it 'The pyramid, the oldest of all surviving antiquities, whole and still undamaged, built by the early Egyptian kings, the descendants of Cham'. He knew that it lay beside the Nile between Heliopolis and Memphis; that it had a flat top and a step-like profile (due to the removal of its smooth limestone casing). The engraver has borrowed the mummy crypts to furnish the pyramid with non-existent doorways. To quote Curl again, 'his improbable Pyramid of Cheops looks forward to Fischer von Erlach and Boullée',[32] architects of the Sublime Baroque and the Titanic Antique.

And what of the sphinx? The only excuse for this ludicrous bust is that the sphinx had long been buried up to its neck in desert sand. Perhaps some traveller reported that there was nothing to be seen but a mighty head and shoulders, with some large broken stones, and the artist's classicizing imagination did the rest. It shows how little disjunction was perceived, at this stage of archaeology, between Egyptian and Graeco-Roman style. But then, as we shall see in the next chapter, the ancient Hebrews wore Roman dress, while the kings and queens of Babylon lived in Baroque palaces.

Strangely enough, the crude woodcut of pyramids (**Ill. 5.27**) is more significant than the preceding engraving, because it is the first known representation of the Pyramids of Dashur, south of the Giza complex. It too was probably based on sketches made on the spot by Burrattini, and for all the distortion, the details bear out its authenticity. In the centre is the large Red Pyramid of

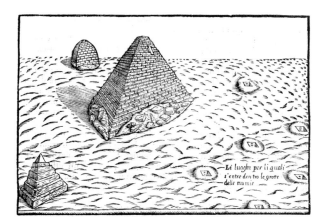

5.27 The pyramids of Dashur, the first known representation, going back ultimately to sketches by Burrattini. (*Œdipus Ægyptiacus*, Volume II, ii, 305)

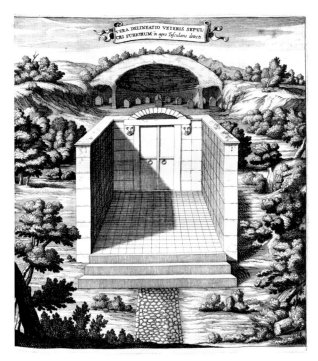

5.29 Tomb of the Furii, near Frascati, Italy. A reconstruction based on verbal reports of its discovery in 1665. (*Latium*, opposite 64)

5.28 Ruins of the Tower of Babel, one from the north (top), the other from the south, based on drawings made on the site of Babylon by Pietro della Valle's artist. (*Turris Babel*, fp. 94/95)

5.30 Ruins of Lucullus's villa. Only the substructure remained, the rest having been recycled into later villas and palaces. (*Latium*, 77)

Snefru; the Bent Pyramid of Snefru is above and to the left of it (the angle of the pyramid being smoothed to a curve), and below is the Black Pyramid of Amenemhet III, which is little more than a heap of mud bricks. To the right are entrances to subterranean tombs, marked 'the places by which one goes into the mummy caves'.

These solecisms were not entirely Kircher's fault, for when it came to places he had not visited, he relied on travellers' reports and the drawings that were sent to him. In the case of Babylon, he was fortunate to have access to the drawings by the artist who accompanied Pietro della Valle on his Asian travels (**Ill. 5.28**). The upper part of the plate shows the view from the north, the lower one that from the south. Kircher quotes della Valle's account in Italian, with a Latin translation. We read how he set up a tent there for his headquarters and walked all round the ruins. He found that the foundations of the famous tower were square, but so decayed that there were no gates, no steps, and unaccountably no sign of a surrounding city. The material of the tower was a mixture of baked and unbaked bricks, with a curious sort of mortar. He brought some specimens home and gave one to Kircher's museum, where visitors could reverently handle 'A Brick from the Tower of Babel'.

Kircher's explorations in Latium, the region around Rome, led to a more disciplined contrast of present-day views and imaginative reconstructions (which are treated in the next chapter). The disproportion between the two types of view reflects the fact that there was simply not very much to see above ground. The practice of reconstructing ancient sites for the sake of preservation (e.g. roofing the remains of Hadrian's Villa in cement) or tourism (e.g. re-erecting columns to make picturesque views) was still centuries away. Anything attractive and portable was likely to be carted away to adorn some Roman palace (see p. 125).

The places that Kircher illustrates in their present state fall into three categories, none of them large. One type records recent findings, as in the case of a tomb near Frascati (**Ill. 5.29**) of which he writes as follows:

In April 1665, while an unnamed peasant was digging around a tumulus in the wilds of Tusculanus Camaldulorum, he struck the earth so hard that the soil of many centuries fell away to reveal a great sepulchre. This was soon made known to the Reverend Camaldulensian Fathers, to whose territory the place belonged, and with much labour the soil was removed. First there appeared a kind of vestibule constructed of

◄◄ 5.31 View of Tivoli, a poorly executed engraving giving only a faint idea of the site. (*Latium*, opposite 168)

◄ 5.32 The Temple of the Sibyl, Tivoli. A more accurate rendition, close to what can be seen today. (*Latium*, 197)

squared stones; then a door of peppered stone, closed by a huge rock with an arch above it, and then a crypt containing a huge tomb, in which they found various vases which we shall describe shortly, surrounded with various objects marked with the singular name of Furii. This year, as I was enjoying my usual autumnal ramblings in the Tusculan countryside, I was asked by the Camaldulenses to examine the inscriptions of the sepulchre and the other antique stuff.[33]

Kircher goes on to try to establish which of the many Furii this tomb belonged to. He gives an account of the inscriptions and of coins and rings from the tomb, but it seems that he did not visit the site himself. His artist has done his best to represent the 'squared stone' vestibule and the crypt beyond, but the illustration is unconvincing.

Another type of illustration is of the ruins of former greatness. Kircher does not appear to have made much, if any, exploration of Hadrian's Villa, which had already been carefully mapped by Pirro Ligorio (see **Ill. 12.20**). Perhaps he had no access to drawings of it. He does, however, show what was believed to be the villa, or villas, of Lucullus (**Ill. 5.30**), with an evocative description:

This whole district from Marino to Monte Portio, for the distance of five or six miles, was built up with so many sumptuous buildings, so many delightful villas, so many houses, that it must have looked more like a vast city than separate villas. You can scarcely go a hundred feet without finding more and more ruins of ancient buildings. As L. Caecilius has shown convincingly in his *Volaterranum*, they were all built through the wealth of Lucullus. As far as we can conjecture, these dark windowless crypts were nothing other than convenient containers for the wine barrels, which abounded there. The *peridromides* or vast avenues and colonnades probably served as lodgings for the slaves, of whom many thousands were used in the agriculture of the villas and other services. And there is no doubt that the magnificent villas that we admire today were constructed in later times from the ruins of them.[34]

The three views of Tivoli in *Latium* are a most revealing case. The first example (**Ill. 5.31**) is a poorly executed engraving from which no one would suspect that there was a flourishing town there. What it calls 'the city of Tivoli' is reduced to a couple of pyramids and some decrepit towers. A large 'palace' and an unidentified building around a courtyard (D) stand isolated, while

VETUS & NOVUM LATIUM.   169

non incurriffe putas fpatio 1600 anno- | neque *Catadupam* illam , quæ modò

5.33 The Temple of the Sibyl seen through rocks. An early example of romantic antiquarianism. (*Latium*, 169)

Time is the devourer of things, and in the course of time forgetful age changes, transforms, alters, dissolves not only the whole earthly globe but especially the site of certain places, such that nothing remains for long in its natural place, nor can it last, owing to the fragility of corruptible things. Whoever wishes may read of this in *Mundus Subterraneus,* where he will find everything about the mutation of the earthly globe thoroughly described. And since we can see that even in a few years river beds can considerably change their position, how much more, do you think, has the Tyburtine City been assailed over 1,600 years by the voracity of a rushing and swirling river?[35]

Kircher's account of how he discovered the sanctuary of Mentorella has something of the same awe before the forces that have moulded the earth:

In 1661, while I was exploring the mountains of Polano and Praeneste, I started in Tivoli and passed through wild mountains and rocks. Around noon I came to a horrid, solitary place, hemmed round with rocks like a crown. It really was a place filled with horror, where the stony pyramids seemed to scrape the heavens, and, falling from hanging rocks in formidable vortices, seemed to express infernal motion. In the midst of all this, among dark trees and rocks, I came across the remnants of a roof: it was a church, all but collapsed. But how could there be a church in this place of terror and solitude? I asked the guide. Going in, I saw the pictures and sculptures of the saints. Everything breathed the devotion of ancient piety.[36]

the Sibyl's Temple (A and B) is alternatively on a low river bank or a high outcrop. To try to correlate this with the plan of Tivoli (see **Ill. 12.22**) only leads to more confusion.

Ill. 5.32, in contrast, shows a more accurate view of the ruined 'Sibyl's Temple'. The fragmentary circle of Corinthian columns is perched above an abyss, through which the river Aniene pours over a cascade, conveniently bridged for the benefit of artists. Kircher's note states that 'its fabric is constructed according to all the rules of the architectonic art, as can be seen to this day'. Once an admired stop on the Grand Tour, it served as the model for innumerable circular temples or *tholoi* in the gardens of northern Europe. Kircher recognized its perfection as an architectural canon, and gives exact measurements in palms and 'minutes' of its columns, doorway, and inner dimensions.

The previous views stand respectively for Kircher's uncritical retailing of stale information, and for his appreciation of scientific accuracy: a contradiction intrinsic to his character. Comparing with the latter engraving a third view (**Ill. 5.33**), one finds a suspicious lack of agreement as to the form of the columns, their capitals, and the entablature. But this artist compensates with his dramatic viewpoint, emphasizing the deep chasm beneath the ruin, and giving Kircher the chance to reveal yet another facet of his personality:

The eighteenth century did not invent the Sublime, nor the Romantic era the melancholy attraction of 'bare ruined choirs'! But for once Kircher did not stop at admiring antiquities that had survived to his own day: he took their preservation in hand himself. Here is an impression of the Mentorella site (**Ill. 5.34**), more likely based on a sketch by Kircher than on a professional topographer's work. On the left is the path descending from Guadognolo, some six miles (ten kilometres) away. In the centre is the church, and on the right the rock on which Christ appeared to St Eustace. It now bears the tiny chapel of the saint with its frescoes by Johann Paul Schor (see **Ills. 3.12–3.14**), and the belfry with its two bells. For comparison, I include a recent photograph of the monastery (**Ill. 5.35**).

A special place in Kircher's antiquarium belongs to the things found at Mentorella. In *Historia Eustachio-Mariana*, his book on the history of the church and monastery, he illustrates wall-paintings of the baptism of St Eustace by the Pope and of an armed monk encircled by a dragon (**Ill. 5.39**), and the few treasures that had survived the ruin of the church and monastery thanks to the local magnate, the Duke of Polana, who kept them in the library of his castle.[37] These included a silver cross of the mediaeval era (**Ill. 5.36**), a large seven-branched candlestick of bronze (**Ill. 5.37**), and an oak tablet about three

Optica Proiectio Rupis et Ecclesiæ Deiparæ de Monterella una cum circumiacentibus locis.

5.34 Sanctuary of Mentorella. This was the place that Kircher knew, sketched, and helped to preserve, where Christ appeared to St Eustace. (*Historia Eustachio-Mariana*, 85)

5.35 The Sanctuary of Mentorella, as it is today. (Author's photograph)

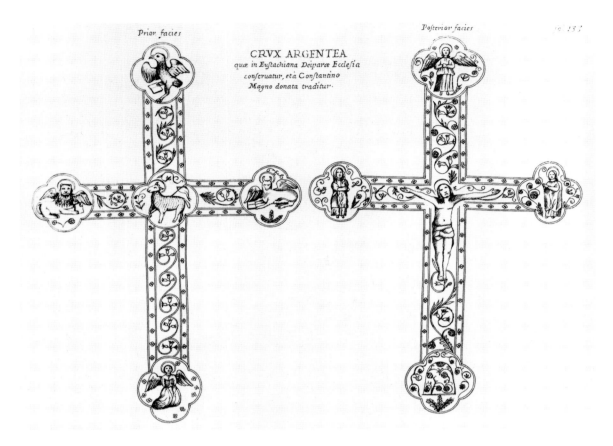

Prior facies

CRVX ARGENTEA
quæ in Eustachiana Deiparæ Ecclesia
conservatur, et à Constantino
Magno donata traditur.

Posterior facies

◄ 5.36, ▼ 5.37, ► 5.38 Three treasures recovered from the ruins of Mentorella: a silver cross, a seven-branched candlestick, and an oak tablet carved with the legend of St Eustace. (*Historia Eustachio-Mariana*, 120/121, 132/133, 134)

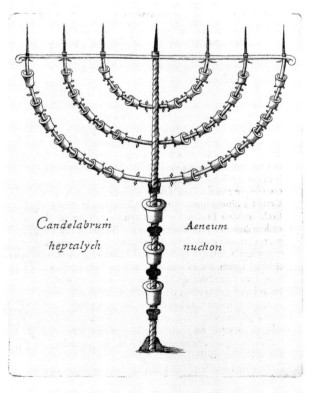

Candelabrum   Aeneum

heptalych   nuchon

5.39 Monk and dragon. From an old fresco in the church of Mentorella. (*Historia Eustachio-Mariana*, 140)

feet (one metre) square, carved with the legend of St Eustace (**Ill. 5.38**). All of these have been preserved to this day, either in the church or in the museum in Palazzo Venezia, Rome.

Kircher's illustrations of these are a rare case, for his time, of antiquarian interest in the Middle Ages.[38] He interpreted the oak tablet as showing Christ (F), Sts Peter and Paul (E, G), St Sylvester (K) and an acolyte (M). This, he says, presents many enigmas, such as why Christ appearing between the stag's horns is not shown on the cross, as is traditional in this scene. Kircher's answer is that it was the ancient custom not to worship Christ crucified, but alive and resplendent.[39] This seems to have been Kircher's own preference, as far as one can deduce from his writings. While they are all suffused with piety, and his books usually end with a kind of ecstatic sermon, the main focus is not on Christ crucified, or even on Christ at all. It is on God as the maker of heaven and earth, who has devised all things with incredible ingenuity for the sake of the greater good, and secondarily on the Virgin Mary.

To accompany the engraving of the monk with the dragon, Kircher recounts the tradition from the Mentorella monastery. Not far off there was once a huge dragon plaguing the countryside. Its very breath poisoned the air, and the inhabitants were powerless before it until a brave monk resolved to save the community, even at the expense of his own life. He dressed himself in armour, took a dagger, and allowed the dragon to wind itself around him. After a long struggle, he forced his dagger between its jaws and killed it, but he too died soon afterwards from having inhaled its breath. Kircher adds that he was shown the dragon's cave, but that he doesn't quite believe the story.[40]

Notes

1 Coincidentally, it was dedicated to Elector Maximilian of Bavaria, who many years before had been the patron of Herwart von Hohenberg. Kircher left out Nardi's last plate, which represented the Phoenician god Attis with his phallus in his hand.
2 He may have got the notion from Pignoria, 15–16, where Pignoria warns his reader not to laugh before illustrating 'Osiris's testicles with eyes'.
3 What follows is paraphrased from *Œdipus Ægyptiacus*, III, 415–416.
4 Compare the planetary ascent described in *Poimandres*, the first dialogue of the *Corpus Hermeticum*.
5 *Œdipus Ægyptiacus*, III, 477.
6 The Iynx is a term found in the *Chaldaean Oracles*. For a rare modern elucidation, see Ronan. What follows is paraphrased from *Œdipus Ægyptiacus*, III, 479–483.
7 Quoted in *Œdipus Ægyptiacus*, I, 211.
8 Pignoria, second unnumbered plate after the illustrations of the Bembine Table; Herwart, figure 50.
9 *Œdipus Ægyptiacus*, II, ii, 468. Gómez de Liaño, II, 258, translates the entire commentary on this figure.
10 From Stanley's *Chaldaick Philosophy*, London 1701, cited in *Chaldaean Oracles of Zoroaster*, 88.
11 Biblioteca Nazionale Vittorio Emanuele II, Rome, Mss. Gesuiti no. 1235, fol. 248.
12 *Œdipus Ægyptiacus*, II, i, 190.
13 *Œdipus Ægyptiacus*, II, ii, 479.
14 *Œdipus Ægyptiacus*, III, 481.
15 Stolzenberg, 'Four Trees', 169, n.40. On Kircher's troubles with, and contempt for, the censors, especially in connection with *Œdipus Ægyptiacus*, see Siebert, 'Kircher and His Critics', 86–91.
16 *Œdipus Ægyptiacus*, III, 521–522.
17 *Œdipus Ægyptiacus*, III, 386.
18 *Œdipus Ægyptiacus*, III, 503–504.
19 *Œdipus Ægyptiacus*, III, 225.
20 *Œdipus Ægyptiacus*, III, 454.
21 *Œdipus Ægyptiacus*, III, 543.
22 What follows is paraphrased or quoted from *Latium*, 83–86.
23 *Latium*, 103.
24 *Latium*, 105.
25 *Latium*, 108.
26 Rachewiltz and Partini, 136.
27 See Beinlich, 'Kircher und Ägypten'.
28 See his biography in *Dizionario biografico degli Italiani*.
29 Beinlich 2002b, 64–65.
30 Beinlich 2002b, 65.
31 Curl, 72.
32 Curl, 72. See ibid., 82, 83, 104, for supporting illustrations from Fischer von Erlach (1721) and Étienne-Louis Boullée (circa 1785).
33 *Latium*, 64.
34 *Latium*, 76.
35 *Latium*, 168–170.
36 *Historia Eustachio-Mariana*, 2 (somewhat abbreviated).
37 *Historia Eustachio-Mariana*, 120.
38 However, he believed the processional cross to date from the time of Constantine; *Historia Eustachio-Mariana*, 133.
39 *Historia Eustachio-Mariana*, 130.
40 *Historia Eustachio-Mariana*, 139–140. The dragon's cave is now the grotto-chapel of St Benedict.

Chapter 6   Antiquity Imagined

Kircher's attitude to antiquity was ambiguous in more ways than one. I have already mentioned his uneasiness about telling his readers too much pagan lore, in case it gave them a taste for illicit magic. Speaking more broadly, he presented antiquity in two quite different ways. One was as a historian, even a pioneer archaeologist, who took seriously his responsibility to show and explain the past. The other way was as the producer of a theatrical entertainment, in which the past was brought to life. Illustrating his books was important for both kinds of presentation: for the first, it served as documentation, while for the second, it fed the imagination. Imagining the past was an essential part of the Spiritual Exercises that every Jesuit regularly practised, and although they were restricted to religious subjects, the capacity must have carried over into secular life.

The illustrations in this section show antiquity not as it had survived in Kircher's day, but as it might have looked originally. Kircher's readers, excusably, may have not made a sharp distinction between the two, and very likely some of them took his imaginative reconstructions as fact. I do not think that he deliberately deceived his readers by showing them something he knew to be inaccurate; he simply did not think about the issue in modern terms. Again, the Spiritual Exercises help one to understand his attitude. Someone meditating on Christ's Passion, for example, might imagine the wrong clothing or visualize Pilate's palace as a Baroque villa, but it did not matter. Painters had been committing anachronisms like these for centuries. The point was to make the images as real and emotionally powerful as possible.

We take Kircher's reconstructions in biblical order, beginning with the plate in *Arca Noë* showing Adam and his descendants (**Ill. 6.1**). It recalls the landscapes with blasted trees beloved of Ruisdael and the Netherlands School, not surprisingly since it was drawn by the Amsterdam artist Coenraet Decker, or someone close to him. Adam and Eve are pictured after the Fall, wearing the garments that the Lord God made for them after they became ashamed of their nakedness; the Serpent keeps company with them.

Kircher had an exalted view of Adam as scientist. He writes in *Œdipus Ægyptiacus*:

No one can doubt that Adam, who had to instruct the rest of humankind about all and every secret of nature, had the most absolute knowl-

6.1 Adam and his progeny. It is after the Fall. Adam and Eve wear clothes to cover their nakedness. Of their three sons, Abel is not included because he had no descendant. Cain's line ends with Tubal Cain, Seth's with Noah, Shem and Abraham. The numbers are their ages at death. (*Arca Noë*, 237)

6.2 Noah and his progeny: Cham (Ham), Shem and Japheth became the ancestors of the various races. Noah holds a model of the Ark. (*Arca Noë*, fp. 226/227)

edge of all these things, divinely infused; thus he knew perfectly the energy and nature of every element, all their mutual combinations, and the complexion of other mixtures made from these by combination and separation. He also penetrated deeply into the natures and strengths of metallic bodies and their generation, their coagulations in the bowels of the earth, and the manner of their depurations, fusions, fixations, calcinations, amalgamations, filtrations, and other actions of the chemists most necessary for the use of the human race; since without these, human life could not subsist.[1]

Genesis records three sons of Adam and Eve: Cain, Abel and Seth. Abel is not included on the tree because he had no descendants. The fratricide's branch is marked 'The accursed line of Cain'. It ends with Tubal Cain 'who was a hammerer and a smith', Jubal 'who was the father of singers', and Jabal 'who was the father of tent-dwellers'. This is the kind of mythic genealogy that explains the great inventions. (Its equivalents in Greek mythology would be the smith-god Hephaestus and Apollo, inventor of the arts, while the beginning of artificial dwellings belongs to the Silver Age.) The more 'blessed' line of descent runs from Seth, through Noah and Shem to Abraham, noting the lifespans of each.

Accuracy was important to Kircher in matters of genealogy and chronology. According to his Bible-based reckoning, Adam lived from the sixth day of the world until the 930th year.[2] Since Kircher dated the Creation 3,984 years before the birth of Christ, this gives Adam's dates as 3984–3054 BC.

A similar picture shows the descendants of Noah (2928–1978 BC) and his progeny (**Ill. 6.2**). He was the father of three sons: Cham (Ham), Shem (or Sem) and Japheth, whose further descendants are named in Genesis 10. On his lap he holds a model of the Ark, and in the distance is Mount Ararat, where it landed after the Flood. The date of the Flood, according to Kircher's calculations, was Anno Mundi 1656, which places it by our reckoning in 2328 BC.[3]

Noah's sons were believed to have gone off in different directions, whence their descendants became the founders of eponymous peoples. This plate names Cham's son Chus, the ancestor of the Ethiopians, Misraim the ancestor of the Egyptians, Nimrod of the Chaldaeans and Canaan of the Canaanites. Among Canaan's sons are Sidon, father of the Sidonites, Hethaeus of the Hittites, Jebusinus of the Jebusites, Amorrhaeus of the Amorites and so on, accounting for all the tribes neighbouring Israel at the time the narrative of Genesis was composed. As Dino Pastine has explained, 'the concept of race was totally foreign to Kircher's mentality'. The fact that Chus was traditionally said to have been the first black man was not a result of God's curse on Cham and his descendants, but a fortuitous condition due to some natural cause. Pastine continues: 'What appeared to the anthropologists of later centuries as racial differences are for him simple accidents, due to a multitude of different causes; they are curiosities that make Adam's descendants multicoloured and picturesque and display the work of the Holy Spirit in its

marvellous, manifold character, while in no way compromising the axiomatic evidence of mankind's unity.'[4]

Kircher's *Arca Noë* is a virtuoso piece of reconstruction, a 'just-so story' that leaves no question unanswered. As all of humanity had to be traced back to Noah's family, so all today's land animals and birds must have descended from the pairs preserved in the Ark. The book thus serves a secondary purpose of taxonomy, naming and classifying as many animals as possible. A third purpose was to capture the attention of its twelve-year old dedicatee, Charles II of Spain.

Some intelligent child might well ask how Noah could possibly have packed them all in. This very large illustration (**Ill. 6.3**) proposes a scheme, which I translate from the bottom row upwards and from left to right (see box on p. 102). Kircher appears to have scoured Aristotle's *History of Animals* and Pliny's *Natural History* for names. Some of the birds named there are unidentifiable (left in italics, untranslated) or uncertain in their English equivalents.

Kircher probably gave all this to the printer in the form of a chart. Not so the next group of illustrations, which are sheer invention on the illustrator's part and full of entertaining details. In this 'Picture of the labours of the workmen in building the Ark' (**Ill. 6.4**) note the forge with bellows on the left, the different types of saw, and Noah on the right giving instructions. The accompanying text goes its own way, like a pious bedtime story. Kircher reminds us that Noah was five hundred years old when he received God's order to build the Ark, and the building took a hundred years. Wood had to be imported from Mount Lebanon and Mesopotamia, bitumen or tar from the Babylonian fields and perhaps Judaea. Tubal Cain, the first smith, supplied the iron and bronze equipment, including the weapons with which he and his family defended themselves against the impious Giants.[5] One issue that is never mentioned, here or elsewhere, is how Noah could afford it. Perhaps Jesuit casuistry could justify issuing promissory notes to those who stubbornly believed that they would live to claim them.

The tale continues with the animals marching in, two by two (**Ill. 6.5**). There is a strangely modern aspect to the terrace-houses in the background and the briefcase carried by one of Noah's sons. Note the social distinction between the lowly donkeys and the noble horses; both pairs seem to be talking to each other. The lions take up a heraldic pose, and the wolves are arrested in mid-leap. The three-storey construction of the Ark is clearly visible, with a door on the third storey for the birds to enter.

Little need be said about the remaining illustrations, striking as they are. The next plate (**Ill. 6.6**) shows 'The miserable condition of men at the start of the flood'. The composition of this plate, and some of the details, are borrowed from one of the most popular series of Bible illustrations, Matthaeus Merian's first volume of *Icones Biblicae* (1625), 27. In **Ill. 6.7**, 'The state of the flood before the ebbing of the waters, in the universal flood', sea monsters come to frolic among the corpses of drowned humans and horses.

THE ARRANGEMENT OF NOAH'S ARK

First (lowest) level, containing animals, side 1:
N: Cistern. Taurus:[6] 2 Beavers. Gemini: 2 Otters. Cancer: 2 Crocodiles. Leo: 2 Hippopotami. M: passage. Virgo: 2 Goat-stags. Libra: 7 Gazelles. Scorpio: 7 Elks. Sagittarius: 7 Bisons. K: passage. Capricorn: 7 Goats. Aquarius: 7 Sheep. Pisces: 7 Cattle. D: passage. Moon: 7 Deer. Sun: 7 Reindeer. Venus: Wild Goats, Gazelles, Chamois, Fallow Deer. F: passage. Mercury: 2 Domestic Dogs. Mars: 2 Aquatic Hare-Hounds. Jupiter: 2 Molossian Hounds. No sign: 2 Maltese Dogs. Saturn: 2 Indian Dogs. H: passage. South node: 2 Sea Cows or Seals. North node: Turtles. No sign: Hedgehogs, Porcupines. Star: Badgers, Dormice, Martens, Weasels. No sign: storage.

First level, side 2:
a: empty. M: 2 Small Indian Pigs. L: 2 Rabbits. K: 2 Hares, Squirrels. I: 2 Monkeys. H: Various species of Ape. L: passage. G: 2 of various species of Felines. F: 2 or several Wild Asses. E: 2 or several Donkeys. D: 2 Horses. I: passage. C: 2 Dromedaries. B: 2 Camels. A: 2 Elephants. N: passage. O: 2 Rhinoceroses. P: 2 Lions. Q: 2 Bears. E: passage. R: 2 Tigers. S: 2 Panthers, Leopards. T: Unicorns, horned animals of Africa. V: 2 Lynxes, Gluttons. G: passage. X: 2 Wolves. Y: 2 Foxes. Z: 2 Wild Boar, 2 Domestic Swine. Libra: Cistern.

Second level, containing provisions, side 1:
S: Agricultural tools for the world reborn. T: Clothes, Household linens. V: Ironmongery, Wool. X: Mills, Bread Ovens, Furnace. [passage] Y: Oil. Z: Salt. Various metals and minerals for use in the new world. aa: Dried fish with fish in brine for the amphibians. Candles, Honey. [passage] bb: Dovecote both for the carnivores and for use in the future world. cc: Chicken-coop for the carnivores, for the quadrupeds, for the birds, and for use in the new world. [passage] dd: Acorns, Nuts. ee: Chestnuts, Dried Grapes. ff: Peas, Pulses, Beans. gg: Lentils, Rice. [passage] hh: Water-casks. [passage] ii: Wheat-straw as food for animals. kk: Hay for Cattle, Asses, Camels, etc. ll: Empty storage for whatever necessity may suggest.

Second level, side 2:
A: Tools for the new world. [empty] B: Ropes and other household equipment. C: Wood. [passage] D: Spices for food. E: Grain of all sorts and Berries for the birds. F: Pears, Apples. G: Twice-cooked Bread, Smoked Meat for the carnivores. [passage] H: Sheep-fold for feeding the carnivores, then for the need of the future world. Butter. I: Goat-fold for use of the carnivorous animals, then of men in the future world. Cheese. [passage] K: Wheat. L: Winter Wheat. M: Barley. N: Oats. [passage] O: Casks full of water for necessary use. [passage] P: Tree-leaves for the use of the animals in wintertime. Q: Hay for the herbivorous animals. R: Some Cattle, Horses, and Asses for use in the coming world.

Third level, containing birds and humans, side 1:
E: Cage for migrating birds, such as River Swallow, *Tanager*, Kingbird, Tit, Corncrake, Creeper, *Phoicus Caerulea*, Pardalus, Shrike, Batis, Long-tailed Tit, *Spinites*, *Chrysometris*, Wryneck, *Glottis*, and the like. F: Gryphon-falcons, Harpies. [passage] G: Doves, Pigeons of different species. H: Fowl of different species, with Chickens. [passage] I: Large aviary for small songbirds, such as Nightingales, Larks, Goldcrests, Buntings, Finches, Robins, Thistle-Finches, and the like. K: Pantry.
L: Kitchen. M: passage. N: Noah's cabin. O: Shem's cabin, P: Cham's cabin. Q: Japheth's cabin. [passage] R: Crows, Hooded Crows, Jackdaws, Woodpeckers.
S: Sparrows, Solitary Sparrow, Witwalls, Hoopoes. T: Different species of Peacocks and Parices. V: Cuckoos, Redstarts, Robins, Caterpillars [sic] [passage] W: Swallows of various species. X: Quails. Y: Birds of Paradise of various species. Z: empty space.

Third level, side 2:
1: Pelicans, Spoonbills, Cochleariae. 2: Pheasants, Grouse. 3: Pernices, Partridges, Attagenes. 4: Kingfishers. 5: Magpies of different species. [passage] 6: Parrots of different species. 7: Peacocks of different species. 8: Peacock-fowl, with Turkeys and Pharaoh's fowl. [passage] 9: Hawks of different species. 10: Vultures of different species. 11: Eagles of different species. [passage] 12: Falcons of different species. 13: Ostriches. 14: Cranes and Storks. [passage] 15: Herons of different species. 16: Geese, domestic and wild. 17: Ducks of different species. [passage] 18: Kites, Meryi, Coots. 19: Fig-peckers, Oyster-catchers. 20: Starlings, Wagtails. [empty] 21: Owls, Screech-owls, Bustards.

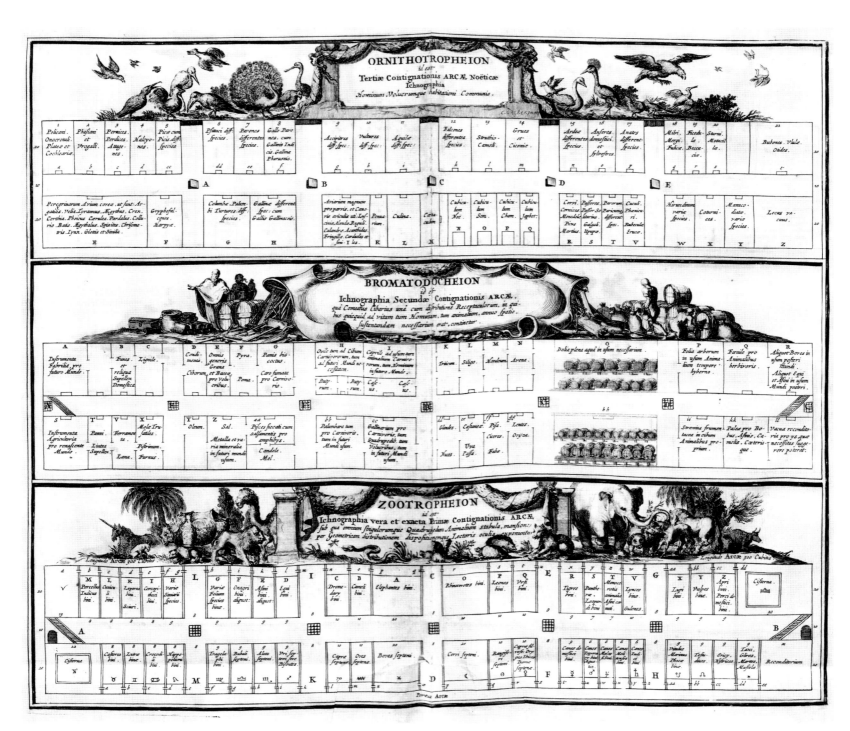

6.3 Plan of the Ark. A key to the letters can be found opposite. (*Arca Noë*, fp. 108/109)

◀ 6.4 Building the Ark. The artist has called on contemporary shipyard techniques. (*Arca Noë*, fp. 28/29)

▼ 6.5 Entry of the animals into the Ark. Kircher's Ark has three storeys with a special entrance for birds. (*Arca Noë*, fp. 122/123)

▶ 6.6 The beginning of the Flood. Kircher's artist borrows from previous biblical illustrations. (*Arca Noë*, fp. 126/127)

▼ 6.7 The Flood. Sea monsters with drowned men and horses. (*Arca Noë*, fp. 154/155)

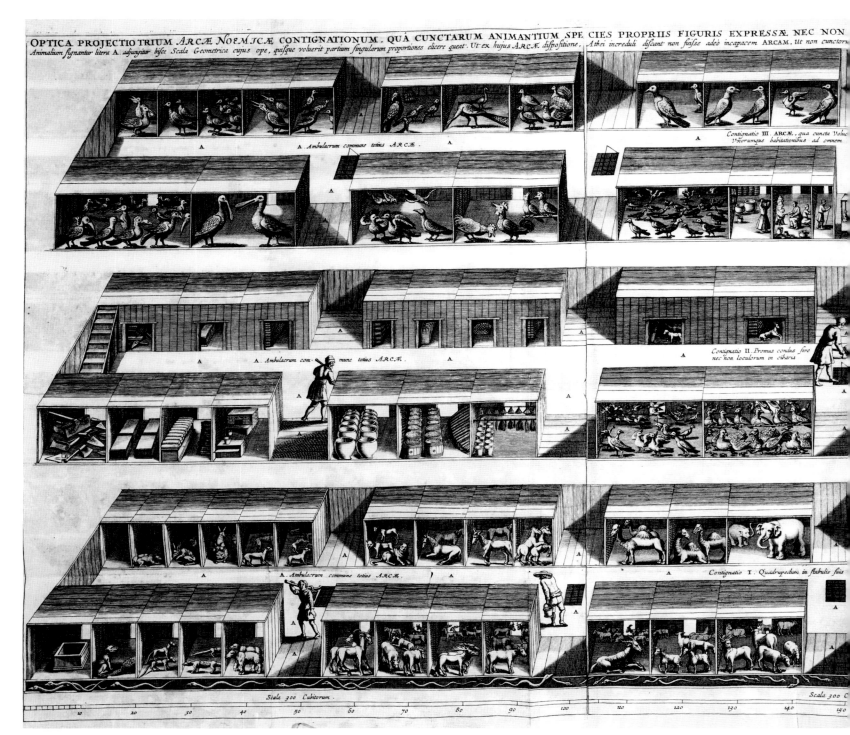

6.8 The inside of the Ark. This is the largest of all Kircher's illustrations. (*Arca Noë*, fp. 46/47)

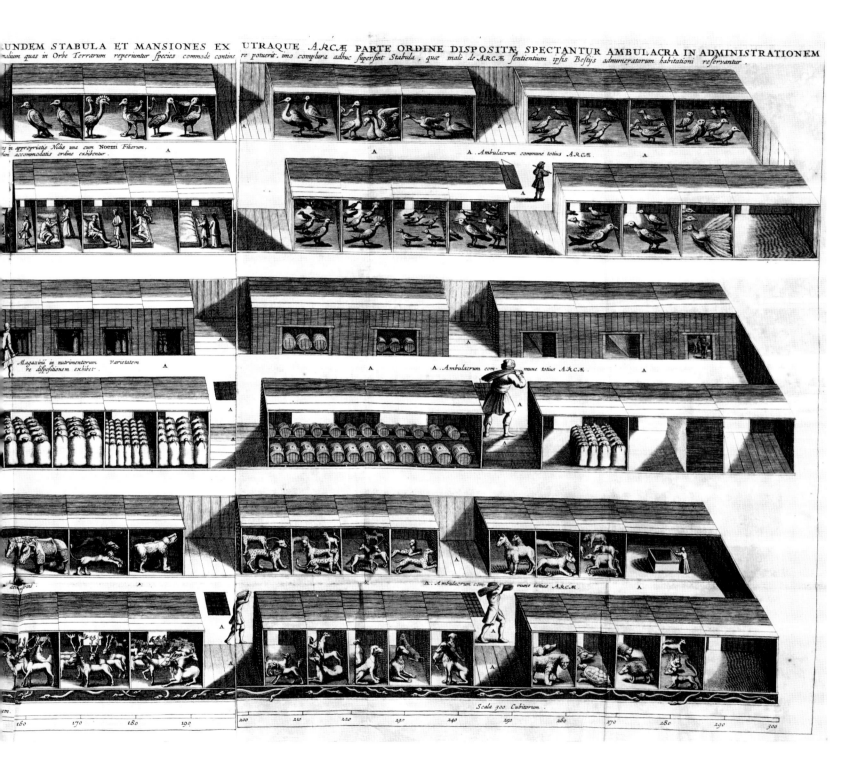

UNDEM STABULA ET MANSIONES EX   UTRAQUE ARCÆ PARTE ORDINE DISPOSITÆ SPECTANTUR AMBULACRA IN ADMINISTRATIONEM
malium quas in Orbe Terrarum reperuntur species commode contine   re potuerit, imo complura adhuc superfint Stabula, quæ male de ARCÆ sentientium ipsis Bestys admuneratorum habitationi reservantur.

as in appropriatis Nidis una cum Noemi Filiorum.
hui accommodatis ordine exhibentur.   A.

A. Ambulacrum commune totius ARCÆ.

Magazinū in nutrimentorum   Varietatem
re dispositionem exhibet.   A.

A. Ambulacrum com   mune totius ARCÆ.

Ambulacrum com   mune totius ARCÆ.

Ambulacrum com   mune totius ARCÆ.

Scala 300. Cubitorum.

6.9 Submerged mountains. The bottom picture shows the Flood at its height; in the upper one the tops of the mountains have begun to appear and the Ark rests on Mount Ararat. (*Arca Noë*, opposite 198)

Before Noah comes to land, Kircher digresses to tell us more about the household economy of the Ark, which requires the largest illustration in any of his books (**Ill. 6.8**): 39 by 17½ inches, made from three separate plates. The engraver was as puzzled as the reader at some of the names of birds and beasts, and simply drew ones he knew, for example, making most of the dogs look alike. The legend at the top reads:

> Here is seen an optical projection of the three storeys of the Ark, whereby the species of all animals are shown in their proper figures, as well as their stables and pens arranged in order on either side of the Ark. The corridors for serving the animals are marked with the letter A. In addition there is a geometric scale with which anyone who wants can find the proportion of individual parts. And from this arrangement of the Ark, let the unbelieving atheists learn that the Ark was not lacking in the capacity to contain comfortably every species of animal found in the earthly globe. There are even some extra stables reserved for the habitation of those who think ill concerning the Ark,[7] and are to be numbered with the very beasts.[8]

A double plate by Coenraet Decker shows the 'before and after' state of the world's mountains (**Ill. 6.9**). The lower half of the plate comes first in order, showing 'the maximum rise of waters in the Flood'. They were fifteen cubits

above the Caucasus (the highest known mountain).[9] The others named are Athos, Olympus, Taurus and Ararat. They reappear in the upper half of the plate, in which the waters have subsided sufficiently for the Ark to rest on the peak of Mount Ararat. Decker, who both designed and engraved the plate, has even managed to show cities and forests beneath the sea.

After this geological interlude, the illustrator of the picture-book story makes one more appearance with Noah's sacrifice (**Ill. 6.10**). From left to right, the eight survivors are Shem's wife, Shem, Noah's wife, Noah,[10] Japheth's wife, Japheth, Cham's wife and Cham. Five of them are kneeling in adoration; two of the wives stand near, still holding their burdens; but Cham, like Judas in paintings of the Last Supper, is a man apart, refusing to join in the ritual of thanksgiving. He is already preparing for the role in which Kircher cast him: the father of false religion, polytheism and idolatry.

Turris Babel continues the story where *Arca Noë* left off. Cham's grandson was Nimrod (**Ill. 6.11**), called by Kircher the first tyrant who tried to extend his rule over other peoples. 'He was the cruellest of men, bloodthirsty, impious, and rapacious, as is clear enough from the picture of his physique here.... He turned men to idolatry, so that they worshipped fire and the sun (which is fire) as God, which error the Persians and Chaldaeans later followed.'[11]

Already in *Obeliscus Pamphilius*, Kircher had stated that Nimrod, Bel, Baal and Saturn were one and the same deified man. In *Turris Babel* he investigates the etymology of their names, and somehow concludes that Nimrod was called Bel 'because of the impure coitus that he practised indiscriminately'.[12] None of these iniquities appear in the Bible, which simply calls Nimrod 'a mighty one in the earth' and 'a mighty hunter before the Lord' (Genesis 10:7–8). Unusually for Kircher, this plate has no didactic purpose. It serves only for decoration and for the engraver to display his mastery of the typical single-figure image. It might equally serve as a picture of Mars. As usual, the 'ancients' of whatever time and place are shown in Roman costume.

The Bible does not say who built the Tower of Babel, but Kircher ascribes it to Nimrod, as the mightiest and wickedest man yet known. In the biblical account, the builders of the Tower of Babel said: 'Come, let us make ourselves a city and a tower whose top will reach Heaven.' The upper part of the illustration (**Ill. 6.12**) shows this phrase written in a few of the post-Babel tongues: Latin, Greek, Samaritan, Hebrew, Arabic and Syrian.[13] Thus Kircher the linguist opened the secondary theme of *Turris Babel*: the taxonomy of languages. But the scientist in him could not resist the passing thought: whatever would have happened if they had succeeded?

Daniel Stolzenberg aptly calls the demonstration 'a pataphysical tour de force',[14] but also a 'thought experiment' of the kind that Galileo frequently used. For example, one cannot perform a physical experiment to discover whether the earth goes round the sun, but by logically thinking through the consequences of what the telescope showed, Galileo in his *Dialogue on the Two World Systems* proved to any unbiased reader that this must be so.

6.10 Noah's sacrifice. Kircher includes the eight survivors – Noah, his wife, their sons and their wives. The beached Ark is top left. (*Arca Noë*, fp. 168/169)

6.11 Nimrod, called 'a mighty hunter' in Genesis, but given a more hostile character by Kircher, who ascribes the building of the Tower of Babel to him. (*Turris Babel*, opposite 112)

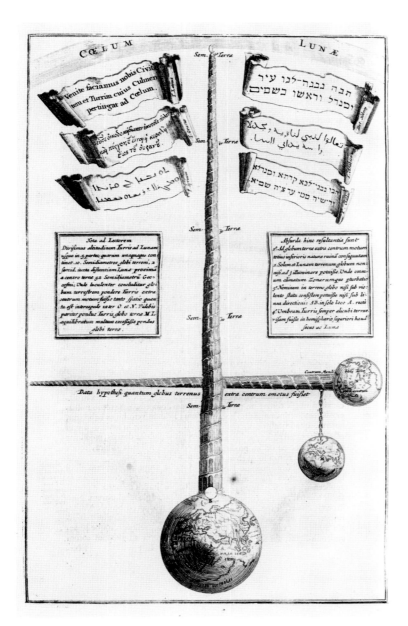

▲ **6.12** 'Why the Tower of Babel could not have reached to the Moon.' The proof involves calculating the number of bricks required (more than the earth could supply) and the time needed to build it (longer than five million lifetimes). (*Turris Babel*, 38)

▶ **6.13** The Tower of Babel, a tour de force of architectural fantasy, partly based on the painting by Jan Breughel. (*Turris Babel*, fp. 40/41)

Such an experiment must begin by defining terms. 'Heaven', in the Aristotelian cosmology, began with the sphere of the moon's orbit around the earth. That must have been what the builders were aiming at. Kircher gives the distance of the moon's sphere from the earth as 52 times the earth's radius, or 178,672 miles. If the tower had a base only eight miles across (and the picture shows it far bigger), it would contain 2,977,850 cubic miles of material, and this would require 374,731,250,000,000,000 bricks. 'The mind can scarcely conceive of such a number,' Kircher writes, 'and countless absurdities follow from this calculation of the tower.'[15] But he presses on: if five million men worked for 426 years, adding a mile a week to the height of the tower, it could not be finished in time. Also, if all the world's forests were denuded of trees, the whole earth turned to clay and all the oceans, seas and lakes turned to bitumen, it would not suffice: it would need another, larger globe to furnish the materials. Then there is the problem of the horses: even galloping up the spiral ramps at thirty miles a day, they wouldn't reach the top of the tower in 800 years. Finally, as shown by the horizontal diagram, the weight of the tower would wrench the earth out of its place at the centre of the universe.[16] So Nimrod's enterprise was not only impious, but also an engineering disaster.

We now pass from the ridiculous to what is arguably the most sublime plate in any of Kircher's books (**Ill. 6.13**), drawn by the nineteen-year-old Coenraet Decker and engraved by Lievin Cruyl. This large engraving (19½ by 18¾ inches) obviously borrows from Jan Breughel's paintings of the Tower of Babel, but adds a system of crossing ramps from one of Kircher's favourite ancient buildings, the Temple of Fortune in Praeneste (see **Ill. 6.27**). The landscape is filled with the typical staffage of the period: Baroque palaces and Roman temples, a winding river with bridges, triumphal arches, courtyards and harbours. There are at least a dozen obelisks, some pyramids, a large building to the right resembling the Temple of Solomon, and a rival tower beyond the city walls. At bottom right Nimrod, dressed as an Ottoman potentate, views the architect's drawing. This may have inspired the theme of Gérard de Lairesse's frontispiece, drawn nine years later (see **Ill. 2.27**).

Although the Tower of Babel failed through its builders' hubris, Kircher extols the grandeur of post-diluvian civilization. He writes that no city has ever compared with Nineveh, neither Egyptian Memphis, Thebes, nor Heliopolis, nor those immense cities that Marco Polo found in China, nor cities of Roman times such as Rome, Syracuse and Carthage, nor modern ones like Rome, Cairo, Paris, London, Amsterdam or Lisbon. His city view (**Ill. 6.14**), is half view, half plan, showing only the major monuments.[17] Most prominent is the Tomb of Ninus in the form of an obelisk–pyramid hybrid.[18] In the lower left corner the prophet Jonah sits beneath his gourd-bush and glumly awaits the city's destruction.

In the Book of Jonah, it says that Nineveh was 'three days' in size. This kind of detail was irresistible to Kircher. What, he asks, could those 'three days' mean? Did it take three days to circumambulate the city, or to go through every street? To do the latter even in modern Rome would take much longer. Or was it

Prospectus Turris Babylonicæ ex Præscripto R. Adm: Patris Athanaſy Kircheri Soc: Jeſu.

TURRIS BABEL.

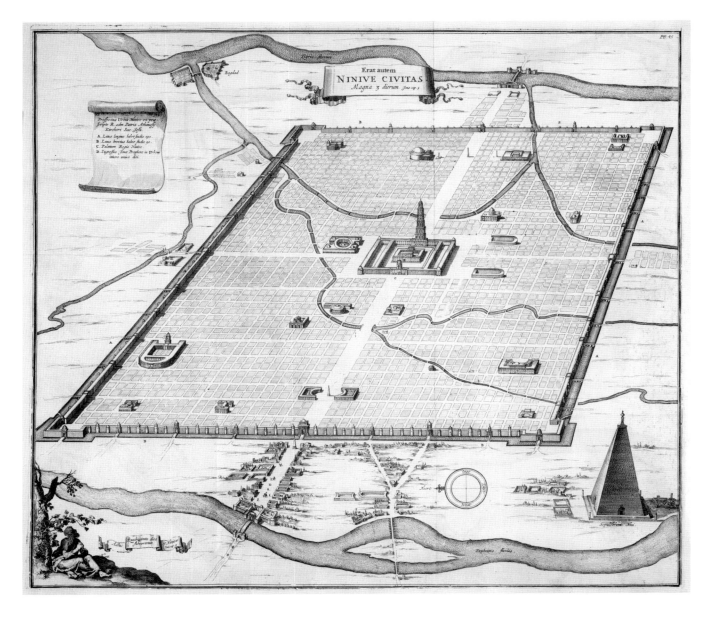

◄ 6.14 A combined plan and view of the city of Nineveh based on biblical description. The prophet Jonah sits lower left. (*Turris Babel*, fp. 44/45)

► 6.15 Babylon. Kircher finds astronomical significance in the figure of 365 stadia given as the circumference of the city. The Hanging Gardens and the Tower of Babylon are prominent. (*Turris Babel*, fp. 52/53)

three days' journey from the sea shore, where the whale deposited Jonah? No, he concludes: it must have taken three days to walk from end to end.[19]

The other pre-classical megalopolis was Babylon. It appears in another masterpiece of engraving by Coenraet Decker (**Ill. 6.15**), headed by a distich: 'This Babylon will never fall with its walls broken, standing to be remembered as long as Kircher endures in the world.' This is a typical indulgence in the conceit that the fame of books and their writers outlasts even empires.

According to Diodorus Siculus, the walls of Babylon were 365 stadia in circumference, which Kircher says must have had an astronomical meaning. He explains that even after the fall of the Tower of Babel had removed their would-be observatory, the Babylonians were keen astronomers. They accepted the 365-day year of Noah's calendar, and made their city correspond to a zodiac divided into 365 degrees, thus perpetuating an astronomical tradition founded by Adam himself. The knowledge had been passed down as follows: Adam instructed Enoch, who after living 365 years was seized up to heaven and 'walked with God, whose admirable works he could then observe carefully'. Enoch taught his son Methusaleh, then the tradition passed through Lamech to Noah, who taught his sons Shem, Cham and Japheth both before and after the Flood. Cham's son was Chus, father of Nimrod; and so the knowledge passed to the great city-builders, including Semiramis, builder of Babylon.[20]

Not to be confused with the biblical Tower of Babel, the Tower of Babylon (**Ill. 6.16**) is described in some detail by Herodotus. Erected by Ninus and his queen Semiramis, it consisted of eight towers of diminishing size, one on top of the other, with a temple of Bel at the summit. Here and there on the spiral ramp were seats for resting and enjoying the view. Inside were rooms for storing archives or supplies, or for public use.[21]

Semiramis, Empress of Assyria around 800 BC, was one of the legendary women of the ancient world. She reputedly reigned for forty-two years, first with her husband Ninus then after his death, building great monuments and cities (including Babylon), waging war and attempting an invasion of India. Kircher had no reason to disbelieve the accounts of her power and personal courage in the histories of Herodotus, Diodorus Siculus and Strabo. However, he had to fit her within the infallible Biblical narrative. He concludes that she flourished around Anno Mundi 2000, i.e. around 2000 BC, and that her husband Ninus was the same as the Assur of Genesis 10:11, who left his father's land of Sennaar (see the maps, **Ills. 12.12–12.15**), conquered the Assyrians and founded the city of Nineveh.[22]

The caption to the illustration of her citadel (**Ill. 6.17**) reads:

Semiramis, with great expense, built two most magnificent palaces in the two regions where the river is bridged. According to Diodorus

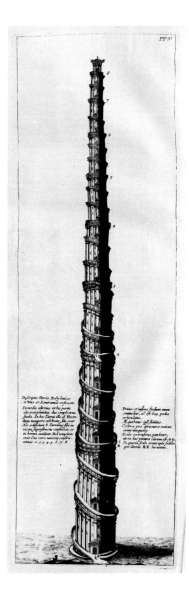

◄ 6.16 The Tower of Babylon follows the description by Herodotus. (*Turris Babel*, fp. 50/51)

► 6.17 Semiramis's citadel, which stood in the centre of the city. This imagined view recalls Plato's citadel of Atlantis with its concentric walls. (*Turris Babel*, 59)

Siculus, the western one had three circuits. The first was 60 stadia and 50 fathoms around, with high and sumptuous walls of fired brick. The tower rose to 70 fathoms. The second circle was forty stadia around and equal in other respects to the first, except that it was made from unbaked brick, on which every sort of creature was painted true to nature. The third and inmost wall, the one surrounding the citadel, is marked C and was thirty stadia around; in length and breadth it exceeded the central structure of the work. The hunt pictured there was especially full of various animals, greater than four cubits in size. And Semiramis was to be seen among them casting a spear at a panther, and nearby her husband Ninus wounding a lion with a lance. For the rest, since the interior structure of the citadel was omitted by Diodorus and Herodotus, the artist's fancy has made a substitute.[23]

Even more of its time is the Baroque fancy with which Kircher's artist recreates the hunting scenes mentioned in the above quotation. In the first (**Ill. 6.18**), the costumes are Roman, and the pyramid on the left is a copy of that of Cestius in Rome. The caption reads: 'A true copy of Ninus and Semiramis, taken from the account of ancient authors and from pictures of the Egyptian Labyrinth.' In the second (**Ill. 6.19**), he adds a group in the distance hunting with firearms.

Among the achievements ascribed to Semiramis was the building of the Hanging Gardens of Babylon (**Ill. 6.20**), one of the Seven Wonders of the World. Since no remnant survives, archaeologists and artists have a clear field in imagining what exactly a 'hanging garden' consisted of. Kircher, as usual, goes to the root of the matter. He writes that each of the four levels of the gardens was 400 by 100 feet in area, so that the entire structure filled a square of 400 feet. He gives the elevations in cubits: the levels from front to

6.18 Ninus and Semiramis hunting. Kircher attempts to reconcile the descriptions of Herodotus, Diodorus Siculus and Strabo, using such models as the Pyramid of Cestius in Rome. (*Turris Babel*, 43)

6.19 Semiramis hunting alone is also based on ancient descriptions, although Kircher's artist permits himself the anacronism of firearms. (*Turris Babel*, 57)

6.20, 6.21 Construction of the Hanging Gardens of Babylon. Kircher imagines four levels of garden, shown first during the process of building and then as completed. (*Turris Babel*, fp. 58/59 and 61)

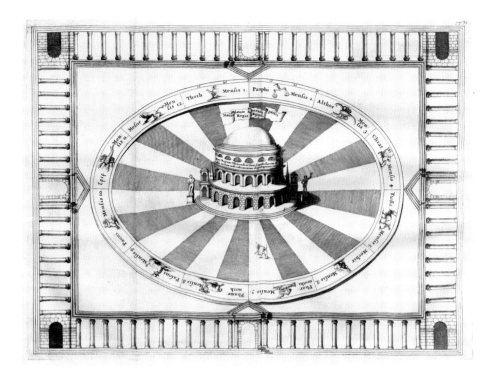

◄ **6.22** The Mausoleum of Mendes. Kircher's description, taken from Diodorus, conveys much more information than the illustration that he provides, including the fact that it was surrounded by a wall four feet thick made of solid gold! (*Turris Babel*, fp. 74/75)

▼ **6.23** The Egyptian labyrinth, another combination of plan (centre) and elevation (surrounding walls). Kircher claims that this labyrinth is impenetrable, as it is; the only entrance leads to a dead end. (*Turris Babel*, fp. 78/79)

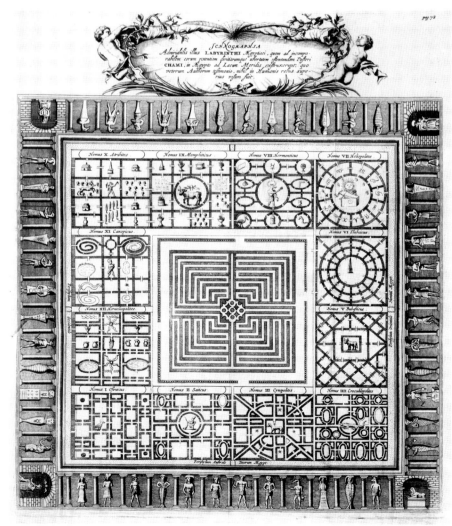

back were 12½, 20, 37½, 50. The purpose of this cut-away diagram is to show how the gardens were built up out of various layers. The lowest level shows the first layer, which consists of slabs sixteen by four feet. Next (shown on the second level) is a layer of beams. Third are sheets of lead. Fourth and last, the level is filled up with earth.

Kircher was trying to solve the problem of making a roof garden that is watertight. There had been partial measures of the kind in the artificial grottoes, arcades and nymphaea of Renaissance gardens (notably at the Villa d'Este), but none of this magnitude. The companion plate (**Ill. 6.21**) shows the gardens completed, though their relation to the river is reversed and the landscape is more specific. The building on the right resembles the Mausoleum of Hadrian (now the Castel Sant'Angelo), and beyond it is another 'Babylonian' spiral tower, like the lantern Borromini placed on the church of Sant'Ivo della Sapienza. On a distant hill is an imitation of the Pantheon.

The structure ingeniously combines two things that are usually separate: a villa and its garden. The support takes the form of an idealized Roman villa in the style of the sixteenth century. Note the herms supporting the left-hand arches – a typical Mannerist motif – and the Palladian arcades. Palladian, too, are the many statues lining the parapets. The gardens, in which there are few trees and no sign of flowers, are geometrical parterres with waterworks. The one concession to practicality is that the fountains become less ambitious as the levels rise.

Kircher's description of the Mausoleum of Mendes, taken from Diodorus, is much richer than the unsatisfactory illustration of it (**Ill. 6.22**). The inscription reads: 'I am Ozymandias, King of Kings. If any wants to know how I was, and where I lie, let him to try to surpass any of my works.'[24] The tomb, domed like the Pantheon, stands in a rectangular arcade resembling the Palazzo del Tè in Mantua. Immediately around it is an oval marked off with the twelve signs of the zodiac and their Graeco-Egyptian names. Two minute figures in the foreground seem to be playing a sort of hockey, with ladle-shaped sticks and a ball. But without Kircher's text, we would suspect nothing of the vastness of the statues, the huge monolithic columns, the wall paintings and the cosmic significance of its 365-cubit circumference. Diodorus also says that it was walled with gold, one cubit thick. Taking a cubit to be four feet, Kircher calculates that a cubic cubit (a four-foot cube) of gold weighs 10,000 pounds (in fact, it weighs much more), so that the entire wall, if only a cubit high, would have taken 3,650,000 pounds of gold – 'which the mind can scarcely conceive of'.[25]

Kircher's account of ancient history has now reached Egypt, which he introduces not with pyramids but with the labyrinth (**Ill. 6.23**). This plate somewhat resembles that of Mendes's Mausoleum, showing its four exterior walls in elevation, but inside the mode of presentation changes to a floor-plan. The Egyptian labyrinth was near Lake Moeris, and enjoyed a reputation as one of the wonders of the ancient world (though not one of the official 'Seven Wonders'). The classical writers explain that its layout reflected the nomes or districts of Egypt, but differ in how many of these divisions there were:

Strabo says thirty, Pliny, twenty, Herodotus, twelve. Kircher follows Herodotus, with a typical allusion to the doctrine of correspondences:

so that the separate parts are equal in size, and according to the mysteries that were offered the gods in the different nomes of Egypt with remarkable, splendid and occult ceremonies; they were very different because of the hidden structure of the houses and dwellings. The immense edifice of this labyrinth expressed nothing less than the temple of the immortal Gods, whither the Kings wished to betake themselves together with their immense treasures. So this building was like an epitome and compendium of that temple that they believed the whole of Egypt to be, full of the cult of the Egyptian gods.[26]

Kircher says that the most precious treasures were kept in the central region, but they could not be found either from within or without, and anyone who did manage to get inside would die before he found an exit.[27] Whether deliberately or not, the labyrinth in the centre of this illustration is impenetrable: the sole entrance, on the right, leads to a dead end.

The illustration of the Cretan labyrinth (**Ill. 6.24**) is titled: 'A fish-eye view of another labyrinth, constructed after the Egyptian model by the architect Daedalus on the isle of Crete, which the fabulous stories of Theseus, Minos, Ariadne and the Minotaur, the ancient poets and orators afterwards made famous.' Quite apart from the tame-looking bull, this labyrinth does not much resemble the Egyptian one. While there each nome is a maze of many chambers, passages and dead ends, through which an endless number of routes are possible, this is a labyrinth with only one entrance and only one possible route. Theseus would not have needed Ariadne's thread, because the route (marked with a dotted line) systematically covers the entire area. Its model is the medieval pilgrimage labyrinth, of which the best-known example is on the floor of Chartres Cathedral.

Kircher seems to skim over Egypt in his survey of the ancient world's wonders, but excusably so. In his time the great Nile temples of Luxor, Karnak, Abydos, Philae and Abu Simbel were unknown in Europe, and even the many pyramids were under-reported. It would remain for later generations to depict Egypt as it had been. He next illustrates the Colossus of Rhodes (**Ill. 6.25**), which was a statue of the sun god, Apollo, bestriding the entrance to the harbour. As it says on the pedestals, it was the work of Cares of Lindos, pupil of Lysippus. It was 70 cubits high (i.e., by Kircher's metrology, between 105 and 280 feet), and perished in an earthquake 56 years after its construction. Kircher goes much into the measurements and other statistics, comparing reports both credible and otherwise. He reflects on how many Greek and Roman monuments have utterly disappeared, whilst those of Egypt (and he must mean the obelisks) still remain to this day, unrivalled.[28]

As dominance passed from Babylon, Egypt and Greece to Rome, we can continue to follow Kircher's historical recreations in *Latium*. Much of the book is

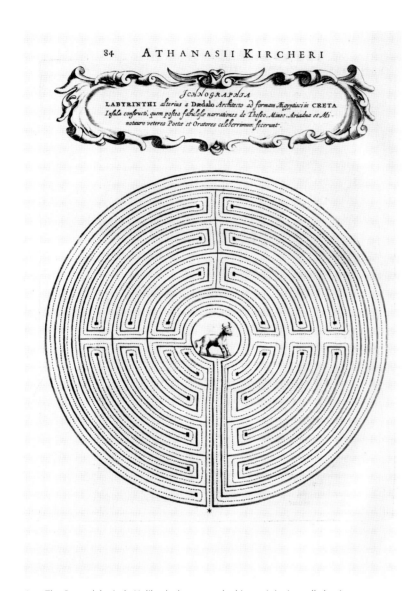

6.24 The Cretan labyrinth. Unlike the last example this one is 'unicursal', that is, there is only one route and no choices. (*Turris Babel*, 84)

6.25 The Colossus of Rhodes, a bronze statue of Apollo, believed in antiquity to have stood astride the harbour entrance. (*Turris Babel*, 89)

dedicated to ancient history, and to determining the exact dates and places of events. In particular, he sought to solve the controversy over where Ascanius, son of Aeneas, built his city Alba Longa. To this end, Kircher illustrates the Alban Lake and its environs as they were in antiquity (**Ill. 6.26**). Consistent with his interest in subterranean things, the plate shows the influx of water from the mountain into the lake, and the channels from which the water flows out of it. Ascanius's city stretches along a single wide street, and if one did not know better, one would think that it contained several churches. At the top left is the 'Field of Hannibal, once the place of the Latins' festivals', and just below it 'Forum of the people, today Rocca di Papa'.

More realistic is the artist's impression of the Temple of Fortune at Praeneste (**Ill. 6.27**), already mentioned in connection with the mosaic of the Nile flood (see **Ill. 5.22**). By the time Kircher visited its remains in 1664, the modern town of Palestrina had all but obscured them, absorbing the temple walls, staircases and 'twelve distinct areas'[29] into its own system of streets ascending the hill (see **Ill. 12.19**). The locations described in this plate (though not all marked) are as follows. A: the citadel of Praeneste. B, C: villas. D: aqueduct. E: 'Cauldron, or Oracle of Fortuna, like a theatre where there were the statue of Jupiter nursing and the chest with the lots'. F: two chapels. G: courtyard. H: temples of Cornelia and Aemilia. I: Serapeum. K: Faustina's

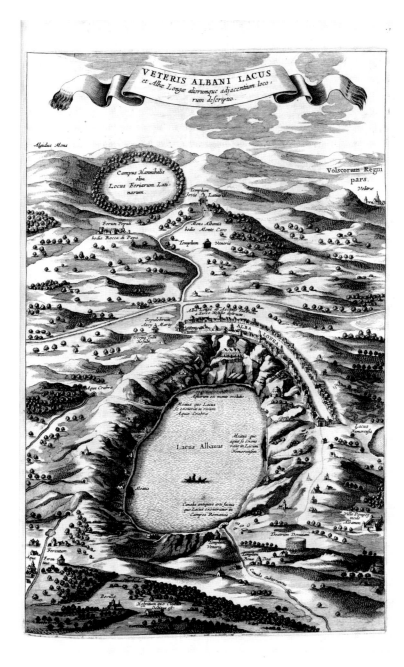

6.26 The Alban Lake in antiquity.
Alba Longa, built by Aeneas's son Ascanius,
is shown as a single wide street to the top
right of the lake. (*Latium*, opposite 32)

school for girls. L: courtyard. M: two ponds. N: crypts. O: terraces. P: stairs. Q: portico or shaded walk. R: inlaid pavement. S: areas decorated with mosaics. T: here lights were lit, visible at sea.[30]

The view of the Temple of Fortune is almost modern in its restraint and plausibility. The reconstructions in Kircher's later works tend to be neither. In *Obeliscus Ægyptiacus* he offered his audience a view of the Temple of Isis Campensis in Rome (**Ill. 6.28**). Caligula built Rome's first Iseum on the Campus Martius in AD 38, and Domitian enlarged it fifty years later. Until the Empire's end it remained one of Rome's most majestic temple complexes, serving Europe's first great wave of Egyptomania,[31] but Kircher's illustrator makes it look as if it came out of an ill-assorted toybox. There is no sign of the avenue that led between sphinxes and 'cynocephalous' baboons, and nothing remotely resembling the great Isis temple, whether this was more Egyptian or Roman in style. Whilst the grandeur of the obelisks was there for any Roman to see (though even these seem to be diminished here), there was as yet no appreciation of the gigantic figural sculpture such as we know from the Nile temples mentioned above. Far from letting his imagination run riot, as Balatri did when he capped the mummy crypt with a cluster of spiky pyramids (see **Ill. 5.24**), this artist seems to have timidly followed Kircher's own best effort.

A far more confident hand was at work in the depiction of Maecenas's villa (**Ill. 6.29**). Kircher notes that the porticos (A, B, C, D) are still extant today, as are the semicircular structures (E, F, G), though devoid of ornament. The rest he has reconstructed 'not as it was, but as it could and must have been' in its days of glory. More than that, he has given his readers a vision of the ideal setting for literary conversation and civilized country living, as he himself must occasionally have enjoyed in the modern villas of the region. He writes wistfully about it:

> In this villa, Maecenas, living in utter quietude, gladdened his soul with the most agreeable studies, far from any stigma of ambition. No one was dearer and more welcome to him than Augustus, who when the weight of the world pressed on him would come to this villa as to a holy hermitage, to free a mind wearied by a multitude of cares and take refuge in the pleasant company of Maecenas. And since Maecenas was always most open and generous to writers, so learned men from everywhere were attracted by his fame and gathered around him. He entertained them at his own expense, not only supplying everything they needed for maintaining the dignity of literary work, but giving in abundance and excess. Consequently, those who support the studies of literary men are called 'Maecenas' to this day. Among others, he showed incredible affection and benevolence to Virgil and Horace, of whose conversation he could scarcely have enough.[32]

While Kircher identified the site of Maecenas's villa within a bend of the River Aniene, that of Varus (**Ill. 6.30**) was on a hilltop on the other side of

ORTHOGRAPHIA TEMPLI FORTUNÆ PRÆNESTÆ.

SCIOGRAPHIA TEMPLI FORTUNÆ PRÆNESTÆ.

A *Arx Prænestina* B *Villa Cetroni*
C *Villa Symmachi*
D *Fontes Aquæductus evariis venis cor-*
    rivatis ad usum Templi et Civitatis
E *Corona sive Oraculum Fortunæ instar Thea-*
    tri ubi simulacrum Deæ Jovem Lactentem gesti-
    tantis et arca cum Sortibus erant & ubi nunc
    quæ Oracula ibi nunc Palatium Principis
F *Sacella duo circa Cortinum*
G *Cavædium magnum inter duas Basilicas*
    sive ut sunt vulgo cortile
H *Duæ Basilicæ hinc Cornelia illinc*
    Æmilia
I *Serapium ubi colebatur Serapis*
K *Schola Faustinæ ab alio latere ubi quæ*
    Faustinæ Augustæ fuerant devota puel-
    læ alebantur
L *Cavædium minus vulgo Cortile inter*
    Serapium et Scholam Faustinianam
M *Piscinæ duæ sive Lavacra variis aquis*
    collectis porexosos Aquæductus ad
    ministeria Sacrificiorum et alios usus
N *Cryptæ substructiones et Exhedræ vulgo*
    Grotte Circuito di muraglie o
    Nicchie
O *Areæ XII. seu Piani ut dici solet vulgo*
P *Gradationes seu Scalæ XII.*
Q *Porticus sive Ambulacra*
R *Lithostraton, seu Pavimentum aliquot-*
    Areæum
S *Musæum quo areæ aliquot superiores et*
    Cryptæ ac exhedræ tam Cortinæ quam
    Sacellorum et Basilicarum erant coronatæ
T *Pharus ubi sacæ accendebantur ut na-*
    vibus prælucerent

6.27 The Temple of Fortune at Praeneste. Kircher's reconstruction of this large Roman site includes the citadel, villas, temple and portico, all recorded in ancient sources but in his time buried under the later town of Palestrina. (*Latium*, fp. 94/95)

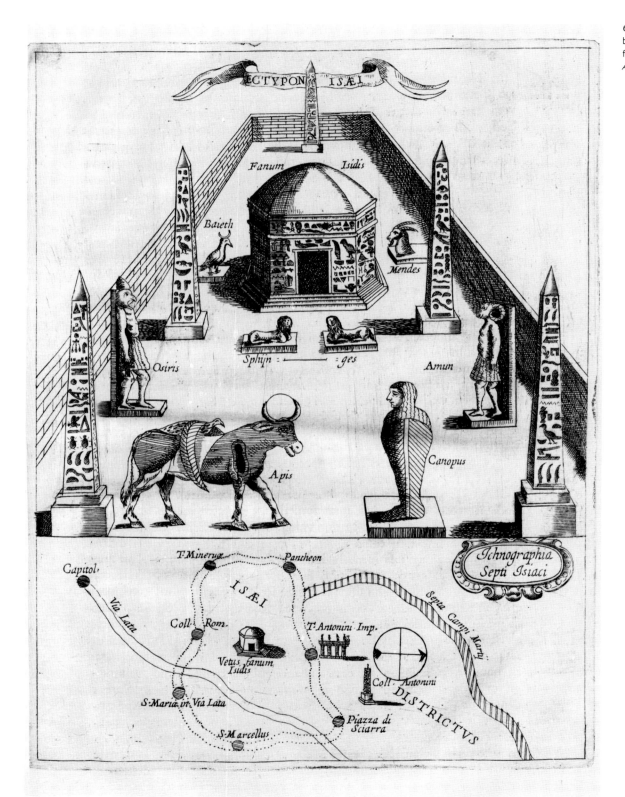

ECTYPON ISÆI

Fanum Isidis

Baieth

Mendes

Osiris

Sphijn : = : ges

Amun

Apis

Canopus

Ichnographia Septi Isiaci

Capitol

T.Mineruæ   Pantheon

ISÆI

Via Lata

Coll: Rom.

T. Antonini Imp.

Septa Campi Martij

Vetus fanum Isidis

S: Mariæ in Via Lata

Coll: Antonini

DISTRICTVS

S: Marcellus

Piazza di Sciarra

6.28 The Temple of Isis in Rome, built by Caligula and incorporating many features of an Egyptian temple. (*Obeliscus Ægyptiacus*, 7)

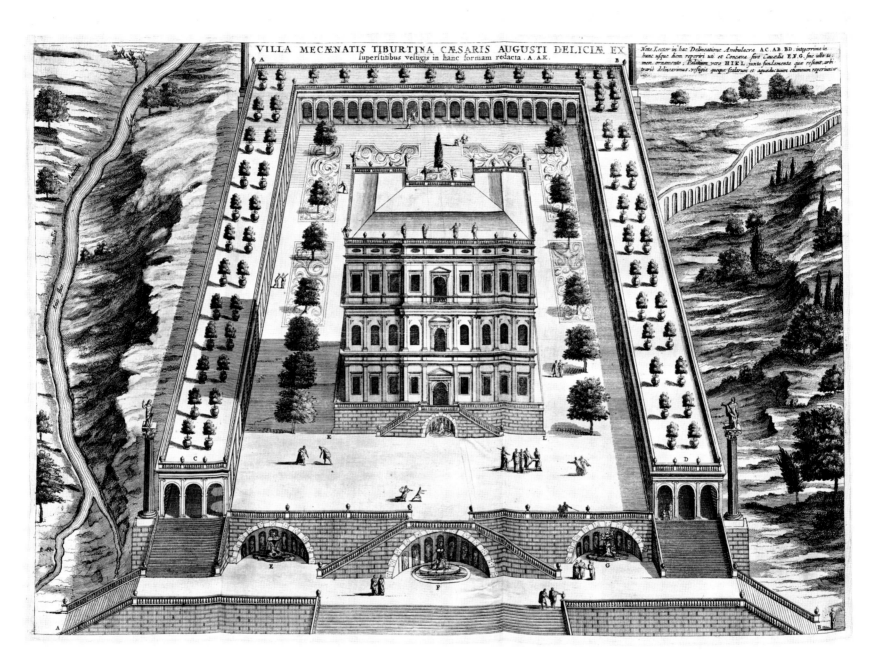

VILLA MECÆNATIS TIBURTINA CÆSARIS AUGUSTI DELICIÆ, EX
superftitibus veftigis in hanc formam redacta . A. A.K.

Nota Lector in hac Delineatione Ambulacra AC.AB BD. integerrima in
hunc ufque diem reperiri uti et Concava. five Cavedia E.F.G. fine ullo tamen. ornamento: Palatium vero HIKL. juxta fundamenta que reftant. arbi
trarie delineavimus. veftigia quoque fcalarum et aquaeductuum. eluuuuun. reperiuntur.

6.29 Villa of Maecenas, some parts
still extant in Kircher's time and others
conjecturally reconstructed. (*Latium*,
opposite 157)

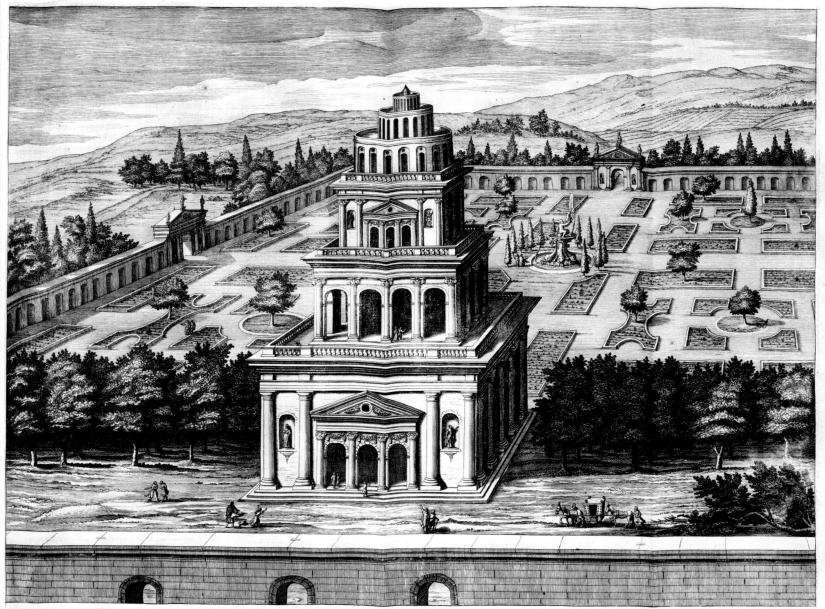

VILLA QVINTILY VARI, PROPINQVI CÆSARIS AVGVSTI.

6.30 Villa of Quintilius Varus, copied
from an earlier engraving and imagined
as a Mannerist pleasure garden. (*Latium*,
opposite 158)

the river. Kircher's artist, however, has copied the picture of Maecenas's villa from Giacomo Lauro's *Antiquae Urbis Vestigia* (1637, plate 104). In the process he has greatly elaborated and beautified Lauro's simplistic engraving, supplying a garden of geometrical parterres, a Mannerist fountain and contemporary staffage, just like the villas of Kircher's time. Not content with that, he crowns it with a structure reminiscent of the Tower of Babel.

Kircher was particularly interested in the remains of the waterworks of Varus's villa and in understanding how its gardens were fed through aqueducts. According to Antonius del Rè, author of a book on Tivoli, the whole villa had been paved in mosaic, sparkling with gemlike colours. Cardinal Montinus, while vacationing there, was the first to discover the remnants of these pavements. He searched the ruins for any remaining stones, and sent twenty horse-loads back to Rome, for his use and as gifts to other princes.[33]

The latest historical event illustrated in *Latium* is the conversion at Mentorella of the Roman officer Placidus, who became St Eustace (**Ill. 6.31**). This is how Kircher relates the story:

> While St Eustace, then called Placidus, was hunting on Mount Vulturellus, he came upon a stag of immense size. He thought that he had it cornered in a narrow passage of the mountain, when suddenly the stag made a prodigious leap and landed on the cliff, 115 palms above him. Placidus was dumbstruck by this marvel, and while his eyes and attention were fastened on the beast, now standing on top of the cliff, behold! he saw Christ crucified between the horns of the stag, opening to him the door of eternal life. He did what he must, and, hastening to Rome, had himself purified in the sacred font of baptism; then returning to this place he obtained proofs of eternal salvation and learned the proper conduct of life.[34]

In the scene, the future saint kneels on the plan of the later church. 'Placidus, why are you hunting me?' says the stag. 'Lord, what would you have me do?' he replies. Constantine the Great, Kircher continues, built a church there, which Pope Sylvester consecrated to the Virgin Mary and St Eustace. It was destroyed by the Gothic invasions, then restored by St Benedict, who built a monastery, but by the time Kircher came upon it in 1661, it had fallen into ruin. He resolved to rebuild the church and reinstate it as a place of pilgrimage, which it remains.

In fact, this episode was probably not imagined by Kircher or his artist, for an identical scene is painted inside the church of Mentorella, on a concave surface less than a foot square above the piscina. Its damaged condition and position make it difficult to judge the style, but I suspect that, like the wall painting of the dragon-slaying monk (see **Ill. 5.39**), it belongs to the late mediaeval period. If so, it served as the model both for the illustration in *Historia Eustachio-Mariana* (1665) and, nine years later, for Johann Paul Schor's fresco in the chapel of St Eustace (see **Ill. 3.13**).

6.31 The conversion of St Eustace. Eustace was the Roman officer Placidus who was converted by meeting a stag with an image of Christ crucified between its horns. (*Latium*, 186)

Notes

1 *Œdipus Ægyptiacus*, II, i, 4–5.

2 *Arca Noë*, 238–239.

3 *Turris Babel*, 216–217.

4 Pastine, 111.

5 *Arca Noë*, 25.

6 Beside letters, Kircher uses for references the symbols of the planets, the zodiac and the north and south nodes of the moon (the symbols resembling earphones).

7 Reading *de ARCA* for *de ARCÆ*.

8 'Creation science', flourishing on the Internet in an unabashedly Kircherian spirit, has now explained what was in those extra chambers. It was dinosaurs, though only smallish ones, whose descendants rapidly mutated into the familiar species. No one thinks that Noah had to deal with *Tyrannosaurus Rex*. See, for example, www. answersingenesis.org (accessed 21 February 2009).

9 Metrology was not of great importance to Kircher, to judge from how he reckoned the biblical 'cubit'. As a traditional measure based on the length of the lower arm, it is about 1½ feet (45 cm), and this sometimes seems to be what he intends. But in his calculations concerning the Mausoleum of Mendes (see Ill. 6.22) the cubit equals 4 feet; when discussing the monolithic temple (see Ill. 10.14) it is 2 feet; and in his discussion of the dimensions of the Ark (see Ill. 15.6), he mentions a 'geometric cubit' of 6 feet (*Arca Noë*, 28).

10 The figure of Noah is taken from that of Noah praying before the Flood in Merian's *Icones Biblicae*, I, 25.

11 *Turris Babel*, 117.

12 *Turris Babel*, 118.

13 Kircher dates this event to Anno Mundi 1984, exactly 2,000 years before the birth of Christ.

14 Introduction to Stolzenberg 2001, 3. The science of pataphysics, founded by Alfred Jarry (author of *Ubu Roi*), is said to bear the same relation to metaphysics as metaphysics does to physics.

15 *Turris Babel*, 39.

16 *Turris Babel*, 40.

17 To judge by the Dutch compass directions (Noort, Oost, Zuyt, West), the printer used an existing plate.

18 Shakespeare immortalized this in *A Midsummer Night's Dream* as 'old Ninny's tomb'.

19 *Turris Babel*, 45–46.

20 *Turris Babel*, 54.

21 *Turris Babel*, 51.

22 *Turris Babel*, 42.

23 Decker's fancy has called on various Roman monuments: the Castel Sant'Angelo at the top, then the Campidoglio as seen from the Forum and the apse of the Vatican Belvedere, which at this time did contain an obelisk.

24 These words served as the theme for Shelley's poem *Ozymandias* (1817).

25 *Turris Babel*, 76–77.

26 *Turris Babel*, 79.

27 *Turris Babel*, 80.

28 *Turris Babel*, 80.

29 *Latium*, 98.

30 For the reconstruction, and for much else that he recounts about the site, Kircher credits Francesco Maria Suares's *De Antiquitatibus Praenestinis*, a book on the antiquities of Praeneste commissioned by Cardinal Barberini.

31 See Baltrušaitis 1967, 7–8.

32 *Latium*, 157–158.

33 *Latium*, 159.

34 *Latium*, 185.

Chapter 7   Naturalia: Fire and Water

In his astronomical writings Kircher took the bold but inevitable step of discarding the Aristotelian cosmology. Aristotle's fundamental principle, as laid out in *De Caelo*, was that the cosmos is without beginning or end; that everything above the sphere of the moon is made from aether, eternal and immutable, and moves in perfect circles, while the sublunary world is made of the four elements of fire, air, water and earth in perpetual flux. By Kircher's time, this tidy scheme was crumbling, along with the Ptolemaic system of planetary motions that had been grafted onto it. As he writes in *Œdipus Ægyptiacus*, 'We know that stars appear and disappear; even the sun has spots; the moon has mountains, seas, and valleys that were unseen for centuries; Venus, the ape of the moon, has horns; Jupiter has satellites; comets are known to be above the sun.'[1] In *Itinerarium Exstaticum*, he expatiates on these discoveries and concludes that the heavenly bodies, like the earth, are created from the elements, subject to change, and scheduled for destruction, as anyone can read in the Book of Revelation.[2] In other words, they are part of the natural order, just as the earth is. With this conclusion, Kircher was moving with a current of scientific opinion whose importance for the history of astronomy cannot be underestimated.

In this and the following chapter, we survey Kircher's views of the natural world, beginning with the heavenly bodies and proceeding through the drama of fire and water that he revealed within the body of the earth, then moving to his depictions of some of the earth's lesser phenomena, animal, vegetable, and mineral. We begin with the sun.

As early as 4 April 1625, in Mainz, Kircher had seen for himself sunspots and solar flares.[3] Ten years later, he worked with his fellow Jesuit Christoph Scheiner (1575–1650) and the telescope called *Rosa Ursina* in the further investigation and drawing of sunspots, but when he published his first picture of them (**Ill. 7.1**), he was still hedging his bets as to what this all meant. He wrote: 'I declare that the sun is a fiery body compounded of ethereal fluid, and a material sphere of light of the firstborn world, filled with a certain universal seed.'[4] In his ecstatic journey (first published 1656), the angel Cosmiel rowed him on the sun's surface in an asbestos boat. The solar nature continued to puzzle him, but it certainly seemed to be a mixture of solid and liquid, and when his artist came to create the spectacular sunscape of *Mundus Subterraneus* (**Ill. 7.2**), the result was surprisingly like the most recent photographs of the solar surface, with its dark spots, swirling currents, and flares.

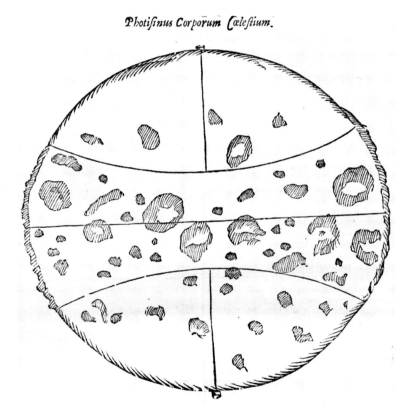

Photismus Corporum Cælestium.

7.1 Sunspots, drawn from the telescopic observations of Kircher and fellow Jesuits. (*Ars Magna Lucis*, 3)

Kircher's ideas about the sun anticipate those of some modern cosmologists who are struck by the incredible finesse of the cosmic balances, and the series of extraordinary chances that have made it possible for humans to exist. He writes:

If the distance of the sun from the earth were much less than it is, then the excess of light that always strikes the greater part of the globe would cause the greatest intemperance among things.... If the sun were smaller than it is, everything would suffer from cold and

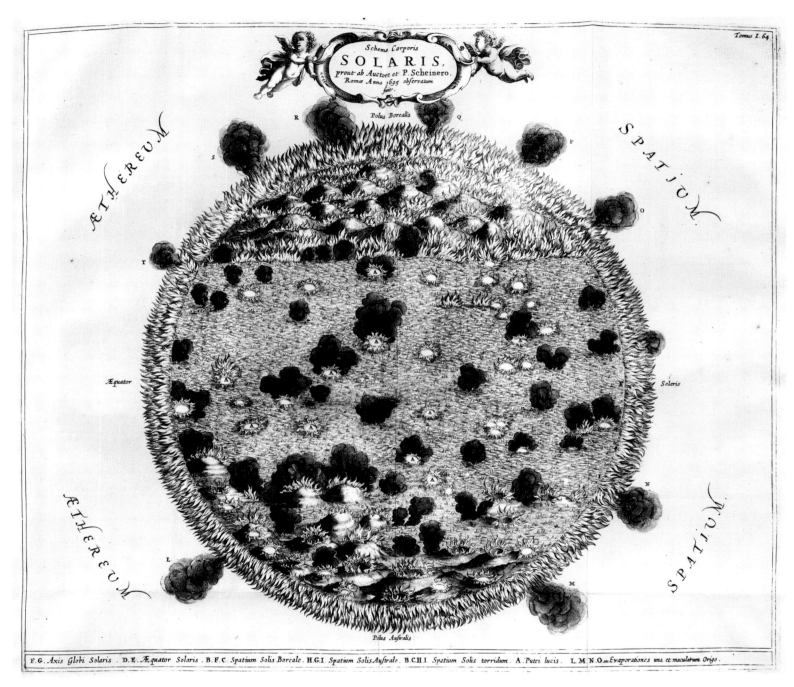

7.2 The sun: Kircher's guess was that the
sun was a mixture of solid and liquid.
(*Mundus Subterraneus*, Volume I, opposite 64)

TYPUS CORPORIS LUNARIS PANSELINI, UNA CUM MACULIS, FACULIS, MONTIBUS,

Fontiumque ebullitionibus, magno studio et labore à Mathematicis Collegij Romani Soc: Jesu duce et Præside P. Scheinero quæ ab Anno 1636 usque ad Annum 1650 novis subinde additis observata et in hanc formam redacta fuerunt.

Tomus I.62

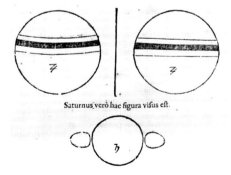

Saturnus verò hac figura visus est.

7.3 Jupiter and Saturn, as revealed by the new telescope. Kircher was sent these images by Florentine astronomers. (*Ars Magna Lucis*, 11)

7.4 The moon, an image based on the latest observations. Kircher believed it also to be solid and liquid, but cold, rough, and dense. (*Mundus Subterraneus*, Volume I, opposite 62)

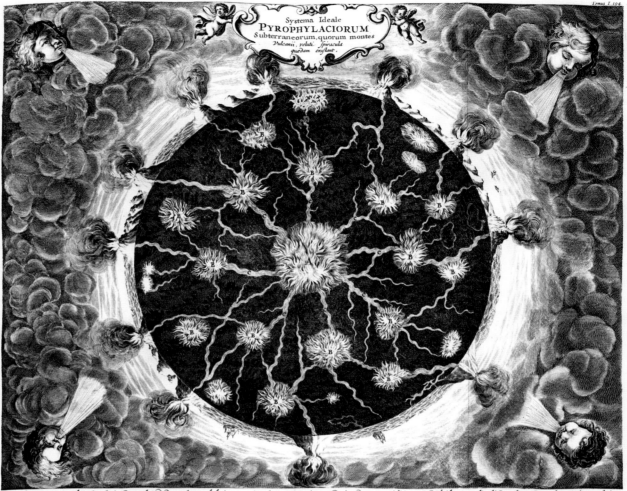

7.5 Subterranean fires. Kircher's very full description follows that of Giovanni Nardi. (*Mundus Subterraneus*, Volume I, opposite 194)

darkness while the hither side of the globe alone was illuminated. Thus the earthly globe is made in such proportion that no race on earth can complain of an insufficient portion of heat or light.[5]

Less spectacularly, but no less significantly, *Ars Magna Lucis* showed the planets Jupiter and Saturn as the telescope had revealed them (**Ill. 7.3**). These images had been sent to Kircher from the Academy of the Lincei in Florence (the academy to which Galileo had belonged), and were based on observations taken in October and November, 1643. The vacillation of Jupiter's belt is easily visible. Saturn's rings, at a certain angle and under low telescopic power, were interpreted as resembling two egg-shaped satellites, but observers soon had to revise this view as the angle of the rings changed and telescopes improved. Kircher took no notice of this, and let his printer use the same blocks for the second edition of *Ars Magna Lucis* in 1671 as for the first.

The sun and moon might seem to have no place in a treatise on the subterranean world, but in Kircher's leisurely scheme they served as a necessary prelude to his theory of the earth. They bracketed it as the two extremes: the sun was a fiery body, the moon a watery one, and the earth's inner mechanism, receiving influences from both of them, was, as we shall see, a blend of fire and water. Kircher's depiction of the moon (**Ill. 7.4**) is less imaginative than that of the sun, being based on the latest observations without any attempt at interpreting the markings. He explains its function thus:

These two bodies, our earth and that ethereal earth of the moon, are very similar, for they cherish and protect one another.... The moon is a rough body, and like our earth very dense and opaque, made from solid and liquid. Not only does it perfectly imbibe the solar rays, but

TYPUS MONTIS
ÆTNÆ
ab Authore
Observati
A: 1637.

7.6 Mount Etna in eruption, observed by Kircher from a safe distance. (*Mundus Subterraneus*, Volume I, opposite 1)

it reflects them to us with a mutual communication of energies. Lest the influx be always the same, the most wise Architect has made it such that in the space of a month it always shows an unequal aspect…. You will see here its extraordinary face, made from shadows and lights, not unlike the preceding phenomenon of the sun, but with this one difference: the torches and spots on the sun are always changing, whereas on the moon they are always the same and unmoved. You would think you were seeing immense seas, washing against the tracts of land.[6]

Since the similarity of the macrocosm with the microcosm was a first principle of Kircher's natural philosophy, he continually drew on human anatomy to explain that of the earth:

Just as in the microcosm of the human body, heat, diffused through all the channels of the whole body, animates everything with its spirits, vivifies it, renews it, agitates it, united with the mass of the humours, even so nature's Artificer has constituted the geocosm no less providentially. He has provided it with copious and plentiful fires in conformity with such a mass, lest anything be lacking necessary for its natural operations.[7]

The illustration of the fires within the earth (**Ill. 7.5**) is deservedly one of the most famous in all of Kircher's works. We have already seen what was probably his own sketch of it (**Ill. 3.5**). But there was another model for it. Kircher's friend Giovanni Nardi, the Florentine antiquarian, had already written a book on the subterranean fire (*De Igne Subterraneo Physica Prolusio*, Florence, 1641). Its frontispiece shows the earth belching forth smoke from many

Tomus I.
in præfatione Caput III.

TYPUS MONTIS
VESUVII
Prout ab Authore
A.º 1638. visus fuit.

7.7 Mount Vesuvius in eruption. In researching Vesuvius, the intrepid Kircher made one of the earliest descents into the crater, leaving a vivid description of what he saw. (*Mundus Subterraneus*, Volume I, opposite 200)

orifices, with the Virgilian motto *Intus alit* that was also a favourite of Kircher's (see **Ill. 2.10**). Nardi's text, too, is like a foretaste of Kircher's much larger work. It includes arguments for the necessity and reality of the subterranean fire, testimonies of classical and patristic authors, what feeds the subterranean fire, its benefits, promoting generation, clouds, rain, frost, dew, snow, hail, winds, thunder and lightning, sources, taste of waters, medicinal springs, tides, earthquakes, fossils, metals, and a hundred questions with answers – for example, why is the sea salty? Why are there prodigious rains of blood, flesh, stones, and milk? *Mundus Subterraneus* ends up treating almost every one of them.

Kircher explains that some of the fires within the earth, notably the central one, are perpetual, while others come and go, depending on the combustible substances they find.

The material of the subterranean fire is not only sulphur, bitumen, or fossil carbon, but also alum, salt, nitre, antimony, carbonized earth, *calcanthum* [limestone?], and that type called metallic. For sulphur and bitumen cannot make so fierce a fire as to overturn mountains and bury cities in the ashes and pumice that the volcano expels; a fire that naturally vomits forth new mountains out of the old ones, as is plain from the foregoing; but something else must be added to it to achieve this effect.[8]

But what makes the subterranean fire so violent? Simple combustion is not enough; it must be some explosive mixture akin to gunpowder. This was Kircher's considered opinion after his own experiences with erupting volcanoes. He was probably the first scientist to study them close up – certainly he was one of the most foolhardy. He had already watched from a safe distance the eruptions of Stromboli and Etna (**Ill. 7.6**) and the total destruction of the island of St Euphemia before he made his famous descent into the crater of Vesuvius (**Ill. 7.7**):

> I reached Portici, the town at the roots of the mountain, and from there was led by a trusty peasant who knew the way, paying him a handsome fee. In the middle of the night I climbed the mountain by hard and rugged paths. When I reached the crater, horrible to relate, I saw it all lit up by fire, with an intolerable exhalation of sulphur and burning bitumen. Thunderstruck by the unheard-of spectacle, I believed I was peering into the realm of the dead, and seeing the horrid phantasms of demons, no less. I perceived the groaning and shaking of the dreadful mountain, the inexplicable stench, the dark smoke mixed with globes of fire which the bottom and sides of the mountain continuously vomited forth from eleven different places, forcing me at times to vomit it out myself.... When dawn broke, I decided to explore diligently the whole of the interior constitution of the mountain. I chose a safe place where a firm foothold might be had, and descended to a vast rock with a flat surface to which the mountain slope gave access. There I set up my Pantometer and measured the dimensions of the mountain.[9]

After this intrepid adventure, Kircher sought in vain for an explanation of mountains in general, and vulcanism in particular. He could not accept the current theories that mountains were merely created by chance or made from heaps of mud left by the Flood. His theocentric conception of the universe led to a far different conclusion. He was convinced that the 'architectonics' of the globe must have some meaning; it must have been designed by God in just as deliberate a way as the human body.[10] With this presupposition, he set out to answer all of Nardi's questions. This is how he explains the mechanics of volcanoes:

> The food and kindling of the subterranean fire follows the movement of the sea, alternating in perpetual flux and reflux. This impulse drives through the hidden channels in which it is often confined; its density and humidity combine with the heat and dryness that nestle beneath the sulphurous soils in the inner passages of the earth, and it restores what was consumed with the ceaseless fruit of a new birth. Then on the outer surface, on account of vapours drawn from the sea and rich in the sea's fruits, it plants a new seed among the porous beds of burnt matter, by means of snows, hail, and rains mixed with dust and ashes; and this matter, now ripened in due course, erupts in a great fire. Thus you see the wondrous and unfailing revolution of nature in its operations.[11]

On the same journey, Kircher saw the Phlegrean Fields, celebrated by many Roman authors (**Ill. 7.8**).

7.8 Volcanic fissures in the Phlegrean Fields, near Naples. (*Mundus Subterraneus*, Volume I, 190)

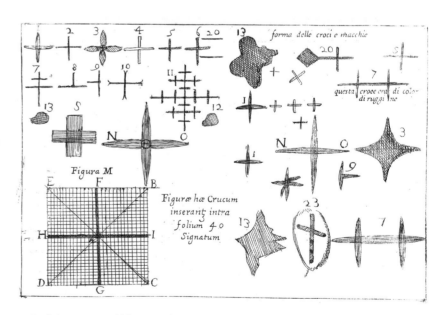

7.9 Prodigious crosses, which appeared on people's clothes in 1660. Kircher thought them too imperfect to be attributable to angels. (*Diatribe de Prodigiosis Crucibus*, 40, 41)

The vast pit in that field aroused my utmost admiration, for the waters there were perpetually boiling, which, with their blackness, struck one with awe. You would think it was pitch and resin boiling in a saucepan, which kept changing place; and with the waters hardening at the edge of the cauldron, it bulged or enlarged along with the greater or lesser impetus of the exhalation. It was a wonder to see the vortex throw the waters up in a pyramid higher than a man, eight to ten feet in the air; also that they were thick and yellow, almost the colour of sulphur.... And horrible as the place is, a lot of profit is made by those who work at making sulphur, nitre, and vitriol.[12]

Following the eruption of Vesuvius in 1660, mysterious crosses appeared on people's clothes, and Kircher, now the recognized expert on all and everything, was asked to explain the phenomenon. This called forth his little book *Diatribe de Prodigiosis Crucibus*, in which he illustrates the various forms that these crosses took (**Ill. 7.9**). Here is his verdict:

It is apparent from all the evidence presented here that such phenomena of crosses cannot strictly be classed among miracles, since they do not exceed the boundaries of Nature. We have an indication of this in the fact that the work of angels, perpetually labouring according to the archetype of Nature, is perfect and shows no defects, whereas crosses of this sort are very imperfect in shape, colour, and quantity. Therefore I would say strongly that they are not to be ascribed to angels, but to Nature.[13]

Observing the peculiar substances thrown up by volcanoes and other geophysical anomalies led Kircher to formulate a theory of metallic formation. The framework within which he develops it was already almost obsolete – the Paracelsian triad of sulphur, mercury, and salt as the parent principles of all substances – and the process he describes is sheer alchemy. This is how he integrates it with his theory of vulcanism (see **Ill. 7.10**):

Let there be a subterranean pyrophylax [fire reservoir] X, whose cauldron is filled with mineral water, or is the mercurio-sulphurous matrix. It diffuses its vapours, exalted by fire, through various tubes into the different matrices of the mountains C D E F. If then the first matrix or cucurbit [alchemical vessel] A is full of sulphur, mercury and salt, from it is born with the help of the said fire a mecurial-sulphuric-saline spermatic vapour, which passes through channel BC. If at the matrix C it meets with a pure vein of sulphur, the cold condenses it all into water, just as in the alembic, and imbues it with the pure ruby-coloured sulphur of the place. Its colour is moderated by channel BC, and with time the humid element is consumed and it is converted into gold. But if the vapour goes through channel BD into the matrix D, it encounters a white sulphur, not yet pure or sufficiently cooked, and then it will produce silver.[14]

He goes on to enumerate the conditions under which the same initial vapour will produce copper, iron, molybdenum, lead and tin. But if the earth's mechanism worked by fire alone, everything would be reduced to ashes. Kircher's theory demanded the complementary action of subterranean waters, just as his planetary theory required the joint action of sun and moon. One plate (**Ill. 7.11**) shows the fire at the centre of the earth (A), diffusing its fiery spirits through subterranean channels and the underground vats and veins of water. The commentary explains that when these spirits encounter subterranean water, they turn partly to hot springs and partly to vapours, which seep through the cavities and condense into water. Some of this emerges as

7.10 Matrix of the metals, which Kircher interprets as if it were an alchemist's laboratory, capable of producing gold and silver. (*Mundus Subterraneus*, Volume II, 255)

7.11 Subterranean waters, turned into hot springs by contact with the subterranean fire. (*Mundus Subterraneus*, Volume I, opposite 180)

springs or rivers; some coalesces to form the 'matrices of metals' or else combustible material to further nourish the fire. The pressure of the winds forces the sea water down through vortices, from which it makes its way into the caves beneath the mountains. Kircher ends the caption: 'But the illustration will teach you everything better than I can explain in a torrent of words.'

Kircher had no experience of water to match that of the subterranean fires of Vesuvius, but he did not have to go far to see an impressive display of water disappearing into the bowels of the earth. At Tivoli, a favourite country resort since Roman times, the River Aniene 'passes beneath a bridge into a deep whirlpool, a horrid spectacle that you would think to be the mouth of Hell, and the part outside the city falls from a high rock into the same abyss, and goes through various underground channels to join all the other cataracts'.[17] In these two scenes (**Ills. 7.12a, b**), the artist has used his freedom to compose a landscape with ruins and to depict the effects of turbulence in water.

Here is Kircher's explanation of the subterranean waterworks (**Ill. 7.13**). The light-coloured channels are rivers. They emerge from the reservoirs that exist beneath every large mountain, and flow to the sea. The dark-coloured channels are the subterranean ones that are invisible to us. They flow in the reverse direction, carrying sea water from abysses in the sea bed into the mountain reservoirs. The places where the sea enters them are marked by vortices or whirlpools. It is the pressure of the wind, says Kircher, that forces water uphill in this way; and he shows many experiments with siphons to prove that water can move upwards.

These mountain reservoirs were a favourite notion of Kircher's, as they solved at a stroke the question of where rivers came from. On the illustration of a subterranean water cave (**Ill. 7.14**) he writes:

The reader will learn graphically from this figure the interior constitution of a hydrophylax [water reservoir]. You will see the lake situ-

◄ 7.12a, b Two views of Tivoli waterfalls, where rivers disappear into the bowels of the earth. (*Latium*, 141, 142)

► 7.13 Origin of rivers. Kircher postulates underground mountain reservoirs fed from the sea, from which the rivers flow. (*Mundus Subterraneus*, Volume I, 254)

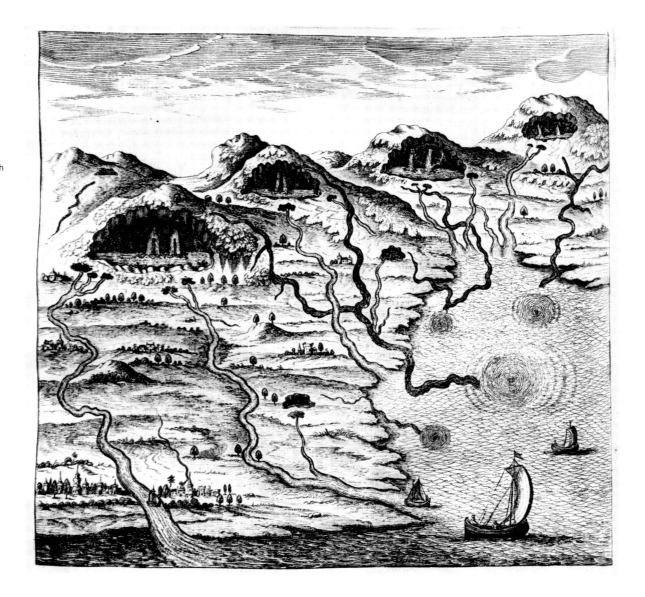

ated inside the mountain, into which the waters from the sides of the mountain pour through subterranean canals. Then they flow out of the subterranean lake through smooth channels into the fields beyond, making rivers and lakes, as the picture shows.[18]

But this was only a local explanation. Some mechanism on a global scale was needed to move oceanic quantities of water around, and Kircher found this in the mythical polar vortices (**Ill. 7.15**) Although explorers had yet to reach the North and South Poles, Kircher felt confident about what was there, and equally certain that no one would ever reach them. His theory of the subterranean circulation of waters persuaded him that at the North Pole (upper diagram), the sea water vanishes down a whirlpool of unimaginable size. At the South Pole (lower diagram), it wells up as though from a spring, causing currents that prevent any ship from proceeding too far south. Incidentally, the

'unknown southern continent' found elsewhere on Kircher's maps (see **Ills. 12.6, 12.7**) has conveniently vanished here.

One of the most puzzling phenomena for early hydrographers was the tides. For any general theory proposed, a local phenomenon could be cited to disprove it. Much earlier, in *Magnes* (1641), Kircher had tackled the subject in the context of magnetism. A simple woodcut (**Ill. 7.16**) illustrates why the tides are higher at new moon. Although this occurs in a chapter on 'magnetism of sun, moon, and sea', Kircher insists that the force involved is not magnetic, but a matter of the sea being infused with 'lunar spirits'. The earth, he says, is always subject to both solar and lunar influences, the sun's rays striking it directly but also reflecting off the moon at various angles, as shown by the positions of the moon around the ellipse. (Note that Kircher draws the moon's orbit as elliptical, but misplaces the earth at the centre of the ellipse, not at one of its poles.) The moon's 'lukewarm' quality tempers the heat of these solar rays and

7.14 Subterranean water cave: the mountain
reservoir that Kircher's theory requires.
(*Mundus Subterraneus*, Volume I, 255)

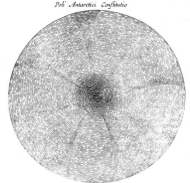

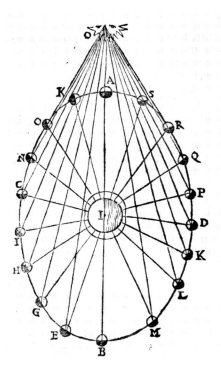

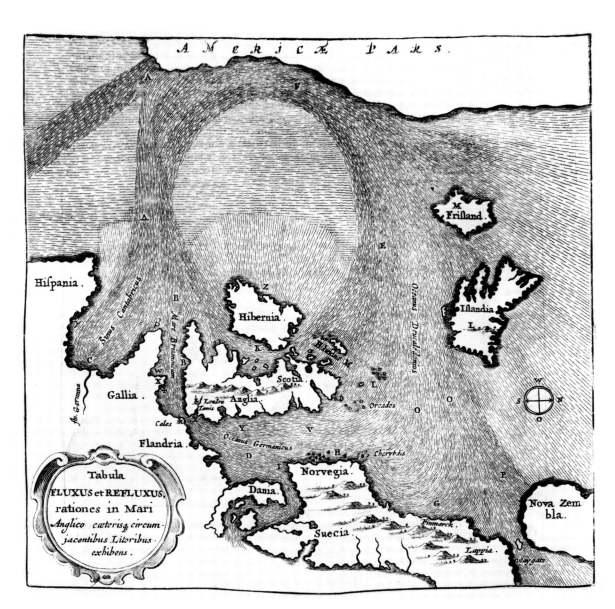

◂▴ 7.15 Vortices at the poles. Kircher believed that vast quantities of water vanish down a whirlpool at the North Pole (upper diagram) to re-emerge at the South. (*Mundus Subterraneus*, Volume I, 170)

◂ 7.16 Causes of the tides was a problem that exercised the early scientists. Kircher noticed that tides were higher at the new moon, which brought him closer than Galileo to the real explanation, the force of the moon's gravity. (*Magnes*, 682).

▴ 7.17 Tides around the British Isles. Unlike the previous explanation, Kircher here posits a geographical rather than an astronomical cause, the English Channel acting like a funnel. (*Mundus Subterraneus*, Volume I, 160)

◄► 7.18, 7.19 The Norwegian Maelstrom, a vortex thirteen miles in circumference. Having accepted reports of this mythical phenomenon, Kircher explained it by positing a subterranean channel linking it to the Gulf of Bothnia. (*Mundus Subterraneus*, Volume I, 152, 159)

converts them, in varying proportions, to a lunar quality. This happens to the greatest degree at A, where the entire output of the sun passes through the moon and is thus 'lunified'. In consequence, the sea then receives the maximum of lunar spirits, which swell and expand it, causing the highest tides.[19]

By the time he came to write *Mundus Subterraneus*, he had discarded this rather occult theory, and had seen presciently that the solution must lie in the interaction of different causes. He devotes a chapter and an illustration to the problem of the tides around the British Isles (**Ill. 7.17**), addressing the question of 'Why the Thames at London reaches its highest tide when the moon is in the south-west quadrant, whereas in the region of northern Europe it attains its greatest swelling when the moon is in the northern signs, namely three hours before the London meridian'. As this map shows, his explanation is that the English Channel constricts the flow of the sea, so

that a local geographical cause modifies a general astronomical one.[20]

To conclude his presentation on the subterranean waters and their effect, Kircher describes the horrendous effects of the Norwegian Maelstrom (**Ills. 7.18** and **7.19**) calling it the largest and most famous vortex in the world. It is thirteen miles in circumference, and for six hours it swallows anything that enters it, including large and small ships, whales, and so on; then for another six hours it vomits them forth again. Olaus Magnus, who is Kircher's source for this, also writes of the terrible noises heard on the coasts of the Gulfs of Bothnia and Finland and in the lakes called Venner and Vetter. The bottoms of these lakes have never been sounded, and Kircher can show the reason why: they must be part of a vast subterranean system that joins the Gulf of Bothnia to the Norwegian Sea. The two seas have different tidal cycles, due to the motion of the moon, and this accounts for the sea rushing to and fro between them.

Notes

1   *Œdipus Ægyptiacus*, I, a[4]ᵛ.
2   *Itinerarium Exstaticum*, 1–12.
3   *Ars Magna Lucis*, 1646, 9; 1671, 3. On Kircher's astronomy, see Siebert in Beinlich 2002a.
4   *Ars Magna Lucis*, 1646, 6; 1671, 2.
5   *Mundus Subterraneus*, 1664, I, 64.
6   *Mundus Subterraneus*, 1664, I, 63.
7   *Mundus Subterraneus*, 1664, I, 175.
8   *Mundus Subterraneus*, 1664, I, 190.
9   *Mundus Subterraneus*, 1664, I, **5. For an explanation of how the pantometer works, see Vollrath, 'Das Pantometrum Kircherianum', 120–124.
10 *Mundus Subterraneus*, 1664, I, **6.
11 *Mundus Subterraneus*, 1664, I, 189.
12 *Mundus Subterraneus*, 1664, I, 178.
13 *Diatribe de Prodigiosis Crucibus*, 77. 'Should any hungry amateur of lies and prodigies be desirous of partaking of a rich and luscious repast, let him read this book, and say grace after dinner to Father Kircher.' Handwritten inscription in the Bodleian Library's copy (Douce K.41), probably by the antiquarian Francis Douce.
14 *Mundus Subterraneus*, 1664, I, 238.
15 *Zahme Xenien*, in *Werke*, Weimar, 1887–1912, Vol. 3, 360.
16 Goethe's source was probably *Œdipus Ægyptiacus*, I, b[1]: 'Sic inconstans continuò rerum vertitur ordo: sic in circulo eunt omnia' (Thus the inconstant order of things continually revolves: thus all things go in a circle).
17 *Latium*, 140.
18 *Mundus Subterraneus*, 1664, I, 235.
19 *Magnes*, 1641, 684; 1643, 600.
20 *Mundus Subterraneus*, 1664, I, 141. This is one of the very few places where Kircher acknowledges the existence of the heretic kingdom of Britain. He had not a single correspondent in England, though his works were read, with varying approval, by the members of the Royal Society. In his *Diatribe*, 96, he calls Elizabeth I 'the image of Jezebel revived', and recounts some of the prodigies with which God showed his displeasure with the English Reformation.

Chapter 8 Naturalia: Air and Earth

After treating fire and water, *Mundus Subterraneus* turned to other phenomena of the earth's interior. In the second edition (1678), he and his correspondents added several novelties, including an account of Mount Testaceo (**Ill. 8.1**) to the south of Rome. (In the distance can be seen San Stefano Rotondo, San Paolo Fuori le Mura and the Pyramid of Cestius.) Kircher was curious to explore the phenomenon of a chilling wind that blows out of a cave there, particularly in summer. He explains that since the hill is an artificial one, made entirely from shattered fragments of pottery, it is easily permeable by air currents. What stirs them into action and chills them is the nearby River Tiber, whose waters penetrate the subterranean channels.

Although he did not explain the mechanics of wind with the same detail and enthusiasm that he brought to fire and water, Kircher had a ready explanation for its causes and an elementary understanding of how differences in air pressure work. In a simple woodcut (**Ill. 8.2**) he illustrates how a cloud (A) heavy with rain, descends and exerts pressure on the air (B–C). The air trapped between the cloud and the sea or land (D) is squeezed out to the sides, and the result can be quite violent. He tells of a windstorm he experienced on a high mountain in the region of Sorano, where the air was squeezed in just this fashion, causing such a gale that no one could stand up in it. And this was not the worst: one of his travelling companions assured him that not long ago in the same place, a tornado had swept up a whole herd of pigs and dropped them to their death on the neighbouring peaks.[1]

In the second volume of *Mundus Subterraneus*, Kircher treats the creatures that live, or lived, beneath the surface of the earth. In pride of place are the giants (**Ill. 8.3**), both real and legendary. This plate shows from left to right a giant whose skeleton Boccaccio reports as discovered in Mount Erice; an ordinary man; Goliath, champion of the Philistines who was slain by David; and giants reported from Switzerland and Mauritania. Of course Kircher believed in Goliath, 'six cubits and a palm in height' (i.e. about ten feet or three metres, as stated in I Samuel 17:4), but only as a special case 'due to God's providence for manifesting the glory of his people'.[2] He gave no credence to the other reports, arguing that even if animals of such size live in the sea, none exist on earth. If they did, they would soon have devoured the available food and exterminated all other creatures. And if a man of this size existed, where would he live? How could he find enough to eat? What would he wear? Then

◄◄ **8.1** Aeolian cave of Mount Testaceo, near Rome, visible in the background. Kircher maintained that the mountain was permeable by air currents because it was made of pottery fragments. (*Mundus Subterraneus*, Volume I, 118)

◄ **8.2** The cause of winds. Here Kircher was basically correct in ascribing winds to differences in air pressure. (*Mundus Subterraneus*, Volume I, 226)

◄ **8.3** Giants: four examples from history and legend, compared to a normal man (the tiny figure near the largest giant's left foot). Kircher was uncharacteristically sceptical when presented with evidence for giants. (*Mundus Subterraneus*, Volume II, 59)

Hic Dracunculus ἄπτερος καὶ ἄπους paulo antequam Hugo Boncompagnus Card. ad Pontificatum assumeretur sub nomine Gregorij XIII. Bononiæ captus etiamnum in Museo Aldrovandi tomento fartus spectatur.

Figura prodigiosi Draconis alati, ex Museo Cardinalis Barberini, apud Terrentium Lynceum.

Hic est Draco ille alatus et quadrupes omni ævo memorabilis, quem Deodatus de Gozon Eques Hierosolymitanus, in insula Rhodo eo quo descripsimus stratagemate confecit, qui et ob beneficium in Insulam collatum postmodum Magnus Ord. Magister creatus est.

Draco Helveticus bipes et alatus.

◄◄ 8.4 Stuffed dragon once in Aldrovandi's museum. Kircher had no problems in believing in dragons, for which there seemed to be a wealth of evidence. (*Mundus Subterraneus*, Volume II, 99)

◄ 8.5 Dragon in the Barberini museum. Kircher accepted the reality of this dragon on the basis of Terentio Fabri's evidence, but did not believe that it breathed fire. (*Mundus Subterraneus*, Volume II, 103)

◄◄ 8.6 Winged four-legged dragon. Kircher here reconstructs a dragon which, according to the story he had been told, appeared on Rhodes in 1345. (*Mundus Subterraneus*, Volume II, 96)

◄ 8.7 Two-legged, winged, Swiss dragon. Another dragon that Kircher accepted on the word of a respected informant, who saw it in 1619. (*Mundus Subterraneus*, Volume II, 100)

there is the question of his weight. Just as colossal statues need extra props, a man of this size could hardly move without collapsing. To clinch the matter, in 1637 Kircher himself had visited the cave in Sicily where the giant had supposedly been found. It was much too small to house him, and there was no sign of his bones. On the same expedition, Kircher consented to view the site of discovery of a collection of monstrous teeth and bones which a historian of Sicily, Marchese Carolo de Vintimiglia, was convinced were those of a giant. After finding not a single human-like bone, Kircher concluded that they were the remains of an elephant, probably left over from Hannibal's campaign.[3]

Although he did not believe in giants, dragons were another matter. Beside the fact that they are mentioned in the Bible, there was the testimony of ancient writers, some of them no less than saints; there were many well-authenticated modern sightings, and there was physical evidence in contemporary museums. For example, Aldrovandi's museum had the stuffed remains of a small, wingless, two-legged dragon (**Ill. 8.4**), captured in Bologna shortly before the accession of Pope Gregory XIII (1572). In the second edition of *Mundus Subterraneus*, Kircher added an illustration of a dragon in Cardinal Barberini's museum, copied from Terentio Fabri's *De Plantis Americae* (**Ill. 8.5**). Fabri's long and learned text, also reproduced, draws on the variety

of hitherto unknown reptiles discovered in Africa and the Americas. He discusses draconic anatomy in the light of classical writings, and questions such as whether dragons lay eggs, and why they appear to grin. As to the reputation of dragons for breathing fire, Kircher could not believe that they really do so; they are probably just phosphorescent, like certain fish and rotten wood, and when seen in dark caves appear to be on fire.[4]

A very different species, winged and four-legged (**Ill. 8.6**), terrorized the island of Rhodes in 1345. This dragon was the size of a bull, its ears like a mule's; with a terrible grin, it revealed its sharp teeth, and breathed fire. A valiant knight, one Deodatus of Gozo, ingeniously made a dragon out of paper and oakum with a movable tail and jaws, painted it red, yellow and blue just like the real one, and for two months trained his horse and hounds to attack it. Kircher recounts the ensuing battle blow by blow, exactly as it was told to him by a knight of Malta.[5] At such points I wonder whether he had, in fact, taken notes when he heard the story (presumably on Malta, twenty-six years before); whether a fertile imagination supplied the details; or, as I sometimes suspect, that one of the components of his genius was the perfect recall of everything he had ever heard or read.

It may surprise the reader to learn that dragons were nowhere more preva-

◄◄ **8.8** Dragons of Lake Lucerne, which lifted a man into the air (upper illustration). The lower picture shows one being killed by a local hero. (*Mundus Subterraneus*, Volume II, 117)

◄ **8.9** Not a dragon but a deformed cock who lived in the Boboli Gardens in Florence and who was illustrated in a work by another famous naturalist, Ulisse Aldrovandi. (*Mundus Subterraneus*, Volume II, 102)

lent than in Switzerland.[6] So writes the Swiss historian Johannes Cysatus, and he gives several historical accounts, which Kircher reproduces. Nearer the present time, Christoph Schorer, Prefect of Solothurn, told Kircher of his own sighting, one night in 1619, of a dragon flying out of a cave on Mount Pilatus and across the Lake of Lucerne (**Ill. 8.7**). At first he thought it was a meteor, but then he saw that it had all the characteristics of a dragon. Schorer added: 'I write this to your Reverence, lest you should have any further doubt about the real existence of dragons in nature.' While Kircher was writing his book, another letter arrived from Schorer, telling him that as recently as 1654, a hunter had discovered a four-legged specimen on the same mountain; and that in 1602, the skeleton of a dragon killed in an earthquake had been found in the nearby Staffelwand.[7]

Another account of strange phenomena in the area reached Kircher in 1667 from his correspondent Elias Georgius Loretus (**Ill. 8.8**). Loretus was a bold explorer of mountains and caves, and a firm believer in the legends of demons that inhabit these remote Alpine places. In April 1666 he saw the Mount Pilatus dragon looking like a flying fire, accompanied by three or four days of dreadful groanings and tremblings of the earth and culminating in the fall of a great rock into the Lake of Lucerne.

That dragons exist in the region is confirmed, says Loretus, by a depiction in the tabernacle of St Leodagarius's Church in Lucerne of a man being lifted up by two flying dragons (on which the upper illustration is based). The legend tells of a man who fell into a mountain crevasse inhabited by two dragons, who however did not harm him. After a winter in which, following their example, he survived by ingesting stones, he caught hold of one of their tails and thus escaped. On returning to civilization he did not live long, being unused to human food, but placed his history in the church as a memorial.

The lower illustration depicts another Lucerne hero, Winckelried, who slew a dragon in what was ever after called the Drakenfeldt. Loretus adds that he has seen a 'draconite' stone larger than a pigeon's egg and marked with various signs. It was spewed out along with flames by a dragon, and picked up by a peasant who saw it while he was reaping. A Lucerne pharmacist uses it against various ailments, especially poisoning.[8]

To conclude his treatise on dragons, Kircher borrowed an illustration (**Ill. 8.9**) from Ulisse Aldrovandi's *History of Serpents and Dragons* of a spectacularly deformed cock that lived for many years in the Boboli Gardens in Florence. 'This cock was bearded, horned and greaved, with a serpentine tail in whose extremity a tuft could be seen. Near the anus, where the tail was joined to the body, a sort of round, tuberous thing was visible, and a white coloured crest, with feathered wattles.'[9] In order to appreciate Kircher's theory of how such a monster came into being, one should know that he believed in spontaneous generation. He did not hold that creatures could arise out of inanimate matter, but he was certain that an embryo could develop from sperm alone, without womb or egg. In *Arca Noë* he explains his theory succinctly:

Many animals, including quadrupeds like mice, moles, and almost all species of frogs and lizards, are born from rot, that is, from the semen of the same kind of animal left somewhere, or from the rotting parts of them, because they actually propagate themselves by a natural mixture of the female [seed] with the male.[10]

He also believed that the fermentation of different types of semen could give rise to many strange, hybrid animals (see p. 152 for some examples). He reminds us that a cock that eats a serpent's egg is known to generate a basilisk, and assumes that the Florentine monster must have arisen from some such accident.

As corroborative evidence, he mentions the venerable case of the Scottish barnacle-goose. This large barnacle, which looks somewhat like an embryo bird folded up in its egg, attaches itself by a stalk to the bottoms of ships. Long tradition held that in time it hatches into a goose and flies away, and Kircher accepted this. He explains that ducks and geese drop their eggs into the sea, where they are whipped into a froth by the rough waves around the north of Scotland. The resultant mixture sticks to ships, and in due course naturally develops into ducks or geese.

THE UNICORN AND THE NARWHAL

When he compiled his catalogue of animals in Noah's Ark, Kircher was of two minds over the unicorn (**Ill. 8.10**). The ancient writers describe it, the Bible mentions it, but now that the whole earth and sea have been explored, none has been found. Yet it verges on blasphemy to suggest that God allowed so famous an animal to perish in the Flood. Probably the Scriptures refer to some other one-horned animal, such as those frequently found in India, or to the rhinoceros.[11]

Kircher had no such doubt about the 'unicorn horns', those long spiral horns preserved in many a mediaeval treasury and Renaissance Kunstkammer. He knew that they came from a fish for which he had no name, but which we know as the narwhal (**Ill. 8.11**).

'There is nothing in the nature of things more valued by emperors, kings, princes and magnates of the world than this horn: gold and gems are nothing to it. However, what it really is, and from what animal it derives, no one can say. To this day physicians, physiologists and explorers of many kinds argue fiercely among themselves, without settling the matter. I will, however, say that if any should deny that this animal, whose horn possesses such efficacy and admirable virtue, exists today, or that it ever existed, their temerity would call into question not only many pages of the Scriptures, but the reliability of all the historians... [Yet] I will say, with due respect, that I believe horns of this type to be not from quadrupeds, but from certain fishes... It occasionally happens that these spearlike snouts are violently broken off between the rocks of icy mountains, and, swept against the shores of neighbouring islands, are collected there. Each year, many have testified to finding them under the sand of the sea. They have also seen the fish, furnished with a proboscis like a great lance, as we show it here.'[12]

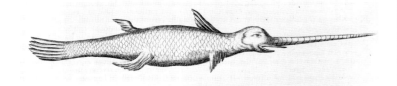

◀ 8.10 Unicorn: Kircher suspected that the unicorn was really a rhino, but illustrates it in classic style. (*Arca Noë*, 57–65)

▼ 8.11 Narwhal. This horn was constantly treasured as a unicorn's, but Kircher knew that it came from a fish. (*Mundus Subterraneus*, Volume II, 67)

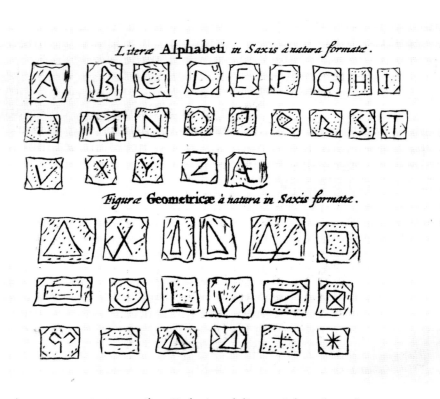

Literæ Alphabeti in Saxis à natura formatæ.

Figuræ Geometricæ à natura in Saxis formatæ.

Pseudocrystallus.

Forma Topaziorum, Amethystorum, Beryllorum.

◄◄ 8.12 Letters in stones. In Kircher's time stones with what looked like Greek and Roman letters seemed to demand an explanation, but he dismissed them as random accidents. (*Mundus Subterraneus*, Volume II, 23)

◄ 8.13 Geometric forms in crystals. The perfect polygons and other geometrical shapes in crystals seemed inexplicable as natural phenomena, and Kircher was driven to offer more abstruse causes. (*Mundus Subterraneus*, Volume II, 25)

▼ 8.14 A city figured in stone: a 'ruin marble', still collected today as a curiosity. (*Mundus Subterraneus*, Volume II, 33)

As soon as one starts to smile at Kircher's credulity, one is brought up short by an example of his rational and sceptical side (see box, 'The Unicorn and the Narwhal'). This happens repeatedly with one of the most famous themes of *Mundus Subterraneus*: the figured stones.[13]

His first experience of the kind happened some years before writing the book, when he was exploring the region of Tolfa northwest of Rome. He came across a hill in which a sort of blue schist-like stone had been found: it was covered with fine white lines that seemed to delineate all the letters of the Roman and Greek alphabets (**Ill. 8.12**). But on reflection he decided that they were merely random combinations of lines (pointing out that most letters, after all, are made from lines), caused by crackling. As often in his observations of natural phenomena, he suggests an experiment that achieves a similar result. In this case, he instructs the reader how to dry a certain sort of clay, and then see the cracks appear.[14]

Crystallography had not yet graduated from the Kunstkammer to the status of a science when Kircher felt obliged to offer a theory of it (**Ill. 8.13**). As a mathematician, he was intrigued by the regular polygons and other geometrical forms displayed by crystals, but lacking a molecular concept of matter, he could not explain the phenomenon without resort to 'virtues', 'spirits' and the 'appetites' of nature:

There is in saline bodies a certain actinobolic virtue, which we call radiative, as many years of experiment have taught us. This force consists in the spirit secreted in the body of the salt, which of itself, its own nature and

Vrbs Turrita

natural appetite, proceeds from the centre to the circumference, and gradually divides by corpuscular protrusion into rays. Thus if the diameter is divided into four parts, that will be the basis and as it were the map upon which the gem is drawn, when nature wishes it to be of a square figure...[15]

And so on, up to the twelvefold division. He was likewise fascinated by the ability of nature to depict almost everything on earth in stones, especially agates. His descriptions move upwards in the chain of being from geometrical

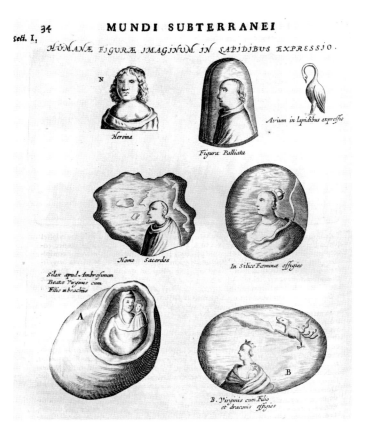

► 8.15 Human
figures in
stones. Chance?
Petrification?
Miracle? Kircher
could not
decide. (*Mundus
Subterraneus*,
Volume II, 34)

▼ 8.16 Birds
figured in stones.
Kircher wondered
whether dead
bodies still
retained 'spirits'
capable of
imprinting
rock. (*Mundus
Subterraneus*,
Volume II, 35)

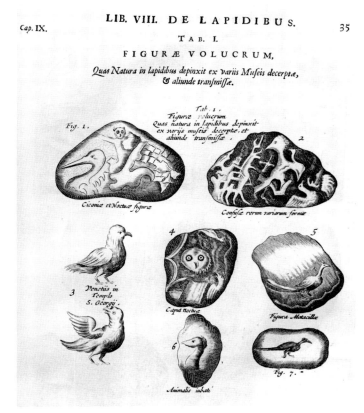

figures to the four elements (pictured as rivers, flames, clouds), trees, birds, quadrupeds, human figures, saints and Christ himself. He notes that the best figurations are found in highly polished marbles and agates. **Ill. 8.14** is an example of the 'ruin marble' quarried near Florence, a favourite of collectors of minerals and natural curiosities.

These human figures found in stones (**Ill. 8.15**) are captioned from top left: 'Heroine; Mantled figure; Expression of birds in stones; Man, priest; Effigy of a woman in flint; Flint from Ambrosinus of the Blessed Virgin with her son in miniature; Effigy of the Virgin with her son and a dragon'. Kircher classifies figures in stones as those on planar surfaces, and those in three dimensions. Both are present here. He also offers four possible explanations of the phenomenon: 1. chance; 2. a disposition of the earthly substance to receive an imprint, which is then petrified; 3. the accidental petrification of a body or an object; 4. a particular divine disposition, carried out by angelic and natural agency.[16]

Some examples of these follow. **Ill. 8.16** shows 'Figures of birds which nature has depicted in stones, gathered from various museums and transmitted from elsewhere'. Kircher offers two explanations of Figure 2, which 'shows various shapes of things and parts of animals, both birds and quadrupeds, but very imperfectly'. First, it may be an example of his first possible cause: sheer imagination on the viewer's part, as when clouds seem to take the shape of figures. He suggests two experiments to discover this for oneself. The first, which can only be performed in freezing weather, is done by pouring coloured waters over ice. The second is pouring gum tragacanth onto water and stirring it into patterns, as is done in the preparation of marbled papers. One will then see forms very like those in real marble, and be able to imagine them as representing creatures and objects.[17]

The other possibility is Kircher's second cause. Under unusual circumstances, even the separated members of dead bodies may retain enough of their 'plastic force' to imprint their images on the material in which they are buried, like a disembodied head or foot; and if this turns to rock, then the images remain.[18]

Most of the images of quadrupeds (**Ill. 8.17**) are of chaotic fragments of animals, thus to be attributed to the sporadic growth of residual energy in their remains. But Figure 7, which 'exhibits the perfect shape of a cat', is a special case. Kircher lists this among several unusually perfect images which he suspects may be due to some work of art that happened to end up buried next to marble or some such receptive stone. Kircher insists that given time and the right circumstances, a painting or drawing can penetrate and tincture the entire stone, and offers as experimental proof a recipe for paints that will do this.

The images of fish figured in stones (**Ill. 8.18**) belong to Kircher's third method: an object is trapped within suitable material, which is then hardened by the 'lapidifying spirit'. He imagines a fish caught in a flood and enveloped in mud. The mud, in the course of time, is converted into stone, and the fish with it. He remarks on how, if one breaks such a fossil apart, there are no

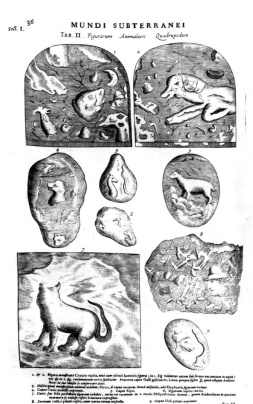

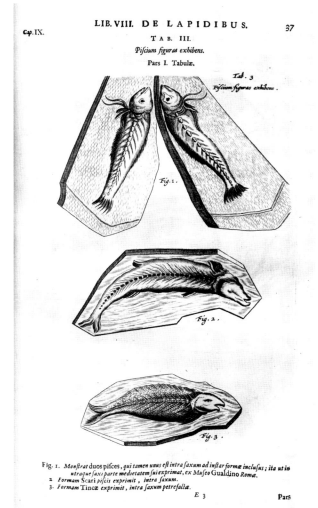

◀ **8.17** Quadrupeds figured in stones. The example numbered 7, 'the perfect shape of a cat', seemed to Kircher too good to be an accident. (*Mundus Subterraneus*, Volume II, 36)

▶ **8.18** Fish figured in stones. Here Kircher stumbles upon a process which is virtually the same as fossilization. (*Mundus Subterraneus*, Volume II, 37)

◀▼ **8.19** Sacred figures in stones. For Kircher these are not miraculous but caused by a sacred image having been dropped in mud. (*Mundus Subterraneus*, Volume II, 39)

▶▼ **8.20** The Virgin and Child figured in a jasper from Chile. Kircher did not absolutely rule out the appearance of miraculous images, but believed them to be very rare. (*Mundus Subterraneus*, Volume II, 47)

intestines visible, which is because all the soft parts have been consumed, or desiccated and turned to dust.

When he comes to sacred figures in stones (**Ill. 8.19**), Kircher gives little comfort to the superstitious. He says that most of them are simply due to sacred images having been dropped or lost in mud, which then hardened into stone following his third process. He attributes the crucifix to the rare circumstance just mentioned: that of a painting penetrating a rock.[19]

Kircher is parsimonious with his fourth explanation of figures in stones, saying that it concerns special, sacred ones, which are brought about through divine providence. Just as on rare occasions a new star appears in the sky or a monster is born, so a sacred effigy may be discovered in a stone. This always has significance and portends great events. For instance, there was the case in China, shortly before the Gospel was preached there, when crabs and lobsters appeared with the sign of the cross on their backs, while in Japan, at a similar time, crosses appeared when tree trunks were cut! The finding of this particular figure (**Ill. 8.20**) in a cave among inaccessible Andean crags is vouched for by Father Alfonso de Valle in his history of Chile. As soon as the local natives saw it and its meaning was explained to them, they all embraced the Christian faith.[20]

Leaving Kircher's geology, we turn now to his zoology, for which Noah's Ark provided the ideal canvas. I give only a few of the many woodcut illustrations in *Arca Noë*, which, from their variety of style, seem to have been gleaned by Jansson from a number of popular natural histories.[21] **Ill. 8.21** is a selection of the thirty-three different animals pictured in the section devoted to quadrupeds, here meaning mammals. Kircher's descriptions contain some of his more engaging writing, with a clear sense of his sympathies and antipathies (see box below).

Arca Noë devotes a special section to hybrid animals (**Ill. 8.22**), which were not included in the Ark, but resulted from inter-species matings after the Flood. Kircher had no doubt that animals of different species could mate and produce young, and as examples he lists the following:

Mule, produced from the mating of a horse and a donkey
Giraffe (*Cameleopardalis*), from panther and camel
Goat-stag (*Tragelaphus* or *Hircocervus*), from goat and stag
Horse-stag (*Hippelaphus* or *Equicervus*), from horse and stag
Horse-panther (*Hippardium*), from horse and panther
Leopard, from lion and panther
Allopecopithicum, from fox and monkey
Chiurcha, parentage uncertain
Armadillo, probably from tortoise and hedgehog[24]
Marmot, from marten and squirrel
Leocrocuta, from lion and hyena
Corcobado: 'I cannot easily say that it is born from the congress of different species, but it is an animal of the bovine species, and perhaps it has been transmuted into this form by a peculiar influx of the heavens or by the nature of the climate and situation, like almost all the animals of America.'[25]

The second great division in Kircher's zoology is amphibians (**Ill. 8.23**), defined as animals that live partly on land, and partly in water. Under this heading he includes the hippopotamus, crocodile, otter, beaver, turtle, seal and siren. Kircher's siren was not the mermaid of legend, for all that he pictures her as such, but some weird sea-creature. It is 'shaped like a woman above, and ends lower down in a fish's tail, and there can be no doubt about it, because our museum exhibits its tail and bones; the bones have a remarkable power of staunching blood'.[26] Whatever its origin, we learn with relief that it was not from inter-species intercourse.

THE SQUIRREL AND THE PIG

'The squirrel is a clean, quick, restless animal, not much different from the rabbit in its members except that it has a long furry tail that can cover its entire body. It lives mostly in beech, oak, walnut, chestnut, and other nut-trees, and lives from their fruits. With great speed it leaps from branch to branch and from tree to tree, so that you'd say it was flying. When tamed, it is very familiar with men, and loves to eat almonds and sugared nuts. When it eats, its actions, gestures and movements are a pleasure to watch. If it is put into a revolving cage, it keeps turning it, and the wheel turns together with the flexible arms of statues attached to its axis, so that the statues seem to be turning the wheel.'[22]

'The pig is a grunting, lustful, dirty, greedy animal, fond of rolling in mud. It likes herbs, fruits and especially the roots of plants; acorns, chestnuts, apples, pears and similar fruit. In a word, it is omnivorous, and when driven by hunger, I would not say it eats corpses, but it does not spare its own progeny. It takes great pleasure in mud, and the fouler the mud, the more it enjoys it. When living, it profits nobody; when dead, many. As long as it lives, it offends everyone with its filthy sight, its stink and its snorting. When it is butchered, its flesh is prepared in various ways and gives no small pleasure to gourmets. From it come lard, together with sausages, bristles that are very widely used, and pigskin used by shoemakers and bookbinders. However, it easily contracts leprosy, and infects others who frequently eat its flesh. Hence this unclean animal was prohibited by the [Mosaic] Law.'[23]

ARCA NOE. 57

proinde satis mirari non queamus Divinæ Sapientiæ altitudinem, dum in principio Creationis, tam provide, & tanto cum ordine mundo mundique filio homini providit, dum *primò* Terrâ & aquis stellisque productis, mox Terram herbis & arboribus, tanquam annonâ, & commeatu animantibus paulò post producendis parato instruxit: productis animalibus, subsecuta fuit hominis creatio, ut homo utroque & vegetabilis & sensitivæ naturæ subsidio, quàm firmissimè, tum ad victum, tum ad vestitum, oblectamentumque possessione perpetuò duraturâ uteretur. Atque hisce camporum sylvarumque recessus conferti sunt, hisce superbit civibus totius terreni globi ambitus. Quibus quidem breviter recensitis, jam ordine singula ex dictis in *Arcam* introductis, juxta naturam & proprietatem uniuscujusque describamus, à majoribus corporis mole orditurι.

Elephas eiusque Natura & proprietas. *Elephas* omnium *Zoologorum* calculo, uti mole corporis cætera excedit; ita quoque meritò primum in *Arca* locum jure suo requirit. *Elephas* brutum quadrupes est, robustum, maximum, etiamsi horridum aspectu, docile tamen est, & nisi irritetur benignum; & materiali quodam ut ita dicam, judicio in rebus agendis pollens: omnium prudentissimum cujus vox naturalis est barrire, foliis arborum, herbis fœnoque, uti & fructibus, utpote Peponibus, imò placentis quoque mellitis pascitur. Delitiæ ejus sunt in *India* Arundines Saccharaceæ, & potus vinum crematum, vel quodcunque tandem aliud vini genus spirituosis halitibus generosum; Mirum tamen est, vitatis superfluis necessaria tantùm appetere; potu tamen aquæ paulò excedit, cum *Aristotele* teste, sex aut septem modios aquæ uno haustu facilè absorbeat; Vastitas tamen corporis id ab hac immoderata potus sumptione facile absolvit; in sociali commoratione, maximus cæteris præcedit; flumina transituri parvulos probissimè, ne absorbeantur, gestant; montes asperiores subituri, proboscide pro baculis utuntur; in Theatris quoque suas partes egregiè peragunt; *Mures* & *Muscas* timet, quas rugis pellis inhærentes, contracta pelle enecat. Sed de his animalibus vide *Zoologos*.

Camelus. *Camelus* est animal quadrupes, gibbosum, gramine, fœno & frugibus, spinosisque fruticibus vitam sustinens, famis sitisque patientissimum; mansuetum quoque, nisi quando in venerem initio verni temporis concitatur; injuriarum à rectore suo acceptarum memor, in illum vehementer sævit; vox ejus est stridere, ad onera etiam maxima aptissimum: unde proverbium: *Camelus* etiam scabiosus pluri-

H morum

ARCA NOE. 59

& minoris momenti in *Arca* animalia conservârit, uti de Reptilibus diximus; hoc itaque asseverare de DEO, blasphemiâ non caret. Non itaque alia ratio assignari potest, illud in *Arca* non fuisse susceptum, nisi quod tale, prout ab *Authoribus* describitur, nullibi in hunc usque diem visum sit. Per *Unicorne* itaque, alia similia huic speciei animalia suprà recensita intelligi debent, ut *Sacræ Scripturæ Textus* servetur. Ego per *Monocerotem* nil aliud intelligi existimo, nisi

Rhinoceros. *Rhinocerotem* animal in naso cornu portans, estque paulò *Elephanto* minus, cum quo & bellum gerit, totum cataphractum.

Bubalus. *Bubalus* sive *Bufalo*, vulgo Bovini generis, ex mundis unum, animal est aspectu formidabile, cornibus præduris & inflexis, quibus pretiosa quævis conficiuntur; corollæ precariæ, reliquiarum capsulæ, vascula, similiaque conficiuntur; aquis & luto gaudet, ferox animal, nulli, ne quidem conductori, si quandoque irritetur, parcit, ex rubri coloris aspectu excandescit, caro olim *Sacris Literis* testantibus, cibus reputabatur delicatus, & inter cæteras carnes, mensæ *Salomonis* deputabatur; hodiè non nisi *Judæis* in escam cedit, inter munda tamen animalia recensetur.

Alce. *Alce* animal quadrupes, velox, bisulcum, unde & mundis animalibus adnumerari potest; flebilem adinstar infantis vocem emittens: *Cervo* majus & hirsutius est; gramine & fœno vivit; ut plurimum in *Lituaniæ* & *Moscoviæ* sylvarum latibulis deprehenditur; Germanicè, *Elendt* à voce flebili: ab Italis *Gran bestia* dicitur, non tam à magnitudine, quàm ob eximiam virtutem, quâ Epilepticos, ungulâ suâ collo, aliisve membris appensa, sanare dicitur; cujusmodi in nostro Musæo videre est.

Equus. *Equus* animal quadrupes hinniens est, generosum, docile, fidele, humanis usibus maximè aptum, gramine, fœno, paleis, avenâ, hordeo alitur.

H 2 Animal

ARCA NOE. 61

meatu medullari, falsum compertum fuit. Salacissimum animal, præsertim fœmina, quæ libidinis œstro percita, etiam *Pardum* admittit; quod si quando sentit mas, tota vi in ultrices pœnas exurgit; odoratu multum valet, indeque masculus femellæ adulterium agnoscit, quæ tamen astutiori instinctu, ne deprehendatur, aquâ se lavat, & hoc pacto marem decipit. Rugitum *Leonis* omnia animalia formidant, quo feras quascunque veluti fascino ligat. Imperterritus Venatoribus se sistit; à quibus si vulneretur, rectà in Venatorem irruit, eumque prosternit. Aliàs hominem nisi læsus ab ipso, aut extrema urgente fame non lædit. Fœminas verò etiam amat, & libenter conversatur cum iis, si quam noxam cæteris brutis intentat, facile à fœmina baculi minis à noxa abstinet.

Cervus. *Cervus* animal est quadrupes, velocissimum cursu, rancans, id est, vocem rancoram edens, quod tametsi vastis & ramosis cornibus constet, timidum tamen est: vescitur frugibus, oleribus, graminibus, aliisque agrorum, hortorumque fructibus, bisulcum est, & ideò mundis animalibus adnumeratur. Tempore mensis Augusti, ardentissima libidine agitatur; denique animal est ad omnes humanos usus aptissimum, carne, corio, cornibus, pinguedine: in varias species dividitur.

Asinus. *Asinus* notum animal, tardum, stupidum, salax, famis, laboris & verberum patiens; vox ejus propria ruditus est; vilissimo alimento contentum; tribulis, carduis, spinis, graminibus, paleâ, fœno; aliisque vilissimis plantis vescitur.

Onager & Bonasus. *Equus* ex *Asina* generat *Mulum*. *Onager* & *Bonasus* etsi differentes aliquo modo quoad exteriorem formam sint, ejusdem

H 3 tamen.

ARCA NOE. 63

avidè arripit; uti bisulcum, ita & ex mundis unum; innumeras enim homini præstat utilitates; Carne siquidem & lacte caseoque nutrimur, corio, velleribusque, lanâque vestimur, aliisque notis omnibus ex ea susceptis emolumentis fruimur; simplicissimum animal est, naturâ suâ inerme; non valet unguibus, non dentibus, non calcibus, non cornibus, ut non immeritò *Christi* ἔκτυπον semper expresserit: qui tanquam *Ovis* ad occisionem ductus, non aperuit os suum; & uti simplicissimum animal est, ita quoque facilè in avia & devia abreptum *Lupis* cedit; multis quoque infirmitatibus exposita est, quas absente pastore, & non curante incurrunt; ut proindè non immeritò, indè Præsules Ecclesiæ, Pastores, & curæ eorum commissi fideles *Oves* dicantur & numerentur.

Ζῦς, Porcus. *Porcus* animal est grunniens, lascivum, immundum, & vorax, luti volutabro assuetum; herbis & frugibus, potissimum radicibus plantarum, uti & glandibus, castaneis, pomis, pyris, similibusque fructibus delectatur: verbo, omnivorum est, & fame stimulante, non dicam cadaveribus, sed ne quidem propriæ soboli parcit; pro deliciis luto delectatur, & si quid luto fœdius est; animam vero pro sale habet: vivens nemini prodest, mortuus multis: quamdiù vivit, omnes offendit torvo aspectu, fœtore & grunnitu. Cùm mactatur, carnes ejus variis modis præparatæ, non exiguam voluptatem præstant gulosis; prosunt & lardo, farciminibus, setis, quorum ingens usus est, tum apud sutores, tum apud compactores librorum pellis. Lepram tamen facilè contrahunt, & alios etiam esu continuo & frequenti suæ carnis leprâ inficiunt; unde tanquam immundum animal in Lege prohibitum est.

Κύων, Canis. *Canis* est animal latrabile, sagax, vigilans, & fidele; nutritur carnibus, ossibus, pane, aliisque, fame stimulante omnia quantumvis vilissima & sordida

devo-

ARCA NOE. 65

men uterum nunquam gerat: Caro à nonnullis improbi succi esse fertur; Martialis tamen reliquis carnibus præfert:

Inter aves Turdus, *si quis me judice certet,*
Inter quadrupedes, gloria prima Lepus.

Cuniculus. *Cuniculus* proximum *Lepori* animal, ut proinde id Leporini generis existiment, & quamvis quoad exteriorem formam prorsus similes sint *Leporibus Cuniculi*; quoad proprietates tamen Naturæ multùm differunt: habitant enim non in apertis campis, sed in locis, seu mæandris subterraneis, quorum suffodicatione, nonnullas urbes in summo ruinæ periculo fuisse, *Historici* memorant. fœcundissimum prætereà animal est, dum semper fere ternos, & quaternos catulos pariat, atque etiam haud secus ac *Lepus* superfœtare soleat; unde brevi in magnam & damnosam multiplicationem propagantur.

Σκίουρος. *Sciurus*, animal est mundum, velox, inquietum, *Cuniculo* haud multum quoad membrorum constitutionem dissimile, nisi quod caudam habeat sat longam & villosam, qua totum corpus contegere potest; utplurimum in Fagis, Quercubus, Juglandibus, Castaneis cæterisque frugiferis arboribus habitat, quarum fructibus victitat, summaque velocitate ex ramo in ramum, & ex arbore in arborem, volare id diceres, se transfert, & cicuratum homini valde familiare est, & præsertim si Amygdalis, & Saccaro imbutis Nucibus alatur; jucundum est videre ejus operationes, gestus, mores in comedendo: Inclusum caveæ rotabili, illam continue versat, rota versata versat unà brachia flexilia statuarum axi rotæ applicatarum, ut statuæ rotam versare videantur, & complura hujusmodi ludicra spectacula exhibet.

Mustela. *Mustela* animal quadrupes, audacissimum in Mures etiam majores, quibus utplurimum vescitur, aviculis quoque insidias tendit, in antris habitat; inquietum semper hinc inde discurrit, mansuescit; cum *Bufone*, seu *Rubeta* immortale gerit bellum, cui tamen posteà succumbit, virulento halitu siderata; contra Serpentes verò in pugnam subitura, priùs rutâ se veluti antidoto quodam munire fertur. Vide de hoc animalculo plura in *lib. 3. Artis Magneticæ*.

Viverra. *Viverra* animalculum, uti lucem odit, ita ferè semper subterraneos mæandros inhabitat, non nisi noctu ad prædam exit; vescitur hordeo, tritico, avenâ, cæterisque frumentis, & leguminibus, quorum pro hyberno commeatu acquirendo-

I rum

8.21 Quadrupeds. Kircher illustrates and describes thirty-three, of which this is a selection (see also **Ill. 8.10**). (*Arca Noë*, 57–65)

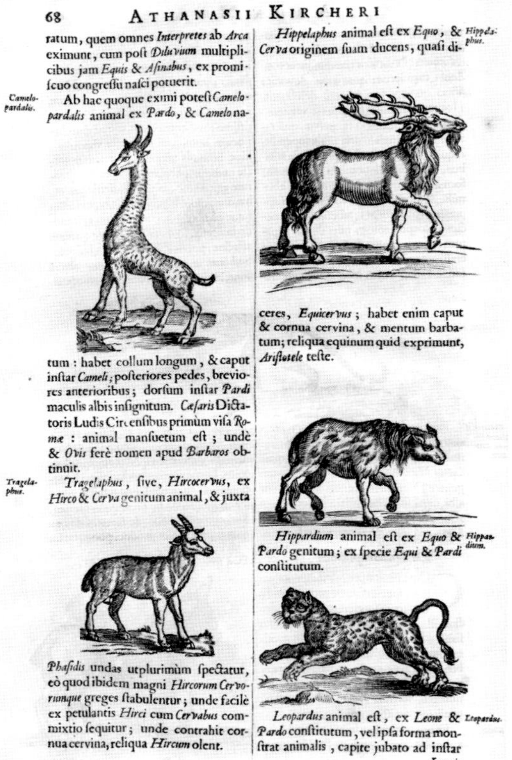

68 ATHANASII KIRCHERI

ratum, quem omnes *Interpretes* ab *Arca* eximunt, cum post *Diluvium* multiplicibus jam *Equis* & *Asinabus*, ex promiscuo congressu nasci potuerit.

[*Camelopardalis.*] Ab hac quoque eximi potest *Camelopardalis* animal ex *Pardo*, & *Camelo* natum: habet collum longum, & caput instar *Cameli*; posteriores pedes, breviores anterioribus; dorsum instar *Pardi* maculis albis insignitum. *Cæsaris* Dictatoris Ludis Circensibus primùm visa *Romæ*: animal mansuetum est; undè & *Ovis* ferè nomen apud *Barbaros* obtinuit.

[*Tragelaphus.*] *Tragelaphus*, sive, *Hircocervus*, ex *Hirco* & *Cerva* genitum animal, & juxta *Phasidis* undas utplurimùm spectatur, eò quod ibidem magni *Hircorum Cervorumque* greges stabulentur; unde facilè ex petulantis *Hirci* cum *Cervabus* commixtio sequitur; unde contrahit cornua cervina, reliqua *Hircum* olent.

[*Hippelaphus.*] *Hippelaphus* animal est ex *Equo*, & *Cerva* originem suam ducens, quasi diceres, *Equicervus*; habet enim caput & cornua cervina, & mentum barbatum; reliqua equinum quid exprimunt, *Aristotele* teste.

[*Hippardium.*] *Hippardium* animal est ex *Equo* & *Pardo* genitum; ex specie *Equi* & *Pardi* constitutum.

[*Leopardus.*] *Leopardus* animal est, ex *Leone* & *Pardo* constitutum, vel ipsa forma monstrat animalis, capite jubato ad instar *Leonis*

ARCA NOE. 69

Leonis insignitum, reliquum corpus maculis pulchris depictum *Pardum* refert.

[*Allopecopithicum.*] *Allopecopithicum* animal ex *Vulpe* & *Simia* genitum, uti vox ipsa composita notat. Hoc animal *Cardanus* in *Æthiopia* nasci scribit, anteriori parte *Vulpi*, caudâ & posteriori *Simiæ* caudatæ, pedibus anterioribus, humanis, auribus Vespertilioni simile, crumenam habens sub ventre, qua catulos gerit, nec dimittit nisi dum lactare vult. Videtur

[*Chiurcha.*] hoc animal *Cardanus*, cum *Chiurcha* animali *Indiæ Occidentalis* confudisse; quod *Scaliger* mustellino generi adscribit; dicitur esse *Viverræ* facie ac magnitudine, capite vulpino, catulosque in bursa sub alvo extensa portare: cum *Chiurca* minimæ molis, illud verò vulpinæ magnitudinis in *Æthiopia* reperiatur. Quicquid sit, ego sanè audacter asseram, hoc animal, uti monstruosissimum est, ita quoque ex diversorum animalium congressu, ortum suum obtinuisse.

[*Armodillus.*] *Armodillus* animal est *Regni Mexicani*, quod in nostro Musæo expositum advenis monstramus, totum instar *Equi* phalerati cataphractum, tessellis seu testaceis corticibus à natura miro ordine distributis instructum, quibus ubi impetitur, mox in globum Erinaceorum more, se contrahit, ita ut nulla ei noxa inferri possit, ore rostrum *Porci*, cauda longa & testacea, lacertæ caudam exprimit; unde & ab *Hispanis Armadillo* illi nomen inditum est, à *Latinis*, *Erinaceus* cataphractus, sive tessalatus, *Tato* à *Barbaris* vocitatum: *Tato* sive *Aiotochli*, quod idem est, ac *Cuniculus* cucurbitalis. Ego sane, quantum conjectura assequi possum, ex *Testudine* & *Erinaceo* originem suam traxisse, non invitus dicerem, cum testudinacei generis, tessellato corpore, reliqua verò membra, moresque *Erinaceum* perfecte, excepto capite, quod *suillum* est, exprimat.

[*Marmota.*] *Marmota* animal ex *Mele* & *Sciuro* natum. *Melem* enim capite, pilo, ungui-

I 3 bus,

70 ATHANASII KIRCHERI

bus, reliquisque membris; *Sciurum* verò moribus exprimit, dum anterioribus pedibus sedens, manuum officio, uti *Sciuri*, utatur.

[*Leocrocuta.*] *Leocrocuta* animal ex *Leone* & *Hyæna* generatum; teste *Plinio*, esse *Asini* ferè magnitudine, collo, cauda, pectore, *Leonis*, capite *Melium*, bisulcâ ungulâ, ore ad aures usque rescisso, humanos mores imitari. Verùm, quæ *Authores de Hyæna*, & *Crocuta* asserunt, fabulis similiora sint, quàm ut certæ alicui animalis speciei congruunt; ideò ea omittenda censui.

[*Corcobado.*] *Corcobado* animal *Americæ Septentrionalis* gibbosum, ex bovino genere, uti testantur fere omnia genera *Tauro* simillima, nisi quod densis pilorum villis, jubisque sit toto corpore vestitum; Turpe aspectu animal, currit, saltat feritque cornibus, formidine ferociæ animalia cuncta fugat, Indigenis tamen mirum, quàm multa commoda præstet: siquidem sanguinem in potum, loco panis carnem in escam, cornua ad conficienda pocula, pellem in vestitum & utres; corium in tegumenta casarum, funes, calceos ac vestes, ossa ad arma conficienda, nervis ad fila, stercus ad ignis fomentum præstat, atque adeò vel hoc unicum animal ad omnes ferè humanæ vitæ usus Indigenis conducit. Ego sanè non facile assererem, id ex diversæ speciei congressu natum, sed esse bovinæ speciei animal, vel cœli influxu peculiari, aut climatis locique natura, uti fere omnia animalia *Americæ*, in hanc formam transmutatum fuisse.

Innumera hoc loco alia animalia adducere possem uti monstruosâ, ita quoque vel ex cœli apporrheâ, vel naturâ climatis, aut etiam ex promiscuo diversarum specierum congressu animalium nata; ut proinde ea in *Arcam* introducta minime putem, cum post *Diluvium* dictæ species animalium, dictis de causis nasci potuerint. Ne tamen quispiam putet, eam ob causam illa non me admittere, quod *Arca* illorum capax non fuerit: Ego ostendam, *Arcam* adhuc ad hujusmodi etiam recipienda, sat amplam capacemque fuisse. Ut verò, quæ hucusque adduximus, vera esse demonstremus, hîc Aristotelis testimonium adjungam lib. 2. de gen. animal. c. 5. ubi sic dicit: *Cœunt animalia generis ejusdem secundum naturam, sed ea etiam, quorum genus diversum quidem, sed natura non multùm distat, si modò par magnitudine sit, & tempora æquent gravidationis, raro id fit, sed tamen fieri, & in* Canibus, *& in* Vulpibus, *& in* Lupis *certum est*; Canes *etiam Indici ex bellua quadam simili &* Cane *generantur, sive ut in Græco est:* ἐκ θηρίου τινὸς κυνώδους.

DU-

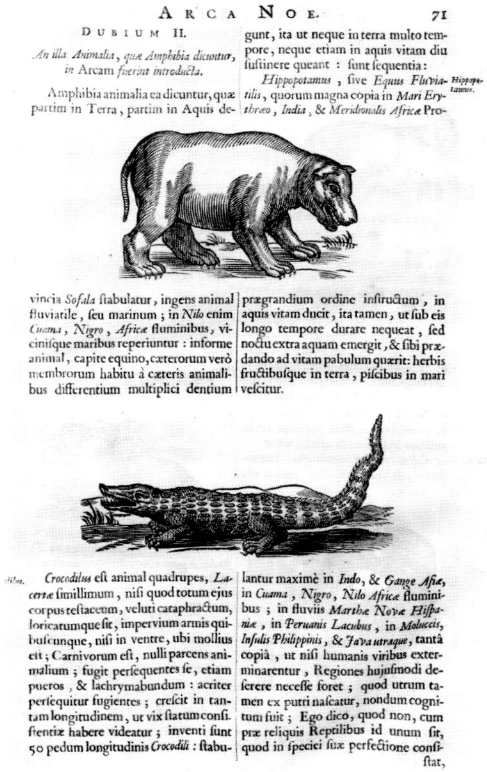

ARCA NOE. 71

DUBIUM II.

An illa Animalia, quæ Amphibia dicuntur, in Arcam *fuerint introducta.*

Amphibia animalia ea dicuntur, quæ partim in Terra, partim in Aquis degunt, ita ut neque in terra multo tempore, neque etiam in aquis vitam diu sustinere queant: sunt sequentia:

[*Hippopotamus.*] *Hippopotamus*, sive *Equus Fluviatilis*, quorum magna copia in *Mari Erythræo*, *India*, & *Meridionalis Africæ* Provincia *Sofala* stabulatur, ingens animal fluviatile, seu marinum; in *Nilo* enim *Cuama*, *Nigro*, *Africæ* fluminibus, viciniisque maribus reperiuntur: informe animal, capite equino, cæterorum verò membrorum habitu à cæteris animalibus differentium multiplici dentium prægrandium ordine instructum, in aquis vitam ducit, ita tamen, ut sub eis longo tempore durare nequeat, sed noctu extra aquam emergit, & sibi prædando ad vitam pabulum quærit: herbis fructibusque in terra, piscibus in mari vescitur.

[...dilus.] *Crocodilus* est animal quadrupes, *Lacertæ* simillimum, nisi quod totum ejus corpus testaceum, veluti cataphractum, loricatumque sit, impervium armis quibuscunque, nisi in ventre, ubi mollius est; Carnivorum est, nulli parcens animalium; fugit persequentes se, etiam pueros, & lachrymabundum: acriter persequitur fugientes; crescit in tantam longitudinem, ut vix statum consistentiæ habere videatur; inventi sunt 50 pedum longitudinis *Crocodili*: stabulantur maximè in *Indo*, & *Gange Asiæ*, in *Cuama*, *Nigro*, *Nilo Africæ* fluminibus; in fluviis *Marthæ Novæ Hispaniæ*, in *Peruanis Lacubus*, in *Moluccis*, *Insulis Philippinis*, & *Java utraque*, tantâ copiâ, ut nisi humanis viribus exterminarentur, Regiones hujusmodi deserere necesse foret; quod utrum tamen ex putri nascatur, nondum cognitum fuit; Ego dico, quod non, cum præ reliquis Reptilibus id unum sit, quod in speciei suæ perfectione consistat,

72 ATHANASII KIRCHERI

stat, atque adeò in *Arca* locum obtinere potuerit.

[*Lutra.*] *Lutra* Græcis ἐνυδρίς, animal quadrupes, tam in aquis, quàm in terra natales suos obtinens, vescitur in aquis piscibus, quas non secùs ac venaticus *Canis* terrestres feras, ita hoc aquatica in cibum sectatur animalia; in terra fructus sectatur, & cortices arborum rodendo comedit; *Felem* magnitudine exprimit. In *Germania*, *Russia*, *Prussia*, *Polonia*, *Lituania*, uti & *Neapoli* in *Italia*, in *Indiis* variis in locis, uti in *Nova Francia*, sed sub differenti forma reperiuntur: Esus carnium hujus animalis in quadragesima; diebusque jejunii, uti piscium, omniumque Amphibiorum, licitus est; pellem habet pilis delicatis instructam, unde & magno pretio in vestium hybernarum usum emitur.

[*Castor.*] *Castor* animal quadrupes Amphibium, si caudam spectes, piscis est, quam & quasi semper, aut sæpiùs aquis ad sui conservationem, immersam tenet; cæterum corpus *Lutræ* non dissimile est, pretiosa pelle ornatum, ex quo pellicea vestimenta contra frigoris hyberni violentiam conficiuntur; dentes acutissimos habet, quibus & frutices & arbuscula, tum ad fructus, quos in cibum appetit, obtinendos, tum ad habitaculorum, quæ in specubus littori maris, aut fluminum adjacentibus fabricat, constructionem amputat: & quamvis nonnulli id piscibus vivere autument, experientia tamen docuit, ea pisces tantum abest, ut appetant, ut potius eorum odorem abominentur; Quod ego tamen non de omnibus, sed quibusdam intelligi velim, cum omne Amphibium ut in utroque elemento, cibum naturæ suæ proportionatum habeat, necesse sit. Ex eo nobile illud medicamentum, quod *Castorium* vocatur, & Theriacæ compositionem præter innumeros alios usus juvat; & nil aliud sunt, quàm *Castoris* testes, qui licet intolerabili pœnè fœtore puteant, histericis tamen mulierum morbis, & odore & singulari medicamento unicè prosunt. Quod verò *Canibus* id persequentibus testes dentibus amputare dicatur, id in hunc usque diem experientiâ necdum innotuit.

[*Testudo.*] *Testudo*: Sunt, qui *Testudinem* quoque inter Amphibia ponant; forsan eâ opinione inducti, quod duplex sit *Testudinum* genus, terrestre & aquaticum: Qui in mari vastissimæ molis testudines viderit, is asserere cogetur, eas Amphibias esse non posse, cùm vastissimo Oceano perpetuò inhæreant, nec ob tarditatem motus insulas appellendi commoditatem habeant; Terrestres verò perpetuò, Hyeme præsertim terræ insepeliantur, atque ex ea vivant, ita quoque præter terrestre aliud elementum non amant; imò experientia me docuit in hujus Collegii Romani horto, ubi plures aluntur, intra fontani crateris

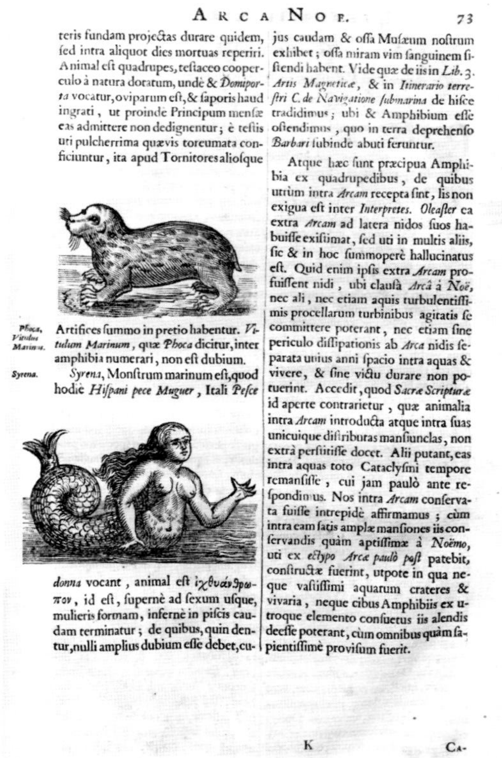

ARCA NOE. 73

teris fundam projectas durare quidem, sed intra aliquot dies mortuas reperiri. Animal est quadrupes, testaceo cooperculo à natura dotatum, undè & *Domiporta* vocatur, oviparum est, & saporis haud ingrati, ut proinde Principum mensæ eas admittere non dedignentur; è testis uti pulcherrima quævis toreumata conficiuntur, ita apud Tornitores aliosque Artifices summo in pretio habentur.

[*Phoca, Vitulus Marinus.*] *Vitulum Marinum*, quæ *Phoca* dicitur, inter amphibia numerari, non est dubium.

[*Syrena.*] *Syrena*, Monstrum marinum est, quod hodiè *Hispani pece Muguer*, Itali *Pesce donna* vocant, animal est ἰχθυάνθρωπον, id est, supernè ad sexum usque, mulieris formam, infernè in piscis caudam terminatur; de quibus, quin dentur, nulli amplius dubium esse debet, cujus caudam & ossa Musæum nostrum exhibet; ossa miram vim sanguinem sistendi habent. Vide quæ de iis in *Lib. 3. Artis Magneticæ*, & in *Itinerario terrestri C. de Navigatione submarina* de hisce tradidimus; ubi & Amphibium esse ostendimus, quo in terra deprehenso *Barbari* subinde abuti feruntur.

Atque hæc sunt præcipua Amphibia ex quadrupedibus, de quibus utrùm intra *Arcam* recepta sint, lis non exigua est inter *Interpretes*. *Oleaster* ea extra *Arcam* ad latera nidos suos habuisse existimat, sed uti in multis aliis, sic & in hoc summoperè hallucinatus est. Quid enim ipsis extra *Arcam* profuissent nidi, ubi clausâ *Arcâ* à *Noë*, nec ali, nec etiam aquis turbulentissimis procellarum turbinibus agitatis se committere poterant, nec etiam sine periculo dissipationis ab *Arca* nidis separata unius anni spacio intra aquas & vivere, & sine victu durare non potuerint. Accedit, quod *Sacræ Scripturæ* id aperte contrarietur, quæ animalia intra *Arcam* introducta atque intra suas unicuique distributas mansiunclas, non extrà perstitisse docet. Alii putant, eas intra aquas toto Cataclysmi tempore remansisse, cui jam paulò antè respondimus. Nos intra *Arcam* conservata fuisse intrepidè affirmamus; cùm intra eam satis amplæ mansiones iis conservandis quàm aptissimæ à *Noëmo*, uti ex *ectypo Arcæ paulò post* patebit, constructæ fuerint, utpote in qua neque vastissimi aquarum crateres & vivaria, neque cibus Amphibiis ex utroque elemento consuetus iis alendis deesse poterant, cùm omnibus quàm sapientissimè provisum fuerit.

K Ca-

◄ **8.22 Hybrid animals.** Kircher believed that animals of different species could mate and produce offspring. Sometimes this is possible (e.g. horse and donkey = mule), but mostly it is not. (*Arca Noë*, 68–70)

◄▼ **8.23 Amphibians.** Along with the crocodile and the otter, Kircher includes the siren, here depicted as being virtually the same as a mermaid. (*Arca Noë*, 71–73)

► **8.24 Gryphon.** Kircher illustrates this animal but describes it as 'chimaerical'. (*Arca Noë*, 77)

Likewise Kircher's griffin (or gryphon) was not the one he misleadingly illustrates and calls the 'chimaerical' creature compounded from a falcon and a lion (**Ill. 8.24**). If the griffin reported by the geographers does exist, he says: 'I would readily ascribe [it] to the genus of vultures or eagles, which have grown to such size either through the nature of the region or the influx of the heavens; wherefore we exclude them from the Ark.'[27]

Kircher's comments on snakes (**Ill. 8.26**) are a mixture of observation, folklore and mistaken theory. Here are a few of his remarks on the ones pictured:

> The virulent bite of the Seps causes putrefaction and rapid death to the person who carelessly treads on it.
> The Viper, six feet long, gives birth to living young, and may be born either from rot or from the copulation of the two sexes. Its venom has claimed many human victims.
> The bite of the Haemorrhous causes bleeding from every part of the body. It appears in America after the rains, with a double-tailed form.
> The Cerastes is named from the horn on its head. Its bite causes an itching over the whole body, then vertigo, loss of mind and swelling of the lower legs.
> The bite of the Dipsas causes its victim to drink water until his stomach bursts.

THE VULTURE AND THE OSTRICH

'Father Joannes Baptista Cysatus, mathematician of our famous Society, in his description of Switzerland, tells of how he climbed with great difficulty to the almost inaccessible summit of a rocky mountain, never before penetrated by man. He found there a formation like a crater with an oak tree in the centre, and in it an enormous nest like the ones that storks build on the roofs of houses. There were three nestlings in it, and as he was examining them down flew the parents and fell on him with such violence that if his companions had not wisely been equipped with weapons, their lives would have been at stake. After killing the mother, they found her wingspan twelve feet long, and seven feet from the point of her beak to the tip of her tail. The larger wing feathers were an elbow's length, or a cubit long. Beneath the tree nothing was to be seen but a huge heap of bodies of the animals that they had seized and transported there. Here were to be seen the skulls of children, hares, dogs, sheep and the boneless pelts of goats, together with the prominent remains of fish. After viewing these with admiration, he afterwards published a picture of what he had seen.'[28]

'The Ostrich is a monstrous animal, participating of quadrupeds as well as of birds. If you look at the mass of its body, it comes closest to the form of a Camel in its humped back, length of neck, sturdiness of legs and twofold claws; if you consider its feathered body and its egg-laying, it is numbered with the birds. It eats seeds, and devours whatever is offered without tasting it. It greedily snaps at iron and eats it, as my experience in Malta taught me, where they are brought from Africa and seen everywhere. Not only does it swallow iron, but digests it through a special quality of its stomach, as we found from the excrement in its pen. I would not think it fit for food, as no animal could be nourished by it, but it ate iron with the greatest avidity, either to strengthen its stomach or as a medicine for a hidden ailment... For the rest, it is a forgetful and stupid animal, for when it is trying to avoid the snares of men, it hides its head among dense shrubs and fancies that if its head cannot be seen, neither can the rest of its body.'[29]

8.25 Vulture and ostrich. Kircher tells lively tales of both. (*Arca Noë*, 78, 79)

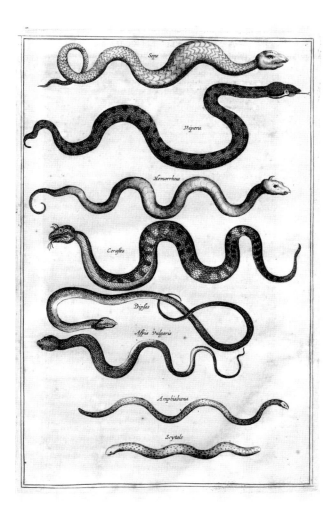

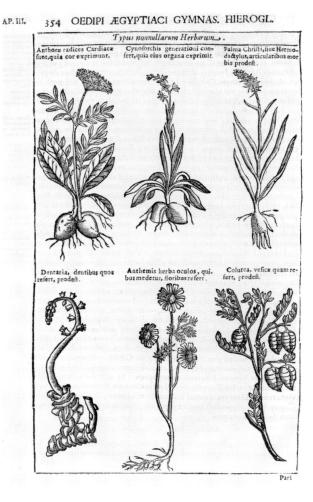

▶ **8.26** Serpents. Kircher combines real information with folklore and even theology. For example, the reason why God created serpents was to remind mankind of the serpent of Eden. (*Arca Noë*, opposite p. 54)

▶▶ **8.27** Hieroglyphic plants: plants whose shapes tell us which diseases they cure. (*Œdipus Ægyptiacus*, Volume II, 354)

The Asp is a degenerate form of the Viper that developed when the latter was imported into Egypt.

The Amphisbaena has two heads, one at either end of its body.

The Scytale is tinged with innumerable colours, and while the curious are staring at it, it kills them with irremediable venom.[30]

After describing these dangerous 'amphibians', Kircher feels that he must excuse God for creating them and Noah for allowing them into the Ark. First, they serve to remind mankind of that first serpent, 'from whom originated the ruin of the whole human race, which was so great that nothing less than the blood of the Son of God could repair it'. Second, the constant vicissitudes of nature, its generation and corruption, cannot prevent such creatures from arising from the malign influence of the stars and from putrefaction on earth; they also serve as food for storks, crows, and so on. Third, they contain excellent medical remedies, such as theriac. Fourth, they purged the Ark and its air from dangerous vapours by attracting them to themselves.[31]

We end this survey of Kircher's natural history with a few loose ends taken from his other books, each of which illuminates a facet of his character and attitudes. In the early book on optics, *Ars Magna Lucis,* he writes of what we

would call psychosomatic phenomena, using the traditional concept of "spirit" (*spiritus*) as a subtle substance permeating organic matter, and develops this into a theory of monstrous births:

> Such is the plastic spirit, that marvellous forms are produced by strong imagination; hence come the stigmata, moles and characteristic markings of fruits, red wine, flesh and animals that are impressed at birth. If cherries, strawberries or wine are thrown or poured in the face or bosom of a pregnant woman, and she is distressed by it, then the said thing is impressed on the foetus and will be seen depicted there. The same thing happens if a cat, mouse or weasel unexpectedly jumps onto a pregnant woman; for it is immediately impressed on the foetus by a radiant species through phantasy, and by the spirits descending to where the foetus is, by a corresponding touch; unless the woman straightaway wipes with her hand the member that the animal has touched, and moves the hand to another, distant part of the body.[32]

Kircher much preferred this explanation to the folk belief that deformed human births resulted from sexual congress with animals, and he deplores the incidents in the past in which women have been so accused. 'Let it be said, against the atheists of our time (who impiously assert that a human can actually conceive by a beast, and even that the human soul is as mortal as an animal's) that this monster cannot have been produced from the semen of a dog.'[33]

His theory of germination meant that he did not have to account for how the vegetable world survived the Flood; Noah did not have to stock the Ark with the seeds of plants and trees. If in Kircher's theory the sperm of a lower animal could fall on the ground and grow into that animal, plant seeds could do no less. He seems to have had no interest in botany as such, only in plants as members of the chain of being which linked every level of the universe through magnetic bonds and magical correspondences. Those which demonstrate this visibly he calls 'hieroglyphic' (**Ill. 8.27**), writing: 'There is an analogy between certain members of the human body and the various characteristics of plants that represent the said members.'[34] In this illustration we see plants whose roots reveal their usefulness for healing the heart, the organs of generation, the hands and joints; and whose stalks, flowers or fruits resemble teeth, eyes and bladders. Kircher adds that the same principle of like curing like applies to the animal world, so that diseases of the liver, for instance, are treated with the livers of deer, doves and other animals of a 'livery' nature.

This kind of argument paradoxically served as a counterweight to the acceptance of other common beliefs. For example, among the many fables that the early scientific revolution weighed and found wanting was that of the 'vegetable lamb' (**Ill. 8.28**). Several of Kircher's sources assured him that this plant is still to be found in Tartary; that it has a seed like a melon's, and from it grows a lamb about three feet high, complete with hoofs and ears, with the stalk ending at the navel. When cut, it bleeds; and wolves like to eat it. Kircher treated such reports with the contempt they deserved, because, as he says, he knows plenty of other instances of plants that resemble animals or body parts.[35]

Another example of Kircher's scepticism is his experiment with rhinoceros horn (**Ill. 8.29**). Here the claim was that the horn of the rhinoceros attracts iron. Kircher says that he has witnessed this experiment several times, in which a sword is held between two fingers and a vase carved from rhinoceros horn is slowly moved around the blade, supposedly causing the latter to move with it. 'But whether it comes from the attractive force of the horn, or the motion of the air, or a defect of balance, I cannot say; and, to tell the truth, I have frequently tried the thing in private with much more exact balancing, but could never detect the slightest movement, either magnetic or electric.'[36]

There was controversy in Kircher's time, as there is today, about the validity of divining (or 'dowsing') for discovering underground water or metals. Kircher illustrates two sorts of divining rod (**Ill. 8.30**), made from hazel, which respond by sudden movement when they cross a vein of silver or other metal. He accepts the possibility on the grounds that all metals continually put out exhalations, which affect different plants in different ways. For instance, the exhalations of antimony, auripigment and arsenic wither all but a few plants, but these exceptions are strengthened thereby. Thus one can judge the mining potential of a territory by the state of its vegetation.

◄ **8.28** Boromez or lamb-plant – a plant that grows in Tartary and is supposed to have the exact shape of a lamb. Kircher cannot bring himself to believe it. (*Magnes*, 730)

◄▼ **8.29** Experiment with rhinoceros horn. The horn was supposed to be magnetic and to attract iron, but Kircher tested it and found that it never worked. (*Magnes*, 19)

▼ **8.30** Divining rods: hazel branches which respond to metals such as silver, a belief still current. (*Magnes*, 725)

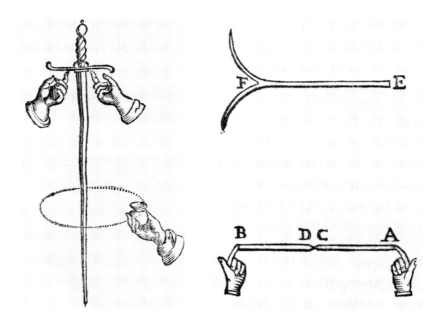

Kircher then quotes Paracelsus on how every plant has its corresponding metal: hazel flourishes above veins of silver, and inclines towards them; ash to copper; pitch-pine to lead. He had tested these woods against the metals themselves, and established that the attraction was not magnetic in nature. Moreover, he had made a simple experimental device from two contiguous sticks of different woods balanced on a pin. One of these woods was supposedly sympathetic to a certain metal, the other not. Experiment showed that there was no natural inclination of wood to metal. He concluded that the effect comes from the hands of the operator, and proceeded to another experiment. Making a rod of elm, he found that it responded to underground water. The reason appeared to be that trees take in metallic vapours through their roots, and these are left in the wood. When a stick imbued with such vapours

8.31 Tarantula and its antidote. Kircher includes a map of Apulia (Taranto) where this spider lives. It was widely believed that the poison could be neutralized by making the patient dance – hence 'Tarantella'. (*Magnes*, opposite 824)

felt strongly compelled to dance, but in vain, because while the venom of one tarantula made him do so, that of the other, being altogether contrary in substance, restrained him from it. They tried again, bringing in other instruments, with strains of a different kind, and indeed he felt that one of them was strongly urging him to dance, but could not... In the end, since there was no way to get the venom out of him, he departed from life, not without pain and the commiseration of the bystanders. Thus he taught by his example how rash and dangerous it is to expose oneself without caution and circumspection to fatal experiment.[38]

Notes

1 *Mundus Subterraneus*, 1665, I, 208.
2 *Mundus Subterraneus*, 1664, II, 58.
3 *Mundus Subterraneus*, 1664, II, 57–58.
4 *Mundus Subterraneus*, 1664, II, 96.
5 *Mundus Subterraneus*, 1664, II, 91–93.
6 *Mundus Subterraneus*, 1664, II, 94.
7 *Mundus Subterraneus*, 1664, II, 94–95.
8 *Mundus Subterraneus*, 1678, II, 117.
9 Aldrovandi, 61.
10 *Arca Noë*, 53–54.
11 *Arca Noë*, 64.
12 *Mundus Subterraneus*, 1664, II, 63–64.
13 See Baltrušaitis 1989, 70–79.
14 *Mundus Subterraneus*, 1664, II, 23–24.
15 *Mundus Subterraneus*, 1664, II, 25.
16 *Mundus Subterraneus*, 1664, II, 31. The first edition had some confusion of the numbering of causes and illustrations, which was corrected in the second edition.
17 *Mundus Subterraneus*, 1678, II, 41.
18 *Mundus Subterraneus*, 1678, II, 44.
19 *Mundus Subterraneus*, 1678, II, 44.
20 Summarized from *Mundus Subterraneus*, 1678, II, 47–48.
21 Gómez de Liaño, I, 69–88, reproduces 96 animals and 39 birds from *Arca Noë*.
22 *Arca Noë*, 65.
23 *Arca Noë*, 63.
24 A version of the same theory appears in 'The Beginning of the Armadillos' in Rudyard Kipling's *Just So Stories*.
25 *Arca Noë*, 70. Kircher's *corcobado* is probably copied from the bison in Francisco Hernandez, *Rerum Medicarum Novae Hispaniae*, Rome, 1651 (see illustration in Desmond, 25).
26 *Arca Noë*, 73.
27 *Arca Noë*, 77–78.
28 *Arca Noë*, 77.
29 *Arca Noë*, 78.
30 *Arca Noë*, 55.
31 *Arca Noë*, 54–55; compare the use of a toad as a plague magnet, p. 18.
32 *Ars Magna Lucis*, 1646, 805; 1671, 707.
33 *Ars Magna Lucis*, 1646, 805; 1671, 708.
34 *Œdipus Ægyptiacus*, II, ii, 353.
35 *Magnes*, 1641, 730; 1643, 639.
36 *Magnes*, 1641, 20; 1643, 18.
37 *Magnes*, 1641, 725–727; 1643, 635–636.
38 *Magnes*, 1641, 880–881; 1643, 767–768.

is pointed at the ground, the vapours flow out of it and are greedily swallowed by the earth. Incidentally, the effect is much lessened after noon.[37]

Lastly, we see how a man who would lower himself into an erupting volcano will still draw the line against rash experimentation. This illustration of the tarantula (**Ill. 8.31**) shows the spider's abdominal and dorsal views, and above them a map of Apulia (the heel of Italy) where it is found, together with one of the melodies that serve as an antidote to its sting. Seven other melodies are notated in the text, in which Kircher speculates on the efficacy of the cure. Among other stories, he tells the following:

A certain Spaniard, staying for a while in Taranto and hearing about [the phenomenon], treated it with derision, and refused to believe the testimony of many trustworthy people unless he should experience the danger for himself. Two tarantulas were then found, of different colour and quality, put upon his hand, and provoked to sting it in different places. As the venom was absorbed through the stings and gradually diffused through his whole body, he soon felt severe paroxysms and feared for his life. Immediately lyre and aulos players, and every sort of musician were summoned, and various kinds of music were tried. At one strain, the patient

Chapter 9   **Music**

Kircher's mastery of music is one of his most unexpected traits. While musical talent typically shows itself in childhood and leads to a lifelong involvement with performance and/or composition, Kircher's biography reveals nothing of the sort. Only once does he mention having had any musical training or inclination in his youth; he never tells anecdotes linking himself with music,[1] and no biographer has shown him doing anything musical. Yet music is not easily learned in later life, while to compose counterpoint, play it on the keyboard, or read it from the score in one's head is no light achievement at any age. Could Kircher do it?

He himself answers the question in the preface to *Musurgia* with a spirited defence, saying that just because he does not perform music or compose for money, it does not mean that he is incompetent. 'The Prince of Venosa [Gesualdo] was not a musician by trade; so was he ignorant of it? Did the great kings Ptolemy and Alfonso, in not professing music or astronomy, know nothing of them?'[2] The idea, he adds, is insolent and absurd! From an early age he has worked at all the noble arts and sciences, including music both theoretical and practical, with attentive study and diligent practice. Not only that, but some of his compositions have been published in Germany under others' names, and heard with considerable pleasure, and there are examples in this book that will serve as his witnesses.[3]

While many pieces in *Musurgia Universalis* are unattributed and may be by him, Kircher states plainly that he composed the example (**Ill. 9.1**) of how to handle three-part writing. He says that the voices can begin together, or else one can lead and the others follow, observing the rules of harmony, diminution and syncopation. In its short compass, this *Paradigma melothesias omnibus numeris absolutae* (example of free composition in all rhythms) contains at least eight different motifs, each treated imitatively and having its own 'affect' or mood. Typically of Kircher's zeal to classify and display the variety of the world, he has here composed a musical microcosm, a sort of miniature specimen chest. Equally typically, he says that his piece 'describes the soul moved towards God in harmonic affection'.[4]

As for the myriad other compositions and musical examples in *Musurgia*, Kircher admits that he had help, and no wonder: at over 1,200 pages it remained for centuries the most comprehensive work on music by a single author.[5] In treating the church style, he was helped by Antonio Maria Abbatini

KIRCHER AS COMPOSER

9.1 'A paradigm of free composition in all rhythms'.

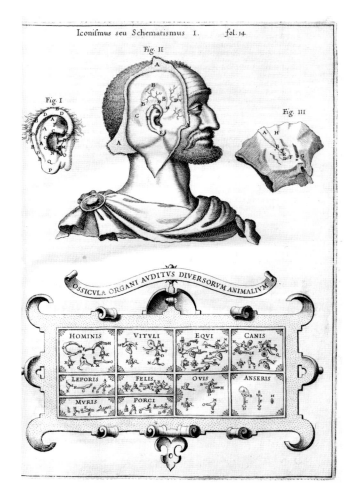

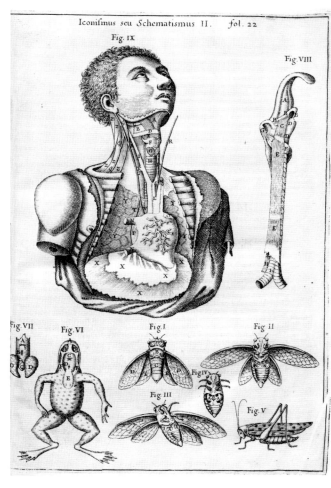

◄◄ 9.2 The anatomy of the ear and its parts, which the small frames beneath compare with the ears of other animals. (*Musurgia Universalis*, Volume I, opposite 14)

◄ 9.3 The anatomy of the voice. As with the ear, Kircher compares the human voice with the sounds made by animals. (*Musurgia Universalis*, Volume I, opposite 22)

and Pedro de Heredia; in the canonic style, by Pietro Francesco Valentini. Silverio Picerli furnished fifty pages of didactic examples. The German lutenist Johannes Hieronymus Kapsberger helped him with the instrumental style, and Giacomo Carissimi with the recitative and other recondite styles.[6] By enlisting these specialists, Kircher overcame the Herculean task of searching out suitable examples of every type of music, and composing hundreds of pieces to illustrate every theoretical point. It left him to apply his stupendous erudition to the historical aspects; to tuning theory, classed by the ancients as a branch of mathematics; to developing a composition machine, an exercise after his own heart; to acoustics, regarded as a sister science to the 'art of light and shadow', which had been the subject of his previous book; and to the Christian-Hermetic peroration that closes the work.

Musurgia opens with the anatomy of the musical parts of man and beast: the ear and the voice. The first engraving (**Ill. 9.2**) shows the outer ear and its parts, and the small bones of the middle ear, namely the hammer, the anvil and the stirrup. The small frames beneath compare these bones in the hearing apparatus of man, calf, horse, dog, hare, cat, sheep, goat, mouse and pig.

For his explication of the ear and how it works, Kircher credits a 'famous surgeon and anatomist of Rome', Ioannes Trullius (Giovanni Trulli, 1598–1661), and the anatomy book of Iulius Casserius (Giulio Casseri).[7] He also acknowledges the authority of Andreas Vesalius.[8] The text describes the three semicircular canals, but says that they have been omitted from the engraving because of the difficulty of illustrating them. It also mentions the cochlea, but hazards no guess as to its function. More important to Kircher is the question of what sort of air is contained in these chambers, which he assumes to be totally isolated from the outside air. He thinks that it must be similar to the air that is treated in the lungs before it is allowed to reach the heart, or the air that enters the nostrils and must be 'prepared' before it can penetrate the brain. This treatment modifies the temperature and humidity of the air, enabling it to nourish the animal spirits. This leads him to consider theories of sound. Some say that it is a real and independent entity, while others, that it only exists as perception. He takes the middle path: sound really exists as waves propagated in the air, but also 'the sounds of sonorous objects reach the auditive potential by the emission of species'.

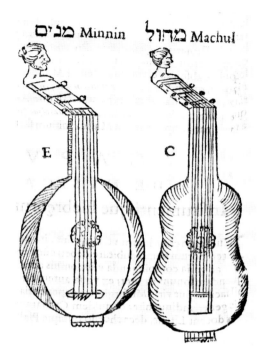

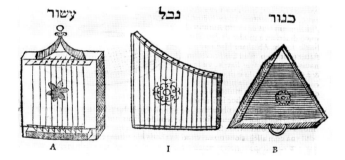

◄ **9.4** Birdsongs: the songs of various birds transcribed into musical notation. (*Musurgia Universalis*, Volume I, opposite 30)

► **9.5** Stringed instruments of the ancient Hebrews. Kircher imagines them as instruments very like those of his own time. (*Musurgia Universalis*, Volume I, 48, 49)

In terms such as 'species' and 'spirits' we hear the struggle of Aristotelian metaphysics to bridge the gap between objective reality and subjective perception. The problems were of a different order when Kircher came to the vocal organs (**Ill. 9.3**).

Who can easily explain the great variety of vocal production in animals? We hear the querulous voice of the toad, the lugubrious cry of the kite, the plaints of the mourning dove, the cuckoo's call, the sweet trilling of the nightingale, the piping of swallows, the cock's crow, the trumpeting of elephants, the bleating of sheep, the lowing of cattle, the barking of dogs, and we wonder what meaning of love, hatred, anger, indignation, sorrow or lamenting lies in them.[9]

Kircher defines the voice thus: 'The voice is the sound produced by an animal from the glottis through the striking of exhaled air, for expressing the affects of the soul.'[10] Consequently he excludes the buzzing or chirping of insects, and, for that matter, the voice that reputedly issued from the stomach of the Pythoness (the prophetic priestess of the Delphic Oracle). The voice of the frog was a borderline case, about whose cause even Aristotle was uncertain, but Kircher settled the matter by experiment. 'We excited [a croak] in a recently dead frog by inserting a pipe through the ribs and into the trachea, then strongly blowing out the water collected in the gullet.'[11] He concluded that the frog's croak is not really a 'voice', but is caused by air violently expelled from the lungs and meeting with moisture: in short, a belch.

The often-reproduced plate of birdsongs (**Ill. 9.4**) shows the song of the nightingale transcribed into musical notation, and the songs of the cock, hen (B: laying an egg; C: gathering her chicks), cuckoo, quail and parrot. The latter has been taught to say 'Hello!' in Greek; but that is nothing compared to a bird of the lark species, called *gallandra*, as we read in the accompanying text. A learned Portuguese friar, Damianus à Fonseca, kept a pet *gallandra* in his 'museum' and trained it to rattle off the Litany of the Saints, and much else, in a quasi-human voice. Kircher would never have believed this, had not he and others witnessed the bird's performance in Father Damianus's cell on 16 March 1648.

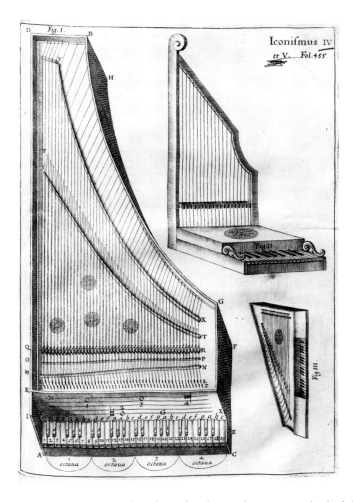

◀ **9.6** Keyboard instruments. Borrowed by Kircher from Marin Mersenne's *Harmonie Universelle*. (*Musurgia Universalis*, Volume I, opposite 454)

▶ **9.7** Plucked instruments. Also from Mersenne. (*Musurgia Universalis*, Volume I, opposite 476)

As we waited in silence for what might transpire, this little bird, after the sweetest cantillations and various murmurings, began to pronounce all the names of the saints, clearly and distinctly in the Italian language. Then it added the words *ora pro nobis* [pray for us], and sometimes *Iesus Christus Crucifixus* [Jesus Christ crucified], and more and more up to 70 different names. It was so marvellously executed that one could scarcely believe that one was hearing a bird's tongue, it was so human-like.[12]

Organology

Reading Kircher on musical instruments and studying his illustrations of them, I have the impression that he knew little about them, and cared less – which is odd in view of his fascination with machines and technology. For all his erudition, his historical anachronisms are quite jarring, especially regarding the instruments of the ancient Hebrews. He credits most of his knowledge of them to a book called *Schilte Haggib(b)orim*, whose Hebrew text he reproduces, and derives his illustrations from a Vatican manuscript (**Ill. 9.5**). While the psaltery (A), *neuel* (I) and *cinnor* (B) look typically antique, the *minnin*

(E) and the *machul* (C) are obviously a lute and guitar of the seventeenth century, drawn by someone unfamiliar with the instruments themselves (and with inappropriate 'graven images' on the pegboxes). Kircher seems to have imagined the ancient Hebrews as playing instruments very similar to those of his own time. In fact, he writes that 'the stringed instrument *haghniugab* (mentioned in the Targum sometimes as *onkelos*, sometimes as *vzielidis*) was scarcely different from the large viol commonly called a viola da gamba'.[13]

Kircher borrowed his modern organology from Mersenne's far superior treatment in *Harmonie Universelle*. In the illustration of keyboard instruments (**Ill. 9.6**), Figure I is copied from Mersenne, right down to the letters on its various parts, and the statement in the text that of the various models of harpsichord, this one is by far the most commonly used. However, one can tell from the two bridges that it is strung in French or Flemish fashion with one 8' and one 4' rank, instead of the two 8' ranks preferred in Italy.

The second instrument is an upright harpsichord, usually called a clavicytherium (though Kircher gives it no particular name). The illustration is again taken from Mersenne, who calls it 'a new form of spinet in use in Italy',

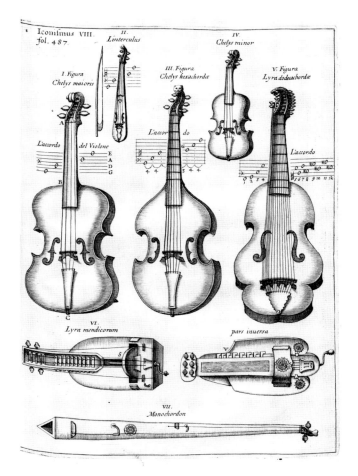

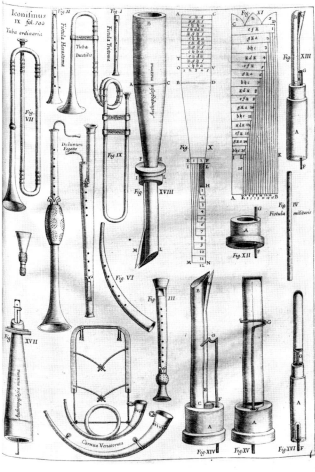

◄◄ 9.8 Bowed
stringed instruments,
from Mersenne.
(*Musurgia Universalis*,
Volume I, opposite
486)

◄ 9.9 Wind
instruments, selected
from Mersenne.
(*Musurgia Universalis*,
Volume I, opposite
500)

while Kircher says that instruments of this kind are frequently used in Germany. 'They are convenient because they take up little space, and serve as an ornament for chambers. Moreover, they have a double function: as harps, and as harpsichords.'[14] Apparently the strings could also be plucked.

The third figure shows a 'spinettino', a miniature harpsichord, 'pitched so high that listeners can scarcely guess what instrument they are hearing; yet it is peculiarly strong and effective in string ensembles'.

Most of what Mersenne and Kircher write about keyboard instruments concerns efforts to achieve perfect intonation, by splitting or doubling first the sharp keys (e.g. to provide different tunings for F-sharp and G-flat), and then the naturals as well, resulting in a keyboard with thirty-two different keys to the octave. This would enable all the diatonic, chromatic and enharmonic tones to be rendered in perfect tuning, but not a word is said about the difficulty of playing on it, nor of the harpsichord builder's problems in cramming thirty-two strings and jacks, instead of just twelve, into the space that one hand can span.

The figures in the engraving of plucked stringed instruments (**Ill. 9.7**) with their tunings all come from Mersenne. They are: I. Fingerboard of a theorbo; II.

Ten-course lute; III. Fourteen-course theorbo; IV. Pandora; V. Cittern; VI. Spanish guitar; VII. Miniature lute or mandora; VIII. Turkish three-stringed colachon. In the brief accompanying text, Kircher gives the following etymology for the theorbo (a name today considered 'of uncertain origin'): its inventor, a Neopolitan street-player, saw a resemblance in it to the *tiorba*, the name given to the mortar used by spice and perfume makers to grind their wares. But giving credit where it is due, he adds that it was a German nobleman, Kapsberger, who brought its playing to perfection and established its superiority to all other instruments.[15]

As a pendant to the engraving of plucked instruments, this one (**Ill. 9.8**) shows the other subdivision of stringed instruments: those played with the bow, or in the case of the hurdy-gurdy with a rosined wheel. Here again, all the illustrations are redrawn after Mersenne, to whom Kircher refers the reader for further details. The instruments, in modern nomenclature, are: I. Bass violin or violone; II. Pocket violin or kit; III. Bass viol or viola da gamba; IV. Violin; V. Lira or lirone; VI. Hurdy-gurdy; VII. Tromba marina.

Wind instruments are the second of Kircher's largest divisions of instruments, coming between strings and percussion. His engraving (**Ill. 9.9**)

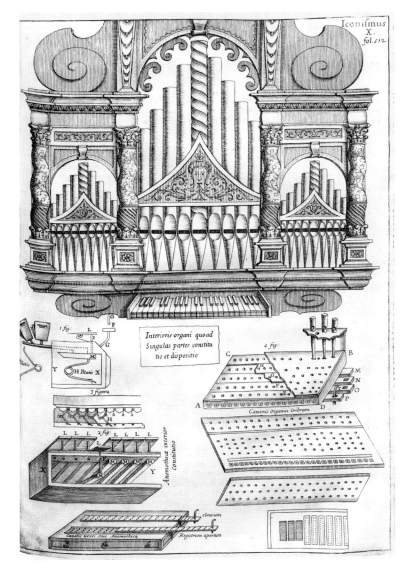

9.10 Organ. The decoration reflects the Italian Baroque, but technically this organ is not very advanced. The diagrams below, showing how it worked, are Mersenne's. (*Musurgia Universalis*, Volume I, opposite 512)

shows a selection from Mersenne's much larger collection. In modern terms they are: I. Three-holed pipe (used with a tabor or small drum); II. Six-holed pipe or flageolet; III. Recorder with eight finger holes and a key; IV. Fife or military flute; [V] Hunting horns, one with a baldric; VI. Cornetto; VII. Trumpet; [VIII] Shawm, with its double reed; [IX] Dulcian or bassoon; IX. Trombone or sackbut; X–XVIII. Details and specifications of organ reed-pipes.

Kircher loved the sound of the wind instruments used in church. After printing the score of a sinfonia for four cornetti and dulcian, he comments:

> The tibiae or horns commonly known as cornetti achieve a wonderful effect in music. I certainly see our Roman musicians having no trouble with them, for no church music could be better suited to them, espe-

cially if three, four or five tibiae are accompanied by a dulcian (commonly called a fagot). In great solemnities and feasts, I think I would far prefer symphonies of this kind over a consort of strings.[16]

Of all these instruments, Kircher treats the trumpet most thoroughly, because its natural scale, following the harmonic series, answered to his concern with number and acoustics. He was fascinated by the gaps in its scale, which he explains thus: when the trumpet jumps from its fundamental tone to the second harmonic, an octave above, the air suddenly has to move twice as fast; at the third harmonic, three times as fast, and so on, up to the practical limit of the 29th or even the 32nd harmonic. Although this is a fallacy (because pitch depends on the frequency of sound waves, not on the speed of sound), Kircher's explanation of the trumpet scale remains purely physical, unlike Mersenne's effort to justify it through theological symbolism.

The upper part of Kircher's organ (**Ill. 9.10**) is decorated in Baroque style, with spiral columns imitated from Bernini's baldacchino in St Peter's, and scrolls like those on countless Italian church façades. In contrast to this grandeur are the single keyboard of three-and-a-half octaves, the lack of pedals and of stops. As Kircher was well aware, Italian organs were very limited in comparison to northern instruments, but not that deficient. Below are Mersenne's diagrams of the workings of the organ, explained in the text, though not sufficiently to instruct a builder. Most of the text on organs is devoted to the measurement and geometry of flue and reed pipes. As he concludes this section, Kircher reveals a conflicted attitude to practical and 'mechanical' matters, which was never in evidence in his books on magnetism or optics. The reason it surfaces here must be the longstanding tradition among music theorists, sanctified by Boethius, of contempt for merely practical musicians.

> Furthermore, there are the wind containers, commonly called *Portaventi*, which are wooden channels of whatever quantity the mass of the organ requires. These channels have their origin in the bellows, with which they are contiguous. The bellows, more or less numerous as the size of the machine demands, have their proportions which can

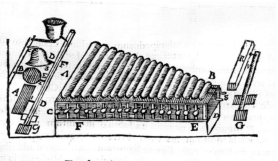

9.11 *Zylorganum*, essentially a keyed xylophone. Kircher makes the point that the same principles could be applied to other materials beside wood. (*Musurgia Universalis*, Volume I, 518)

9.12 Echoes. After analysing an echo acoustically, Kircher typically proposes ways of turning it into a curiosity or game. (*Musurgia Universalis*, Volume II, opposite 264)

9.13 Acoustic theatres. Following Vitruvius, Kircher describes the properties of resonators inside chambers behind the stage. Figure II shows an 'echo theatre' near Milan. (*Musurgia Universalis*, Volume II, opposite 282)

be seen in Causius and Marsennus [i.e., Salomon de Caus and Marin Mersenne], from which we have largely taken these things. Here I could add much more about the quality of bellows that I have learned by word of mouth from organ builders, but we deliberately omit them, lest we should seem to be busying ourselves too much with mechanical things and other trite matters accessible to the vulgar. But anyone who desires more recondite things should consult our 'Musical Magic', where we certainly hope to have adequately satisfied the reader's curiosity.[17]

Like Mersenne, Kircher was much interested in the properties of the various materials used for musical instruments. He discusses the different

animal guts and metals from which strings can be made, and explains how the guts are twisted and the metals are formed into wires. In two cases he gives the quantitative results of his experiments, comparing the pitches rendered by different species of wood and by bells forged from different metals. In both cases he tabulates Mersenne's figures against his own, and records his puzzlement that they do not agree.

Among his few percussion instruments is the *Zylorganum*, or wooden organ, in effect a keyed xylophone (**Ill. 9.11**). The wooden blocks are suspended on wires over a resonant chamber, and sounded by a simple pivoting action (shown on the right) resembling that of the clavichord. As a corollary to this experiment, Kircher suggests that the principle can be extended to any substance in the world, but the more resonant it is, the better. Some of these appear on the left, where the key (G) causes tangents or hammers to strike a wood block (A), a 'tintinnabulum' (B), a glass bell (D) and/or some other bell-shaped body. Finally, Kircher describes the infamous 'cat organ', in which the sounding objects were cats of various sizes, and the keys prodded spikes into their tails, 'which produced a harmony that moved men to laughter, and might cause the very mice to jump for joy'.[18]

Acoustics

In the second volume of *Musurgia*, Kircher addresses a favourite subject: that of the analogy between sound and light. Having exhaustively treated the latter in *Ars Magna Lucis et Umbrae*, he was on the lookout for acoustical refractions, reflections, amplifications and multiplications. In the plate illustrating echoes (**Ill. 9.12**), Figure I makes the point that a series of equally spaced walls, or towers, will reflect the voice in a multiple echo. Kircher discovered the effect in Avignon, where the city walls favoured the phenomenon, and repeated it at the walls of Rome. The trick was to stand at the same distance from the first wall as the distance between the walls, and then to speak however many syllables could be fitted in before the first echo returned. Ideally, one would then hear one's syllables echoed successively by the more distant walls.

In Figure II, the experimenter is causing the echo to return a different word from that which he spoke. He has chosen the word *clamore*, which has the peculiarity that as the initial letters are removed one by one, what remains is still a real word.[19] As the walls are more distant, their echoes are more abbreviated. Still more wonderful is the case in which words spoken in one language cause an echo in another one. To this end, Kircher provides a list of Greek phrases whose last syllables can be construed as Latin words: a good example of how readily his science wandered off into 'curiosity'.

Figure III takes a further step from experience into fantasy. It suggests building a circular enclosure with inner walls or baffles designed to produce successive echoes. Kircher calls on Euclidean geometry to argue that the baffles will all bounce the sound to point G, from which it will return to the auditor at A as a distinct series of echoes.

Other echoic phenomena are illustrated by the two buildings in **Ill. 9.13**. Although they look superficially similar, they illustrate entirely different acoustic phenomena: resonance and reflection. As to the first, the Roman architect Vitruvius set a puzzle for future generations when he recommended installing tuned resonators of bronze in theatres, to amplify the actors' voices. After careful examination of Vitruvius's text and criticism of the architect's musical errors, Kircher arrives at the design in Figure I. The resonators are suspended inside chambers behind the stage, with mouth-like openings through which the vibrations of the voices supposedly enter, stimulate the resonators, and emerge louder.

Kircher also reads into Vitruvius's text a hint that the resonators could be used to play an overture to the drama:

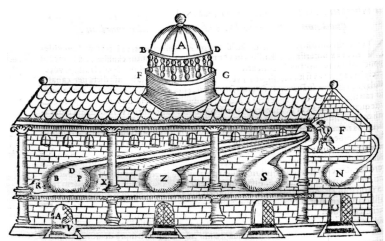

▲▲ 9.14 The 'Ear of Dionysus', part of a quarry near Syracuse, which still exists. (*Phonurgia Nova*, 84)

▲ 9.15 Acoustic system for palaces, a device for eavesdropping on private conversations. (*Musurgia Universalis*, Volume II, 296)

In order to excite the audience, and to sharpen their expectation of what was to come, before the actors came on stage the Echaea [resonators] were sounded; but this could only be done if iron wires furnished with hammers were strung through all the cells. Once this wire was diligently installed, someone specially appointed to the task could set all the vases going in perfect harmony. These vases made a powerful noise in the cells that could be heard loud and long, and was all the more wonderful because the musical apparatus was hidden.[20]

Figure II shows a contemporary 'echo theatre', that of Villa Simonetta near Milan. It was rumoured that if one shouted through a certain window (RS), one would hear twenty-four or more echoes. Kircher would not take this astonishing report on trust, but sent a fellow Jesuit to investigate: one Matthaeus Storr, noted both for his erudition and his 'German candour' – a quality often praised by the still patriotic Kircher. After studying Storr's findings, Kircher concluded that the echoes were the result of two exactly parallel walls, standing an optimum distance apart. This enabled a sound hitting the wall exactly opposite the window to bounce back and forth again and again.

A third acoustic phenomenon, that of propagation through a tube, is shown in the next illustration (**Ill. 9.14**). Near Syracuse in Sicily, among the quarries formerly used as a prison, there is a cave called The 'Ear of Dionysus', because the tyrant Dionysus is said to have used it to eavesdrop on his prisoners' conversations. Kircher visited it in 1638, and his Jesuit contacts in Sicily later provided him with measured plans of it. Kircher concluded that for maximum acoustical effect, the tyrant had deliberately had it made in the form of the human ear. Admitting that it is difficult to picture it on account of its twists and turns, he offers this woodcut. At the bottom are the 'slave quarters', and at the top of the cliff the 'house of Dionysus the Tyrant', where he secretly listens to them.

This became the inspiration for Kircher's many plans for snooping or intercommunication devices. For instance, in **Ill. 9.15** he devises a system by which the proprietor of a palace can eavesdrop on his servants or guests. Here the prince sits in his private chamber and overhears what is going on in the downstairs rooms, or listens to music from them.

> Make a room big enough to hold a few people, eight spans[21] long, as shown in the figure, and equal in length and height. It should have a low and narrow door A, which can be tightly closed, and windows of the thickest glass inserted in the walls, so that the sound of the voices resonating inside can escape neither by the door nor window, but is led via the channel DE through a secret passage into the chamber F. You should make it continuous from D, the ceiling of the chamber (which should be highly polished, like the spiral tube just mentioned), so that it forms one unbroken surface.[22]

Another acoustic phenomenon, analogous to the focusing power of lenses or mirrors, occurs in some circular, domed buildings: a person on one side can be clearly heard by someone diametrically opposite, no matter how far the distance or how much ambient noise there is (see **Ill. 9.16**). Kircher mentions as examples the round tower of Heidelberg Castle and a hall of the 'subur-

ban palace' (presumably the Palazzo del Tè) in Mantua.[23] In *Phonurgia Nova* he describes his own experiments in the dome of St Peter's (shown very approximately here), where 'inside the cupola the corona is so wide that one could safely drive a carriage around it'.[24] He explains that a quiet murmur at point A propagates in circles, reflecting off the walls at every point, until all the reflections converge on the listener at point B.

An oft-reproduced engraving (**Ill. 9.17**) instructs one 'How to construct in any building a cone twisted in a spiral, or a shell-like tube, so that it will render any articulated sounds clearly and distinctly inside a room, no matter how distant from the outside, just as if it were next to the ear, with no one suspecting where it could come from'.[25]

Kircher built something of this kind in preparation for the visit of Queen Christina of Sweden to his museum, calling it the 'Delphic Oracle' that answered whatever questions it was asked.[26] No doubt it impressed her, but to us it is the enormous spiral tube that dominates the image. Kircher adds:

> One may well wonder why the multiplication of sound is so strong in a cone twisted in a spiral. I have certainly pondered long over this matter, finding at last that a helical cone, twisted in a certain ratio, makes some kind of parabola which brings about infinite conglomerations of sound. So it is no wonder that it achieves such energy in the multiplication of sound.[27]

Figure III combines the spiral tube with the 'whispering gallery' phenomenon (see **Ill. 9.16**), only here using an elliptical rather than a circular vault. The idea is that the sounds outside the room are reflected off the ceiling and concentrated at the point at the other end, where a speaking statue is placed. The voices outside then seem to come from the statue.

Kircher was convinced that the multiple reflection of sound in tubes, especially spiral and elliptical ones, actually amplified the original signal. This would later be demonstrated to be an acoustical fallacy, but it is easy to see how Kircher's experiments led him to believe it, and to design apparatuses exploiting it. A further variation on the principle of the 'Ear of Dionysus' requires a sealed chamber (**Ill. 9.18**) with a concave plastered ceiling, from which a tube twenty-two palms (or feet? See note 21) long leads to the outside of the building. The music played in the chamber will be so greatly amplified as to be audible two or three miles (three or four kilometres) away. Kircher assures the reader that he has tested this by having music played at the other end of his intercom (see **Ill. 9.19**) and hearing it in his study, 'which I add so that the reader may know that I write nothing here that I have not tested by experiment'.

Kircher had been experimenting with intercommunication for many years. Already in the 1640s he had a system in the Roman College by which he could talk to the porters at the entrance, or to visitors if they were to be admitted to his museum.

9.16 Acoustic dome – the well-known 'whispering gallery' phenomenon exemplified at Heidelberg and Mantua (and later at St Paul's, London). (*Phonurgia Nova*, 69)

9.17 Speaking statue, a typically Kircherian trick, which he constructed to entertain Queen Christina. He believed that a spiral tube could amplify sound. (*Musurgia Universalis*, Volume II, opposite 303)

DE FABRICIS DIVERSORUM ORGANORUM. 143

9.18 Broadcasting music. Kircher claimed to have amplified music played indoors to such a degree that it could be heard two or three miles (three or four kilometres) away. (*Phonurgia Nova*, 143)

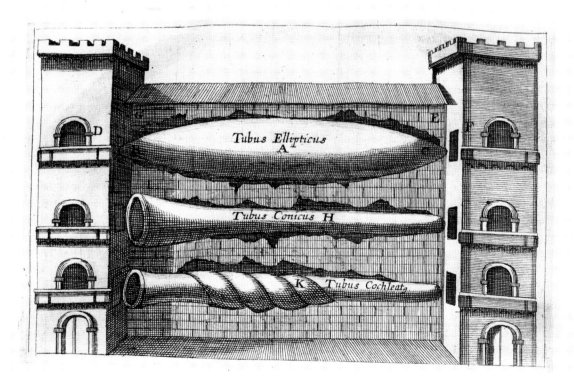

100 PHONURGIÆ LIBER I. Sect. IV.

9.19 An intercom: ways in which two princes would be able to converse over a distance of more than a hundred feet. (*Phonurgia Nova*, 100)

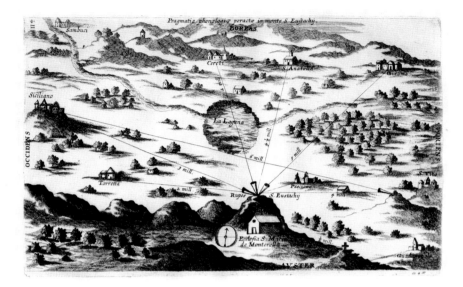

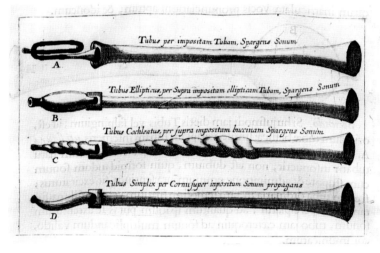

▲▲ 9.20 The loudspeaker system at Mentorella. Kircher assures his readers that by this system he was able to make his voice heard over a distance of five miles. He suggests that it could be used to mislead a Turkish army by broadcasting orders in their language. (*Phonurgia Nova*, 115)

▲ 9.21 Amplifying devices. These could be used to communicate with the inhabitants of a besieged city. (*Phonurgia Nova*, 138)

I saw fit to point this out to the reader, lest he should be persuaded that it was a new invention of today, brought from England, whereas it was often exhibited about twenty-four years ago in the Roman College, as many living people can testify, both our fathers and outsiders, who have honoured with their visits my museum of rare objects.[28]

Developing this idea, Kircher suggests a system by which two princes can have private conversations, each in his own chamber (**Ill. 9.19**). He says that they could be one hundred feet apart, or even more. Ideally, he recommends

building in a polished elliptical tube between two walls, in which the sound can echo and re-echo, increasing in volume as it does so. If this is too difficult to construct, he allows that one can make a narrower tube in conical or spiral form. The plate shows all three shapes.

Kircher also conducted acoustical experiments at the sanctuary of Mentorella, which stands on a spur overlooking a wide valley dotted with villages (**Ill. 9.20**). He found that by using a 'cleverly constructed' tube fifteen palms long, a voice could be heard at Toretta, two miles away; Siciliano (now Ciciliano), three miles; Cereti (now Cerreto Laziale), two miles; S. Anatolin, four-and-a-half miles; and even at Giramo (Gerano), five miles. The illustration shows several conical tubes aimed at the surrounding hilltops.

Kircher took delight in the wonder aroused in all who heard this mysterious sound. He writes that as many as 2,500 people at once obeyed its summons, flocking even by night to satisfy their curiosity or perform their devotions at the shrine.[29] The local wolves, too, answered when one of his friends tried howling through the loudspeaker: it set them all a-howling in response, and all the neighbouring dogs barking, in a 'not unamusing concert'.[30] The reader might pause to imagine Kircher and his mule lugging a six- or eight-foot (two-metre) megaphone from Rome, along miles of winding mountain tracks through wolf country.

The success of his loudspeaker gave Kircher the idea of its potential as a secret weapon in the war against the Turks. Commanders could use it, 'directing at the Turkish army previously prepared words in Arabic or Turkish, and causing consternation and flight, since they would not know the true origin of this sound that seemed to come from the sky'.[31] The ever-present Ottoman threat was also in his mind when he designed a series of amplifiers (**Ill. 9.21**). They work through blowing a trumpet or horn into a larger trumpet-shaped tube (A, D), by adding an elliptical resonating chamber (B), and by coupling two cochleate tubes. The context is a discussion of how to send secret messages by audible means, for which Kircher gives the example of a siege. How are the besieged to communicate with their allies outside the walls, without the enemy learning the intentions of both? He suggests that they should have a code already prepared, in which the various options and replies are numbered. Then they could use one of these devices to send whatever number of sounds corresponds to the question or answer intended.[32] He then suggests building a series of towers around the coast of Sicily equipped with these long-distance communicators, from which warnings of Turkish or pirate incursions could be rapidly relayed.

A third military application, based on the anatomy of the ear (**Ill. 9.22**), was intended to extend the audible range of the drum. According to his theory of amplification, the sound of the drumsticks on the drumhead ought to be doubled by the vibrations of the skin at the other end of the drum, and these greatly amplified in their turn as the sound passes through the trumpet-shaped tube.

Kircher applied the same acoustical principles in miniature for making aids for the deaf (**Ill. 9.23**) He was convinced that circular, elliptical, hyperbolic and parabolic spaces all serve to amplify sound, but that the ellipse and

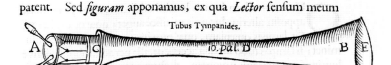

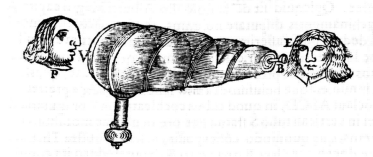

the spiral tube prove most effective as magnifiers of the voice. In the text he adds a third suggestion. Since the hearing of some animals, notably dogs and hares, is so much more acute than human hearing, one might make a device shaped like a hare's ear, attached to a twisted conical tube. At the end of the tube there would be a membrane like the eardrum, and then versions of the hammer, anvil and stirrup bones. The air contained within this inner chamber would be agitated to an extreme degree, magnifying the sound just as it occurs in the animal.[33]

When Kircher was researching material for *Œdipus Ægyptiacus* in the Vatican Library, he came upon the *Book of the Secrets of Aristotle to Alexander the Great*, in which there was a drawing of the horn by which Alexander summoned his army from distances up to one hundred stadia (or twelve-and-a-half Italian miles). The horn itself was five cubits or fifteen palms across, and formed as in **Ill. 9.24**. Although Kircher was not able to reconstruct it experimentally, he recalled his experiences as a boy in Germany, where shepherds used cow horns for signals audible a mile or more away. The cows in the town would hear the sound, and come out to pasture without any need for servants to drive them, then in the evening the horns would summon them back to their stables. As for Alexander's horn, Kircher found its range credible on account of its great size, and due to his conviction that the volume would be redoubled as the sound passed by two different routes from the mouthpiece to the bell.[34] By combining this with his spiral 'amplifier', Kircher comes up with an improvement on Alexander's horn, and says that it ought to be audible twenty miles away.[35]

The reader is probably aware that all of Kircher's schemes for amplification are based on a fallacy. Sound vibrations contain a finite energy that cannot be increased by reflection or multiplication. It may seem to be so, as when one shouts through a megaphone or through a tube, but all that is happening is that the energy is being concentrated in a smaller volume of air. It carries the sound further because the vibrations are being inhibited in their natural tendency of spherical propagation. Kircher's enthusiasm for spiral and other amplifiers, based as he says on his own experiments, is perfectly understandable, but it is still an example of the fallibility of experimental science when backed by mistaken principles and as yet uncontrolled by quantitative data.

Musical Magic

As with every subject he treated, music provided Kircher with resources for the magical devices of which he was so fond. I use 'magical' in a broad sense to cover phenomena that are not visible or obvious to the five senses, or which tap into some human or natural faculty of which most people are unaware. The results belong more to stage magic than to magic in the occult sense, and Kircher's role is often like that of the stage performer who displays some baffling illusion – only, unlike a professional, he then whisks the curtain away to show how he did it.

Nothing in *Musurgia Universalis* excited more interest than the eighth book, 'Musurgia mirifica' or 'Marvellous music-making'. It is a composition manual

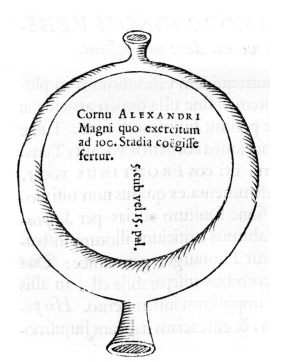

▲▲ **9.22** Amplified drum: another military application, based on the anatomy of the ear. (*Phonurgia Nova*, 135)

▲ **9.23** Two aids for the deaf. Among Kircher's endlessly inventive (and optimistic) proposals was a deaf-aid modelled on the ear of dogs and hares. (*Musurgia Universalis*, Volume II, 304, 305)

◄ **9.24** Horn of Alexander the Great, illustrated in a manuscript in the Vatican Library. Kircher compares it to the horn used by Alpine shepherds. (*Phonurgia Nova*, 132)

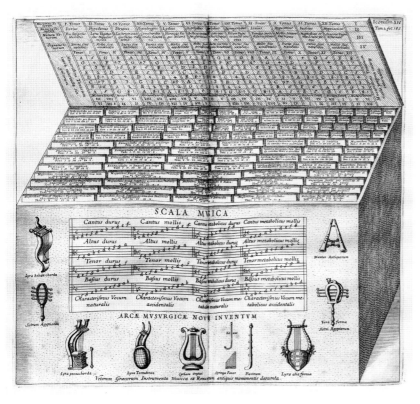

9.25 'Musurgical Ark': a device for composing a melody to a particular text and harmonizing it. This was useful to Jesuits working in foreign languages. At least three versions of these machines still exist. (*Musurgia Universalis*, Volume II, fp. 184/185)

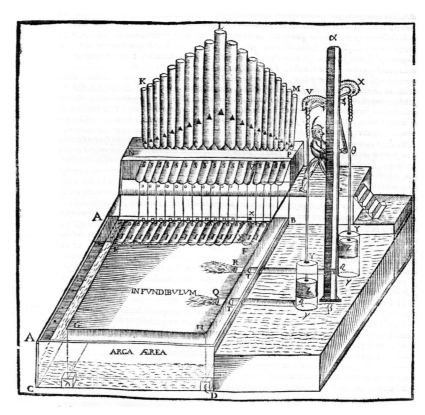

9.26 Vitruvius's organ: an attempt to reconstruct an ancient Roman organ from a written description. Vitruvius calls it 'hydraulic', but Kircher failed to find a function for water. (*Musurgia Universalis*, Volume II, 332)

that teaches how to compose a melody to a given text and harmonize it correctly in four parts. Kircher insists that anyone can do this, even someone who has never composed music before. He had invented at least the basic system by 1628–1630, while teaching mathematics in Würzburg.[36] As Ulf Scharlau points out in his study of *Musurgia*, the idea appealed greatly to Jesuits working in foreign missions.[37] Convinced of the value and power of music for converting the heathen, they needed help in composing suitable hymns in the languages of their hosts. Armed with this manual, anyone who could read Latin could do so, hand the results to a choir, and lo!, like a well-executed card-trick, it worked perfectly.

In *Musurgia*, Kircher only revealed the elementary part of his composition system, sufficient for making hymn-like settings with simple chord progressions. Far more complex was the 'Musurgical Ark', pictured above (**Ill. 9.25**), which allowed for further rhythmic and melodic subtleties. This was one of several such machines, made in small numbers and presented to favoured recipients.[38] At least three specimens survive in public collections. Kircher gave one to his patron and correspondent the Duke of Brunswick, and it is now in the Herzog August Bibliothek in Wolfenbüttel. Another is in the Herzog-Anton-Ulrich Museum in Braunschweig.[39] A third was bought by Samuel Pepys, the English diarist, and is in the Pepysian Library of Magdalene College, Cambridge. No one has yet made a special study of them, or tried to dis-

cover how effectively they produce music.

For no obvious reason, the engraving of the Musurgical Ark is ornamented with small pictures of 'The musical instruments of the ancient Greeks, taken from the antique monuments of the Romans.' Kircher did not try to integrate them into his text or otherwise explain them. The only ancient instrument that aroused his technical curiosity was the 'hydraulic organ' described by Vitruvius in his book on architecture (**Ill. 9.26**). Vitruvius's sketchy description was a challenge to him, and this illustration is Kircher's answer to it. He was quite scornful about the instrument, comparing its handful of pipes to the '1,152 pipes and twenty-four stops' of the larger German organs, and saying: 'There are many things, indeed, that this most enlightened century has invented to which the inventions of the Ancients can in no way be compared.'[40] Besides, the most laughable thing about this so-called 'hydraulic' organ is that water plays no essential part in its mechanism. (Despite appearances, the pistons YY and YY are pumping air, not water, into the reservoir ABCD.) The only purpose of the water that Kircher can think of may have been to impart a tremolo to the air contained in the same chamber with it.

Kircher improved on Vitruvius's design by showing how to make a hydraulic organ worthy of the name (**Ill. 9.27**). Here the water not only powers a mechanical playing device, but also supplies the air to the pipes. Falling or pressurized water (T) enters a sealed chamber (V) and increases the air pressure inside. Air escapes (Z) to supply the pipes, while the water escapes through a drain (R) to power a water-wheel (M). This is geared (L) to drive a cylinder (K) which is pinned, as in a music box or barrel organ, and operates the keys (EF) that let air into their respective pipes. To the viewer, the instrument plays as though by magic.

To the left is a smaller design, taken (with acknowledgement) from Robert Fludd's 'Great Instrument' in his treatise on music.[41] This contraption serves to slowly lower a grilled framework through a triangular harp. The protrusions on the vertical bars are placed analogously to those on a barrel, and twang the harp strings as they descend. Kircher was no more impressed by this device than by Fludd's work in general: 'Note, however, that this machine requires the greatest equality in movement, without which you will achieve nothing. It is especially inconvenient in that every time it was let down, it would have to be laboriously drawn up again'[42] – playing the piece backwards.

Among the magical instruments that seem to play by themselves, Kircher includes 'The giant hanging star, cast in bronze and equipped with innumerable bells, which is seen and heard in the church of Fulda, to the great admiration of all' (Ill. 9.28). Twenty-four feet across, it hung high above the nave, driven by a man in a treadmill hidden between the vault and the roof of the church.

It was intricately decorated, all fourteen rays being different, and it bore the inscription (visible in Gothic letters on the outermost circle): ANNO+DOMINI MILLESIMO QUADRINGENTESIMO XIIIII ('In the year of the Lord 1415').

Kircher obtained his description and drawing from contacts in Fulda, where he had received his schooling. 'The most illustrious and most reverend Abbot Ioachim of the Monastery of Fulda, Prince of the Holy Roman Empire and Arch-Chancellor of the Empress, had it most accurately drawn and sent by his secretary, Christopher Emerus, a man not only expert in hand but also in mind.'[43] Here as elsewhere in his works, he gave extra space – in this case, the largest folding plate in the book – to items sent him by highly placed benefactors, and was always careful to give them credit.

The Fulda star, for all its majesty and craftsmanship, was mechanically simple and musically trite. After printing the secretary's plodding description, Kircher adds a typical improvement of his own: 'This sort of wheel could also be made to go by perpetual motion, if outside the temple roof an Aeolian machine, constructed like windmills, should drive the axle inside.'[44]

Penelope Gouk, who calls the sixth book of *Musurgia* 'the central seventeenth-century treatise on automatic instruments',[45] situates Kircher's enthusiasm for them in a context of the discovery of the *Pneumatics* and

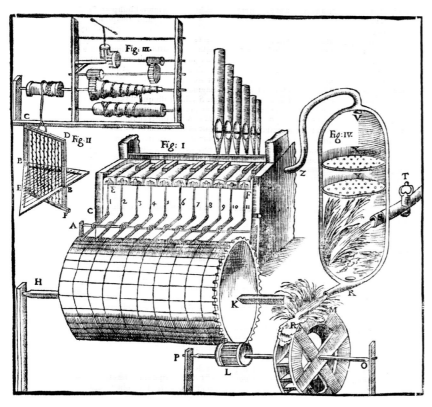

9.27 Hydraulic organ and automatic harp. Here Kircher improves on Vitruvius by designing an organ in which water actually does play a part. The smaller design on the left is taken from Robert Fludd. (*Musurgia Universalis*, Volume II, 534)

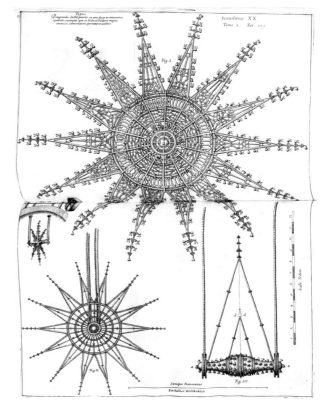

9.28 Giant cymbelstern, an instrument that seemed to play itself, but was worked by a man hidden in the roof. It existed in the church of Fulda, whose abbot supplied Kircher with the drawings. (*Musurgia Universalis*, Volume II, fp. 338/339)

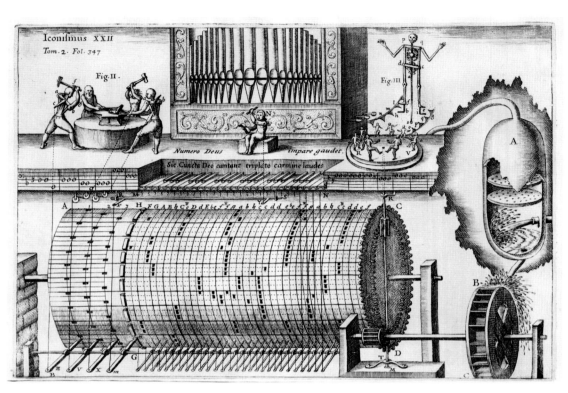

Mechanics of Hero of Alexandria (first century AD). The mechanical marvels described by Hero cried out to be recreated, and so they had been in the gardens and grottoes of the Villa d'Este in Tivoli, Villa Aldobrandini in Frascati, Francesco de' Medici's villa at Pratolino, and the Quirinal Palace in Rome.[46]

Kircher was involved with the last of these (**Ill. 9.29**), which had been built in 1594 and by the 1640s was in need of reconstruction.[47] Its mythological subject was the god Pan and the nymph Echo: a doubly appropriate one for Kircher, in view of his interest in echoes and his esoteric knowledge of what was really signified by the goat-footed god (see **Ill. 14.1**). The Greek inscription reads 'Pan, the harmonious god, Echo to whom he gives all things'. The visible part of the organ shows Pan in a grotto, playing his panpipes to the accompaniment of a cuckoo and a cock. In a separate grotto to the right, Echo repeats his song. The description in the text and the cutaway view are as clear as an instruction manual. The grotto with a cuckoo, a chicken and a pointy-eared Pan reduces the whole contraption to the fairground level, as a mechanical toy made to amuse and at the same time mystify. The reader has the satisfaction of being in on the secret, because he knows how the trick is done.[48]

This sense of complicity with the reader runs through Kircher's scientific works. Time and again, he writes of the astonishment, amazement and wonder of those who witness his machines in action; of how some fear that there must be a demon inside, until he shows them that it is all done by mirrors, magnetism or hydraulic power. But members of the elite who not only read,

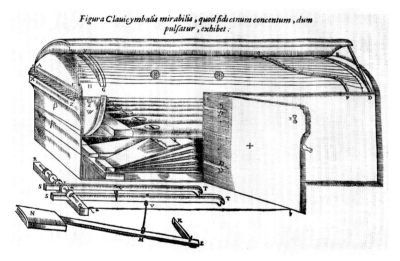

◄◄ **9.29** Organ in the Quirinal Palace gardens: a complex mechanical organ which featured the god Pan playing his pipes to the accompaniment of a cuckoo and a cock. (*Musurgia Universalis*, Volume II, opposite 342)

▲▲ **9.30** Pythagorean organ. This was Kircher's own organ. When set in motion Vulcan and three Cyclopes hammer at a forge, and Pythagoras discovers the physical origin of the musical scale. (*Musurgia Universalis*, Volume II, opposite 346)

▲ **9.31** Claviorganum, containing organ pipes as well as strings sounded by the turning wheel on the left. (*Musurgia Universalis*, Volume II, 341)

9.32 Michele Todini's prodigious instrument. Todini was a Roman musician whose giant mechanical orchestra took up two whole rooms. An organ and three harpsichords (B, C, D) could be played from a console (A), as well as devices that sounded like a violin and bagpipes. Parts of it survive, including figures of Polyphemus and the nymph Galatea, not shown in Kircher's illustration. (*Phonurgia Nova*, 168)

but read Latin, are not to be fooled. To them it is given to comprehend the mysteries of *natural* magic.

Another automatic organ (**Ill. 9.30**) appears to have belonged to Kircher himself, if we believe him when he says that he has displayed it in many places before many princes, who could hardly have enough of it. He adds that ideally it should be combined with live actors, who sing an eight-part madrigal (composed by himself and given in score) with appropriate leaps and gestures.

The automaton blends two mythological scenes. One is of the lame god Vulcan, overseeing the three Cyclopes at work in his forge; these are the figures seen on the left. The other is of Pythagoras, whose discovery of the link between tone and number was sparked off by hearing the clang of hammers in a smithy. From him comes the motto beneath the central figure: 'God rejoices in odd number.' The motto above the keyboard, 'Thus all things sing praises to God in threefold song', reconciles these pagan scenes with Kircher's vision of world harmony.

When set in motion by water power, the barrel plays the eight-part song on the organ, while Vulcan and the giants move in time to the music, and the hammers produce the correct Pythagorean tunings. The figure in the centre beats time, and those on the right-hand side dance. (The skeleton is not part of the display, but an illustration of how to articulate the bodies of the Cyclopes.)

Even an instrument played by visible human agency could have a large component of magic. The woodcut of a claviorganum (**Ill. 9.31**) is titled: 'Picture of a wonderful harpsichord, which when played gives forth the symphony of bowed strings.' The concept begins with the mechanism of a hurdy-gurdy, whose constantly turning wheel, coated with rosin, substitutes for a bow. However, while a hurdy-gurdy's wheel is always touching and playing all the strings, in this more refined instrument each string must be playable separately. Each key (N in the illustration), pivoted at L, pulls a wire (VM) that causes a bar (ST) to descend and depress its string (AB). The beaked end of the bar (T) thus serves a dual function: like the tangent of a clavichord, it acts as one end of the sounding string, and it also pushes the string down the short distance necessary for it to touch the wheel. Kircher says that the strings should be of gut, and that a clever artisan could wind the wheel with horsehair, like a bow, to better simulate the sound of the viol or violin family. A love of hidden mechanisms leads him to add that it could be played automatically, using a pinned barrel to depress the keys and powering it by water, like his hydraulic organs.

This is only the beginning of Kircher's instructions 'For making an automatic machine that exhibits the symphony of every sort of instrument'. Already in the illustration we can see a rank of organ pipes beneath the strings, and a pair of bellows beneath those. He now recommends adding organ pipes 'of every kind', including flues, reeds and regals. Next comes a harpsichord (wire-strung) with three registers: 1. a normal harpsichord; 2. imitating a harp 'by a certain accommodation of the jacks, known to the better technicians'; and 3. 'through hollow jacks equipped with little dies, jump-

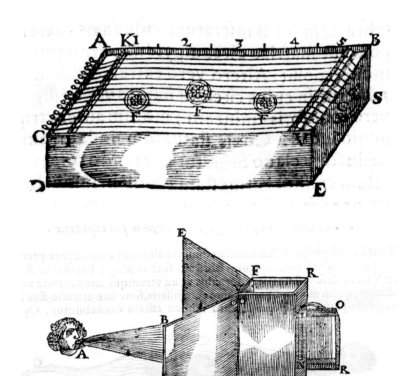

9.33 Æolian harp, which produces music by the action of wind controlled by opening and closing a window. (*Musurgia Universalis*, Volume II, 352, 353)

ing up from below the strings, they give forth a sound very like those wind instruments called *surdinas*'.[49]

Kircher admired the ability of this three-registered harpsichord to imitate three different families of instruments: harpsichord, harp and woodwind. Combined with the imitation viols and the organ, it allowed

> an almost infinite variety, which you could change by working the registers, so that now one would hear a symphony of viols, now one of harps, wind instruments, harpsichords; and a little later, organs, flutes of every kind; and lastly the variously mixed ensemble of them all. And thus a single instrument would exhibit every kind of musical instrument, with no one playing them.[50]

The nearest realization of this fantasy was the Galleria Armonica of Michele Todini (1616–1690), a private museum in Rome to which paying visitors were admitted. Kircher illustrates part of it in *Phonurgia Nova* (**Ill. 9.32**), writing that

the Roman musician took eighteen years of 'incredible labour and perspiration' to set up this instrument in two adjacent chambers near his house. Everything was controlled from the console (A) which resembles a clavicytherium. There was an organ, seen in the background, and three harpsichord-like instruments mounted on pedestals (B, C, D), all of which could be played separately or in combination. Some other unseen contraption imitated the sound of a violin by the continuous rubbing of gut strings, and another hidden source sounded exactly like a musette or bagpipe.[51] Out of respect for a fellow magician, Kircher refuses to disclose the complicated mechanism that made all this possible.

By a fortunate chance, the Metropolitan Museum of Art in New York owns some parts of Todini's display. One would have no idea from Kircher's illustration that they were so splendidly carved and gilded, which must be the reason they were preserved long after the Galleria Armonica had closed its doors. The surviving pieces illustrate the myth of Polyphemus the Cyclops and his love of the sea-nymph Galatea. A large harpsichord forms the centrepiece, mounted on a base simulating the ocean and carried by tritons. On one side is Polyphemus with his bagpipe, on a rock that concealed an organ; on the other, Galatea, who once held a lute that was simulated by the harpsichord.[52] As with Kircher's automatic instruments, Todini followed the fashion of the time in clothing his devices with classical mythology.

Kircher was the first to depict the instrument that plays without any human or mechanical assistance, now known as the Æolian harp (**Ill. 9.33**). It is made from a chest with fifteen gut strings tuned in unison. The diagram is inadequate, but the text explains that the harp is placed in a window, outside which two shutters or baffles serve to concentrate the airstream on the strings. Here is his description:

> This machine is novel, very simple and entertaining, and listeners in my museum hear it with the greatest admiration. The instrument is silent as long as the window is closed, but when it is opened, lo! it straightway makes a harmonious sound that renders them all dumbstruck. For they do not know where the sound is coming from, or from what instrument, for it the sound is not that of strings nor wind instruments, but as it were in between, and very strange.[53]

Particularly strange was the fact that identical strings should give off such a range and variety of sounds. 'For depending on the strength or weakness of the wind, you hear a wondrous harmony inside the room: now all the strings give off a kind of trembling sound; now the songs of birds; or the harmonious pipes of a hydraulic organ, or some other strange sounds.'[54] It would be a century or more before the acoustics of the instrument were properly understood.

This did not exhaust the possibilities of the instrument. Kircher found that the Aeolian harp could be freely used outdoors whenever the wind was

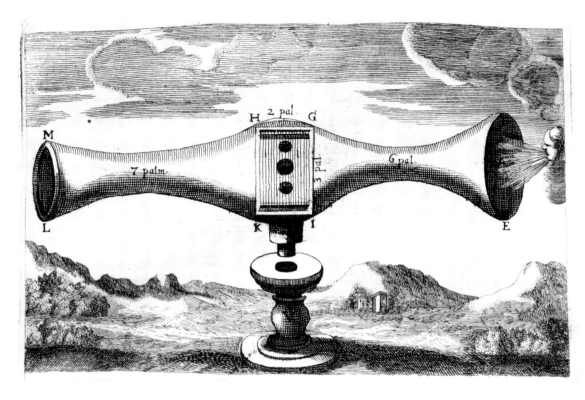

◄ **9.34** An outdoor Æolian harp. (*Phonurgia Nova*, 144)

◄▼ **9.35** A musical kite, essentially an Æolian harp sent up into the sky. (*Musurgia Universalis*, Volume II, 354)

▼ **9.36** Musical glasses. The well-known musical effect caused by rubbing the rim of a glass with a finger was used by Kircher to support the 'doctrine of the affections' by filling the glasses with different liquids. (*Phonurgia Nova*, 191)

Machinam memoratam perpetuo resonantem fabricari.

SI quis vero huiusmodi harmoniosum sonum in perpetuum continuare vellet, is machinam apparabit in turris alicuius patente loco, ea ratione accommodatam, vt in morem aplustri siue indicis ventorum ad eum ventum, qui actu spirat, versetur, & sic concepto aere animata suapte sponte ad quemcumque ventum semper resonabit.

Corollarium II.

Vt in alto aere prodigiosa Musica percipiatur.

VT verò prodigiosus ille harmonicus sonus in alto aere cum stupore percipiatur; pisce vel Dracone volante (cuius fabricam fusè in Magia Parastatica Artis Magnæ Lucis & Vmbræ descripsimus) ita adornabis vt ad vtrumque latus chordæ ad æquisonū extendantur, quem mox vt liberiori aurę commiseris, fune siue attracto, siue laxato, magno semper impetu chordę cum intento musicæ effectu excitabuntur. Quod si loco

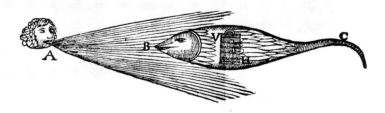

Typus Tarantiacorum Saltantium.

9.37 Tarantella dancers. Kircher expands his treatment of tarantula poisoning (see **Ill. 8.31**). Here he includes in the cure not simply non-stop dancing but also the particular ways in which the music is produced. (*Phonurgia Nova*, 206)

blowing. He fixed it inside a funnel and used strings all of different gauges, tuned at random (**Ill. 9.34**). The resultant sound

> is heard like wailings and moanings, to the stupefaction and admiration of all; for whence such exotic and lugubrious music comes, those ignorant and absent will surmise after long pondering that it is some 'prodigious polyphonism' fallen from the sky, while those present will indeed see a machine, but will remain at a loss to say what art and industry produces the sound.[55]

Here he makes a dig at the non-experimenters and their habit of explaining away the unknown by inventing high-sounding terms. It was a small step from taking an Æolian harp outdoors to sending it up in the sky. With his musical kite (**Ill. 9.35**), Kircher hit on the perfect way to stage a miracle:

> In order to astonish the listeners with a prodigious sound from high up in the air, make a flying fish or dragon ... and furnish it on either side with strings tuned in unison. Let it go free with the breeze, and soon, as the string tightens and loosens, the continuous buffeting

will excite the strings to the desired musical effect. If instead of a dragon, you make a flying angel, the machine will cause all the more prodigious a spectacle, as the sound will be stranger and more remarkable.[56]

There was nothing magical about the musical glasses (**Ill. 9.36**), but Kircher's experiment with them was significant. By showing how music could set liquids in motion, it supported the theory that the effect of music on humans comes from moving their 'humours'. This was at the heart of the Baroque 'doctrine of the affections' which Kircher, famously, was the first to describe.

> Take five glasses, all of the same size and capacity, and place them contiguously in the arrangement shown here. Fill one glass with aquavitae, another with the better sort of wine, another with subtle water, another with dense water such as sea water or oil, and the middle one with common water. Then rub the mouth of the glass with the end of a moistened finger until you hear a ringing, such as we taught you to do in the first experiment.
>
> Thereupon a very high sound will agitate all the other humours in a remarkable way, and do so more violently in proportion to the subtlety of the different humours.

ate in quality, music will incite it to love, joy, happiness and venereal affections; if it is more compressed, it will move it to tears, religiosity, continence, and other pathetic affects; and lastly, if it is thick as in people weighed down with sorrow, it will be incapable of any motion, and therefore music is in fact an ineffective address to grief.[57]

This mechanistic theory of music also served Kircher as explanation for the periodic epidemics of tarantism that afflicted southern Italy (**Ill. 9.37**). He first discussed the tarantula in *Magnes* (1641; see **Ill. 8.31**), and again in *Musurgia Universalis* (1650), where he went more deeply into the phenomenon and its causes. He reproduced the latter section in *Phonurgia*, adding this illustration of people affected by the spider's bite.[58] The text discusses the different types of spider and especially their colours, which Kircher correlates with the four humours (choleric, sanguine, phlegmatic and melancholic). His explanation hinges on the assumption that the *spiritus* or subtle spirits in the body are responsive to music in various degrees (like the liquids in the musical glasses), and that when they are infected by poison, music can be effective, through sympathetic resonance, in dispelling it. Once started on the topic, he spins out anecdotes about misguided efforts to cure victims by explosions; a spider that danced in perfect time with the music; fabric woven from an Indian spider's web; a Capuchin monk who unwisely tried to cure himself by dashing into the sea; the bite of rabid dogs; and the effects of aconite or the bite of the dipsas serpent, which cause one to see people transformed into fish, geese, ducks, and so on.[59] As far as I have discovered, this is the only time Kircher refers to psychedelics.

At the ends of his books, Kircher tends to give everything that has preceded a spiritual consecration. In *Musurgia* he uses for this a symbolic 'organ of the world's creation' (**Ill. 9.38**). 'Thus God's eternal wisdom plays on the orb of the worlds', reads the inscription beneath the keyboard. The six registers correspond to the six days of creation, each imagined as a 'harmony' made by God, the maker and player of the organ of the universe. The small circles illustrate the events as described in the opening chapter of Genesis:

Day I. This image is taken from Robert Fludd's treatise on the macrocosm.[60] It shows the Holy Spirit as a dove, dividing the light from the darkness, with the words 'Let there be light'.

Day II. Collecting of the waters in one place; appearance of dry land.

Day III. The earth brings forth vegetation.

Day IV. Lights are placed in the firmament of heaven: the sun, moon, planets and stars are created.

Day V. The waters and the earth bring forth animals.

Day VI. Man is made in God's image.

Kircher describes all this in the exalted and picturesque language of a sermon. He involves the reader emotionally as he imagines God playing on one stop after another, then, when his creation is complete, making a superb symphony that uses the full resources of the instrument:

9.38 Organ of the world's creation: a complex image that seeks to sum up Kircher's doctrine of music. The six registers correspond to the six days of creation illustrated in the picture in the six circles. The organ is the universe, the organ-player God. (*Musurgia Universalis*, Volume II, opposite 366)

Thus the aquavitae, which answers to the igneous or choleric nature, will jump up much more than the others; the wine, answering to the sanguine or airy complexion, suffers a moderate commotion; the subtle water, showing a phlegmatic constitution, causes a slower and more obtuse motion; and the dense water contained in the glass will scarcely be capable of movement on account of its earthy complexion. If therefore our *spiritus* should be subtle and hot, music will arouse it to proud, immoderate and angry motions; if it is more subtle and moder-

Thus that eternal arch-musician, after the prelude of the six created things, when he produced man, the most excellent of corporeal creatures, pulled out all the stops of the world-organ and played on it with a universal harmony, as it were the measure and end of all things.[61]

Those unmoved by the pious and exultant text may wonder what the smiling satyr heads and the spread-eagled siren are doing at the bottom, while organists will notice something decidedly odd about the keyboard, stops and pipes. The cynic may even suspect it of being another fairground instrument, or a prop in the Jesuit theatre of didactic entertainment.

Notes

1 If we except the concert by two violinists and a theorbo-player that set him on his ecstatic journey. See *Itinerarium Exstaticum*, 1656, 33.

2 The reference is to Claudius Ptolemaeus, whom Kircher still confused with the Egyptian Ptolemaic dynasty, and to Alfonso the Wise of Spain, who codified the planetary motions.

3 *Musurgia Universalis*, I, xxiii.

4 *Musurgia Universalis*, I, 311–313.

5 Only exceeded in 2005 by Richard Taruskin's *Oxford History of Western Music*.

6 *Musurgia Universalis*, I, xx.

7 Giulio Casseri and Adriaan van Spiegel, *De Humani Corporis Fabrica Libri Decem*, Venice, 1627.

8 What follows is summarized from *Musurgia Universalis*, I, 18–19.

9 *Musurgia Universalis*, I, 19.

10 *Musurgia Universalis*, I, 20.

11 *Musurgia Universalis*, I, 33.

12 *Musurgia Universalis*, I, 30–31.

13 *Musurgia Universalis*, I, 49.

14 *Musurgia Universalis*, I, 454.

15 *Musurgia Universalis*, I, 476.

16 *Musurgia Universalis*, I, 501.

17 *Musurgia Universalis*, I, 513.

18 *Musurgia Universalis*, I, 519.

19 Cartari's *Immagini*, 1626, 119–122 gives numerous words that work thus. A well-known example is the echo duet at the beginning of Monteverdi's *Orfeo*, Act V.

20 *Musurgia Universalis*, II, 288.

21 Kircher sometimes uses *palma*, meaning a palm or span, when one suspects that he means *pedis*, a foot. His *palma* is 1/3 of a cubit, or 6 inches, which is absurd in this context (but see Chapter 6, note 9 on his 'cubit').

22 *Musurgia Universalis*, II, 294.

23 *Musurgia Universalis*, II, 275.

24 *Phonurgia Nova*, 68.

25 *Musurgia Universalis*, II, 303.

26 See letter from Kaspar Schott, April 1, 1656, APUG, 561, f.40, cited in Schott 2000, 275n.

27 *Musurgia Universalis*, II, 303.

28 *Phonurgia Nova*, 112. The rival claimant was Samuel Morland, who published an account of his 'Tuba Stentoro-Phonica' in *Philosophical Transactions of the Royal Society*, January, 1672; see Gouk, 77.

29 *Phonurgia Nova*, 114.

30 *Phonurgia Nova*, 228.

31 *Phonurgia Nova*, 138.

32 *Phonurgia Nova*, 137–138.

33 *Musurgia Universalis*, II, 305.

34 *Phonurgia Nova*, 132–133.

35 *Phonurgia Nova*, 134.

36 Gouk, 72.

37 Scharlau 1969, 210.

38 For other examples, see Wilding, 100; Fletcher, 'Athanasius Kircher and Duke August,' 102.

39 Gouk, 82, n. 5.

40 *Musurgia Universalis*, II, 333.

41 In Fludd 1618, 245–258. See Godwin 1973, 4–7.

42 *Musurgia Universalis*, II, 336.

43 *Musurgia Universalis*, II, 338.

44 *Musurgia Universalis*, II, 339.

45 Gouk, 77.

46 On the mentality and mythology behind these enterprises, see Godwin 2002, Chapters 7–8.

47 On the Quirinal organ and its restoration, see Donelli, specifically the article by Olivieri.

48 John Evelyn also drew a diagram of the organ's workings in his manuscript *Elysium Britannicum*; see British Library Add. Ms. 78342, ff. 177ᵛ–178.

49 After reading this improbable description, I tried striking the bass strings of a harpsichord (with the jacks raised) with a small hardwood stick, and could just imagine a resemblance to staccato notes played on the sordoun (a kind of early bassoon with a muted tone). More intriguing is the thought that Kircher came within an inch of inventing the pianoforte.

50 *Musurgia Universalis*, II, 343.

51 *Phonurgia Nova*, 168–170.

52 On the Galleria Armonica, see Barbieri.

53 *Musurgia Universalis*, II, 352.

54 *Musurgia Universalis*, II, 353.

55 *Phonurgia Nova*, 144.

56 *Musurgia Universalis*, II, 354.

57 *Phonurgia Nova*, 191–192. This experiment also appeared in *Musurgia Universalis*, II, 212.

58 Note the presence of swords as well as spiders, which may have some folkloric significance if we follow the musicologist Marius Schneider, who combined the Tarantella and the Sword-dance in a single mythological study (see Schneider).

59 *Phonurgia Nova*, 215.

60 Fludd 1617, 49.

61 *Musurgia Universalis*, II, 367. For a translation of the final pages of *Musurgia*, see Godwin 1986, 160–161.

Chapter 10   Machines of Past and Present

Machines of the Past

While Kircher was in Würzburg (1628–1631), he spent much of his time, and won his first renown, as an inventor and operator of machines. One of these showed Jonah swallowed by the whale: a device simple enough in itself, but which has struck later scholars as a symptom of a mentality all but incomprehensible today. The machine worked thus: the two protagonists floated in a large bottle; Jonah's head contained a piece of steel, and the whale's belly a magnet. The magnet could be rotated by means of a thread passing outside the vessel, so that the operator could turn it, first to repel Jonah, then to suck him into the whale's gaping mouth.

True, Jonah's story in the Old Testament has its comic aspects, but it is Kircher's further remarks that astonish: 'By this art the Ascension of Christ Our Lord into heaven, the mission of the Holy Spirit, and other stories both sacred and profane can be exhibited with no less amazement than delight.'[1] From the catalogue of his museum (see next chapter), we know that he made just such a 'resurrection machine'. The Kircher scholar Michael John Gorman wonders: 'How could Kircher dare to make a joke of the central mystery of Christianity? How could he place the resurrected Christ in a glass sphere, alongside genies, water-vomiting snakes, and pagan goddesses?'[2] And I might add, who is supposed to respond to the exhibition with 'amazement and delight'? Perhaps it delighted the in-group at the Roman College, well accustomed to dramatizing sacred stories, and amazed the ignorant masses, especially those in heathen nations who would gawp in astonishment and be moved to conversion. If so, one cannot overlook the parallel with the pagan priests, whom Kircher accuses of just the same deception with their ingenious automata, speaking statues, miraculously opening doors and the like.

The Romans used the word *machina* for any device that extended the human capacity to move, lift, throw, shape, measure, calculate or trick.[3] That is a broad field, but almost everything within it comes under what we now call technology. Some machines worked in a mysterious way – that was part of their tricky side – but their secrets were open to the elite, which included the readers of Kircher's books. There was no technology here whose basic principles and construction an educated person could not grasp, and a mathematically gifted man like Kircher could design it, too. We will see how earnestly he tried

10.1 Nilometer. In ancient Egypt (note the crocodile and pyramid) the level of the annual Nile flood could be calculated using this cyclindrical enclosure with a calibrated column. (*Œdipus Ægyptiacus*, Volume I, 34)

to explain the workings of machines of almost[4] every kind, and how, as in any instruction manual, the illustrations were indispensable.

Those machines that were so highly regarded in antiquity held no mysteries for Kircher. One of the simplest, though perhaps the most useful in its time, was the Nilometer (**Ill. 10.1**) described in an Arabic work, *Nubian Geography*. The cutaway diagram makes it clear that as the Nile rises, water flows into the cylindrical enclosure, where its height can be read from the column. Many of Kircher's own hydraulic machines exploit the same principle of the equal height of connected bodies of water. But that is not enough: the artist has added crocodiles and pyramids (signifying Egypt), he has modelled

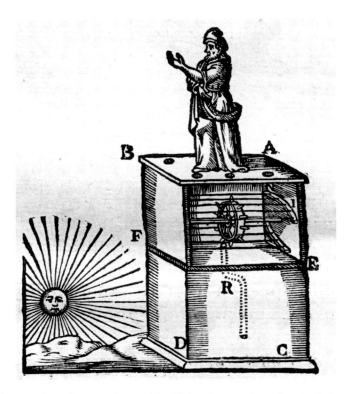

10.2 Statue of Memnon. Kircher's somewhat desperate explanation of its so-called 'cry' was an imprisoned demon, but his illustration shows how it could be simulated mechanically. (*Œdipus Ægyptiacus*, Volume II, ii, 326)

the building on the Coliseum of Rome (signifying the grandeur of antiquity), and shrunk the Nile to a brook.

Hydraulics and pneumatics were at the basis of many of Kircher's machines. The illustration of the statue of Memnon (**Ill. 10.2**) introduces the latter principle, using the expansion of heated air. The Colossus of Memnon of Egyptian Thebes was in fact one of a pair of seated figures of Amenhotep III, surviving the destruction of his temple on the west bank of the Nile. It was famous in ancient times for the 'cry of Memnon', variously described as resembling the twang of a lyre, a trumpet or a copper gong, that came from it at sunrise.[5] Many Greek and Roman tourists testified to hearing this sound, and carved poems to that effect on the statue's base, but no travellers of Kircher's day had gone so far up the Nile as to report on it at first hand.

First Kircher had to explain the prodigy itself. He came to the conclusion that it was probably caused by a demon that had been enclosed in the statue by conjuration. This was not his usual solution of ancient enigmas, but a last resort when rational explanations failed. His reasoning is that if the Memnon phenomenon had been artificially caused, it could not have kept working for thousands of years.[6] However, lacking any idea of what the real Memnon statue looked like, he designed an artificial statue that would have a similar effect. It stands on a box containing a wheel equipped with plectra, which strike a bank of strings somewhat like those of a harpsichord. The lower chamber is tightly sealed, except for a narrow tube which points at the 'paddles' of the wheel. When the sun rises, it heats the air in the lower chamber, which suddenly expands, exits through the tube, and sets the wheel in motion. For extra effect, Kircher recommends adding an organ pipe in the statue's throat, and having it roll its eyes.

Although Kircher believed that the ancients were habitual traffickers with demons, he attributed most of their wonders to the trickery of the pagan priests. Here he shows how a statue of many-breasted 'Isis' (better known as Diana of Ephesus) could have been made to produce milk at the time of sacrifice (**Ill. 10.3**). The hemisphere ABC is sealed, its only outlet being a tube that leads from X down through a column to the lower chamber MN. This chamber is filled with milk, and connected through the tube I to the breasts of the statue. To operate the miracle, the candle-holders ST are swung on their hinges so that the candles heat the hemispherical chamber. The air within it expands, and having nowhere else to go enters the chamber MN and forces the liquid upwards (as in some coffee machines). Milk spurts from the breasts and falls into the basin, to the astonishment and pious admiration of the populace.[7]

In a similar vein, Hero of Alexandria tells of an altar in Sais in which, when the fire was lit, Dionysus and Diana poured out wine and milk, and a snake-like dragon hissed. The mechanics, as Kircher interprets them (**Ill. 10.4**), are similar to that of the fountain of milk, but the base should show two reservoirs for the two liquids. When the fire is lit, the air within the altar expands and issues through E, forcing up the liquids. Wine and milk pour from the ewers in the hands of the statues – incongruously wearing the crown of the two Egypts – and extinguish the fire. The hissing of the dragon is easily made by the same means. Kircher adds a theological explanation: 'Isis of the Nile was the genius of water, the asp the agathodaimon of the sun, cause of all the things I have explained elsewhere; and they perform sacrifices to procure common benefits for all and for pleasing the gods.'[8]

Hero also wrote of how the doors of temples could seem to open without human agency. Kircher responds with a design for a pneumatic machine (**Ill. 10.5**). When fire is kindled on the altar ED, hot air goes into the water-filled globe GHK and forces out the water through the pipe L. It falls into a suspended bucket NX which descends under the weight of the water. This pulls the ropes wound around the rollers, which rotate and swing the doors open. 'Some think that when the doors open, various apparitions of the gods and groups of dancers appear, and it is not difficult to imagine how this would be done.' But the water in the bucket gradually drains out through the pipe V, allowing the weight F to descend, and the doors close again, to the stupefaction of all present.[9]

The next specimen of ancient Egyptian machines derives from the dubious authority of the late Greek author Horapollo. In his *Hieroglyphica* (I, 16), he writes enigmatically of the cynocephalus (the 'dog-headed' Egyptian baboon), which at the equinoxes urinates punctually at every hour of the day and night.[10] Horapollo adds that for this reason the Egyptians place an image of this beast on top of their water-clocks. Kircher's interpretation of such a clock (**Ill. 10.6**) begins with the hollow brass figure of a seated cynocephalus, 'as it is shown today in the royal museum of the Pincian Hill by Francisco Gualdo of Rimini, Knight of St Stephen'.[11] The ape, which symbolizes the Nile, is filled with water, and the piping is calibrated so that it takes exactly

CLASS. VIII. MECHANICA ÆGYPTIORVM. 333

Tempore itaque facrificij , candelis E, D accenfis, tholi fundus B C calefactus, latentem intra tholum aërem rarefaciebat; hic rarefa-ctus , dum locum euadendi non reperiebat, trochlea obftructo tholo, per X B K I abitum parans, dum arulæ interiora iam lactis humore repleta reperit, illum impetu fuo per canalem N M in vbera ftatuæ protrudit ; hæc largifluum humorem foras, non fine admiratione infpectantis populi, fingulari Deorum beneficio conceffum putantis, intra arulæ craterem G H difpergunt , durabatque folùm facrificij tempore . Patet itaque ex dictis propofitum.

10.3 A fountain of milk. By heating the interior chamber milk is forced through a tube to spurt from the statue's breasts. (*Œdipus Ægyptiacus*, Volume II, ii, 333)

10.4 Altar of Sais. Like the previous figure, this one (described by Hero of Alexandria) uses heat from a fire to force wine and milk to flow into ewers held by Dionysus and Diana. (*Œdipus Ægyptiacus*, Volume II, ii, 334)

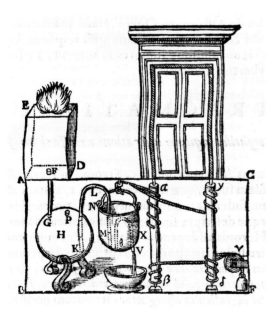

10.5 Miraculously opening doors: water from a globe is forced into a bucket which descends, pulling ropes wound round rollers. (*Œdipus Ægyptiacus*, Volume II, ii, 335)

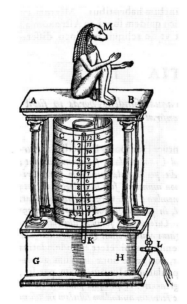

10.6 Water-clock with an ape. By maintaining a constant flow of water into a calibrated cylinder the time can be read off. (*Œdipus Ægyptiacus*, Volume II, ii, 340)

10.7 Petroleum light. By feeding petroleum at a constant rate, the light can be kept permanently burning. (*Mundus Subterraneus*, Volume II, 76)

KIRCHER AND THE OCCULT

Kircher was not a magician like Marsilio Ficino, who summoned the planetary influences with Orphic songs and perfumes. He is never known to have drawn up horoscopes, like Johann Kepler or Jerome Cardan. Unlike Tommaso Campanella, he did not perform ceremonies of astrological magic for his patron Pope Urban VIII.[12] Nor had he any respect for alchemy, either physical or spiritual. He despised all forms of divination, especially the geomancy that infatuated Robert Fludd. One cannot be sure that he never indulged in erotically energized meditations, like Giordano Bruno, but it seems unlikely. He never, ever summoned spirits or attempted to converse with angels, like John Dee and Edward Kelley; it would have been a sure way to invite demons to the party.

Moreover, he considered Paracelsus a dangerous lunatic, and loathed the Rosicrucians, with their Calvinistic plots for world reform. He knew next to nothing of Jakob Boehme and the Christian theosophic tradition that followed him, and in any case, Kircher did not presume to plumb the mystery within the Godhead or to forge a new theosophic language out of his private revelations. In short, he did not belong to any of the esoteric currents represented by these people. For all his revelation of Hermetic mysteries and Sphingian secrets, for all his hundreds of pages expounding Hebrew and Arabic Kabbalah,

these neither supplanted, nor even supplemented, the doctrines and practices of the Roman Church.

Daniel Stolzenberg writes with passion of how scholars have misinterpreted Kircher as a promulgator of the Hermetic tradition within Counter-Reformation Catholicism. 'The scholarly persona that Kircher presented to readers of the *Œdipus Ægyptiacus,* under which guise he wished them to understand his authorial intentions, was not the persona of a magus-philosopher in the style of Ficino, Pico, Agrippa or John Dee, who studied ancient esoteric texts as part of a search for timeless, transcendent truths. Instead, Kircher presented himself as an antiquary, an investigator of the material remains of ancient civilizations, who, by combining knowledge of "recondite" antiquities and Oriental literature, had been able to decipher the most perplexing of all ancient inscriptions.'[13]

While he wrote unhesitatingly about magnetic magic, musical magic, hieroglyphic magic and many other magics, the only ones Kircher considered licit were natural. That is, they were based on the knowledge and exploitation of nature's hidden laws, which not even angels and demons were free to disobey.[14] That these laws included correspondences between entities on the different planes of being (planets, plants, parts of the body, etc.) was not

supernatural: it was simply the way the natural universe was put together, 'bound by secret knots'. Few people of his time had any problem with the idea. For better or worse, it ruled their medical treatments, but it did not make occultists in the modern sense out of them. Nor did a belief that angels and demons might sometimes be persuaded to intervene in human affairs.

What makes Kircher seem like an occultist is that his world-view made no sharp distinction between the realm of matter and that of spirit, or between the sense-world and the unseen. His geology, magnetism, chemistry and optics were suffused – some would say infected – by religious dogmas and spiritual notions. In the course of the next century, the natural sciences would be purged of all that, and focused on the material world alone. By the nineteenth century, the only people who resisted this purgation were the Christian fundamentalists and – for entirely different reasons – esoteric groups like the German *Naturphilosophen,* the French *occultistes,* the Theosophists, and some strains of Freemasonry. For those of them who discovered Kircher, his universe had an understandable attraction, and he became a kind of honorary occultist, misplaced as a link in the chain from which these groups claimed descent.

twelve hours for the water to run out of it. The outside cylinder CD is made of glass, and the inner one has notches at the bottom, so that the water falling from the ape fills both of them. It rises every hour in accordance with the markings inscribed on the outer cylinder (the right-hand column of numbers denoting the hours of day). When it reaches the top of the inmost pipe IK, it begins to drain out, and it takes another twelve hours for it all to exit through K into the lower chamber GH. One reads off its falling level on the left-hand column of numbers, which mark the hours of night. The water is let out at L, poured back into the ape, and the process repeats. So says Kircher, who bases several designs on this siphoning principle. Incredibly, he seems to assume that the weight of the water in the outside cylinder will force the water in the inside cylinder upwards and out of the drain pipe. Kaspar Schott pointed out the fallacy in his book on hydraulics, but blamed it on Kircher's source, Hero.[15]

Kircher did not believe the claims of modern authors of occult leanings such as Della Porta and Trithemius that it was possible to make a perpetually

burning lamp. But since such lamps were reported in antiquity, he sought a rational solution to them. Again his mastery of Arabic sources came to his aid, for there he learned how lamps can be fuelled from wells of petroleum or bitumen. The diagram (**Ill. 10.7**) shows how one could light an underground chamber with an apparently inexhaustible lamp, by feeding petroleum to it through a lead pipe.

Another marvel of antiquity was Archimedes' sphere, in which the motions of the planets and the fixed stars were supposedly reproduced in miniature and in perpetual motion (**Ill. 10.8**). Kircher did not believe in the possibility of perpetual motion (see below), but as with the ever-burning lamps, he suspected the ancients of cleverly simulating it. This sphere, he says, can only have worked in one of three ways: either by weights (i.e. clockwork), by some hydraulic-pneumatic device (i.e. by air and water), or else by magnetism. He doubts that Archimedes knew how to exploit magnetism, and that the famous sphere was as wonderful as the ancient poets pretend. Confident that modern technology surpasses that of the ancients, he describes his own

solution to the problem, assuring the reader that he would not do so if he had not already demonstrated several experiments of this kind before witnesses.[16]

In **Ill. 10.8** we see what the astonished viewer sees: two glass globes filled half with spirits and half with coloured oil, which do not mix but distinguish the two hemispheres. Floating on the heavier liquid is a smaller globe. The one on the left represents the heavenly spheres, or the sphere of the sun, enclosed within the sphere of the fixed stars, which can be seen painted on it. The one on the right has a small figure with a pointer directed at the twenty-four hours. If the machine works properly, the inner globes revolve without visible cause. The banner carries one of Pico della Mirandola's gnomic Conclusions: 'He approaches Nature and Proteus in vain who does not attract Pan.'

Kircher then removes the tablecloth of the previous plate (**Ill. 10.9**) to reveal the secret mechanism. It is a magnet that rotates beneath the table, causing a corresponding rotation in the floating spheres, which contain magnets or carry a magnetic figure. Moreover, there are several glass globes nested inside one another, representing the spheres of the sun, the moon, and the planets.

10.8, 10.9 Archimedes' sphere, a model of the planets and fixed stars, as it appeared and as Kircher suggests it actually worked. It consisted of two glass globes, each filled with spirits and oil, which do not mix. In both, a smaller globe floats on the heavier liquid. The first represents the sun and the fixed stars, the second the sun and the planets, which seem to move of their own accord but are in fact controlled by concealed magnets. In his second drawing this is revealed. But since Kircher did not believe that Archimedes understood magnetism, he is forced to concede that he must have used clockwork or some hydraulic device. (*Magnes*, opposite 344, 346)

If you wonder how they can get inside each other, he says, know that they are made by cementing together hemispheres of glass with a mixture of wax, marble dust, and Greek pitch.

This device contains a further refinement: it causes the planets within the glass sphere to perform epicycles, in response to the turning of the secondary wheel on the edge of the large one. Something of the mood in which these experiments were conceived transpires from Kircher's comment: 'This artifice is full of admiration and pleasure, so that you may know through this very experiment that there can be no joy, nor any true felicity in this world, except that which we perceive from the contemplation of the true.'[17]

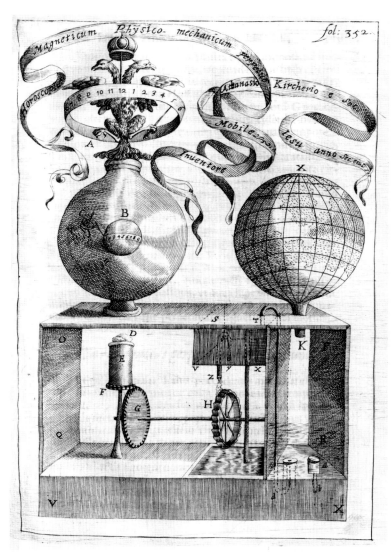

10.10 Perpetual magnetic horoscope. Here Kircher offers further speculation on Archimedes' sphere. The heat of the sun forces water into a chamber where it works a water-wheel. (*Magnes*, opposite 352)

10.11 Archytas's dove – another device depending on a hidden magnet to cause the dove to fly. (*Magnes*, opposite 358)

In a third illustration derived from Archimedes' sphere, Kircher hits on a way to introduce quasi-perpetual motion into it (**Ill. 10.10**). On the left is the same kind of glass sphere containing a floating sphere and a pointer. The latter is controlled by the magnet D, which revolves driven by a little water-wheel H. The right-hand sphere is metal, airtight and exposed to the sun. When the sun shines, the air inside it heats up and expands into the separate chamber KPR. This forces the water in the chamber up through the siphon X into the container ST, from which it descends at Z to drive the water-wheel. Every time the sun shines, the machine is set in motion. At night, when it cools, the air contracts into the metal sphere again and sucks up water through the valve ab. And so it can go on working, in the temperate zone, from the beginning of April until November.[18]

Kircher's scepticism (with which he is seldom credited) extended to all the magnetic marvels told of in ancient times, such as the iron chariot or the statue of Arsinoe at Alexandria, said to have been suspended in mid-air beneath a magnetic dome, the tomb of Muhammad, the golden calf of Jeroboam, or the iron horse of Bellerophon, held aloft between two magnets. As to the last phenomenon, Kircher points out that the equilibrium would be so fine that the slightest movement of the air would be enough to disturb it and make one magnet prevail over the other. He does, however, suggest a means to achieve the effect, which is to have the 'floating' object anchored by a thin thread, against which the magnet pulls it from above.[19]

In this illustration (**Ill. 10.11**), Kircher applies the principle to replicate the flying dove attributed to the Pythagorean mathematician Archytas. This must be the machine described in the catalogue of Kircher's museum as 'The dove of Archytas reaching towards a crystalline rotunda and indicating the

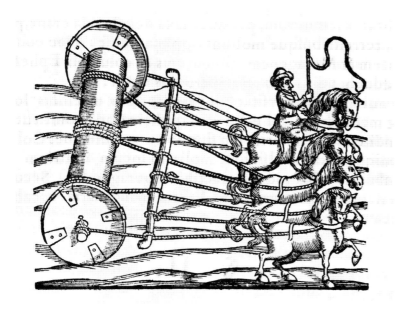

FANUM MONOΛIΘION
ab
Amafi Rege Ægypto ex unico Saxa
Minervæ confecratum.
Herod. Euterp.

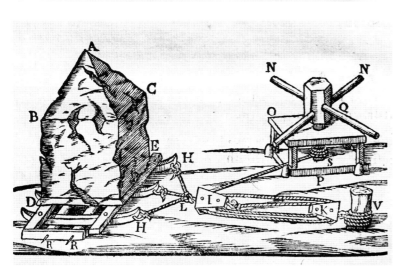

◄ **10.12** How Ctesiphon moved the columns. Large wheels are fixed to the ends of the columns which can then be rolled along horizontally. (*Œdipus Ægyptiacus*, Volume II, ii, 314)

◄▼ **10.13** Monolithic temple, described by Herodotus as made from a single stone. Kircher gives its dimensions as 42 x 28 x 16 feet. (*Turris Babel*, 72)

◄▼▼ **10.14** Egyptian 'polyspastos' was an arrangement described by Herodotus by which the monolithic temple was moved by means of a sledge, a fixed capstan and pulleys. (*Œdipus Ægyptiacus*, Volume II, ii, 520)

▼ **10.15** How the ancients transported obelisks. Following a text by Pliny, Kircher shows how a canal was dug to join the Nile with the obelisk. Boats filled with stones were then placed underneath the obelisk, and as the stones were removed the boats rose until they supported the obelisk. The engraving also shows it being transported to Rome. (*Obeliscus Pamphilius*, opposite 91)

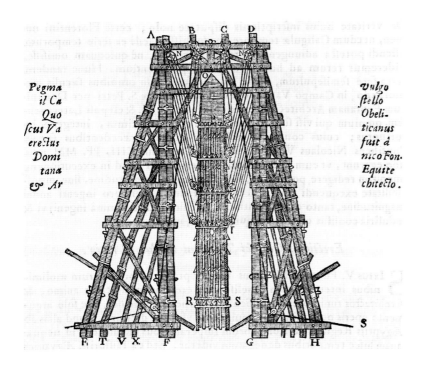

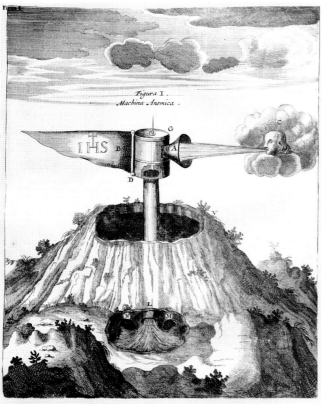

▲ **10.16** Erecting the Vatican obelisk – a famous feat carried out by Fontana in 1586. (*Œdipus Ægyptiacus*, Volume III, 372)

►▲ **10.17** Ladder in the mines of Peru, made with leather thongs and rungs of wood; information provided by a fellow Jesuit in South America. (*Mundus Subterraneus*, Volume II, 228)

◄ **10.18** Ventilator for mines. A weather vane turns a funnel to face into the wind. (*Mundus Subterraneus*, Volume II, 210)

► **10.19** Bucket-pump, a drawing sent to Kircher by a Jesuit colleague in Burgundy. A treadmill works a chain of buckets to extract salt-bearing waters. (*Mundus Subterraneus*, Volume II, fp. 248/249)

hours by its free flight' (see p. 192). It is like a peepshow enclosed in a thin copper or brass case. The wheel at the top conceals a magnet on its upper rim, invisible to the viewer. Archytas, standing on the hillock, is made from paper and dried hemp-stalk, so light that the slightest breath will spin him round. An almost invisible thread joins his hand to the magnetized dove, which must be no more than four fingers' breadth from the magnet above. Thereupon the operator turns the wheel, the dove flies round, and Archytas turns to face it wherever it goes.[20]

Whatever his doubts about the technological claims of the ancients, Rome itself held palpable evidence that they could move stupendous weights. Kircher illustrates a few of their methods, such as Vitruvius's description of how Ctesiphon moved the immense columns of the Temple of Diana in Ephesus (**Ill. 10.12**). Bronze axles were inserted into the ends of the columns and large wheels affixed, so that the columns travelled slung between them. A cruder method, which Kircher describes disdainfully, uses a sledge, a fixed capstan and a sheaf of pulleys (**Ill. 10.14**). Herodotus calls this machine a *polyspastos*, and says that King Amasis used it to move a prodigious temple made from a single stone from Elephantine to Sais, a twenty days' journey, in three years.[21] Kircher remarks on the weight of the machine itself as being no small matter to transport, and on the inconvenience of having to take it down and re-erect it every hundred paces, but concludes that no better or quicker method was then available.

In *Turris Babel*, Kircher illustrated this temple (**Ill. 10.13**) and gave Herodotus's figures: twenty-one by fourteen by eight cubits (exterior), eighteen by twelve by five (interior). He invites the reader to calculate the weight by subtracting the inside from the outside volume. (In his chart of calculations, he gives one cubit = two feet). The artist's impression, with a pyramidal roof and hieroglyphs on the walls, is as fanciful as the European foliage around it; no such building is known.

The biggest Roman obelisks had already been moved under Sixtus V, before Kircher was born, but he witnessed the erection of two mid-sized ones (those of Piazza Navona and Piazza Minerva), and argued unsuccessfully for the rescue of several more. The upper half of a plate in *Obeliscus Pamphilius* (**Ill. 10.15**) follows Pliny's description of how the architect Satyrus moved an obelisk 'extracted from the Theban rock'. First a deep canal was dug from the Nile to the place where the obelisk lay. Then two boats were floated under it, laden with stones twice the weight of the obelisk. As the stones were removed, the boats rose in the water and eventually supported the weight of the obelisk, which could then be floated down the Nile to Alexandria.[22]

The lower half of the plate follows Ammianus Marcellinus's description of the ship on which Emperor Constantius brought the Ramessean obelisk(s) to Rome. The incongruities of Pierre Miotte's interpretation are the most striking thing about this plate. His drawing of the ship has elements of a cutaway diagram: the upper rank of oars on the starboard side has no corresponding rank on the port side. There is no sense of scale: if the obelisk is correctly

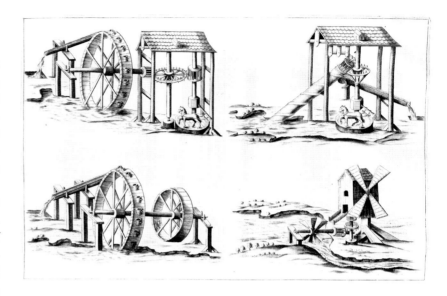

▲ **10.20** Apparatus for draining the Pontine Marshes, a subject of widespread concern in Kircher's time, when all previous attempts had failed. The four solutions illustrated here involve horsepower, treadmill and windmill. (*Latium*, opposite 258)

◄ **10.21** Kite in the shape of a dragon. Typically Kircher improves the occasion by giving the kite a message – 'The Wrath of God' – and suggests adding whistles and bells. (*Mundus Subterraneus*, Volume II, 499)

sized, then the oars are of superhuman dimensions. But from the upper plate, one would conclude that the obelisks are about a dozen feet long, and the Nile a few feet wide.

Machines of the Present: Mechanical and Chemical

Kircher was convinced that his modern age was superior both in wisdom and technology to any age of fallen mankind. In the preface to *Œdipus Ægyptiacus*, he writes of how the ancients reported things that seem to exceed human ingenuity, such as Archimedes' glass sphere, Archytas's flying dove, and Daedalus's self-moving statue; yet every day now such things are being rediscovered. 'Indeed, I have seen such works made in Frankfurt that go beyond anything the

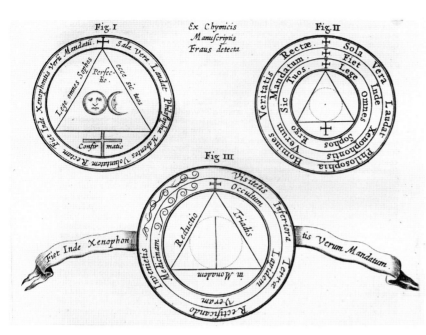

10.22 Alchemists' diagrams: Kircher reproduces these only in order to demolish them. (*Mundus Subterraneus*, Volume II, 311)

▶ 10.23 Distilling apparatus. For Kircher distilling is an image of nature and life. (*Mundus Subterraneus*, Volume II, opposite 411)

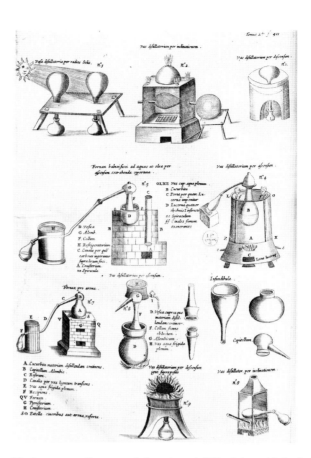

ancients could have done! Moreover, things unknown to us, such as gunpowder or the typography invented by Gutenberg, have long been known in China.'[23]

Kircher never devoted a book specifically to machines – an omission made good by Kaspar Schott (see p. 19) – but several of his works are full of designs and explanations of them. Among these I would include *Musurgia Universalis* and *Phonurgia Nova*, for the definition of 'machine' certainly covers organs, harpsichords, loudspeakers, intercoms and perhaps any musical instrument. He often digresses to describe contemporary technology, such as that wonder of recent Roman history, Fontana's wooden 'castle' built in 1586 to move the Vatican obelisk (**Ill. 10.16**; see also **Ill. 4.16**). His worldwide correspondents provided descriptions and drawings of other machines. Acosta, a fellow Jesuit working as a missionary in South America, described to him the incredible richness of the gold and silver mines in Peru and Potosi. Kircher admired from a distance their vast scale and low-tech ingenuity, typified by a lightweight ladder (**Ill. 10.17**) made from leather thongs with rungs of wood, but he was sensitive to the human cost. He writes, probably translating from Acosta's report:

> The first worker carries a candle to give the necessary light to himself, then to his companions following after. The depth is so horrible as to strike terror into those who merely hear of it; and the miserable miners meet a frightful death, either from the leather ladders snapping, or from the great weight of the veins in which they are working being broken and collapsing through their labours.[24]

Kircher was well aware of the miners' difficulties with foul air, and designed a rotating wind machine that would hopefully transmit fresh air to the bottom of a mine shaft (**Ill. 10.18**). The principle is simple: the vane B causes the funnel A to face whatever direction the wind is coming from. However, the scale is so exaggerated – the machine so large, the mountain so small – that the whole thing seems more like a pipe-dream, sanctified by the Jesuit monogram on the pointer.

Another correspondent, Johannes Menecard, Canon and Succentor of St Maurice in Salines, Burgundy, sent Kircher an illustration of a bucket pump (**Ill. 10.19**) with a minutely detailed explanation. The purpose of the device is to extract salt-bearing water from a number of different underground sources, using a bucket-chain mechanism. The small wheels at the bottom, whose function is unclear from the illustration, ring a bell to warn the operator when the water level falls. The hollow wheel that drives the whole machine is a treadmill, worked by a donkey or horse. The Canon boasts that visitors deemed the Salines pump the eighth wonder of the world. Kircher must have been under some obligation to him to have lavished a double-page plate on such a simple machine.

He himself had much bolder hydraulic ambitions, as he showed when Cardinal Pamphili set him to study the draining of the Pontine Marshes (**Ill. 10.20**). These were a perpetual source of aggravation, and from Roman times onwards various schemes for draining them had been proposed. The advantages would be an increase in habitable and arable land, an easy route from

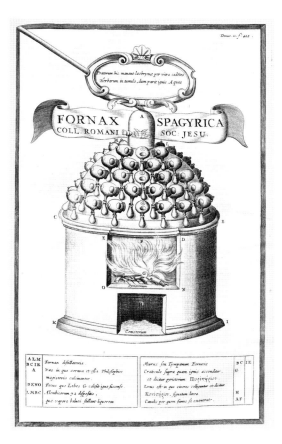

► **10.24** The Jesuits' distillery; its function is to reduce herbs – and practically anything else – to their quintessence. (*Mundus Subterraneus*, Volume II, opposite 412)

►► **10.25** Alchemical apparatus. Kircher's purpose is to rule out supernatural features and reduce the activities of the magus to rational procedures that anyone can repeat. (*Mundus Subterraneus*, Volume II, opposite 414)

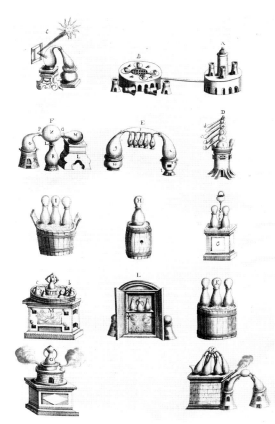

Rome to the sea coast, and the elimination of a source of malaria (blamed, as the name shows, on 'bad air' rather than on mosquitoes). Yet as Kircher says, there are four perennial obstacles: plague, war, the depravity of the natives of the region and Nature herself.[25] In the last book of *Latium* he lists the failed attempts. Most recently, Pope Urban VIII was offered a bold but viable scheme by Dutch experts, whose own country was sufficient proof that land lying below sea-level could be reclaimed and made profitable. But they made conditions (which Kircher does not specify) that caused the Pope to reject the offer. Kircher illustrates four pumping devices, two driven by horsepower, one by a man in a treadmill, and one by a windmill. The latter, he says, is widely used in Belgium and the lower parts of Germany, and when many are used together they are very efficient in draining large fields; also they work day and night without requiring any assistance.

Another of his ideas is to build a series of oaken barriers to prevent the sea from flooding up-river (like the modern Thames Barrier in London). Obviously all this would be horrendously expensive, but Kircher has one more suggestion up his sleeve: it is to drive herds of fifty buffalo along the marshes, urging them onward with the help of dogs. They would stir up the mud and weeds and allow fresh water to flow in their place.[26]

While in sheer inventiveness Kircher sometimes resembles Leonardo da Vinci, it seems not to have occurred to him that man could ever fly. But he had flown kites (**Ill. 10.21**). His instructions for making one out of thin struts of cane and paper, and his advice about flying it, obviously come from experi-

ence. Like a modern kite carrying an advertising logo, this specimen advertises Kircher's own preoccupation with its inscription 'The Wrath of God'.[27] He suggests that one could achieve a great effect on Ascension Day by using a kite to simulate flying angels, and all the better if equipped with whistles and bells.

Much has been written about Kircher's attitude to alchemy.[28] Living as he did at the close of the golden age of European alchemy, he cordially disliked its pretensions – perhaps in part because so many practitioners were Protestants. When he reproduces some of their diagrams (**Ill. 10.22**), he starts to fume: 'These are those wondrous arcana that the fatuous hair-curlers exhibit to the world in ridiculous figures and emblems. We now add an explanation of them, lest *Oedipus* should appear to be fooled by their guile and falsehood.' He adds that not only are these alchemists full of nonsense, but they cannot even write correct Latin![29]

The first two diagrams, taken from some unnamed alchemical treatise, contain acrostics concealing the words 'SULPHUR FIXUM'. Their meaning is that there is a tincture called fixed sulphur that penetrates all metals, like lightning, and gives them their colour. The third diagram is taken from Paracelsus, whom Kircher loathed perhaps above any other philosopher. He devotes two pages of fulmination to the sins and follies of the Swiss alchemist, then shows how Paracelsus's recipes could not possibly work. The diagram contains the well-known adage: 'Visit the interior of the earth; by rectification your will find the hidden stone, the true medicine.' The initials of the letters produce another acrostic, VITRIOL.

Some of the principles of alchemy, however, were acceptable to him, such as distillation (**Ill. 10.23**). According to his world-view, distillation imitates what nature performs in the interior of the earth. In that 'workshop of Vulcan' it is distillation that produces the *panspermia*, the universal seed of things from which man and animals proceed. All the chemical apparatus shown here merely emulates the tubes, cucurbits, alembics and furnaces within the earth itself.[30] The simplest kind of distillery (No. 3) works by the sun's rays. Others employ furnaces that send the vapours either up or down. Each has its own special purpose. Kircher saw the human body, too, as a distillery:

> What is the stomach but a sort of chemical cucurbit which receives the food and subjects it to natural humidity and heat, so that once attenuated it seeks the cold alembic of the head and brain, where it is resolved and finds exits via the mouth, nose, ears and eyes; thence it descends and lubricates the nerves, cartilages, tendons and muscles so that they can move. Thus it maintains the whole body in its healthy state.[31]

The 'spagyric furnace' at the Roman College (**Ill. 10.24**) stood in haughty contrast to the primitive furnaces and distilleries of the alchemists, showing that Kircher's own institution was at the cutting edge of chemistry. The furnace is comprised of six main elements: an ashtray (H), a firebox (G), a cauldron (B, C), a copper dome containing 66 alembics (L, M, B, C), a copper vase for the calcination of horns and bones (A), and, at the back, a register that could be opened and closed to regulate the heat. Usually the alembics are filled with herbs, then as the water in the cauldron boils, its steam enters the alembics and 'resolves the herbs into vapour'. This condenses and can be siphoned out. The uppermost chamber contains an iron mesh on which the animal bones, horns, and teeth rest. The steam softens them, says Kircher, to such a degree that they can be reduced to powder between the fingers.

'Philosophical' or alchemical distillation, according to Kircher, was different from the chemical kind that the Jesuits' equipment performed to such perfection. The alchemists, he says, aim to extract the quintessence from plants and liquors, for which they generally use a continuous distillation in a process lasting for months. The apparatuses marked G–O serve this purpose (**Ill. 10.25**). As the substance boils in the athanor, its vapour condenses in the globe above, and falls back into the vessel to be boiled again. Some of the athanors are furnace-driven; others use the gentler heat of sand, ashes or just the warmth produced by manure.[32]

The machines described and illustrated in this chapter cover almost the whole field of natural magic – that is, the exploitation of the hidden forces and qualities of the natural universe. The magus who could do this had esoteric knowledge, but only in the sense of being inaccessible to the unlearned and unscientific public. Anyone who read Kircher's books could figure out how this magic worked, and, given time and funds, should be able to build the machines for himself and produce the same astonishing phenomena.

In this sense, Kircher's natural magic followed the principle of the scientific method, which rules that an experiment, to be valid, is replicable by anyone who can create the same circumstances. It is the contrary of the occult sort of magic, which, even if one allows the possibility of its existence, can only be performed by persons specially gifted and trained. Like a modern stage magician, Kircher enjoyed playing the role of the latter kind of magus, and nowhere more than in the purpose-built theatre of his own museum.

Notes

1   *Magnes*, 1641, 360; 1643, 316.
2   Gorman, 68.
3   We have preserved the latter meaning in our word 'machinations'.
4   Unlike Schott, Kircher does not discuss Otto von Guericke's experiments with a vacuum, which were inexplicable within the framework of Aristotelian physics.
5   On the cry of Memnon, see Gould 1965, 26–36.
6   *Œdipus Ægyptiacus*, II, ii, 325.
7   *Œdipus Ægyptiacus*, II, ii, 332–333.
8   *Œdipus Ægyptiacus*, II, ii, 334.
9   *Œdipus Ægyptiacus*, II, ii, 335–336.
10   If there is any sense to this, it is to be found in the unequal 'hours' of ancient chronography, which divided day and night respectively into twelve portions. Only at the equinoxes would all the hours be equal.
11   *Œdipus Ægyptiacus*, II, ii, 339.
12   See Walker, 205–210.
13   Stolzenberg 2006, 178. See also Hine, 90, on Frances Yates's mistake in putting Kircher on the 'wrong' side of her Renaissance–modern watershed because she misunderstood the practice of natural magic.
14   'But what exactly is the order of nature that even demons cannot pervert? Schott's answer [in his Kircherian works] is unequivocal: demons are bound to obey the laws of Aristotelian natural philosophy!' Gorman and Wilding in Schott 2000, 275.
15   Schott 1658, 36–37.
16   *Magnes*, 1641, 348; 1643, 307.
17   *Magnes*, 1641, 346; 1643, 305.
18   *Magnes*, 1641, 353; 1643, 311.
19   *Magnes*, 1641, 357–358; 1643, 315.
20   *Magnes*, 1641, 359; 1643, 315.
21   Herodotus, *Histories*, II, 275.
22   *Obeliscus Pamphilius*, 88.
23   *Œdipus Ægyptiacus*, I, a[4]*verso*.
24   *Mundus Subterraneus*, 1664, II, 210.
25   *Latium*, 244–245. The marshes were finally drained in the 1930s, as part of Mussolini's programme of public works.
26   *Latium*, 258–259.
27   See Ill. 3.3 for Kircher's sketch of this kite. In German a kite is still called a 'dragon' (*Drachen*).
28   The definitive study of Kircher and alchemy is Partini 2006.
29   *Mundus Subterraneus*, 1664, II, 292. 'Hair-curlers' is a snide reference to the heated curlers used by hairdressers in Roman times, and in Kircher's day for dressing wigs. Notice that he still thinks of himself as Œdipus.
30   *Mundus Subterraneus*, 1664, II, 390.
31   *Mundus Subterraneus*, 1664, II, 391.
32   *Mundus Subterraneus*, 1664, II, 393.

Chapter 11 Machines: Magnetic and Optical

Magnetic Machines

Kircher's museum was crammed with an extraordinary number of machines. Who made them? The Roman College, as we know, had a superb furnace and presumably a chemistry laboratory to go with it. Did it also have its own machine shop, foundry, carpentry and glassworks, where Kircher's junior colleagues hitched up their soutanes and laboured at his projects, or was the work contracted out to local artisans? At all events, much effort and expense went into this collection, as we can see from de Sepi's catalogue (see box on p. 192), and it explains Kircher's constant need for gifts of money from his patrons.

This chapter treats the machines driven by magnetism and those that exploit the laws of optics, culminating in the magic lantern. The chief application of magnetism was, of course, the compass, which revolutionized surveying no less than navigation. Kircher had been interested in surveying since his twenties, and proved his competence by mapping the domains of the Archbishop of Mainz and the area around Narbonne. It was left to Kaspar Schott

to describe Kircher's own invention, the Pantometrum, in a separate work of 1660.[1] The secret of the Pantometrum was that it combined directional surveying with a magnetic compass. So does an even more ingenious machine described in *Magnes* (**Ill. 11.1**). One straps it to the belt and ties the string (H) to the knee, so that at each pace, the large wheel (D) turns one notch. At every hundred paces, a spring (G) is activated that causes the three pinpoints (c) on the magnetic needle (bo) to pierce a strip of paper (TS). After the journey is over, the paper is removed and the directions of the pinpoints noted. These can then be translated into vectors on a map. This object was not Kircher's invention; someone apparently offered it to Emperor Rudolf II, a collector and connoisseur of such things. Kircher remarks on the difficulty of making and operating it, then outlines some simpler and more reliable mapping methods of his own.

Another contemporary machine that Kircher explains, only to reject, looks to magnetism as a source of perpetual motion (**Ill. 11.2**). The idea is that a hollow

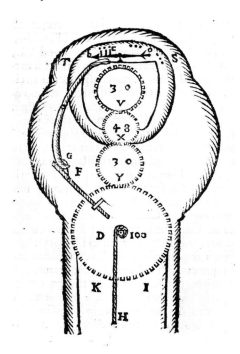

◄ **11.1** Device for mapping itineraries. It works like a pedometer by measuring the paces and direction of the person walking. Kircher did not invent it and in fact considered that he could do better. (*Magnes*, 248)

► **11.2** Perpetual motion machine. This depends on a ball attracted by a magnet, but at the last moment it falls and begins the process all over again. Kircher knew that it would not work. (*Magnes*, 331)

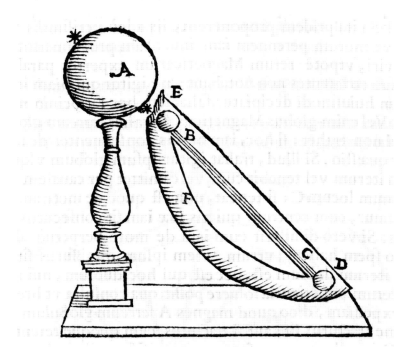

THE MACHINES IN KIRCHER'S MUSEUM

As listed and described in Giorgio de Sepi's catalogue of 1678.

1. Two helical spirals most skilfully measuring cycles with the twisted coils of snakes. An organ, driven by an automatic drum, playing a concert of every kind of birdsong, and sustaining in mid-air a spherical globe, continually buffeted by the force of the wind.[2]

2. A hydrostatic-magnetic machine, representing the hours, zodiac, planets and the whole fabric of the heavens. The hours are described by means of a very simple motion, in which images of the sun and moon alternately ascend and descend vertically. The divisions of the hour are marked by the sympathetic motion of the flight of small birds.

3. A magnetic-hydraulic machine displaying the time all over the world, as well as the astronomical, Italian, Babylonian and ancient hours.

4. A little fountain moving the globe weighing down on the head of Atlas in a circle by hidden movements.

5. A fountain that lifts a genie fixed in the water up and down, with a perpetual motion of tossing about and turning.

6. A fountain in which the Goddess Isis, contained in a crystalline sphere, is sustained, and greets guests by spraying water everywhere.

7. A hydraulic machine that apes perpetual motion, recently invented by the Author, consisting of a clepsydra that flows out when it is inverted, and again when it is turned the right way up, wetting a watery heaven with its spray.

8. A hydraulic machine most skilfully representing the Primum Mobile, and violently impelling a brass snake resting on top of the water in twists and turns by water.

9. A water-vomiting hydraulic machine, at the top of which stands a figure vomiting up various liquids for guests to drink.

10. A hydraulic clock urging or carrying globes or genies up and down inside crystal tubes five palms in height, indicating the different times.

11. A hydraulic machine which supports a crystal goblet, from one side of which a thirsty bird drinks up water, than a snake revomits from the other side while opening its mouth.

12. A hydrotectonic machine moving armed knights from one place and a crowd returning from another by means of continual drops.

13. A two-headed imperial eagle, vomiting water copiously from the depths of its gullets.

14. A crowd of dancing genies driven by the silent approach of water.

15. The dove of Archytas reaching towards a crystalline rotunda and indicating the hours by its free flight.

16. The catoptric theatre, completely filled with a treasure of all sorts of delicacies, fruits and precious ornaments.

17. An architectural perspective representing the arrangement of the rooms inside a magnificent palace.

18. A perpetual screw, the invention of Archimedes, by which it is an easy matter to lift 125 pounds with the strength of a very weak small boy.

19. A large crystalline globe full of water representing the resurrection of the Saviour in the midst of the waters.

Various thermoscopes or thermometers, which indicate the daily growth of simples, the mutations of the air, the ebb and flow of the tide, and the variation of the winds, together with experiments on the origins of springs.

An extremely large concavo-convex burning mirror, with a collection of many mirrors, some of which show ghosts in the air; others show objects unchanged, others show them multiplied and others reconstitute completely undetermined species from a confused series into a beautiful form. Among these there is one which reconstitutes the effigy of Alexander VII. [...]

A large number of mechanical clocks, one of which plays harmonious music by a concert of bells with an elaborate movement; at any hour it plays the sound, also every half-hour with a marvellous harmony of notes and sweetness of sound it plays the hymn *Ave Maris stella.* Another one indicating the time of day by the movement of a pendulum. Another, finally, giving the minutes and seconds of time. The part of the world illuminated by the sun, the increase and decrease of day and night. The current sign of the zodiac, the astronomical and Italian hours, as well as the ancient hours, or the unequal hours, which it describes along a straight line by a singular artifice. Many sundials. [...]

The Delphic Oracle, or speaking statue.

A Divinatory Machine for any planetary influence at the circumference of two glass spheres by genies moved uniformly by a mutually sympathetic motion. Twisting themselves to the same degree at a large distance, each of them in his sphere indicates the same point of the sign.

Various motions of solid globes bearing a resemblance to perpetual motion.

A hydraulic perpetual motion by rarefaction and condensation, an Archimedean screw carrying globes up with a continual motion through helical glass channels.[3]

11.3 Universal horoscope. By using a ship's compass and a magnetic needle one could discover the time anywhere in the world. (*Magnes*, 320)

11.4 Chart of magnetic declination. Kircher was one of many who hoped to enable seamen to establish longitude by means of the compass. The heart-shaped diagram suggested a mystical analogy – as the compass needle inclines to the north so our hearts incline to God. (*Magnes*, 404)

11.5 Walking statue of Daedalus in the labyrinth: the paper figure contains a steel plate that responds to a hidden magnet (marked 'B'). (*Magnes*, 362)

device (EFD) contains an iron ball (B, C) which is attracted by a fixed magnet (A). The magnet pulls the ball up, but at the last moment (position B) gravity prevails and the ball falls down the curved chute (F) to position C. From here it is again attracted by the magnet, and so moves perpetually up and down. In a way, this is a 'thought experiment' that may have seemed persuasive to those with no direct experience of how magnets behave. Kircher demonstrates that it is dynamically impossible, for either the magnetic force is sufficient to draw the ball from C to B, and then will suffice to hold it there; or else, if it is not strong enough to hold the ball, then it will not draw it up in the first place.[4]

Some of Kircher's ideas seem simple to us, but cannot have been easy for his audience to grasp. How could they understand that at one moment it may be Sunday in one place, but Monday in another? This is one consequence that Kircher draws from his 'Universal magnetic horoscope, through which the hour can be seen anywhere on earth' (**Ill. 11.3**). It is made like a ship's compass, with a card driven by a magnetic needle rotating over a bowl or cylinder. On the card are the names of countries and their principal cities all round the world, and on the edge of the cylinder are the twenty-four hours of the day and night. By rotating the device, one can see what hour it is anywhere in the Catholic realm, on which the sun never sets.[5] Later he would develop this into one of his most elaborate plates (see **Ill. 11.17**, below).

Another magnetic device with a religious subtext is the 'Instrument of magnetic inclination for the whole world' (**Ill. 11.4**). From this one is supposed to read off the angle of declination performed by a freely suspended magnetic needle. There was much interest in this dimension of compass-reading in Kircher's time, and he collected tables from forty-four people all over the world, thirty-six of them Jesuits.[6] It was hoped that navigators could use these to establish not only the direction of magnetic north, but their longitude at sea. Unfortunately the reports did not match, because magnetic declinations vary not only with location but with time. By 1667, the Royal Society under Henry Oldenburg was collecting data for the change of declination over time, but as the tables became ever more complicated the attempt was abandoned, and attention focused on establishing longitude through a chronometer. Kircher's diagram comes from the time when the declinations were believed to be regular and invariable, and the symmetry of the diagram expresses this hope. Beside that, it has a religious dimension. The inscription on the concentric circles continues: 'Just as the magnet points to one centre, so our hearts incline to God, the centre.' It may have been the cordiform shape of the diagram that suggested putting in the mystical symbol of the eye in the blazing heart.[7]

Turning to more frivolous matters, one of the magnetic toys that delighted Kircher's visitors was a peepshow depicting Daedalus in his labyrinth (**Ill. 11.5**)

The statue is made of paper, dried hemp-stalk, or the lightest of wood, and, as in similar machines, contains a small steel plate that responds to the hidden magnet B. As the wheel turns, apparently driven by weights and pulleys, the magnet on it causes the statue to rush around the chamber, the effect being greatly enhanced by lining the latter with mirrors, so that innumerable images of the statue are also seen in motion. And all this, to the amazement of the viewers, happens without any visible threads, weights or other mechanism.[8]

The upper part of the plate shows a magnetic sundial. The hours are inscribed on the bottom of the vase, beneath the water, and the little figure in the boat points at the appropriate hour with his fishing rod. If he is disturbed, he returns to the correct hour. The viewer does not know that the boat is under the influence of a magnet beneath, which reorients it north–south. A further complication is the fact of refraction, as the lines of the sundial are seen through water, hence the title: 'Anaclastic magnetic sundial, demonstrating the hours through refraction'.

While Kircher was in Malta, he made a magnetic wind indicator for the Jesuit College, which may have resembled the one pictured here (**Ill. 11.6**). One inspiration for it came from the octagonal Tower of the Winds in Athens, originally topped by a statue of Aeolus. As the wind blew, the statue would swivel around and point its trident to the face of the tower on which the image of the appropriate wind was carved. Kircher's invention was more sophisticated, and shows the direction of the wind in two ways. As the weathercock (here an imperial eagle) moves with the wind, it turns the cogwheel C, whose movements are transferred through wheel D to the pointer S on the dial XY. Here the viewers can learn from where the wind is blowing. More mysteriously, they can also see the glass sphere H, half-filled with water and inscribed with thirty-two winds and their properties. A magnetized figure of Aeolus floats in the water, and turns without visible agency to point with his sceptre to the current wind. The secret motive power is supplied by a magnet beneath it, on the column A, which turns along with the other wheels.[9]

When the machine was unveiled, its viewers thought at first that there must be a demon inside the glass globe. When Kircher told them that it was done by magnetism, they would not believe him, for what could magnetism have to do with the winds? Only when he showed them the mechanism did they admit that they had been deceived.[10]

Kircher did not believe in the kind of 'magnetism' that was widely believed to communicate over distance, and went to some length to mock and discredit those who attempted it. He tells a story about a nobleman who had lost his nose through syphilis, and had a false nose made from flesh cut from the arm of a servant. When the 'donor' sickened and died, so did the nose. He also tells of an experiment in which two dear friends tried to communicate with each other by pricking themselves in numbers corresponding to the letters of the alphabet. When the other friend felt the sympathetic pricking in his own flesh, he could decode the message by counting the pricks.[11]

Instead of these and other superstitious or demonic devices, Kircher suggested some of his own (**Ill. 11.7a, b**). In the horizontal plate, the two glass globes A and E are separated by a number (up to an infinite number!) of other globes, each with a magnetized pointer inside it. So long as they are all equal in strength, Kircher says, the direction of the pointer in A will be communicated to B, and vice versa.

In the other plate, the impulse is carried from one globe to another via a pulley system, which rotates the magnets concealed beneath each globe. Thus all the globes point to the same letter. Elegant as the architectural setting is, the whole notion of communication has been lost in the process.

Many of Kircher's machines are just variations on a single theme, but the graphic skills of his illustrators made them all look novel and different from one another. He also varied their symbolism, meaning and historical references, as we have seen in his recreations of the wondrous machines of antiquity. Once he had found that a figure suspended inside a glass globe could be turned by an unseen magnet, the stage magician in him took over. Here is one of his favourites, in which the fiction is that of an oracle (**Ill. 11.8**). The visitor is invited to ask some question about signs of the zodiac, planets, winds or the system by which the date of Easter is calculated. The operator then moves the pointer T to cause the magnet S to revolve, in turn causing the figures in the globes to point to the answer. To give it an atmosphere of Egyptian mysteries, the magnet is hidden beneath an obelisk adorned with hieroglyphs, and the operator is actually named 'Oedipus' – Kircher's alter ego.

After describing the magnetic oracle, he tells a story of how he was showing the 'trifles' in his museum to the usual crowd of visitors. One of them, more simple or more curious than the others, asked whether the oracle could tell what the weather was going to do (it being calm at the time). Kircher happened to have a hydraulic machine in his museum, with which he used to entertain people by making a shower of rain at will. The moving figure, controlled in the usual way, announced that a great shower was imminent, which the visitors found laughable. While they were guffawing over it, Kircher slipped away and turned on the tap of his hydraulic machine, taking cover himself, and had the pleasure of seeing them all soaked to the skin. But they could not blame anyone but themselves: they had been warned![12]

The second edition of *Ars Magna Lucis* contained three novel clocks: two of them hydraulic, which Kircher suggests an adept mechanic might build,[13] and one which was actually in his museum (**Ill. 11.9**). It is driven by a combination of clockwork and magnets, and marks the hours in two different ways. The columns at the sides are hollow, containing the cords and weights that drive a clockwork, and one of the weights is a strong magnet. As it rises up, a little model of a lizard or crab, made of paper with a needle inside, seems to crawl up the outside of the column and marks the hours. The three glass globes contain Kircher's favourite device of magnetized pointing figures which rotate as though by magic, but actually because a magnet is turning in the column beneath them. In this machine, the magnet is also turned by clockwork.

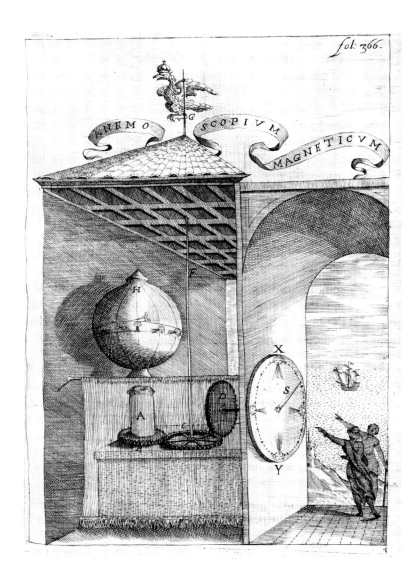

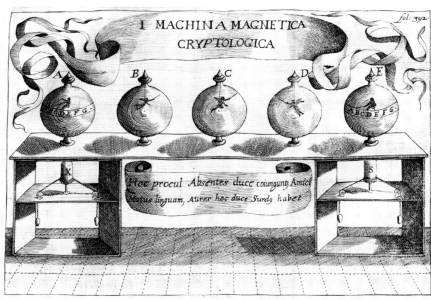

▲ **11.6** Magnetic wind indicator: a complicated form of weathervane. The eagle, moved by the wind, turns a cogwheel, whose movement is transferred to a pointer on a dial. At the same time a hidden magnet floating in water turns a figure of Aeolus, whose sceptre points in the same direction. (*Magnes*, 366)

▶▲ ▶ **11.7a, b** Cryptological machines. A demonstration of magnetism. If each globe has a magnet inside it, they will all point in the same direction, no matter how many there are. In the second design the globes are too distant to affect each other, but a system of pulleys causes hidden magnets to turn, controlling the magnetic pointers in each globe. (*Magnes*, 392, 393)

▲ **11.8** Magnetic oracle, one of Kircher's machines that show him more as an entertainer than a serious scientist. It pretends to answer astronomical questions. By moving the pointer (T), an unseen magnet in the base of the obelisk (S) causes the figures on the globes to point to the answer. (*Magnes*, 237)

▶ **11.9** Multiple magnetic clock, another conjuring trick. By a combination of magnets and clockwork, a model crab or lizard crawls up the column in the middle. (*Ars Magna Lucis*, 1671, 701)

11.10 A sunflower clock. The flower turns naturally to the sun. A pointer fixed to the flower (F) indicates the time on a ring (DE) that encircles it. (*Magnes*, 644)

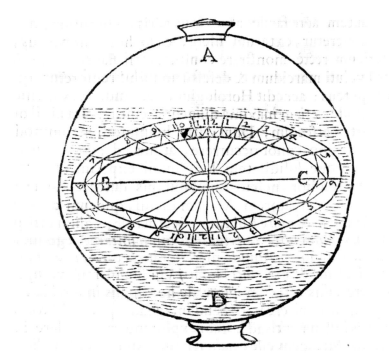

11.11 Heliotropic clock. An Arab merchant provided Kircher with an unknown substance which, fixed at the centre of a floating disc, caused the disc to rotate in conformity with the course of the sun. (*Magnes*, 738)

on the cork, or even penetrates through the cork to the water, as shown in the illustration opposite. Tie a skein of wool around the roots and hanging down into the water, so that the water, attracted by the wool, will provide nutriment for the plant, lest it be dried out by the sucking of the sun. After this, surround the flower with a circle of the hours, divided according to the latitude of your region, so that the centre of the flower, equipped with the pointer F, can point to the hours on it. Expose the machine in the open air to the rising sun, and the face of the flower, attracted by the sun, will easily turn about to face it, since there is no resistance of the stalk to hinder it. The success of the thing requires industry and skilled workmanship, but I have tested it most successfully...[14]

He warns that the slightest breath of wind can upset the device, and suggests enclosing it in glass. He also admits that it becomes 'lazy' when the sun goes in, and that at best it scarcely lasts a month.

When he was in Marseille, he showed his sunflower clock to an Arab merchant, who assured him that in Arabia they had clocks that showed the hour both day and night, made from a material that always faced the sun (**Ill. 11.11**). The merchant did not know what this material was, but happened to have

One of Kircher's most famous 'magnetic' inventions was the sunflower clock (**Ill. 11.10**), for which he gives precise instructions:

Take a large and capacious tub, fill it up with water, and fix in the centre of it a spike, then adapt a cork to the size of the vessel and of the sunflower stalk, such that the cork can move easily and unimpeded around the spike as if around an axle. Onto this cork, fix the bloom of a sunflower that you know to be particularly imbued with its effective virtue, complete with its root and stalk, such that it stands normally

some of it which he gave (or sold) to Kircher. After repeated experiments, Kircher fixed it on a circular dial which floated on water inside a glass globe, and found that it worked, but only for a few days before it was 'corrupted' by the water.[15]

While there was no doubt in Kircher's mind that it was the sun's magnetism that worked on the sunflower and made it revolve, he rejected Kepler's suggestion that this also causes the earth to go around the sun. He offers this experiment to demonstrate the heliocentric theory and its falsity (**Ill. 11.12**). The large globe is filled with a heavy liquid, and the glass bulb filled with lighter oil or spirits floats on it. Inside the latter, a wick is kindled to represent Kepler's central sun (I), while the earth–moon system (T) revolves around it once a year. The magnet representing the earth (A) rotates once a day, delighting viewers with the sight of its regions passing alternately through light

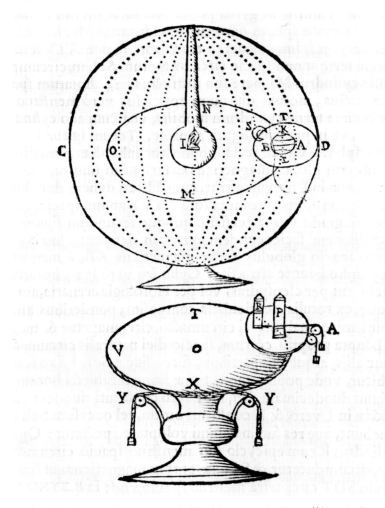

11.12 Machine demonstrating a moving earth. The globe representing the sun (I) has a candle inside it. The earth (A) rotates on its axis, producing the effect of night and day, and also goes round the sun. It assumes the Copernican model of the solar system that Kircher was officially obliged to deny. (*Magnes*, 573)

and shadow. Kircher does not explain the mechanism, but leaves the inventive reader to devise a power source such as weights, cogwheels, sand (like an hourglass) or steel springs. To improve it further, one can include another magnet (R) representing the moon, which is driven around the earth (P) once a month. This will show to perfection how the moon shows its various phases to the earth, and occasionally eclipses the sun. It is only after praising the ability of such machines to illustrate any and every cosmic system that Kircher proceeds to demolish Kepler's theory.[16]

Sundials and Moondials

Although Kircher's museum contained a large number of mechanical clocks,[17] he never wrote about how they work. For him, timekeeping was much more a branch of optics, and that was part of the 'great art of light and shadow' that included those ultimate timekeepers, the sun, moon and stars. This focused his attention and ingenuity to an obsessive degree on the sundial and its variations.

Early in his career, Kircher had made sundials both large and small, notably one that occupied a whole tower at the Jesuit College in Avignon.[18] To design them was a complicated exercise of mathematics and astronomy. They would then be installed, beautifully painted, gilded and inscribed, at an architectural focal point.[19] The Museo Astronomico e Copernicano in Rome owns four extremely complex dials, inscribed and painted on large slate tablets, which were made in 1635–1636 and were probably among the first productions of Kircher's residence in Rome.[20] His early books *Magnes* and *Ars Magna Lucis* illustrate dozens of dials, all based on the same technical principles but each with a different symbolism and set of learned references. Most of them did not yet exist, but were offered as a pattern-book for the use of patrons. One of these is a homage to Emperor Ferdinand (**Ill. 11.13**), the letters of whose name stand vertically, each a separate sundial. The corners (or in the case of closed letters, the holes) act as gnomons, and the hours are inscribed at the appropriate places. The eagle, too, traces the hours by casting shadows from its beaks, wingtips and sceptres. As a timekeeper it is full of redundancies; a single, large-scale dial would have been much more useful and accurate. But efficiency was not the point, as we see if we examine the symbolic dimensions of this and other dials.

The 'Astronomico-physical dial, showing the doctrine of the whole Primum Mobile' (**Ill. 11.14**) shows how Kircher could design a machine to convey a whole cosmology, a theology and a theory of empire. First, it is set out, like many of his frontispieces, as an image of three worlds: Archetypal, Sidereal and Elementary. Since it is an astronomical machine, the middle world occupies most of the picture, bounded by the four winds, symbols of the four cardinal directions and the four seasons of the year. They are the link between time and space, between the seasonal phenomena of earth and the structure of the sidereal world (the planets and fixed stars, including those of the zodiac). The double-headed eagle of the Habsburg dynasty looks both

11.13 Imperial sundial. This is an elaborate homage to the Emperor Ferdinand, the letters of whose name form sundials. The time is indicated by the shadows cast by parts of the eagle. (*Ars Magna Lucis*, 1671, 364)

11.14 An astronomical sundial, combining a whole host of meanings. The signs of the zodiac take up most of the picture. From the crucified Christ at the top streams of blood flow onto the Emperor's crown, sanctifying his rule over Europe, below. (*Ars Magna Lucis*, 1671, 383)

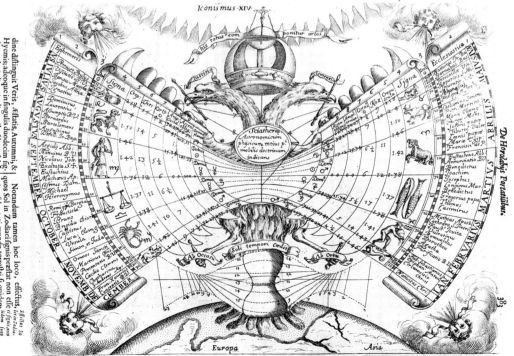

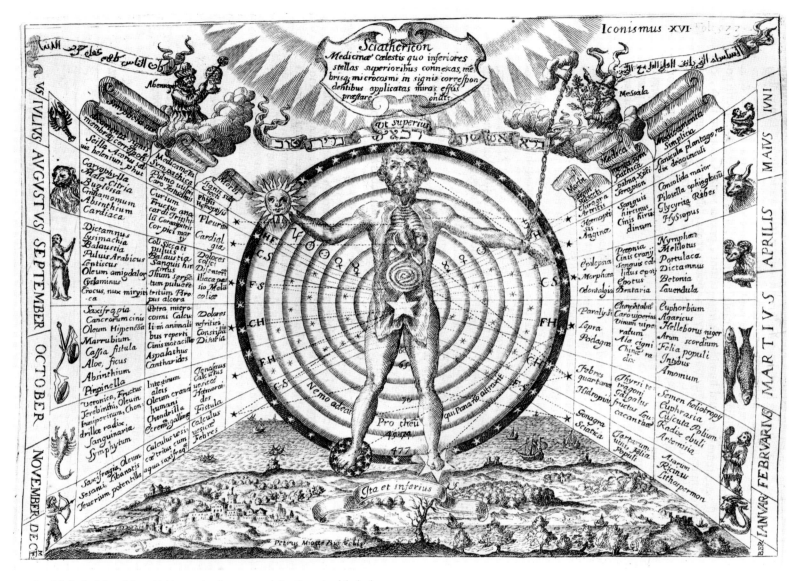

11.15 Sundial of celestial medicine: a highly complex diagram, correlating the parts of the body with the signs of the zodiac, following Arab sages and Hermetic philosophy. (*Ars Magna Lucis*, 1671, 396)

ways, dispensing justice to the west and mercy to the east. From its imperial crown to the feathers of its tail, it fills the whole distance between heaven and earth. At the very top is the crucified Christ, with two streams of blood flowing from his hands onto the horns of the crown, signifying that the Holy Roman Emperor enjoys a direct mandate from God.

In practical terms, this is a calendar as well as a clock, marking not only the course of the day but of the year, which is shown as the monthy signs of the zodiac and the Church's calendar of saints' days. The butterfly shape is due to the varying declination of the sun through the seasons; the shadow cast by

the gnomon varies in length, as does the amplitude of its course from sunrise to sunset. Kircher explains:

If for example the feast of St John the Baptist falls on 24 June, in the first degree of Cancer, which is the maximum declination of the sun at twenty-three degrees, thirty minutes, the feast commemorated is inscribed on the line of the summer tropic. Likewise the feast of the Assumption of the Blessed Virgin Mary falls on 15 August, where the sun is in the 22nd degree of Leo. Look up the declination of this degree in the table of Book

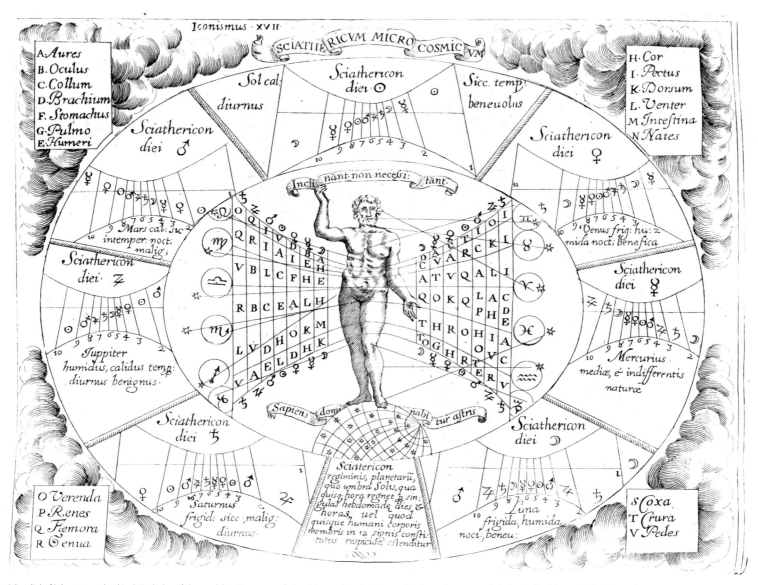

11.16 Sundial of 'planetary rulerships'. Each day of the week has its own sundial and its good and bad hours for the various parts of the body. (*Ars Magna Lucis*, 1671, 402)

III, and you will find it to be eighteen degrees. Then you put the feast of the Assumption in the column of feasts.[21]

The other columns of the dial show other consequences of the phenomenon of the seasons, which in Kircher's geocentric cosmology was due not to the inclination of the earth's axis but to a regular dipping motion of the sun's passage through the zodiac. The seasons affect the lengths of day and night, the times of sunrise and sunset throughout the year, the degrees of right ascension and the houses of the planets. The eagle holds two sceptres which serve

as gnomons for dials of 'Italian' hours, counted from sunrise, and 'Babylonian' hours, counted from sunset. In the text, Kircher celebrates his invention with a Latin sonnet.

Another compound sundial illustrates the correspondence of macrocosm with microcosm. It is called 'Dial of celestial medicine, showing the lower stars connected with the higher stars, and their marvellous effects when applied in the corresponding signs to the members of the microcosm' (**Ill. 11.15**). The gnomon at the figure's navel casts a shadow whose length varies with the seasons. In the upper corners are the Arab sages Abenragel with

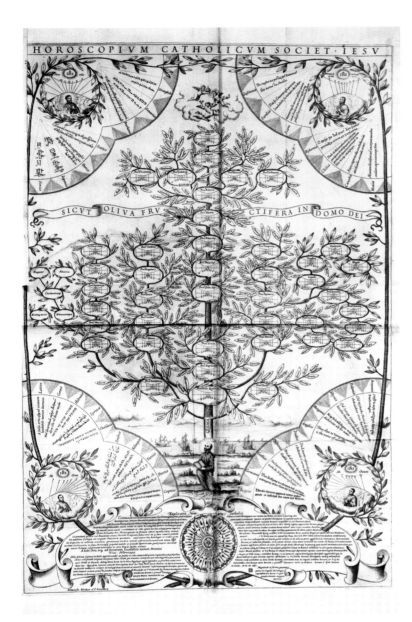

11.17 Jesuits' horoscope, a diagram for telling the time in all the parts of the world where Jesuits were active, to be used in conjunction with a sundial. (*Ars Magna Lucis*, 1671, 3)

a globe and Messala with a plant. The Hermetic saying 'As above, so below' adorns the head and feet of the microcosmic figure, who spans the cosmos from the sphere of Mercury to that of the fixed stars. In the sphere of Jupiter is written the adage 'No one approaches Proteus without attracting Pan' (compare **Ill. 10.8**). The parts of the body, with their ailments and cures, correspond to the twelve signs of the zodiac.

A third variation is a 'Dial of planetary rulerships, which shows by the sun's

shadow which planet rules on any day of the week and hour, and which member of the human body it affects when in the twelve signs' (**Ill. 11.16**). The directions are to place the instrument in the sun, and to consult whichever of the seven dials in the outer oval corresponds to the day of the week. The position of the shadow gives both the time of day and the planet that rules that hour. Then one looks at the chart on the inner oval and finds the current sign of the zodiac. Where the sign's horizontal row of letters meets the vertical column of the currently ruling planet, there is a letter denoting the part of the body currently affected; the keys to these are in the four corners. The banners contain cautionary sayings about astrology: 'They incline, they don't compel' and 'The wise man will rule the stars'.

The catoptric sundial of Kircher's Avignon days already told the time in all the countries of the world where the Jesuits were active. While a simplified, magnetic version has already been shown (**Ill. 11.3**) the great folding plate at the beginning of *Ars Magna Lucis* takes the idea to its graphic limit (**Ill. 11.17**).[22] Kircher still intended this as a practical device, and suggests that it be mounted on wood, then oriented exactly, along with a sundial. The rose should be cut out and mounted on stiffer paper so that it can be rotated and the hours read from it. He even shows a little square, 'the size and shape of the gnomon which should be erected in the individual sundials, perpendicularly above the line of the twelfth hour'. The rose at the bottom comes recognizably from the 'universal horoscope', and the purpose is similar: it is to show the time in all the places of the world where the Jesuits have established their provinces. On the trunk of the tree are European provinces that share the same time zone as Rome. To the left are those whose time is behind Roman time, such as Chile, where it is 6 a.m. when it is noon in Rome. To the right are places whose time is ahead, the furthest being Japan, where it is 9 p.m. Thus it celebrates the realization of the Psalmist's verse: 'From the rising of the sun until the going down of the same, the Lord's name is to be praised' (Psalm 113:3).

Beside its practical use, the plate has a symbolic meaning. The provinces are like so many fruits on an olive tree, while the missions or Jesuit houses within them are like the leaves. The grouping of the fruits is in the shape of the Jesuits' monogram: IHS with a cross above, three nails beneath. Ignatius of Loyola, founder of the order, kneels at the foot of the tree, while behind him the ships depart on their missionary journeys. In the corners, the souls of departed Jesuits repeat the prayer in all the languages of the world.

More entertaining than his endless series of sundial designs is Kircher's proposal for a 'Heliocaustic or sun-ignited clock' (**Ill. 11.18**),

ingeniously constructed so as not only to show the hours by light, but to mark the hours by igniting fire and making a noise, just as normal clocks do with the help of wheels. Three things are necessary to begin with. First, a crystal ball, or if you cannot have that, a spherical phial filled with liquid. Secondly, a spherical shell. Thirdly, the drawing of

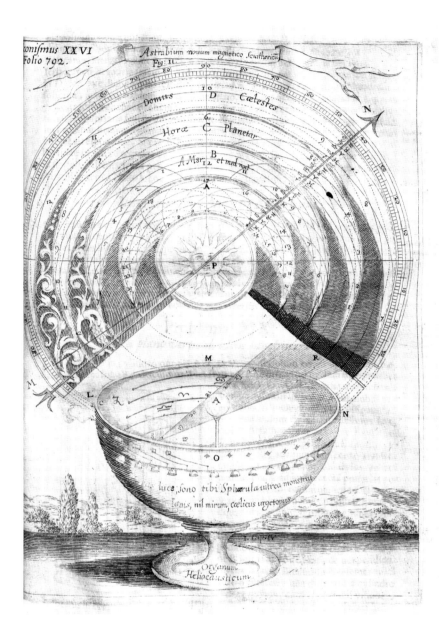

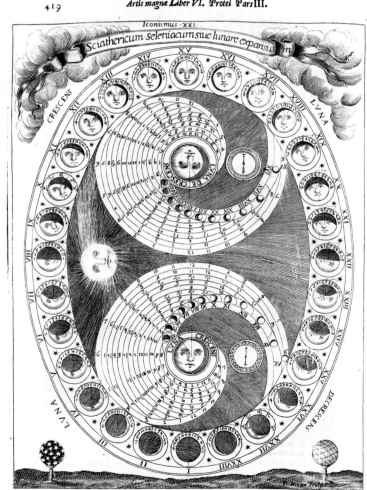

11.18 Explosive sundial, a complicated machine by which the concentrated rays of the sun detonate small amounts of gunpowder in iron channels every hour. The illustration is not easily understood since Kircher omits the channels. The upper part of the plate illustrates a 'magnetic dial' which has no connection with the explosive sundial. (*Ars Magna Lucis*, 1671, 692)

11.19 Moondial. The twenty-eight small circles forming an oval represent the days of the lunar cycle, each with its gnomon. One of the drawbacks of this idea is that there are several nights when the moon does not shine, even in good weather, but Kircher is not discouraged. (*Ars Magna Lucis*, 1671, 419)

circulum 28. ætatis Lunaris: habebis tot horologia Lunaria feparata, quot circuli in præcedentibus duobus continentur. His fic delineatis, horum fingula fuo ftylo munies; phafique Lunari circa centrum, unà cum numero ætatis Lunaris defignata; habebis fyftema horarum Lunarium, ex quo, quemadmodum paulò ante diximus, facillimè nocturnam horam difcas; illud enim horologium illa nocte horam demonftrabit. cui ætas

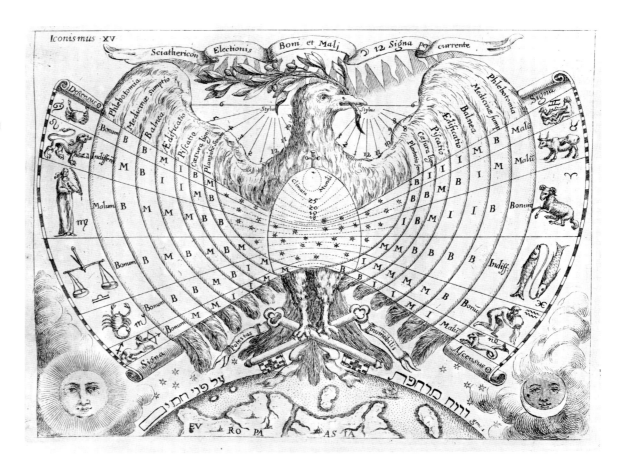

11.20 Moondial of good and bad days, a specialized astrological form of the previous illustration to indicate, from a moondial reading, which days would be good or bad for such things as blood-letting, planting and other activities. (*Ars Magna Lucis*, 1671, 391)

the clock in the shell, together with the things necessary for firing and making sounds.

The crystal ball must focus the sun's rays exactly on the hemispherical shell. The latter has a number of little iron channels, one for every hour, and these are stuffed with gunpowder, but they are not shown 'so as not to perplex the reader with a complicated illustration.' As the sun's magnified rays fire the miniature cannons, they also ring the bells, and it can even be arranged for multiple bells to sound each particular hour. Kircher assures his readers that he has often exhibited this machine, causing enormous delight and admiration, and that nothing would be more appropriate for the entertainment of princes.[23] (The upper part of the plate illustrates a 'magnetic dial' which has no connection with the explosive sundial.)

It seems incredible that a moondial could be of any possible use, since the moon is seldom strong enough to cast a shadow and rarely shines all night, but Kircher's world-view made it at least symbolically necessary to give the moon its due as a timekeeper. The mysterious-looking spiral moondial (**Ill. 11.19**) is a horizontal device, in whose outer circle are twenty-eight little moondials corresponding to the twenty-eight days of the lunar cycle, each with its gnomon (shown in dotted lines) and hours. For example, the 15th dial at the top of the plate shows the full moon, which shines from 6 p.m.

until 6 a.m. At the other end of the oval, even the days on which the moon is invisible, or scarcely visible, have their own dials. The purpose of this is to know the hours of the night. But to make it more useful, Kircher recommends putting two larger dials inside the oval, one for the waxing half of the cycle, the other for the waning half. The spirals coming out of each moon phase then allow the gnomon to indicate the current hour of the night.

As with sundials, Kircher applied moondials to other fields, in this case to the astrological belief that the moon's influence makes certain days more propitious than others. The practical purpose of this complex moondial (**Ill. 11.20**) is to show, by the position of the gnomon's shadow cast by the moon, whether a day is good (B), bad (M), or indifferent (I) for activities under lunar influence: phlebotomy (blood-letting), taking medicine, bathing, building, hunting and fishing, cutting wood (for carpentry), and planting. 'Thus if the moon's shadow falls in the space of Aries, with the letters I, B, M, I, I, B, it is an opportune time for bleeding, also good for taking medicine, indifferent for bathing or for building, bad for hunting, very good for woodcutting, as for agricultural work, seeding, and planting. But we have made the dial in the form of a mystic dove with an olive branch, which are the arms of nobility of Innocent X, Roman Pontiff as we write this, raised to the papacy from the family of the Pamphili.'[24] The structure is the familiar three-world system, with heaven and earth separated by the heavenly bodies

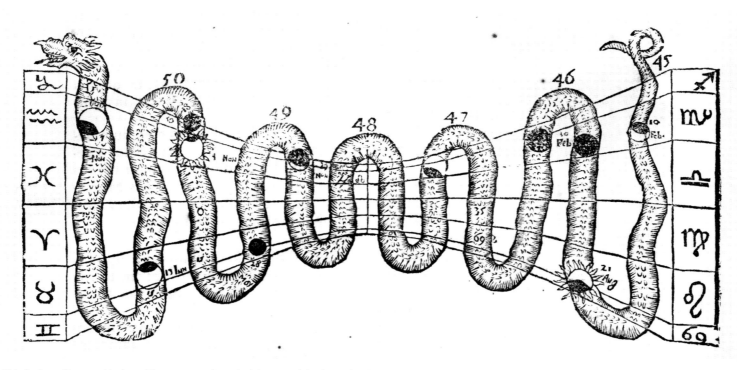

11.21 Dial of eclipses. The curved horizontal lines represent the path of the sun, and the dragon the phases of the moon. When they intersect an eclipse occurs. The flaw is that it applies to only six particular years, 1645–1651, and so was quite useless when this edition was published. (*Ars Magna Lucis*, 1671, 410)

(here, the sun and moon) and filled by the dove. It is the dove released from the Ark by Noah, which returned with the olive-branch of peace in its beak, and incidentally – or especially – the heraldic bird of the Pamphili. It clutches the keys of heaven and hell over which the Pope, heir to St Peter, claims control. The Hebrew quotation from Genesis 1:2 ('the breath/spirit was on the face of the waters') assimilates Noah's dove and the Pope's spiritual authority over land and sea to the Holy Spirit on the first day of creation. Kircher accordingly gives each of these lunar activities a mystical correspondence with the sacraments of the Church: bathing = baptism, confirmation, and extreme unction; bleeding = penance; taking medicine = eucharist; hunting and fishing = ordination (the Apostles being 'fishers of men'); planting = matrimony.

The intersections of the moon's orbit around the earth with the plane of the earth's orbit around the sun are the points where, if the moon is present, eclipses occur; hence the name of 'ecliptic' for the latter plane. These points are known in traditional astrology as *Caput* and *Cauda Draconis*: 'Dragon's head' and 'Dragon's tail'. Consequently Kircher used the image of a dragon or serpent when he designed a sundial to predict eclipses (**Ill. 11.21**). He tells us to place this dial in the sun, and see where the sun's shadow intersects the current turn of the dragon's tail. There one will find whether an eclipse will occur, and if so, when. However, he allowed only for the six years beginning

in 1645, and did not even change this in the 1671 edition. The information would have been more accurately given by an almanac, yet once again Kircher designed a scientific instrument of whose inaccuracy, even uselessness, he must have been aware. This part of his creative work resembles science fiction, in which an idea with a scientific basis is developed into a chain of fantasies, to entertain the reader or arouse his awestruck admiration.

Optical Machines

Most of Kircher's writing on optics is illustrated with plain textbook diagrams. An exception in *Ars Magna Lucis* shows the figure of Death (**Ill. 11.22**) with the motto 'Always and everywhere, sudden Death spies his own,' and two soldiers aiming an arquebus and a crossbow at the viewer. This representation of figures in contemporary dress is almost unique in Kircher's work. Its purpose is to explain how painters create portraits whose eyes always seem to be looking at the viewer. The reason given is that the eyes of the observer radiate in the form of pyramids whose bases are the eyes of the painting. This radiation corresponds precisely to the pyramid that culminated in the eyes of the painter, when he made the image from the living subject. This analysis also explains why the eyes of statues do not have the same property: it is because they are carved in the round, protruding from the plane surface, so that when the viewer moves, he ceases to see the entire eye. 'Thus the image

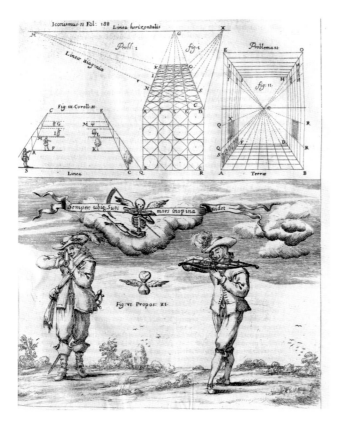

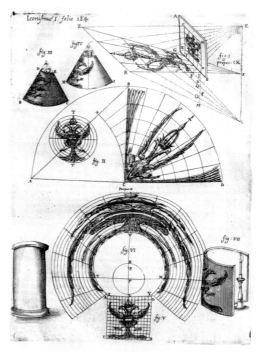

◄◄ 11.22 Tricks for artists: the point of this engraving is to show how the laws of perspective always make it appear that the eyes in a portrait are looking at the viewer. Kircher chose to illustrate this with an image of two men aiming an arquebus and a crossbow at the viewer. The upper part of the engraving instructs artists how to represent a pavement or other perspectival design. (*Ars Magna Lucis*, 1646, 188)

◄ 11.23 Anamorphoses: it was popular in the 17th century to paint distorted pictures whose distortions can only be corrected by viewing them in a conical or cylindrical mirror. (*Ars Magna Lucis*, 1646, 188)

of Death with a crossbow can be painted so cleverly that wherever you turn, you will be horrified to see the arrow fitted to his bow about to fire at you.'[25] The upper part of the engraving instructs artists how to represent a pavement or other perspectival design.

Kircher loved to puzzle people, showing them objects that turned out to be something quite different once he divulged their secrets from his superior knowledge. The graphic phenomenon of anamorphoses (**Ill. 11.23**) was a perfect example. They are drawings or paintings that make no sense whatever until viewed from the right perspective, or in a cylindrical mirror.[26] Figure I of the plate shows how an image is deformed when projected onto an angled surface. The image of an imperial eagle is pricked on a screen AB, and the light coming from E makes a deformed pattern RG. Figure II shows how to draw an image on the outside of a cone, so that it looks correct when viewed from the apex. Kircher adds that one can use the same principle to draw an image on the inside of a cone. Figures III and IV are methods of projecting images from a paper cone with a candle inside, either as shadows or as points of light coming through pinholes. Figures V and VI show how to create an anamorphic image (though Kircher does not use the term) that resolves into correct proportion when viewed in a cylindrical mirror placed on its centre. Figure VII is another image made with prinpricks, which looks nonsensical until seen in a cylindrical mirror. As so often while describing his machines, Kircher remarks on the viewers' incredulity as they witness them.[27]

Like the artist, Nature also has the capacity to project a *parastasis* or representation of something that is not there. The top part of the plate illustrat-

ing this (**Ill. 11.24**) shows her imprinting images and letters on stones and plants: a theme that Kircher would take up at length in *Mundus Subterraneus* (see **Ills. 8.12–20**). He comments on the items marked *Pyri Ramus* and *Papilio*: 'As I write this, I find in a small branch of pearwood, fresh and cut by chance, the pectoral image of an oval figure, inserted by nature with such skill that it could well compete with art. At the same time, I caught in the garden of our house a butterfly on whose wings nature had perfectly expressed the face of the Saviour.'[28] He continues by describing the many places where a natural feature seems to resemble something else. Among those he himself has seen are mountains in Sicily shaped like triremes, like men on horseback, or Bacchus seated on a cask. He discourses at length on an image of the Virgin and Child which can be seen in a rock in Arauco, Chile. Although the church authorities decided that this was a freak of nature, not a miracle, they allowed the popular devotion to flourish around it.

The middle part of this plate does not illustrate 'Nature as artist', as do the objects in the top part, but a whim of Kircher's. After describing how realistic a painted scene looks if viewed with one eye through a peephole, he suggests making one that looks like a landscape, then when turned on its side reveals itself as a human head. His artist has copied a well-known anthropomorphic landscape by Matthaeus Merian the Elder.

The lowest compartment of the plate shows a machine that Kircher saw in Germany, consisting of a double chamber and made from some lightweight material. The man crawls into the inner chamber through the hole marked F, and sees whatever is outside projected onto the paper walls. Kircher assures

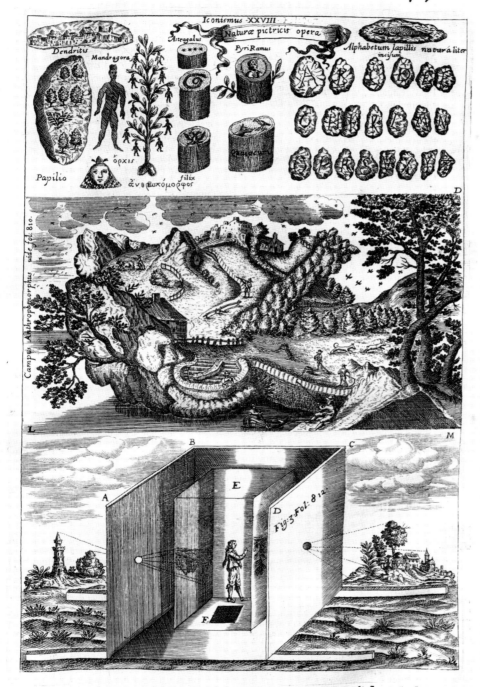

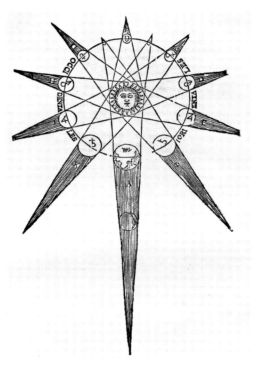

◄ **11.24** Anthropomorphic landscape. Top: letters and images occurring accidentally in nature. Middle: a landscape that turns into a face when viewed sideways. Bottom: a machine that projects an image onto transparent paper. (*Ars Magna Lucis*, 1671, 709)

▲ **11.25** Cosmometric sphere, a demonstration of the cones of shadow cast by the planets and the moon on the side away from the sun. Kircher rightly points out that this only works if one assumes the Copernican system. (*Ars Magna Lucis*, 1671, 671)

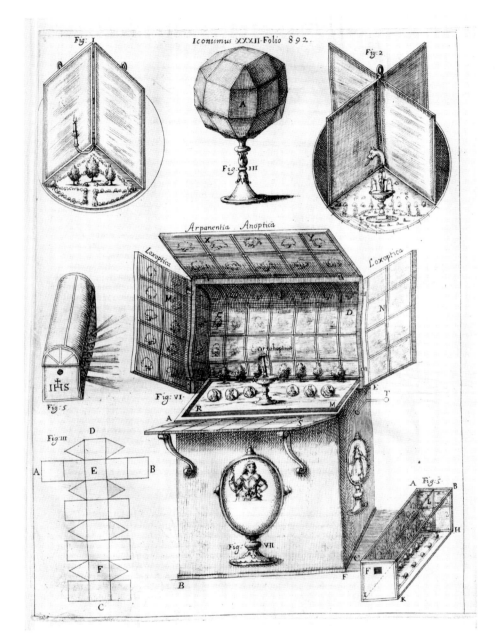

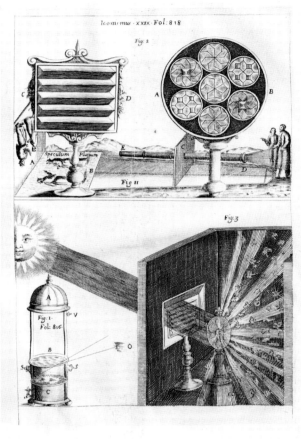

◄ **11.26** Catoptric theatre, a box lined with mirrors which multiplies whatever is inside it to infinity. (*Ars Magna Lucis*, 1646, 892)

▲ **11.27** Reflection and refraction. The surprising effects to be produced by light either reflected in a revolving sphere or refracted in a prism. (*Ars Magna Lucis*, 1646, 818)

us that he could even see the teeth of the men standing outside, and praises the usefulness of the device, for it enables one to see anything with an accuracy that no painter can rival. What exactly its use was is not specified, since one could see the teeth and so on, without the machine, but perhaps the man inside is supposed to trace the outlines of the image on the wall as preparation for a painting.

Ars Magna Lucis, beside the thirty-four numbered engravings, contains innumerable woodcuts. This one (**Ill. 11.25**) occurs at the end of Book IX, 'Cosmometria Gnomonica', which treats of the location, size, quantity, altitude, light and shadow of the planets, sun and moon. Having determined all of these, Kircher devises various machines for demonstrating them,

especially the cones of shadow that they cast on the side opposite to the sun. These machines, he says, help to answer questions such as whether the stars shine with their own light or with the sun's; or whether the moon, at new moon phase, can receive the sun's light reflected from the earth. This design for a 'cosmometric' (i.e. cosmos-measuring) sphere places all the planets at the same distance from the sun, but according to their relative sizes. It is chiefly of interest for Kircher's offhand remark: 'This sphere can be better constructed according to Copernicus's system. Make, then, a circle in the largest possible room, according to Copernicus's system; for this will be found most apt for our machination, since a glass sphere placed in the sun's position at the centre will be better able to do its

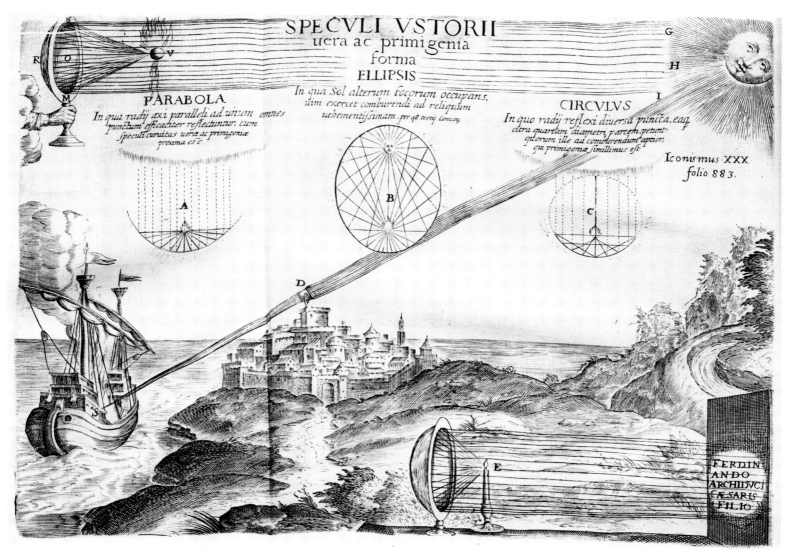

11.28 How Archimedes burned the ships. Here Kircher the sceptical scientist tests the story that Archimedes was able to burn ships in the harbour of Syracuse by focusing the sun's rays on them by a lens or mirror. The conclusion of his researches is that, in spite of his illustration, Archimedes probably never did burn the ships. (*Ars Magna Lucis*, 1646, 883)

work.'[29] The censors apparently had no problem with the Copernican hypothesis, so long as it was used as a mathematical convenience and not presented as fact.

While Kircher was not the first inventor of the magic lantern, he was the first to illustrate and explain 'parastatic' or projecting machines. He was already working on them in his Avignon period (1630–1632), as witness an insignificant woodcut which shows: 'How to draw a fantastic sundial on the wall so that even in the dark, with the windows closed, it shows the hours by a reflected ray of the sun; then when the windows are opened, the whole fantastic device, with all its lines and colours, vanishes in an instant, and the wall remains without any lines on it.' The viewers are invited to look out through a peephole at an arrangement of poles that replicate the lines on a sundial. Then they look inside the dark room, and the same pattern is seen on the wall. (The explanation is not entirely clear, since some letters on the illustration are lacking.) Kircher says that he exhibited this device in Avignon, to the viewers' great astonishment, and that (once again) some of them suspected demonic influences at work.[30]

Another attraction in Kircher's museum was the 'Catoptric theatre' (**Ill. 11.26**), which he built in emulation of one in the Villa Borghese. It is basically a box lined with mirrors that multiply the images of whatever is on the horizontal table RM. This in turn is one side of a parallelepiped, which can be turned by the handle T to present different spectacles. Kircher says that

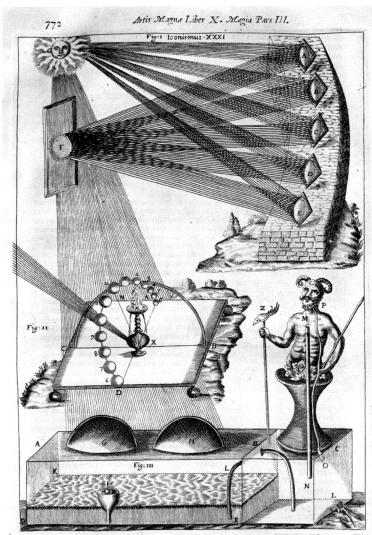

772

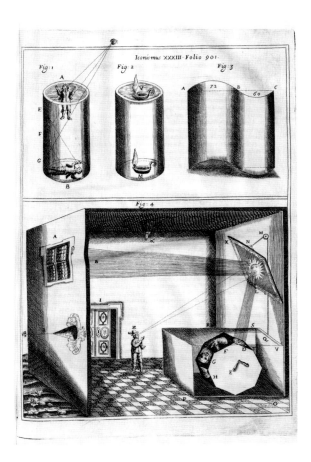

▲ 11.29 Burning mirror. Three ways in which heating water by sunlight using mirrors or lenses could actually produce effects. In Figure I Kircher illustrates a device similar to that attributed to Archimedes which he thinks really would work. Figure II shows that heating water in this way could produce a fountain. Figure III: how the statue of Memnon might have been made to sing by water being forced through a siphon. (*Ars Magna Lucis*, 1671, 772)

►▲ 11.30 Projected images, another case of Kircher testing experiments invented by others – one in which an image enclosed at the bottom of a cylinder is made to appear at the top; the other in which a person looking into a mirror sees an animal's head in place of his own. (*Ars Magna Lucis*, 1646, 910)

it so amazes the viewers that they try in vain to touch what they see inside it. Greedy folk, especially, try to grab the coins (shown here), but recoil with groans and indignation when they find them to be insubstantial phantasms. The best entertainment of all is to confront a cat with its own reflections in the machine: 'for when it sees it full of an innumerable multitude of cats, it thinks that they are real, and I can scarcely tell you what tricks it plays in this theatre. It tries to catch them, stroke them with its tail, kiss its own image, and break through the obstacles in every way, striking them with its claws, wanting so much to reach them; and it expresses with various cries and miserable groanings its many emotions: indignation, anger, jealousy, desire and love. And the same may be said of other animals.'[31]

Kircher well knew that images seen through convex lenses appear reversed, even if he could not fully explain it. This is what the two figures at the top of the next illustration are discovering (**Ill. 11.27**). The plate shows several different devices that exploit the properties of reflected and refracted light. Figure I consists of three vessels, A, B, C, of which B is open and has some image painted inside it. To the viewer, who must look precisely from point O, the image is only visible when B is filled with water and the phenomenon of refraction bends the light rays. To his amazement, as water pours in from the

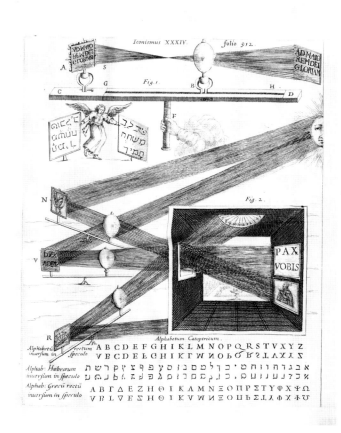

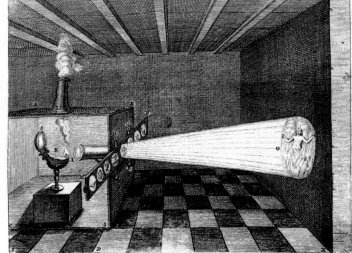

reservoir A, the image floats into sight, then as the water is let out into the container C, the image vanishes again.

In Figure II, CD is a frame filled with triangular prisms, which break the light into rainbow colours so beautiful that Kircher likens them to a vision of Paradise. AB is a revolving frame with polyhedral glass insets. In Figure III the two instruments are combined to turn the sunlight entering a dark chamber into a revolving spectacle of stars, coloured like emeralds, sapphires, amethysts, gold: you will never have seen anything like it! (1646, 816–818; 1671, 716–718) Once again, Kircher anticipates a modern invention: the turning sphere studded with mirrors used in dance halls.

The power of lenses and mirrors to amplify the sun's heat has already been exploited in the exploding sundial (see **Ill. 11.18**). The next plate refers to a famous historical instance of applying this power (**Ill. 11.28**). Ancient historians assert that during the Sicilian wars, Archimedes succeeded in setting the enemy's ships on fire by means of a burning mirror (or lens), variously said to be three stadia (about 1,800 feet) or 3,000 paces (three miles) away. Kircher examines this claim with exceptional care and rationality.[32] He points out that, as any experimenter knows, combustion with a burning glass requires three things of the object: first, that it remain steady; second, that it be pre-

◄◄ **11.31** Figures projected by sunlight. Kircher claimed to be able to project images amazing distances, but it is highly doubtful that he could. (*Ars Magna Lucis*, 1646, 912)

▲ **11.32** Above is a projecting lantern: a device to enlarge a mere candle-flame to make it seem a great fire. In the illustration below is a magic lantern showing a soul in Purgatory. One of Kircher's most famous illustrations, which supports the claim that he invented the magic lantern. (*Ars Magna Lucis*, 1671, 768)

cisely at the focal point; third, that it be of combustible material. The historian's picture of ships tossing at anchor violates the first two requirements. Moreover, based on his own experience, a lens as big as the dome of St Peter's could not even reach the Roman College, 1,200 paces away. He says in an aside that if the historians were right, and lighting fires at a distance were so easy, someone would already be marketing such devices.

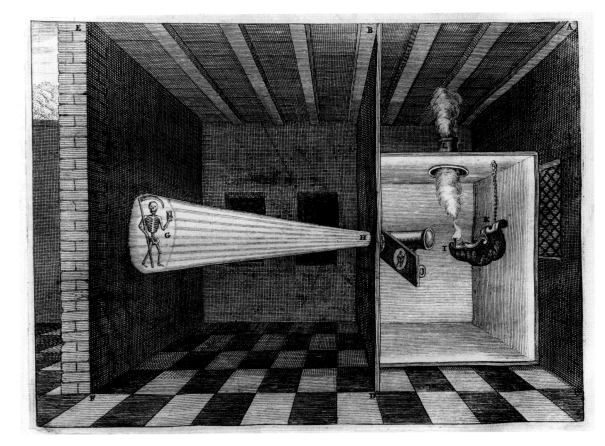

◄ 11.33 Magic lantern showing Death: the same principle as the previous illustration. (*Ars Magna Lucis*, 1671, 769)

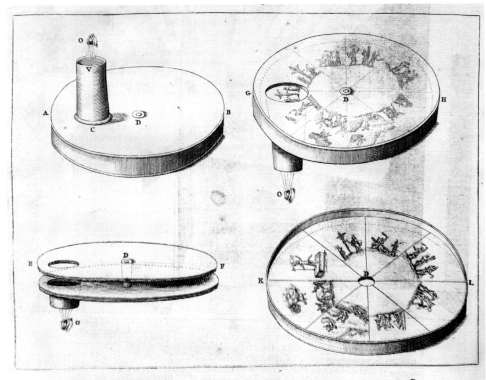

► 11.34 Parastatic microscope. The wheel carries eight different images, viewed one by one through the tube. It has been pointed out that if these images could be shown sequentially and sufficiently fast the illusion of movement could be created. (*Ars Magna Lucis*, 1671, 770)

However, when Kircher visited Sicily in 1636, he took the trouble to examine the place where the feat was said to have happened. He found the minimum distance between the besieging ships moored in the harbour and a burning mirror protected by the city walls to be a mere twenty-five to thirty paces. Could a parabolic mirror or lens be made that would function as described?

In all his researches, Kircher found no evidence of such a mirror being effective at more than fifteen paces (he includes a letter from a fellow Jesuit describing such a one), and every indication that its power decreases greatly with distance. Another difficulty lay in the grinding or forging of a perfect parabolic lens, that being the only shape that sufficiently concentrates the rays. Every time he tried, or had his workmen try, it turned out to be merely spherical. For all the plausibility of the illustration, Kircher leaves the reader sharing his own scepticism.

The challenge remained to design an effective burning mirror (**Ill. 11.29**) Unlike the claims made for Archimedes' machine, this one would work, and at a considerable distance. Instead of a single parabolic lens, it consists of a number of flat mirrors, so angled that they focus the sun's reflection at a single point F, thus multiplying the sun's heat. The historian Zonaras tells that Proclus destroyed the Byzantine fleet with such a device, and this Kircher finds credible.

The lower part of the plate shows two machines based on this principle. In figure II, glass globes or lenses are so placed that every hour the sun shines through them, heats up the water in the reservoir X, and makes a fountain erupt. Figure III is a mechanical toy imitating the famous Memnon of Egypt (compare **Ill. 10.2**), whose statue greeted the dawn with a mysterious twanging sound. When the sun shines through the large lenses G and H, it expands the air in the sealed chamber KL, forcing water through the siphon E into the other chamber N. Thereupon, air rushes up into the statue, causing the bird Z to sing, the breast of the statue M to groan, the eyes to roll and the tongue to protrude. Moreover, the two devices could be combined into a kind of clock that produces these phenomena on the hour.[33]

Just as Kircher tested the story of Archimedes by experiment before rejecting it, so he did with Giambattista della Porta's claim that a cylindrical mirror, enclosed in a box, could project images outside the box. He writes that he has tried della Porta's directions more than a hundred times, without any success. However, he knew of ways to achieve a similar effect, one of which he illustrates in the upper part of this plate (**Ill. 11.30**). It is a cylinder whose inner surface is coated with mercury, and whatever is pictured or enclosed on the bottom appears at the top. Kircher says that he has exhibited such a device showing the Lord's Ascension, with all the figures seemingly hanging in mid-air.[34] By the same means, he astonished some visitors by holding his hand unharmed in the visible flame of a lamp (Figure 2).

The lower part of the plate shows a machine based on a claim of Trithemius: that one can make a person see himself in a mirror with an animal head in place of his own. The principle is that the mirror KL reflects the heads painted on the drum, invisible to the viewer Z. If he stands in the right position, he will see that head in the mirror. Although Kircher claims to have made such a machine, there is no way in which it could have shown the person's own body simultaneously with the strange head.

One of Kircher's own claims seems to stretch credulity. In this plate (**Ill. 11.31**), a lens of the right focal length is used to project an inscription or other image into a dark room, using the sun's light as vehicle. Kircher says that he has projected legible inscriptions as much as five hundred feet away, using a plate half a palm across and a lens a third of a palm. If they were eight palms in width, he says, one could without a doubt project the letters twelve miles away. Then one could converse with someone at that distance, though it might be only one letter at a time, and the distance would increase them to the size of a tower. He suggests that someone with more leisure and money than himself might be able to develop the idea into something truly remarkable.[35] Then, with a characteristic swerve of attention, he supplies reversed images of the Latin, Hebrew and Greek alphabets that would be necessary if the thing were ever done.

Another little woodcut, this time from the second edition of *Ars Magna Lucis*, introduces the crucial element that combines with projecting an image on a darkroom wall to create the magic lantern: 'an artificial lantern, which makes writing legible at a remote distance' (**Ill. 11.32**, above). It is nothing more than a cylinder with a concave mirror AB at its base, 'as parabolic as is possible to make', a handle E, a chimney C, a candle F, and a window D. Seeing it from afar, one thinks it not a candle but a great fire.

Kircher now combines the magnified lantern with transparent slides. (**Ill. 11.32**, below). This and the next are among his most celebrated illustrations, establishing his claim, if not as the inventor of the magic lantern and hence the ancestor of the cinema, then at least as its best promoter. While these plates and their accompanying text did not appear in the original edition of *Ars Magna Lucis*, Kircher points out that he did describe there the projection of coloured images into dark chambers by means of the sun. Although he himself had not developed it further, other inventors took up the idea.

The first of these was a Dane, Thomas Walgenstenius, quite a famous mathematician, who, thinking over my inventions described there, turned the lantern on page 767 into a better form. He afterwards sold it to various rulers in Italy, to his great profit, so that it has become almost common knowledge in Rome. But there is no difference between it and the lantern we described, except that Walgenstenius showed multiple images in a dark chamber, so neatly and cleanly as to arouse high admiration from the spectators. In a dark chamber of our college, we have been exhibiting the four latest ones [?], to the viewers' greatest astonishment. Indeed, it is a thing well worth seeing, since it enables one to show whole satyrical scenes, tragic plays, and things of the kind, true to life.[36]

The second magic lantern (**Ill. 11.33**) is identical in principle to the first, and likewise shows a gloomy image: a skeletal Death with scythe and hourglass. At the very beginnings of the technology that would lead to the cinema, one of its chief attractions was its ability to scare people! Kircher's instructions apply both to this and to the previous plate:

Make a receptacle ABCD out of wood, with a chimney at L where the lantern can emit its smoke. Fix the lantern K in the middle, either by an iron wire or on a stand M, in the region of the aperture H, in which a palm-wide tube is inserted; then insert into the hole at the front of the tube I the best possible glass lens, and at the end of the tube H a well-made flat glass, on which is painted whatever you wish in transparent watercolours. When this is done, the light of the lantern will show the image painted on the flat glass H (which is placed upside-down) properly and in larger size on the white wall of the chamber VTSX, showing all the colours true to life. Note, however, that the light of the lantern must be intense, and to achieve this, we put a concave steel mirror S behind the flame, thereby remarkably increasing its light.[37]

If the twentieth-century equivalent of the magic lantern was the slide-projector, then the battery-powered slide viewer found its predecessor in Kircher's 'Parastatic microscope' (**Ill. 11.34**) This makes visible in daylight any of the images that can be projected with the magic lantern. It consists of a circular glass plate KL with eight painted images – in this case, those of the Passion of Christ – mounted so as to rotate inside a wooden case GH. The eye-piece VC contains a magnifying lens, and the images are viewed one at a time. Although we should imagine it as being used to project static figures, there would have been the potential here to create a primitive moving picture.

Notes

1 For illustrations and history, see Vollrath.
2 A globe kept aloft by a stream of air was one of the curiosities of the Villa Aldobrandini grotto, which also had a hydraulic organ.
3 Di Sepi, 2–3, translated in Schott 2000, 259–260. Translation used by kind permission of Michael John Gorman.
4 *Magnes*, 1641, 331; 1643, 292.
5 *Magnes*, 1641, 320–321; 1643, 284–285.
6 See Radelet de Grave, 215.
7 See Smith, 36 (figs. 18, 19), 48 (fig. 27), for Jesuit devotional images involving the heart, and for an explanation of the spiritual exercises connected with them.
8 *Magnes*, 1641, 364; 1643, 319.
9 *Magnes*, 1641, 366–367; 1643, 322.
10 *Magnes*, 1641, 368; 1643, 322–323.
11 *Magnes*, 1641, 380–381; 1643, 334. Umberto Eco uses this theme in *The Island of the Day Before*.
12 *Magnes*, 1641, 375; 1643, 328.
13 Illustrated in *Ars Magna Lucis*, 1671, 698 (clock with two snakes) and 700 (clock with eagle).
14 *Magnes*, 1641, 736–737; 1643, 644–645.
15 *Magnes*, 1641, 737–738; 1643, 645–646.
16 *Magnes*, 1641, 504–506; 1643, 572–575.
17 Thus De Sepi's catalogue, quoted in Gorman, 60.
18 '…using mirrors placed outside the tower to reflect the light of the sun and moon onto the ceiling, where he traced all the necessary uranographic projections, adding a series of meridians giving the time in all the countries of the world.' Gorman and Wilding in Schott 2000, 255–256.
19 In England, some well-known complex dials are those of Caius College, Cambridge, Corpus Christi College, Oxford, and the 'Seven Dials' column near Covent Garden, London.
20 See Monaco in Lo Sardo 2001, with coloured illustrations of the dials.
21 *Ars Magna Lucis*, 1646, 519–520; 1671, 384–385.
22 A smaller and simpler version appears in *Ars Magna Lucis* opposite page 553. It probably corresponds more closely to the Avignon dial. Uniquely among Kircher's illustrations, it is signed *Athanasio Kirchero S.I. Inventore*. See also Smith, 2, for an illustration of an earlier image (circa 1620) of the Society of Jesus as a tree, with its worldwide houses as the leaves.
23 *Ars Magna Lucis*, 1646, 790–792; 1671, 690–691.
24 *Ars Magna Lucis*, 1646, 526–527; 1671, 391.
25 *Ars Magna Lucis*, 1646, 191; 1671, 140.
26 The classic, if not the only, full-length study of anamorphoses is Baltrušaitis 1977, which has a chapter (79–90) on Kircher and Schott.
27 *Ars Magna Lucis*, 1646, 187; 1671, 136.
28 *Ars Magna Lucis*, 1646, 807; 1671, 709–710.
29 *Ars Magna Lucis*, 1646, 766–767; 1671, 670.
30 *Ars Magna Lucis*, 1646, 779–780; 1671, 681–682. On Kircher's audience's attraction to the demonic, see Gorman, 63.
31 *Ars Magna Lucis*, 1646, 894; 1671, 777–778.
32 *Ars Magna Lucis*, 1646, 874–883; 1671, 757–765.
33 *Ars Magna Lucis*, 1646, 889; 1671, 773.
34 *Ars Magna Lucis*, 1646, 899; 1671, 781.
35 *Ars Magna Lucis*, 1646, 911; 1671, 791.
36 *Ars Magna Lucis*, 1671, 768–769.
37 *Ars Magna Lucis*, 1671, 769–770.

Chapter 12   Maps and Plans

Kircher's Amsterdam publishers, the house of Jansson van Waesberge (see box, p. 55), had always been a major contestant in the profitable business of drawing, printing and selling maps: maps of the world, the continents, countries, regions and cities, shading off into town and topographical views. It is this shading off that is so interesting when one considers Kircher's use of maps. As an experienced surveyor, he well understood the techniques and problems of mapping on a provincial scale.[1] But the severely practical maps that a surveyor or ship's captain might produce do not necessarily attract or assist readers. Kircher's maps are of a piece with his programme of illustration: they were meant to excite the imagination and bring his texts to life. They have the same blend of scientific reconstruction and fantasy that pervades his historical and geological work.

Kircher has several cartographical 'firsts' to his name. Maria Bertini, in her history of geography, writes that he has the merit of illustrating in three maps the source area of the Nile, and of making the first map of tides and ocean currents, the first imaginary map of the island of Atlantis, and a map of the world after Noah's Flood.[2] The last of these sounds fanciful, but it shows a prescient awareness of how coastlines change with the rise and fall of sea-levels.

The plates of the source of the Nile (**Ill. 12.1a, b**) appeared first in *Œdipus Ægyptiacus* as part of a long discussion of the search for Egypt's sacred river.[3] The first shows a map of southern Africa 'according to the observations of Odoardus Lopez', a Portuguese explorer. As in all early maps, the Nile originates from two separate sources (marked *Fons Nili* – source of the Nile), which are linked by numerous other rivers to the west, south and east coasts. Although Odoardus criticized Ptolemy's account of the matter, most of what he added (says Kircher) is fiction.

The second map is 'taken from the geography of the Arabs', reputedly from a manuscript in the Medici library.[4] Since north is at the bottom of this map, the 'circulus aequinoctualis' must be the Tropic of Cancer. In this version, the Nile issues from ten separate sources in the Mountains of the Moon, beyond the sixteenth degree of southern latitude. They all come together in Lake Zambia. Out of that lake issue three rivers: one the Zaire (or Congo), one ending in the 'Land of the people of the Niger', and one running through Egypt. Also marked are 'The land of serpents', 'The Golden Mountain' and 'The mountain of the Egyptian Temple'.

The third map is 'The true and genuine topography of the sources of the Nile, made by Father Pedro Páez of the Society of Jesus on 21 April 1618, in the presence of the Emperor [of Abyssinia]'. With justifiable pride, Kircher highlights the discovery – actually of the Blue Nile – by a fellow Jesuit. Pedro Páez (1566–1622) was one of the most intrepid of the Society's missionaries, working in Goa, on the west coast of India, and in Yemen, where he served seven years as a slave of the Pasha, before ending his life in Africa. The crudeness of the engraving suggests that it was copied directly from topographical drawings sent by Páez to his superiors in Rome, rather than being imaginatively reconstructed in Kircher's studio. The mountain which is the Nile's source is towards the top right of the map (again oriented with north to the bottom). Páez writes that while accompanying the Emperor's army he climbed to this place, and found two round wells, each about four palms in diameter, out of which issued the purest water. These are the 'eyes of the Nile' (*Oculi Nili*). But the river itself issues from the bottom of the mountain, which is full of subterranean water channels.

Besides its source, the other great enigma about the Nile was what causes its sudden annual flood. Páez's mountain source offered a solution that became fundamental to Kircher's geological theory. The rainy season causes water to accumulate in the cavities within the mountain until they can hold no more, then they overflow. The maps of *Mundus Subterraneus* all illustrate this principle of mountains as the primary sources of rivers.

The map of southern Africa (**Ill. 12.2**), titled 'Hydrophylacium of Africa, situated in the Mountains of the Moon, supplying the main lakes and rivers, wherein is shown the new discovery of the source of the Nile', is a simplified version of the *Africa Nova Tabula* first published in 1631 by Johann Jansson, Senior, and Hendricus Hondius.[5] While mapmakers had yet to admit that this was *terra incognita*, it shows how vague and legendary the inland geography of Africa was. Beside the fact that it was simply unexplored, no one suspected that the Nile might originate from such widely separated regions: the mountains of Ethiopia, from which the Blue Nile flows, and, far to the south, Lakes Edward, Albert and Victoria, which feed the White Nile. The two rivers unite at Khartoum. Ancient geographers wrote of the 'Mountains of the Moon' as the river's source, and Kircher shows them as a stupendous peak filling most of southern Africa, but they might as well have been on the moon, for all that was known about them.

12.1a, b The source of the River Nile. The first map is based on that of a Portuguese explorer which Kircher does not endorse, the second on a map in the Medici library, and the third on one made by the Jesuit missionary Pedro Páez which shows accurately the Blue Nile, not the White. Note that, like the second map, north is at the bottom. (*Œdipus Ægyptiacus*, Volume I, fp. 56/57, 52/53)

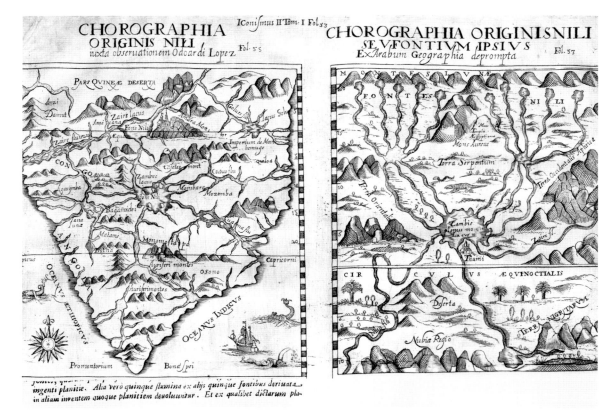

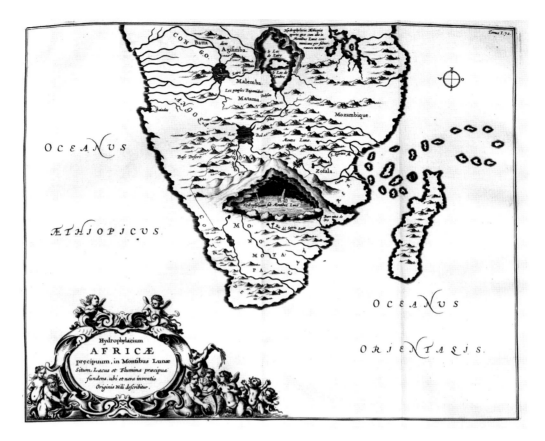

▶ 12.2 Southern Africa. The source of the (White) Nile is shown as the 'Mountains of the Moon', a vague term for a region totally unexplored. (*Mundus Subterraneus*, Volume I, opposite 72)

▼ 12.3 South Asia. The Himalayas are the predictable source of the Indus and the Ganges. (*Mundus Subterraneus*, Volume I, 70)

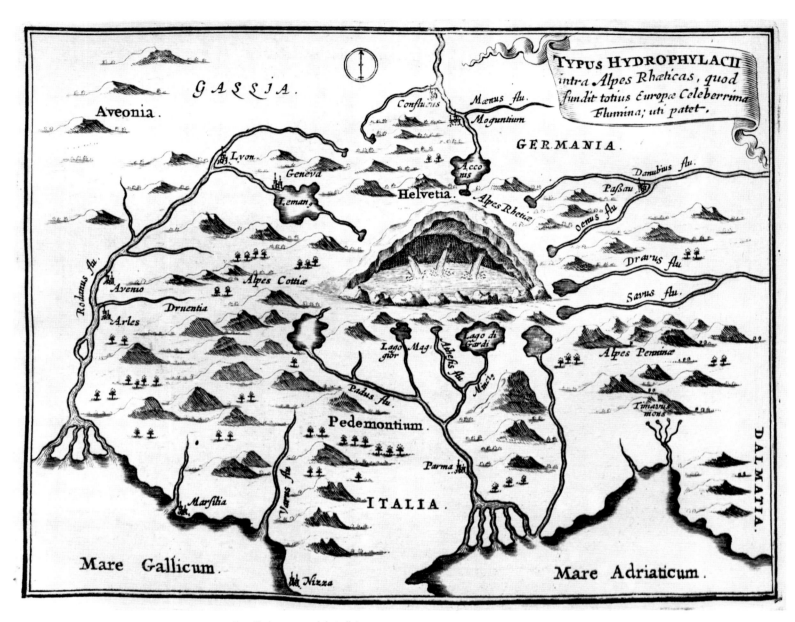

12.4 Alps. Kircher assumed that all rivers originated in mountains. From the Alps he traced practically every river in Europe. (*Mundus Subterraneus*, Volume I, opposite 70)

Once supplied with a theory to account for the sources of rivers, Kircher sought and found one on every continent. He writes: 'I have sufficiently proved that mountains are not made casually or chaotically by Nature, but following the wisest of counsels [i.e. that of God] in their protuberance from the surface of the globe.' Thus every continent has its own mountain range, covering its divinely decreed 'hydrophylacium' or subterranean reservoir. For Europe, the source of rivers is naturally beneath the Swiss Alps (**Ill. 12.4**). He continues:

> From this whole Alpine complex, as from a fertile womb, flow the great rivers. The Danube, Rhine and the Oder bless Germany with their irrigation; the Rhone, Arar, Mosa, Mosella flow into Gaul and Belgium; the Po, Athesis Mincio, Ticino into Italy; Savus and Davus into Illyria. And from this not only the rivers, but great and mighty lakes have their origin: in Germany, the lakes Acronius, Lucerne, Tigurinus; in the region of Gaul and Insubrium, Leman, innumerable lesser lakes; in Cisalpine Italy, three lakes called Maggiore, Como (anciently Larium) and Garda.[6]

In the case of South Asia (**Ill. 12.3**) the reservoir is beneath the Himalayas, from which the Indus issues directly and the Ganges indirectly. In South America it is in the Andes. In this illustration (**Ill. 12.5**) the reservoir looks open, suggesting that Lake Titicaca might be intended. But this was a mistake, and not on Kircher's part. On the back of his manuscript draft, discovered by Gerhard Strasser, he wrote in Latin: 'Instruction for the engraver: in this figure, the lake or sea should be shown in the interior of the mountain, of which only part is indicated.'[7] It should therefore have been shown as a cavern beneath the Andes (compare **Ill. 3.12**).

Apart from the hydrophylacia, drawn disproportionately large, these maps are quite sober and unadorned. The time of maps filled with imaginary denizens of land and sea was passing; indeed, it was Johann Jansson [I] in 1612 who, in copying Ortelius's map of Iceland, cut out the wondrous monsters derived from Olaus Magnus that filled the surrounding ocean.[8] However, while leaving the sea calm and empty, the engraver of Kircher's maps of South Asia and South Africa decorated the cartouches in accepted Baroque style with playful sea-beings and voluptuous mermaids. Strasser notes that in the copy of *Mundus Subterraneus* in the Pontificia Università Gregoriana (formerly Kircher's own Collegio Romano), the mermaids have been decently censored.

Anyone today will notice in these maps the distortion of India and the squashed aspect of South America. These are due to the impossibility of accurately measuring longitude, that is, of correct east–west mapping. Until Ortelius's world map of 1586, South America had looked far more grotesque, with a huge bulge in its south-west portion.[9] Since the books in question were being published by one of the foremost map-makers in Europe, Kircher would have had no reason to question their wisdom in the matter. But it is surprising that when it came to maps of the world, Jansson's engraver took as his model

12.5 South America. The source of the rivers should have been shown as a cavern beneath the Andes. The mistake was not Kircher's. (*Mundus Subterraneus*, Volume I, opposite 74)

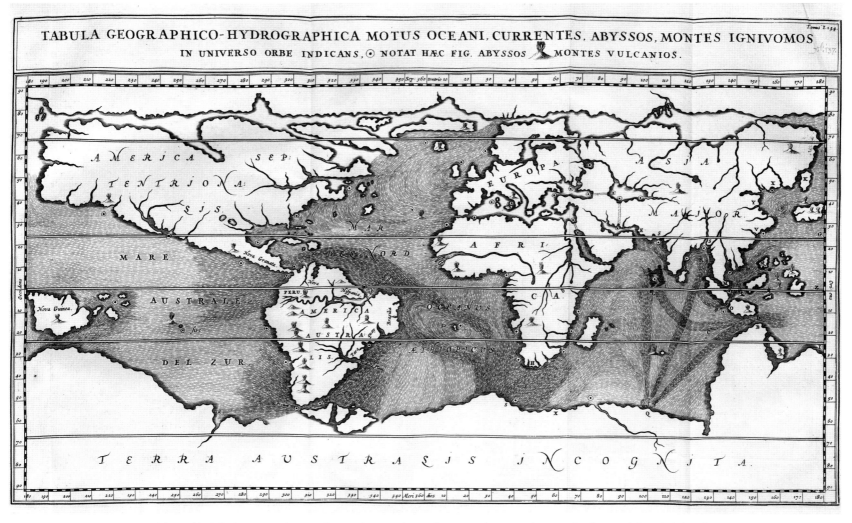

12.6 Ocean currents of the world. Kircher's map contains many features that turned out to be true. But he assumed a series of underground channels linking the oceans. (*Mundus Subterraneus*, Volume I, opposite 134)

this old map of Ortelius, ignoring the improvements of decades of navigation and the efforts of Mercator, Blaeu, Hondius and the Janssons themselves. The two examples are the map of ocean currents in *Mundus Subterraneus* (**Ill. 12.6**) and the map of the world after the Flood (**Ill. 12.7**) in *Arca Noë*.

The margin of tolerance acceptable in high-class publishing of the 1660s–1670s is startling to those who have been familiar since childhood with the shapes of all the continents and many of the countries. Part of the trouble, as mentioned, came from the longitude problem; another part, from the exaggeration of the northern and southern regions that is inevitable in Mercator's and similar projections that stretch a spherical surface onto a rectangular grid. But that such wildly different interpretations of South America or East Asia could appear between the same covers, or that the long familiar

regions of Asia Minor and the Black Sea should be so grossly distorted, is a reminder that their 'canonical' shapes were a long time coming.

Note the 'Terra Australis Incognita' (unknown southern land) filling the bottom of the map. Although Antarctica had not yet been discovered, the early map-makers habitually put a large unknown continent in its place, which also served to cover rumours of Australia. As time went on and nobody landed on it, the more advanced cartographers stopped making it up and left a blank. By mid-century, they were able to show instead the west and north coasts of Australia.[10]

None of this affects the fact that Kircher's map of ocean currents was a most significant contribution to cartography. As in the case of the tides, he did not seek a single explanation for them, but a combination of factors.

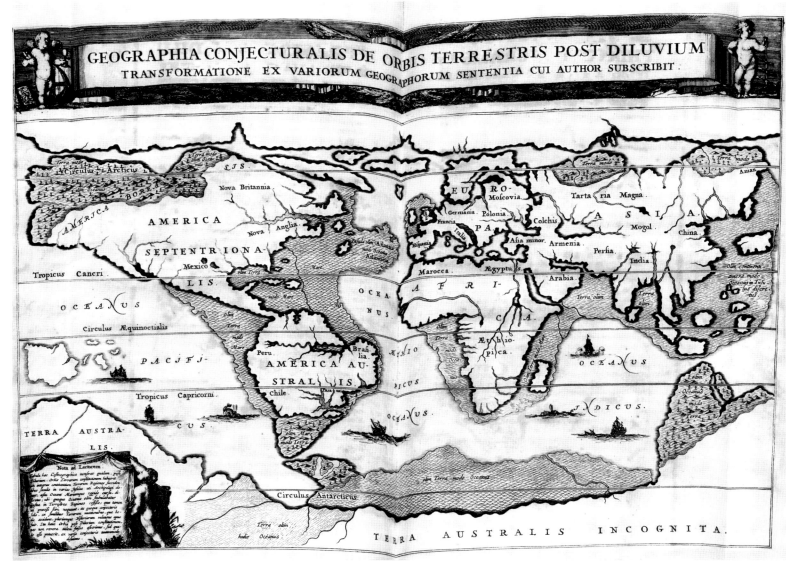

12.7 The world after the Flood. Australia remained a mystery until long after Kircher's time. (*Arca Noë*, fp. 192/193)

He mentions the general east–west movement and its reflux, known as the mariners' current, which he says is caused by the sun and moon, the wind, and the fact that the sea bed is not smooth but mountainous, just like the land. The circled dots on the map represent whirlpools by which the sea is sucked down, thereby entering the subterranean system of channels that is essential to Kircher's geology. These channels, memorably traversed in *Itinerarium Exstaticum II*, enable sea water to cross from the Pacific to the Atlantic Ocean beneath the Isthmus of Panama, and from the Red Sea to the Mediterranean at the site of the present-day Suez Canal; they also link the Black and Caspian Seas to the Persian Gulf. The marking of the principal volcanoes refers to the complementary system of subterranean fires.

The north polar projection (**Ill. 12.8**) reminds us that much of the seventeenth century's geographical imagination came from looking at globes. This polar view made it easy to calculate the time zones (shown on the rose-like diagram at bottom left), though we should remember that in Kircher's cosmology they were not a phenomenon of the turning earth, but of the sphere of the fixed stars, hurtling around the universe every twenty-four hours and carrying the sun, the moon and the planets along with it.

Mundus Subterraneus contains a famous map of Atlantis (**Ill. 12.9**), which Kircher introduces in the context of a discussion of the mutability of the earth's surface. There was no reason for him to doubt the substance of Plato's account in the *Timaeus* and *Critias*, since the island of St Euphemia had vanished almost before his eyes, and other islands in the Mediterranean and

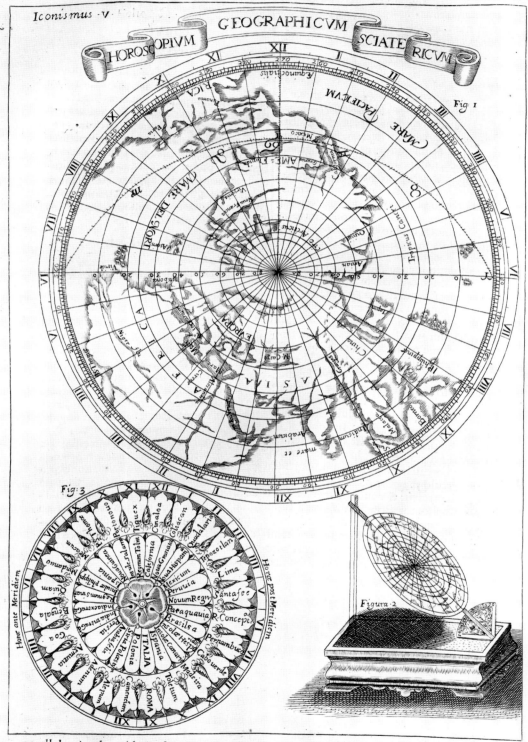

12.8 Polar projection. The rose-like diagram bottom left is to calculate time zones. (*Ars Magna Lucis*, 334)

parallela; circuli verò latitudinum, erunt arcus declinationum Solis. Idem dicendum de meridiano plano, quibus una & eadem mappa applicata serviet in toto orbe.

In inclinantibus, & declinantibus planis leges procedendi in præcedentibus traditæ servabuntur. Spacium igitur ἡλιοδ ρομον declaravimus, quod erat faciendum.

Problema

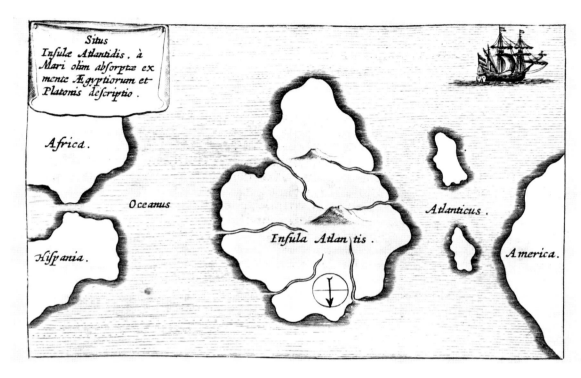

12.9 Atlantis. Kircher had no reason to doubt Plato's account of the disappearance of Atlantis; indeed, in accepting the enormous changes in the land masses and oceans throughout history he was not far from the truth. (*Mundus Subterraneus*, Volume I, 82)

among the Canaries were known to have appeared and disappeared. He draws this conclusion from the fate of the mythical island:

> From this perhaps overlong discourse, it is as clear as day that the earth has a far different constitution today from what it had before the global cataclysm, and even for forgotten centuries after the Flood. Islands exist that did not exist before. Where once were fierce whirlpools, it has turned to land. On the other hand, we know tracts of land that were once rich and fertile, but are now under the sea's dominion and a lurking-place for fishes. Mountain ranges disappear in one place, while others grow elsewhere. Great lakes have exchanged the rule of Neptune for that of Rhea or Vesta, and vice versa.... And these changes in the terrestrial globe, however horrible, exist that they might show forth the infinite power of God and the incertitude of human fate, and warn the mortal inhabitants of this Geocosm that nothing is perpetual or stable, but all things are fleeting and subject to the variable fates of fortune and to destruction; so that they might raise their minds, their studies, their soul and intellect, which no created things can satisfy, to sublime and sempiternal possessions, and gaze at God alone, in whose hand are all the powers of the realms and the destinies of universal nature.[11]

Charles Hapgood and his followers are convinced that Kircher's Atlantis is really based on an ancient mapping of Antarctica, which he is presumed to have found in some forgotten archive.[12] The plausibility of the theory aside,

Kircher habitually revealed his sources, especially when they did credit to his ingenuity, erudition and good luck. If he had made such a discovery, I think he would have mentioned it, sending scholars on a futile quest like the one for Barachias or for the Greek musical manuscript he found in Messina.[13]

He also marked the place where Atlantis was on the map of the world after the Flood: 'Once the island of Atlantis, now the Atlantic Ocean'. The areas of land and ocean that are unchanged are unshaded. Portions of land that were once ocean (*terra modo olim oceanus*), such as the Arctic regions, are shaded with hills and trees. Portions of ocean that were once land (*olim terra modo oceanus*) are shaded with waves. It is an ingenious way of showing two maps superimposed. Kircher admits in a note to the reader that this map is only conjectural, based on the opinions of various geographers. In an era before deep-sea soundings there cannot have been any real oceanological basis to it. However, just as Kircher's inadequate microscope led him to the true conclusion that plague is caused by germs, so his conjectures about the historical rise of sea-levels anticipated a serious concern of our time.

Several of Kircher's maps compare their regions in ancient and modern times, using two images. The large folding plate at the beginning of *Œdipus Ægyptiacus* (**Ill. 12.10**) shows ancient Egypt divided into its thirty nomes or administrative districts, following the geographical writings of Strabo and Ptolemy. Among the landmarks (from north to south) are the nine mouths of the Nile delta, the mummy crypts, the Pyramids of Giza, the labyrinth, Thebes, Philae, Syene, the Nile cataracts and the mountains of Ethiopia. The inset map of 'more recent Egypt' shows the delta in more accurate fashion,

◄ **12.10** Ancient and modern Egypt. Kircher's map of ancient Egypt is taken from Strabo and Ptolemy, that of modern Egypt (inset) from more recent Arabic sources. (*Œdipus Ægyptiacus*, Volume I, fp. 8/9)

▼ **12.11** The region of Eden, incorporating the four rivers of Paradise: Tigris, Euphrates, Geon and Physon. (*Arca Noë*, opposite 22)

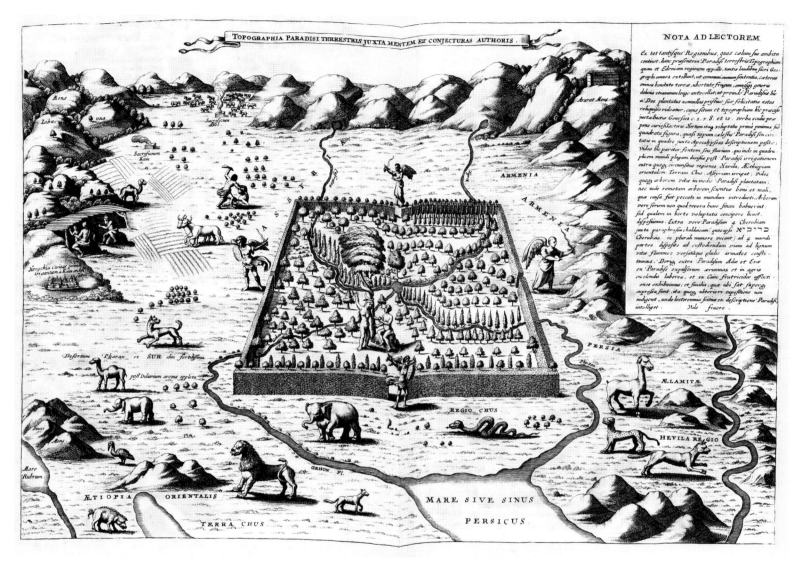

12.12 The Earthly Paradise, an attempt to make sense of Genesis, including pictorial representations of many of the biblical stories (*Arca Noë*, fp. 196/197)

and gives the Arabic, rather than the Greek names. But what is being compared here? Is it a political or a physical map – is it intended to show changes in the human settlements and boundaries, or changes in the natural disposition of the land? Or, a third possibility, is it a demonstration of progress in cartography, contrasting the old, stylized impression of the Delta with one based on modern surveys? It would not have occurred to Kircher's readers to ask such questions; but that again goes to show how greatly expectations and standards in this field have changed.

The region bounded to the north by the Caucasus Mountains, to the west by Lebanon, and to the south by the Red Sea and the Persian Gulf greatly interested Kircher because it was the site of the earliest events in biblical

history: the creation of the Earthly Paradise or the Garden of Eden, the proliferation of mankind before the Flood, the fresh start of humanity from Noah and his sons, the building of Babylon, Nineveh and the Tower of Babel, and the migrations that somehow managed to populate every corner of the globe. While one purpose of his illustrations in these popular books was to delight and aid the imagination, another was to settle some long-standing debates among geographers, so that again we have a mixture of motives and a sometimes jarring graphic blend of information and fantasy.

The account in Genesis (2:10–14) requires there to be four rivers flowing out of Eden: Physon, Geon, Tigris and Euphrates. These would cause endless trouble to map-makers, as no four known rivers satisfied the description. Kircher

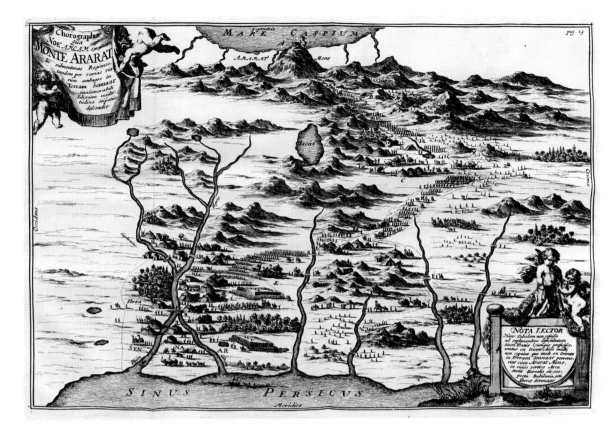

◄ 12.13 Mount Ararat. Kircher had problems in reconciling apparently contradictory accounts in Genesis relating to directions. (*Turris Babel*, fp. 12/13)

▼ 12.14 Migration after the Flood, an attempt to show graphically how the Earth was repopulated by the descendants of Noah. (*Arca Noë*, fp. 222/223)

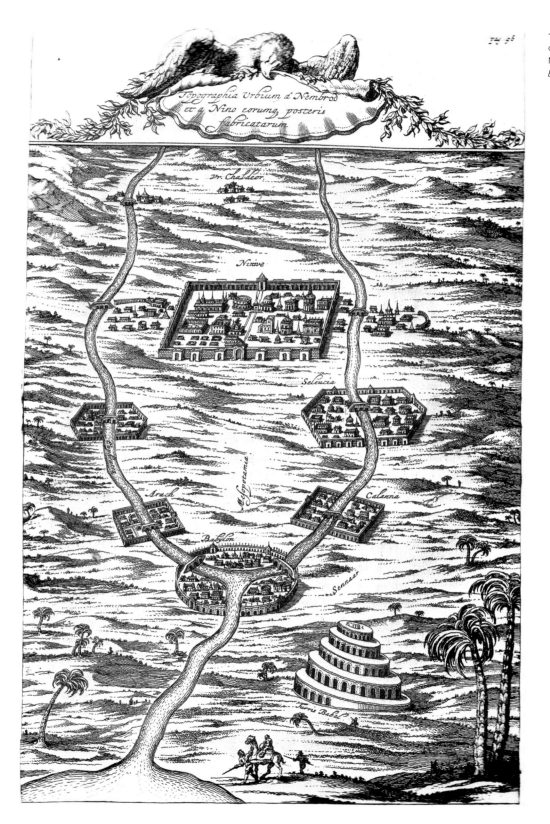

12.15 Cities of Nimrod, Ninus and their descendants, including the Tower of Babel, Nineveh and Ur of the Chaldees. (*Turris Babel*, opposite 96)

offers his solution in two different illustrations, which only a very charitable eye could credit as representing the same region. In the 'Description of the region of Eden, seat and fatherland of the Patriarchs before the Flood, as the author imagines it' (**Ill. 12.11**), the four rivers are clearly marked: the Euphrates flowing east from the mountains of Lebanon, the Tigris rising from a lake near the Caspian Sea. They meet in the land of Sennaar, then diverge as the Geon and Physon, which flow into the Persian Gulf. Near the centre of the map is the place where the Ark was built, and elsewhere Kircher indicates where the wood and pitch for it came from. The desert of Sur between the Red Sea and the Persian Gulf 'was once, before the Flood, very fertile, and afterwards filled up with stony mud'. At the top left is 'Henoch, the city of the Giants', and at the bottom right in Greater Armenia, Mount Ararat, with the Ark resting on it.

The more picturesque view of the Earthly Paradise (**Ill. 12.12**) centres on the enclosed Garden of Eden, with Adam, Eve and the Serpent. Other biblical events and a whole menagerie of animals decorate the surrounding countryside, in which the Latin legends read, clockwise from bottom left: Red Sea; Mount Sinai, Desert of Pharan and Sur, once most fertile, filled with sand after the Flood; city of Enoch, first built by the Giants for Cain; Mount Libanus; sacrifice of Cain; sacrifice of Abel; River Euphrates; River Tigris; Mount Ararat; Armenia; Persia; River Physon; Elamites; region of Hevila; region of Chus; Persian Sea or Gulf; River Geon; land of Chus; Eastern Ethiopia.

Mount Ararat is the centre of the next map in the series (**Ill. 12.13**), which addresses another problem for geographers bound to the biblical account. The story of the Tower of Babel begins in the second chapter of Genesis: 'And the whole earth was of one language, and of one speech. And it came to pass as they journeyed from the east, that they found a plain in the land of Shinar [Vulgate: Sennaar], and they dwelt there.' As Kircher puts it in the tablet on the right: 'Note, reader, that this table cannot explain the difficulty of the Sacred Text (how they came forth from the east), while many do not understand how they reached the land of Sennaar from the east, since Mount Ararat, on whose top the Ark rested, is to the north with respect to Babylon, or the land of Sennaar.' In fact, Kircher does devote some pages to solving the difficulty, and to explaining how many generations it took, and how much zigzag wandering, before the descendants of Noah and his sons became so numerous as to populate Sennaar, the future megalopolis of Babylon. Here they are encamped with their camels, elephants and regiments of pikemen drawn up in seventeenth-century square formation.

The next episode concerns the migrations after the Flood (**Ill. 12.14**). According to the Book of Genesis, all the peoples of the world descend from one of Noah's three sons. Kircher conjectured which son's descendants went where, 'with incredible labour from various versions of the Holy Scriptures in Latin, Greek, Hebrew, Chaldaic, Syriac and Arabic, and from many interpreters' (note to the reader at top left). But it was not until 124 years after the Flood that the dispersion began. Thereupon Cham's descendants, who had already founded the city of Babylon and attempted to build the Tower of Babel, migrated to

Africa. On this map, the four rivers have vanished, leaving only the Euphrates. Along the North African coast one can see the names of Cham's son Chus, his son Misraim, and further descendants. Likewise, Japheth's son Gomer and his descendants spread over Europe, and Sem's progeny began to move towards Asia, which is not shown here. Later they would be the founders of the Indian, Chinese and Japanese civilizations.

Cham, as we know, was Noah's bad son, who fell away from the true religion and fathered the races given to polytheism and idolatry. Even believing this, Kircher could not but feel awe before the achievements of these misguided peoples, and a nagging doubt that his own time had really surpassed them, as he often asserted that they had. In Chapter 6 we saw his reconstructions of their monuments. Here is one of his maps which, like modern tourist maps, shows the chief monuments of the region in pictorial form (**Ill. 12.15**). The unfinished Tower of Babel is at the bottom right, and in the middle is the square city of Nineveh. Near the top is Ur of the Chaldees, home of Abraham. If there is any consistency between the various maps of the Middle East that appear in Kircher's books, we discover the remarkable coincidence that the city of Babylon, shown here as a circular, walled city embracing the confluence of the Tigris and Euphrates, occupied the former location of the Earthly Paradise.

China Illustrata contains two important maps of China. The first (**Ill. 12.16**) shows how much was already known of the hinterlands – or, if not known, conjectured.[14] The second (**Ill. 12.17**) extends from the Persian Gulf to Formosa (Taiwan), taking in India and the steppes of 'Tartary' in order to map St Thomas's presumed route to Malabar (*Iter S. Thomæ Apost:*), the famous journey of Marco Polo (*Iter M.P. Venetii in Cathaiium*) and the no less intrepid missionary journeys of Benedict Goes, Antonio Antrada, D'Orville and Grüber. Among the many topographical features are the Great Wall of China and the 'Desert of Lop, infested with diabolical illusions' (top centre). Compared to the map of Asia in *Mundus Subterraneus*, there is a noticeable improvement in accuracy, due to Jansson's having taken Blaeu's 1648 world map,[15] not Ortelius's of the past century, as his model.

We turn now to maps and plans of Kircher's adopted homeland, the area around Rome which he studied and illustrated in his late work *Latium*. In these illustrations, we can see the shading-off mentioned above, and consider the shifting intention vis-à-vis the reader or browser in his books. A map, ideally speaking, represents the features of a geographical region, ranging from the whole world to a single town. Beyond that we usually speak of a 'plan' – for example, of part of a town, a garden or a house. As the focus becomes closer, so the third dimension becomes perceptible. The seventeenth century was the great era of topographical views and cityscapes, especially as engraved by Kircher's contemporaries, the Merian family. Here a town is seldom mapped, but often pictured as it looks from a suitable vantage point, perhaps a semi-bird's eye view. Closer still, when it comes to picturing an individual building, most readers would rather see its elevation (i.e. what it looks like) than

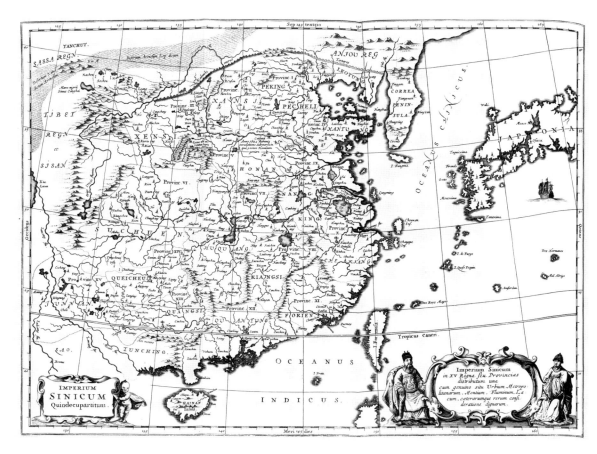

12.16, 12.17 Maps of China and of Asian explorations. Kircher was a pioneer in his study of China, relying on the travels of Marco Polo, St Thomas and later missionaries, as well as Blaeu's world map of 1648. (*China Illustrata*, opposite 1)

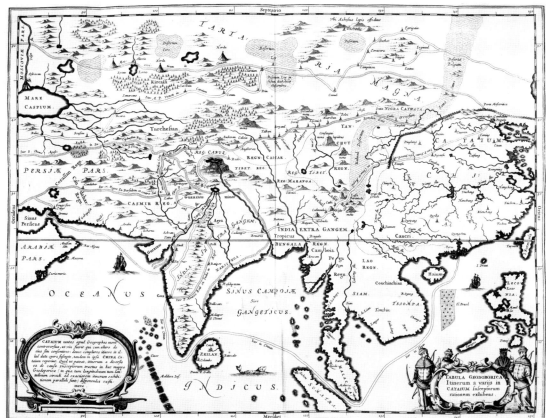

▶ **12.18** Latium, modern Lazio, an area that Kircher knew very well, including Lakes Albano and Nemi and the towns of Palestrina, Frascati and Tivoli. (*Latium*, before 1)

▼ **12.19** The town of Palestrina, formerly called Praeneste, largely built over the vast Roman Temple of Fortune. (*Latium*, opposite 112)

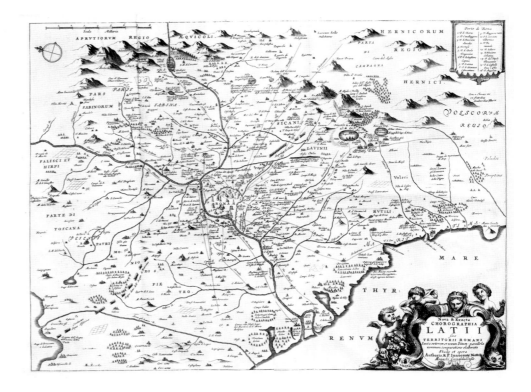

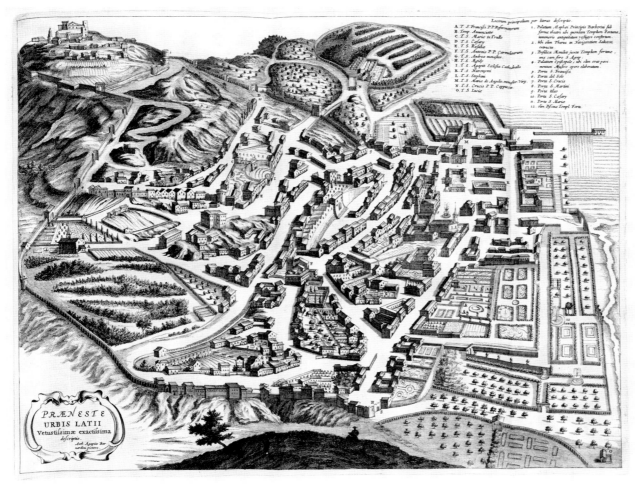

its ground plan; and with that, we have arrived at pure illustration. Here I give representative examples of every kind.

At the beginning of his regional study, Kircher presents 'a new and exact map of Latium or the Roman territories, both ancient and modern, with a parallel comparison of the place names' (**Ill. 12.18**), crediting it to the studies and labour both of himself and of Father Innocentius Matteus, a Camaldulian monk. (The Camaldulians or Camaldolites were a Benedictine order founded at Camaldoli in 1012, whose monastery at Frascati was probably among Kircher's regular stopping places.) Among the main landmarks is the River Tiber, which traverses the map in a southerly, then south-west direction, passing through Rome. In the text, Kircher pays much attention to the two oval lakes, Albano and Nemi; to the towns of Praeneste (top centre), Frascati (directly below) and Tivoli (on the River Aniene, to the left). Near the latter are the sites of the villas of Hadrian, Varus and Maecenas, all of which Kircher illustrates. On the coast, he has marked the landing place of Aeneas, and everywhere the territories of the indigenous tribes (Sabini, Sicani, Volsci, etc.) who figure in early Roman history.

Kircher does not seem to have spent much time in the northern part of Latium, where so many Etruscan sites were subsequently discovered. He concentrated on three easily accessible centres east and south-east of Rome: the town of Palestrina, with its fascinating archaeological remains; the territory around Tivoli, at that time a city of some political and ecclesiastical importance; and Frascati, the summer playground of the Roman aristocracy.

Kircher's plan of Palestrina (**Ill. 12.19**) was provided by a local artist and antiquarian, Agapito Bernardini. It conveys the important fact that much of the town was built over the ruins of the tremendous Temple of Fortuna Primigenia. If one compares this plan with Kircher's reconstruction of the Temple (see **Ill. 6.27**), one can see how the town followed the contours of the latter. When Kircher visited Palestrina in the autumn of 1664, he was delighted to find there Cardinal Francesco Barberini, his patron for almost thirty years. The learned Cardinal in person guided Kircher around, explaining the remnants of the ancient site. The number 1 is 'The palace of Prince Maffeo Barberini in the shape of a theatre, where once was the Temple of Fortuna with innumerable vestiges of antiquity'. The number 2, with a long wall corresponding to T in the temple reconstruction, is 'where once stood the lighthouse for the safety of mariners' that was visible from the Tyrrhenian Sea. Kircher describes it as 'resembling a shell of enormous capacity, with a vaulted roof, about ten feet in diameter, completely blackened by smoke, with the signs of the old lantern'.[16] Descending further, the number 3 on this plan marks 'Basilica Aemiliae at the Temple of Fortune, together with the forum of St Agape', which would bring us to the forecourt (O in the reconstruction). Finally, the gardens marked 12 are in the place of the temple ponds (M in the reconstruction).

The plan of Hadrian's Villa (**Ill. 12.20**) is the result of surveying of a very high order, again not by Kircher himself. This plate, measuring 43 by 15 inches (109 by 38 centimetres) when unfolded and made from three separate engravings, is a monument of early archaeology. It is based on the excavations of

Pirro Ligorio, commissioned by Cardinal Francesco Barberini and completed by Francesco Contini. The publisher Jansson has put his name on it, stating that it is a gift from him to the Cardinal. Kircher's text includes a key of six closely printed pages, probably the work of Contini, which explains or suggests the nature of every place marked on the plan. This includes the names of the proprietors of the various fields and olive groves, and measurements in palms. Much of what today's visitor to Hadrian's Villa sees has been tidied up, re-erected, and even rebuilt, but Ligorio's survey, made under difficulties that can well be imagined, still holds good.

When Kircher could not rely on local experts for mapping the places he visited, his scientific standards suffered and his imagination made up the deficit. His map of the Tivoli region (**Ill. 12.21**) brings it to life with a combination of myth and history, folklore and hearsay. Here are some of the landmarks, starting from the bottom and going clockwise:

> This whole flat space is covered with baked stone, which they call *testino*
> The place where sugar is collected, commonly called *confetti di Tivoli*
> The Albula, a sulphurous river
> Floating islands
> The Albunean Lake, commonly called the sixteen Ships
> Pit of unplumbed depth
> It is thought that the Albunean Sibyl lived here
> Tomb of Queen Zenobia, today Colle di Ferro
> Villa of Queen Zenobia
> The Tiburtine quarries, which from the founding of Rome to this day have supplied the city with an inexhaustible quantity of stone called Travertine
> The Sabine Way
> Monte Gennaro; from here come storax and manna
> [to the right of the river]
> The Madonna of Mentorella
> Place of the Conversion of St Eustace
> Remains of Emperors Trajan and Hadrian's naumachia (lake for staged naval battles)
> Monte Spaccato, which split apart at the time of the Passion of Christ
> Villa of Emperor Hadrian

In the case of Tivoli, Kircher could use existing views of the Villa d'Este (see below) and of the 'Temple of the Sibyl' (see **Ills 5.32, 5.33**), but had no good town plan. The one he offers (**Ill. 12.22**) is quite crude, and the compass directions, indicated by the four winds, are out of order (north should be in the place of Zephyrus, the west wind, and so forth). The plan does show how the ancient town was built within a bend of the River Aniene, and that much of the modern town is taken up by the gardens of the Villa d'Este. The river runs through the town in several streams and ends in waterfalls (marked *Cascata*); one of them is an aqueduct that feeds the gardens of the villa and its famous

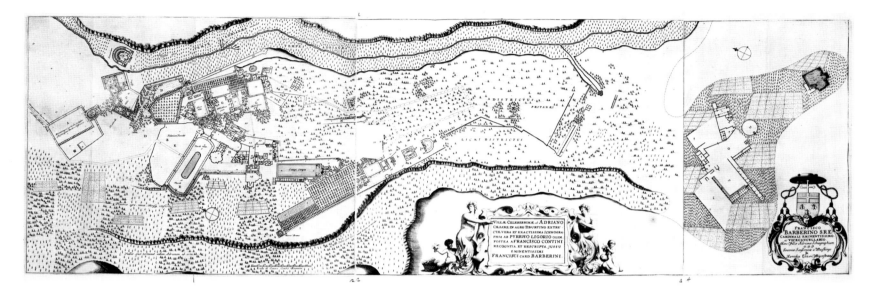

▲ **12.20** Hadrian's Villa at Tivoli, accurately drawn by an expert surveyor, a valuable record of the villa before modern restoration. (*Latium*, fp. 144/145)

▶ **12.21** The territory round Tivoli, with plentiful annotations from myth and history, given in the text on page 231. (*Latium*, opposite 143)

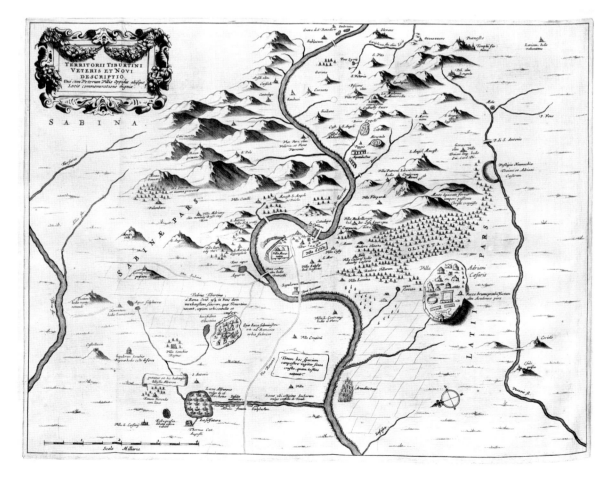

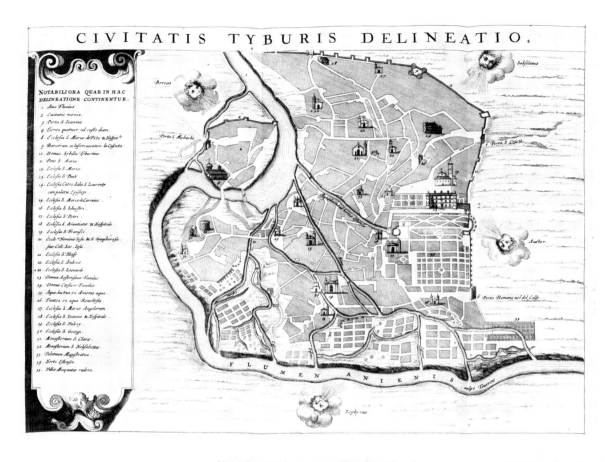

◀ **12.22** The town of Tivoli. Kircher's map is deficient in accuracy and the compass directions are wrong. (*Latium*, opposite 128)

▼ **12.23** The Villa d'Este, a combined map and bird's-eye view, based on an engraving by Dupérac of 1573. (*Latium*, 174)

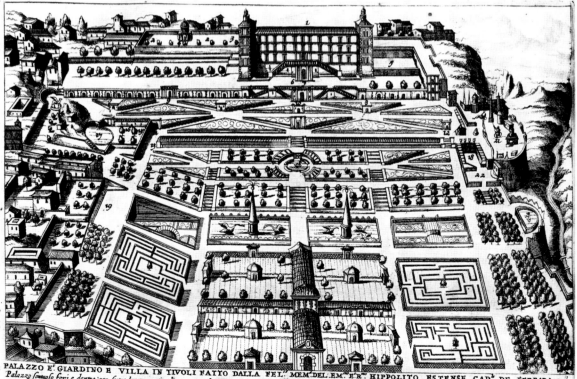

12.24a, b, c Town and villas of Frascati, three large illustrations of the villas built by papal and aristocratic families near Rome, copied from an engraving of 1620. (*Latium*, fps 78/79)

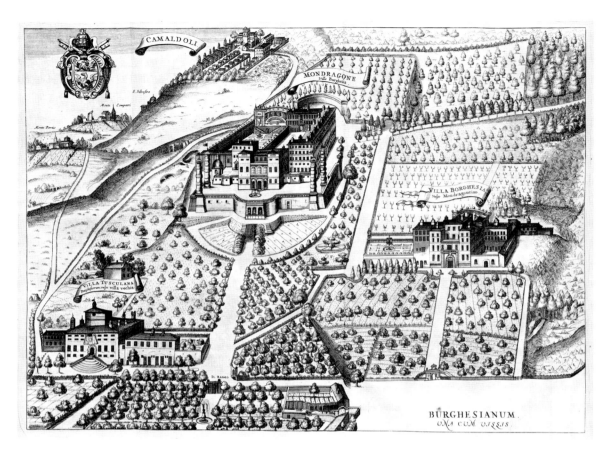

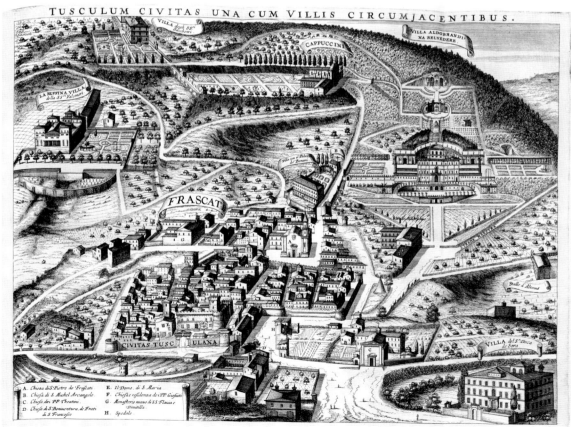

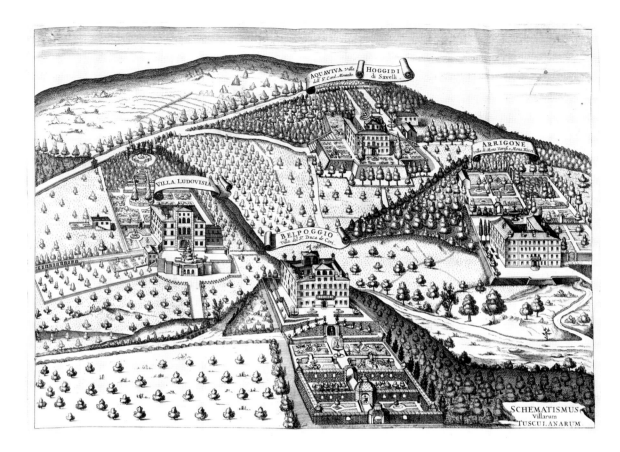

fountains. The number 10 marks the circular temple supposedly dedicated to the Tiburtine Sibyl.

For the Villa d'Este itself (**Ill. 12.23**), Kircher's illustrator made a simplified version of the superb engraving by Étienne Dupérac (1573), perhaps mediated through a later source such as Giacomo Lauro's *Antiquae Vrbis Vestigia* (1637). This is half-way between a plan and a bird's-eye view. Like many a later writer, Kircher enthusiastically describes his itinerary through the palace and gardens. He praises the rooms painted floor to ceiling with gods, goddesses and heroes, and the crypt of the Nymphs decorated with mosaic work. In the gardens he walks from the Pegasus fountain (number 17 on this plan) along the Alley of the Hundred Fountains, with its sculptured scenes from Ovid's *Metamorphoses* (number 13), to the Rometta (number 21) whose miniature buildings imitate those of Rome itself, just visible on the skyline. Then he admires Mount Parnassus, a mound planted with trees 'in which the cuckoo cuckoos, the nightingale modulates, the goose hisses, and the canaries cantillate'. Meanwhile, water springs up from the pavement and sprays the visitors. The Dragon Fountain vomits water to the four corners of the earth, and on its back a great pipe called the Girandola sends up a stream as high as the cypresses. From there the water falls back into the garden, where the visitor delights in watching the various fish and birds that are kept there. Lastly, the waters channelled from the River Aniene pour down in a cataract into a magnificent theatre, in whose recesses an automatic organ plays.[17]

When he came to describe Frascati, Kircher's main object was not to guide his readers, but to impress them. Another series of three large engravings grouped together in *Latium* (**Ill. 12.24a, b, c**) pays tribute to the aristocratic and papal families who went there to escape the summer heat and bad smells of Rome. Kircher calls Frascati 'truly the paradise of the city of Rome', and compares its present splendour favourably with that of the ancient Roman villas – whose foundations often served the modern builders for their own. Visitors were invariably awestruck by the fountains and waterworks that adorned the villa gardens, so that Kircher adds: 'Today it abounds not only in fountains, but in whole rivers of water.' Of the twelve villas that he lists, he singles out three above all: Aldobrandini, Mondragone and Ludovisi. 'If you consider the size and magnificence of their buildings, the excellence of their statues and paintings, the ingenious structure of their hydraulic organs and the pleasing sports of their waterworks, I believe nothing can equal their rarity and truly regal excellence.'[18]

Kircher's engraver was not recording the Frascati of Kircher's time, but dutifully copying from Matthias Greuter's view of 1620, already half a century out of date. When the three plates are assembled in a continuous print, they make a panorama seen from the west, so that the northernmost group of villas (here titled 'Burghesianum') is on the left, the town of Frascati in the middle, and the southern group ('Schematismus') on the right. It goes without saying that the villas are magnified out of all proportion relative to the humbler buildings, and that the modern visitor who expects to see this vista will be disappointed. Almost all the villas have changed hands many times since their building, and undergone both enlargement and destruction. As their owners have changed, so have their names, so that the ones Kircher gives them are not the names by which they are known today. No one source, to my knowledge, has correlated all the villas in Greuter's print with their present identities, so for the benefit of any who might wish to explore Latium in Kircher's footsteps, I do so here.

In Kircher's time the first group ('Burghesianum') had all come into the possession of the Borghese family. Later the Jesuits owned them, using them as the summer retreat of the Collegio Romano. Now the whole complex belongs to the Università di Roma di Tor Vergata, which uses the largest one, Mondragone, as a conference centre and occasionally offers public exhibitions and concerts there. Its dependency 'Villa Borghesia, commonly known as Mondragoncino' is called Villa La Borghesiana. At the lower left, adjoining the main road, 'Villa Tusculana Burghesiorum, commonly known as Villa Vecchia', is a hotel and restaurant called Villa Vecchia. At the top of the view is the monastery of the Camaldulian Order.

In the second plate, centred around the town of Frascati, 'La Ruffina' is now state property and called Villa Falconieri. It is the seat of the Istituto Nazionale per la Valutazione del Sistema Educativo di Istruzione e di Formazione. 'Villa degli Signori Sacchetti' was generally under the same ownership as Villa Falconieri, and, from its smaller size, called 'La Ruffinella'. In the eighteenth century the Jesuits acquired it and had it rebuilt on a much larger scale. It then passed for a time to the Italian royal family, and is now the Grand Hotel Villa Tuscolana. Immediately below it is San Francesco, the monastery of the Capuchin Friars, with an Ethiopian Museum.

Almost in the town, near the cathedral, is the modest 'Villa con il Palazzo de' Bonani' – modest, because it was built not by princes of the church but by the Oratorian Order. Other names for it are Villa Piccolomini and Villa di Roberto Primo. It is now called Villa Lancelotti, after the family that has owned it since the nineteenth century. Its gardens are being restored and have partly become a public park, Parco dell'Ombrellino. 'Villa del Sr Duca de Sora', at the bottom of the plate, was also called Villa del Papa. Since 1896 it has been a school run by the Salesian Order.

Pride of place goes to Villa Aldobrandini, which looms over the lower town square, Piazza Marconi. Beside the parterres and bowers stretching on either side of the villa, one can see the successive stages of its famous waterworks. They begin on the hill, with the water issuing from two gigantic masks, and continue via a water-stair and a pair of column-fountains to the great hemicycle of the nymphaeum behind the villa. This is where Kircher found the hydraulic organ that so impressed him, in a grotto with moving figures of Apollo and the Muses.[19] The organ is silent today, but the water flows, and the Aldobrandini, who still own the villa, open the gardens to visitors.

The right-hand plate of the group, entitled 'Schematismus Villarum Tuscu-lanarum', shows a group of four villas that all suffered in an Allied bombing attack on the day of Italy's surrender, 8 September 1943. Villa Ludovisia was destroyed, but its water-stair and nymphaeum have been restored as the focal point of a public park, now called Villa Torlonia. What remains of Belpoggio is now called Villa Sciarra; it contains state schools and a public park. 'Arrigone', of which Kircher mentions the 'incredible hanging gardens', is now called Villa Muti and is under restoration. Finally, Villa Acquaviva, which Kircher adds is 'nowadays called Savelli', has been transformed into another luxurious hotel under the name of Park Hotel Villa Grazioli.

In this chapter we have come from world maps to plans of areas within walking distance, and from mankind's beginnings in Eden to the new Paradise of aristocratic *villegiatura*. This was the term used for the custom of making prolonged stays in the country, ideally in one's own villa, enjoying a more salubrious climate and a more select company than in the city. Knowing that the ancient Romans had done the same gave men of Kircher's time the feeling of participation in the antiquity they so admired, and the adornment of their villas and gardens was a conscious emulation of classical models. In choosing the illustrations for *Latium*, Kircher returned the compliment by depicting the villas of Romans like Maecenas or Varus in Baroque style. Thus exaggerated plans like Greuter's view of Frascati shade into illustrations that are frankly imaginary.

Notes

1. He mapped the Bergstrasse region for the Kurfürst of Mainz in 1624, and in 1629 the region around Narbonne; see Kelber and Okrusch, 140.
2. Bertini, 80.
3. Kircher used them again as a single large plate in the second edition of *Mundus Subterraneus*, 1678, 73.
4. See *Œdipus Ægyptiacus*, I, 53, for text and Latin translation.
5. For a reproduction, see Klemp, no. 17.
6. *Mundus Subterraneus*, 1664, I, 71; 1678, 70.
7. Strasser 1982, 368–369.
8. Battini, 212–213 illustrates the two versions.
9. Ortelius's map of 1586 is illustrated and discussed in Shirley, XXIX, pl. 8, no. 153. His world map of 1570, with South America as described, is illustrated in Ndalianis, 135.
10. On the first appearance of Australia on maps and its subsequent refinement, see Shirley, 355–356. Among those that showed it clearly are Blaeu's 1648 world map (Shirley, pl. 280, no. 371) and Jansson van Waesberge's world map of 1673 or 1676 (Shirley, pl. 252, no. 334).
11. *Mundus Subterraneus*, 1664, I, 83.
12. Hapgood 1966, 69ff.
13. Transcribed and discussed in *Musurgia Universalis*, I, 541–542.
14. The first accurate survey of China was the 'Confidential Map of the Qing Empire', made from 1708–1718 with the help of Western cartographers.
15. See note 10.
16. *Latium*, 95.
17. *Latium*, 173.
18. *Latium*, 78.
19. *Latium*, 78.

Chapter 13   **Exotica**

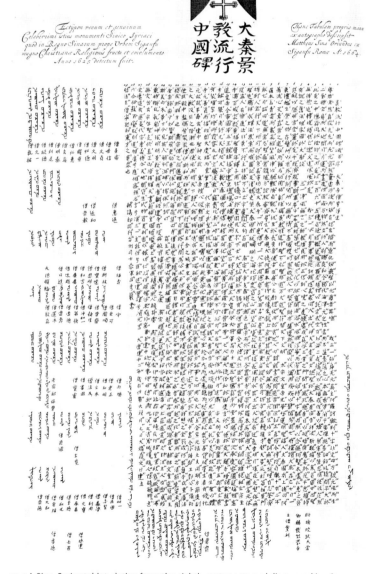

The worldwide efforts of the Society of Jesus to convert the heathen had always been close to Kircher's heart. If he had had his way, he would have gone to China as a missionary, and then his career might have resembled that of a latter-day Matteo Ricci or Adam Schall, settling there, learning the language, and winning the Celestial Emperor's patronage as an expert in applied science. On the other hand, he might have ended up cruelly martyred: a possibility that Jesuit missionaries faced, even courted, in the certainty of a heavenly reward.

Perhaps Kircher's superiors thought him too good to waste on a hazardous mission. As it was, he ended up in the centre of the Jesuit web, enjoying a vicariously global existence as information poured in from all quarters.[1] Often hardly bought and with little thanks (for Kircher's correspondents repeatedly complain that he has not answered their letters), this not only swelled the stock of useful knowledge, but also fed a taste for the exotic. Every Kunstkammer needs some exotica in it, to bring the spice and wonder of far-off lands. Elias Ashmole's Cabinet of Rarities had Turkish thumb-rings and the shell-embroidered cloak of Princess Pocahontas. Kircher's museum had African ivories, a Sioux costume decorated with porcupine quills, and a samurai sword venerated as an instrument of martyrdom.[2]

At least three motivations were behind Kircher's interest in the world beyond Europe. One was to fill in the gaps in a knowledge that aspired to universality, and especially to complete the tale of how languages and religions had evolved after the Universal Deluge. A second was the passion for curiosities, whether material objects or reports of strange creatures and customs. A third was the missionary zeal that proclaims itself in the frontispiece to *China Illustrata* (see **Ill. 2.16**).

The desire to bring light to those walking in darkness was genuine, but it coexisted with a spirit of adventure and the thrill of exploration. *China Illustrata* begins by recounting the great voyages over land and sea by St Thomas to Malabar in south-east India, Marco Polo and Benedict Goes to China, Heinrich Roth to India, and the astonishing overland journey by the Franciscans D'Orville and Grüber (see the map, **Ill. 12.17**). But these were not the first Christians in the region, as was proven by Kircher's prize exhibit, the Sino-Syriac tablet (**Ill. 13.1**). In 1625, a marble tablet with inscriptions in Chinese and Syriac was unearthed in the village of Shang-hsien (Sanxuen), near the ancient Chinese capital of Hsi-an (X'ian) on the Yellow River.[3] Three years

13.1 A Sino-Syriac tablet, dating from the eighth century AD, and discovered in 1625, was a sort of Chinese Rosetta Stone. The Chinese part was translated in 1631 and Kircher translated the Syriac part in 1636, giving phonetic equivalents to the Chinese characters. Its subject is the early, short-lived Christian mission to China. (*China Illustrata*, opposite 13)

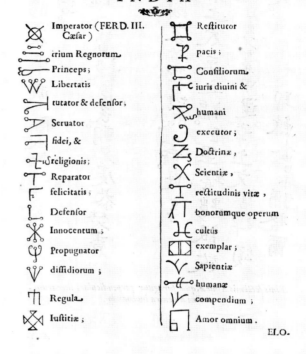

later, a Portuguese missionary examined it and brought news of it to his community in Malabar. The Chinese part was translated with the help of a convert, Leone Mandarino, and published in 1631. According to the best authority on Kircher's version of sacred history, the coincidence of this with Kircher's discovery of Coptic probably sparked the idea of a historical-theological system to which he would dedicate the rest of his life.[4]

Kircher translated the essentials of the Syriac part of the tablet in *Prodromus Coptus* (1636), but only in *China Illustra* did he go into its whole history and significance. The exquisite facsimile with over 1900 Chinese characters was probably the work of W. van der Laegh, who signed several of the other engravings of exotic alphabets. Kircher numbers the characters, keying them into a word-for-word Latin translation and phonetic transcription of the Chinese, and supplying a smoother Latin paraphrase.

The inscription deserved the attention he gave it, for its historical significance was and is considerable. It dates from the year 781/2 and commemorates an annual reunion of Nestorian Christians. After a summary of Christian doctrine, it tells of the arrival in 635 of a Syrian monk in China, the Emperor's approval of his mission, and the ups and downs of the Christian community which, by the time of writing, was active in at least eight Chinese cities. Always at odds with the local Buddhist clergy, it succumbed along with them in the ninth century to an imperial decree banning all foreign religions, and by the end of the first millennium the community was extinct.[5]

Kircher was struck by the resemblance of the cross on the tablet to the one on the altar of St Thomas in Malabar (**Ill. 13.2**). One of the great surprises of early voyagers to India had been to find a Christian enclave in the southeast corner. The Indian Christians had also embraced the Nestorian heresy,[6] but it only remained for the Catholic Church to take over the shrine and to correct the accumulated errors of doctrine. And these appearances of the sign of the cross in the two greatest nations of Asia were not the only ones: white crosses had appeared on the shells of Chinese crabs, while in Chile a tree had grown in the shape of a cross, in both cases shortly before the missionaries arrived.[7] Prodigies apart, Kircher knew that his order was taking up an Asiatic mission that had flourished centuries before, and hence had every chance of future success.[8]

The Malabar cross was a miraculous one, behaving suspiciously like the blood of St Januarius, which liquefies (or doesn't) on his annual feast day. Of special interest to Kircher was the inscription around it in 'mystical Brahman characters', which a Portuguese Father, Johannes Lucena, translated (surely with a little troping from local legend) as follows:

On the 21st day of December in the 30th year after the preaching of the Gospel to the whole world, St Thomas the Apostle died in Meliapore. From him was learned the knowledge of God, the change of the Law, and the destruction of the Demon. God was born of the Virgin Mary and lived thirty years in obedience to her. He was Eternal God. This God taught His Law to Twelve Apostles, and one of that number came to Meliapore holding in his hand a staff. (Others say a carpenter's ruler made of wood and a stake.) They say that this stake, cast up by the sea onto the shore, was so large that many elephants couldn't move it from that place, but that the king gave it to the apostle to use for the foundation of his church. The king of Meliapore, Coromandel, and Pandi, and the heads of diverse nations and sects quickly made a voluntary submission to the Law of St Thomas, for they had seen the great miracle. The time came when St Thomas died by the hand of a certain brahmin and this cross was formed by his own blood. Thus says Fr Lucena. Moreover, on 18 December, the Feast of the Blessed Virgin (which the Spanish call the Expectation of the Birth) at the annual sacrifice of the Mass this cross changes to various colours and suddenly drips much sweat and blood. Experience has shown that this is always a forecast of some great and imminent calamity.[9]

Kircher lacked the resources to study the scripts and languages of East Asia as thoroughly as he had those of the Near and Middle East, but this did not prevent him from using them in his own way. Among the Elogia in praise of Emperor Ferdinand III that preface *Œdipus Ægyptiacus* is one in the 'secret writing of the Indian Brahmans' (**Ill. 13.3**). Kircher writes:

Dominus Franciscus Stellutus was the first to communicate these notes to me. His Excellency Caesius, Duke of Aqua Sparta, had once taken the trouble to collect them, on account of his curious disposition and his love for recondite letters. Then, about six years ago, Father Antonius Ceschius sent me from the East Indies a great quantity of them for elucidation; he was a priest of our Society, most religious and learned in every sort of virtue and science, who had extracted them from a certain mountain of India called Mount Pagodum, in the Chau-

lensian territory. Now this mountain is famous throughout India, and often thronged with people who come there on pilgrimage; it is so full of them that one can only enter the interior from one side. The whole mountain is inscribed with characters of this kind, which are held by all in great veneration and respect. Therefore the aforementioned Father Ceschius sent me a transcription of them, out of his love for promoting the common good, so that he might test my diligence in expounding them.[10]

Strictly speaking, Kircher says, these are not hieroglyphs, which are either sacred signs denoting arcane things, or else signs of the great mysteries made from animals, birds, objects, and so forth. The Brahmanic signs are abstract, direct symbols of what they denote, somewhat resembling the magical characters called sigils. But there is no doubt that the Brahmanic wisdom derived from Egypt. Therefore we can expect it to include the concepts of the three

13.4 Prayers in Sanskrit. Kircher was the first to publish Sanskrit, together with a grammar and translation. (*China Illustrata*, 5th plate after 162)

worlds, intelligible, celestial and elementary; the twelve signs of the zodiac; the seven planets; and the four elements.

Kircher gives some hundred Brahmanic signs and their meanings, classifying them according to the effects of the seven planets in the various zodiacal signs.[11] Unfortunately almost none of them correspond to the signs used in the dedication to the Emperor, so their origin remains a mystery. Both these and the letters in the inscription on St Thomas's altar are entirely different from the Sanskrit alphabet, which Kircher's book was also the first to publish, along with a brief grammar and some translated prayers (**Ill. 13.4**).

Whereas the mystical Brahman script and the Sanskrit alphabet, each in its own way, could be fitted into Kircher's theories of the evolution of writing, the Chinese characters were another matter. Madeleine David has written on how important their discovery was to Kircher, to Leibniz and to the wider efforts in the seventeenth and eighteenth centuries to arrive at a universal language.[12] The essential point had been made by a French Jesuit, Nicolas Trigault, who published his chronicle of Jesuit expeditions to China in 1615:[13] it was that the Chinese characters were a purely *written* language, which the literate could read whether in China, Korea, Japan, Cochinchina or Tonkin.[14] But these peoples pronounced them in completely different ways, according to their different *spoken* languages. The Chinese characters were a non-alphabetic script which Trigault actually calls 'hieroglyphic' and compares to that of the Egyptians. He comments: 'Thereby they say not only in a few words but in a few syllables what we, perhaps, would say less intelligibly with long discourses full of ambiguity.'[15] Kircher used a similar principle in his *Polygraphia Nova* (1663), which was a design for a hieroglyphic writing system that was not dependent on the language of its readers. However, he presented it more as a secret code for his patrons (the most important of whom were equipped with a special encoding machine) than as a benefit to the world in general. Leibniz, after a brief enthusiasm and exchange of letters with Kircher, saw this 'new universal writing' as a dead end,[16] though he never lost his respect for Chinese ways of thought, especially as contained in the *I Ching*.

From Kircher's point of view, Chinese writing was a living survival of the hieroglyphic principle. This is how he describes its origins:

> The ancient Chinese were descended from Egyptians, from whom they derived their writing system. Both writing systems were based, not on letters, but on pictures drawn from various natural things. The first Chinese emperor, Fohi, found the first type of characters made from serpents and dragons, as described in the *Chinese Annals*. Therefore, the book on Mathematics and Astrology is called *The Book of Dragons*.[17]

Already in *Œdipus Ægyptiacus* Kircher was able to publish sixteen small engravings of archaic and modern Chinese characters, in order to demonstrate how they have evolved from picture-writing. Some of these are shown in **Ill. 13.5**,

13.5 Evolution of Chinese characters. Kircher's theory was that, like Egyptian hieroglyphics, they originated as pictures. (*Œdipus Ægyptiacus*, Volume III, 18)

where characters are traced to animal and vegetable forms. Kircher does not try to answer the question of how certain formations of worms, birds, and so on, had come to signify certain words, or to find any constant principles in the many styles of script. Haun Saussy has traced Kircher's source to a Chinese manuscript that he knew in Rome, written in characters made from serpents, turtles, phoenixes, and the like. But what Kircher took to be the original *Book of Dragons* of the god-king Fohi was probably no more than 'a manual of fanciful calligraphic styles'.[18] By the time he came to compile *China Illustrata*, he had made no further progress in this field, and simply reproduced the illustrations along with the same theory.

When *China Illustrata* turns from history to anthropology, it is overshadowed by the missionary attitude. Kircher lets no opportunity slip for painting the 'heathen' in the worst possible light, and there are many such opportunities as he describes the customs and costumes of the various peoples of Asia (**Ill. 13.6**). This is one of the illustrations engraved from drawings by Father Johann Grüber (1625–1665), during his journey from Beijing that began in 1661 and finally brought him to Rome, and Kircher's study, in 1664. While the costumes are of minor interest, this drawing of Tanguth men also shows 'the demonic boy called Phut, who slaughters men'. Here are the details:

> They choose a robust and strong boy, and give him the authority to kill on certain days of the year whatever human he meets, showing no respect for sex or age. He kills them with the weapons provided. They are stupidly and madly convinced that people killed in this way, as if dedicated to the wretched deity Manipe, whom they worship, will receive eternal honor and a blessed condition. The boy is outfitted with a marvellously variegated cloak, a sword, quiver, arrows and trophies of flags. At certain times he is possessed by a demon, to whom he is said to be consecrated. After he has slipped out of his home, he wanders quite mad over the highways and byways. He kills at his pleasure everyone he meets, and no resistance is made. In their native tongue they call him 'Buth', which means 'executioner'. The Fathers drew him exactly as they had seen him while they were staying there.[19]

Grüber also drew the Potala, the monastery-palace of the Dalai Lama in Lhasa, and Kircher's book was the first to publish a picture of it (**Ill. 13.7**). Here, too, appeared a portrait of the Potala's first builder, the Great Fifth Dalai Lama (Lozang Gyatso, 1617–1682), one of the most distinguished of his line (**Ill. 13.8**). According to Kircher, the missionaries were not allowed into his presence, but Father Grüber was able to copy a picture of the god-king then hung in the palace. Here is his annotation on the plate, with typical asides:

> He sits on a raised place on a pillow under which precious carpets are strewn. Before him the visitors fall prostrate and place their heads on the ground. They kiss his feet with incredible veneration, as if he were the Pope. Thus, even by this the deceitfulness of the evil spirit is marvellously shown, for veneration due only to the Vicar of Christ on earth, the Pope of Rome, is transferred to the heathen worship of savage nations, like all the other mysteries of Christianity. The Devil does this with his natural malevolence... Lest he seem to lose his immortality, after his death the Lamas search the whole kingdom for a man similar to him in every respect. When such a one is found, he is substituted on the throne for the former Grand Lama. In this way they persuade the whole kingdom, ignorant of this fraud and deception, of the eternal

XII. Habitus communis in Regno *Tanchuth*.   XIII. Habitus ejusdem Gentis.   XIV. Effigies Pueri dæmoniaci, dum mactat homines, *Phut* nomine.

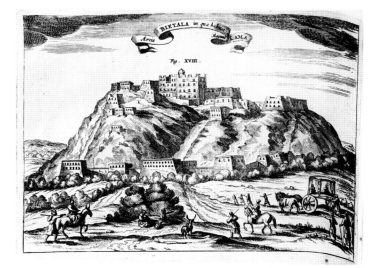

XIX. Effigies Magni *Lama* seu *Patris æterni*.   XX. *Han* mortuus Rex *Tanguth* divinis honoribus colitur.

◀ 13.6 Costumes of the Tartars, copied from the drawings of the Jesuit missionary Father Johann Grüber, who travelled in China from 1661 to 1664. This one includes the demon Phut, a sort of holy murderer. (*China Illustrata*, 71)

▼ 13.7 The Potala, Lhasa: the first picture of the Potala to reach Europe, drawn by Father Grüber and published by Kircher in 1667. (*China Illustrata*, 74)

▼▼ 13.8 Dalai Lama, whom, in spite of Kircher's claims, Grüber may actually have been permitted to see. (*China Illustrata*, 73)

survival of the Eternal Father, who has been revived from Hell seven times already in this century.[20]

Aldo Mastroianni comments:

> The picture of the Dalai Lama drawn by Grueber and published in *China* shows a youthful figure with energetic features, answering closely to the character of the real man, offering us a psychological depth rarely met with in the otherwise iconic and symbolic art of eighteenth-century Tibet. This leads us to believe that, contrarily to what Kircher says, Father Grueber may actually have been able to see the great Dalai Lama in person.[21]

After Tibet, Grüber and D'Orville continued through Kathmandu into Agra, capital of Mughal India, where the Emperor Akbar (reigned 1556–1605) had first summoned Christian missionaries 'not so much from curiosity as from his love of the Gospel and a certain natural inclination toward faith in Christ'.[22] He was nominally a Muslim, but, Grüber was told, habitually mocked both that religion and that of the Brahmans. This illustration (**Ill. 13.9**) comes from a likeness sent by the Fathers to Rome, and shows the Emperor in his throne room holding a sphere 'through which he showed himself to be the lord of the world and the greatest power'.[23] By the time Akbar's portrait appeared in *China Illustrata*, the Mughal Empire was ruled by Aurangzeb (1658–1707), who imposed the Sharia (Islamic law) on his unhappy subjects. There is no evidence that Grüber obtained an audience with him.

Kircher's account of the first emperor of the Ch'ing (Qing) Dynasty, Shun-Chih (lived 1638–1661; **Ill. 13.10**), pictured in very similar style to his Indian counterpart, celebrates the brilliant success of the Jesuits in obtaining his patronage. Two reasons for this emerge from the text. First, the Ch'ing Dynasty was not Chinese but Manchurian, or what Kircher calls Tartar. The

▶ **13.9** The Mughal Emperor. This was identified as Akbar, who did indeed receive Christian missionaries, but by the time of Grüber's visit he had been succeeded by Aurangzeb. (*China Illustrata*, opposite 78)

▶▶ **13.10** Emperor of China, a friend and patron of the Jesuits whom he favoured, says Kircher, because he was not Chinese but Tartar and felt closer to the West. (*China Illustrata*, 1st plate after 112)

Emperor declared that he felt closer in spirit to the 'Far West' than to his Chinese subjects, whose customs, Kircher says, he detested. He only observed Chinese religious rites out of political necessity and kept to his native Tartar costume, as did his whole court. Better yet, he acknowledged the Far West as the source of his ancestral culture, writing and even religion. 'The king was certainly much inclined towards Christianity, which he said his ancestors had followed, and was convinced of the truth of our holy faith. He would have been baptized except for his love of polygamy, which he would have had to give up if he was a Christian.'[24]

The first of the Jesuits to gain a foothold in the imperial court was Matteo Ricci (1552–1610; **Ill. 13.11**), shown here before an altar with an aristocratic convert. A little later, Adam Schall von Bell (1591–1666; **Ill. 13.12**) survived the fall of the Ming Dynasty in 1643 and was kept on by the new Ch'ing Dynasty rulers.[25] The portrait of Schall with his map, cross-staff, quadrant, astrolabe, armillary sphere, celestial globe and well-stocked library, shows

the second reason that the emperors tolerated these visitors: they brought Western science with them. As Kircher relates it, the Chinese calendar had degenerated from lack of revisions, and the court astronomers were unable to predict eclipses. The Emperor realized that the missionaries could help to rectify the system, and in 1611 the project was begun with the accurate survey of the latitude of Beijing. Finding the Chinese still bound to a flat-earth cosmology and a mythical astronomy, the missionaries became the scientific enlighteners of an empire, educating their charges in European astronomy, surveying, medicine, optics and mathematics. The Emperor was fascinated by the new sciences and by the advanced astronomical instruments that the missionaries imported. He protected them against the inevitable court intrigues and supported them in regal style. 'Also, he put Father Adam Schall in charge of a hundred Chinese astronomers and he served over them as head or judge in any decisions, and was like a teacher for them. He made Father Schall a Mandarin of the First Order.'[26] It is in this resplendent costume that

P. Matthæus Riccius Macerat: è Soc: Jesu primus Chrianæ Fidei in Regno Sinarum propagator.

Lÿ Paulus Magnus Sinarum Colaus Legis Christianæ propagator.

◄◄ 13.11 Matteo Ricci, died 1610, the first Jesuit to be accepted at the Chinese court, shown here before an altar with a Christian convert. (*China Illustrata*, 1st plate after 414)

◄ 13.12 Adam Schall von Bell, who succeeded Ricci and lived until 1666. He is shown dressed as a mandarin and surrounded by scientific instruments. (*China Illustrata*, 4th plate after 412)

13.13a, b Chinese
ladies, for Kircher
an example that
Christian ladies
could well follow,
except for the
cruel custom of
binding the feet.
(*China Illustrata*,
2nd and 3rd plates
after 414)

Kircher presents his compatriot, implicitly defending the Jesuits' much criticized tendency to 'go native' and make extreme concessions to those they hoped to convert.

The other full-page portraits in *China Illustrata* are of two palace noblewomen, engraved from drawings sent to Kircher by the Fathers in China (**Ill. 13.13a, b**). In his commentary, Kircher (or his correspondent) is torn between horror at the custom of binding the feet of infant girls, crippling them for life but making them beautiful by Chinese standards, and approval of their mores: 'The dress of the women is modest and grave, and covers every part of the body except the face. If some European women would follow this example, they would certainly behave more modestly.'[27] The two ladies are shown in the futile activities of their sequestered life, passing the time 'playing with birds, puppies, and other diversions'. We can sense the early stirrings of Chinoiserie: the representation

of China as an exotic Arcadia, already present in a European passion for blue-and-white porcelain and imported silks, and soon to become a veritable craze.[28]

With only 237 pages, *China Illustrata* is one of Kircher's shortest works, and it must have been judged his most readable, for it is the only one that was widely translated from Latin to the vernacular. It is stuffed with anecdotes and travellers' tales of the sensational aspects of Oriental culture and superstition. Readers found there a horrifying description of a *suttee* or widow-burning, ending with the complacent remark: 'she in all her ornaments was burned to cinders and died, destined not for the Elysian Fields, but for eternal torment'.[29] Philosophical beliefs and harmless customs come in for equally scathing criticism. The doctrine of reincarnation, for instance, was taught to the Chinese by 'a very sinful Brahman imbued with Pythagoreanism', which taught that souls are reincarnated in animals and even trees.[30] Without using the term *feng shui*, Kircher described the Chinese art of geomancy, or as he puts it, 'choosing the site for a house, temple or grave according to the location of the head, tail, or feet of the dragons whom they imagine to live under the ground'.[31] He ridiculed all spiritual practices, such as the spiritual alchemy of the Taoists who 'prescribe certain exercises, ways of sitting, prayers, and even drugs, by which they persuade themselves that they will achieve a longer mortal life with the favour of the gods',[32] and their practice of meditation, described thus:

> Those who are better trained, or perhaps I should say, more insane, in their philosophy, say that a man by thinking is really able to achieve the desired object, that a man can stop all activity to the point that no life remains in him. They think that he does this not only by his intellect and his will power, but also by his cognitive, appetitive and imaginary powers. They add that when a man has made such intellectual progress, he falls into ecstasy and an unmoving stupor. Then finally he can be said to have arrived at the greatest possible happiness and he is said to be among the gods in the pagodas.[33]

The said pagodas (**Ill. 13.14**), suggestively called 'pyramids', are among the proofs that Kircher adduces for an Egyptian origin of Chinese religion. This illustration of the Pagoda of Novizionia in Fukien province derives from Father Martini's *Atlas*, which states that it is 900 cubits high; the outside is 'ornamented with raised pictures and figures on the thin porcelain finish', hung with bells that tinkled in the slightest wind, and veneered inside with polished marble.[34] But to what purpose? Everything about Oriental religion, to Kircher, reeked of Satanism. Alluding to the most controversial passage in the *Corpus Hermeticum*, he writes: 'The Chinese, like the ancient Egyptians, lock up demons in statues and dedicate temples to them, where they ask questions of them.'[35]

Already when writing *Œdipus Ægyptiacus* in the 1640s, Kircher included East Asian religions in his broad vision of Egyptian origins and influences, and included several exotic illustrations in that book. Jurgis Baltrušaitis, one of the first modern scholars to appreciate Kircher, has shown[36] how these were improved for use in *China Illustrata*. The first, called 'Amida, Deity of the Japanese', was reproduced in *Œdipus* with a careful avoidance of stylization (**Ill. 13.15**), and obviously copied from an imported painting, drawing or print. When Kircher re-used the image in *China*, his illustrator Westernized the face and modelled the body, turning it into an idol in an imaginary temple and combining it with the three-headed idol (see below) (**Ill. 13.16**).

For his skimpy knowledge of Buddhism, Kircher was at the mercy of his missionary informants, who told him that the Japanese have two very different sects. One is called the 'Xenxus'; it has splendid temples and is patronized by royalty, but does not believe in life after death. Obviously this is the indigenous religion of Shinto, spelled in Portuguese fashion. The other sect

▲ **13.14** Pagoda, which Kircher, obsessed by the Egyptian origin of everything, calls a pyramid. (*China Illustrata*, opposite 134)

◄ **13.15** 'Amida, Deity of the Japanese', retaining the style of an Oriental picture. (*Œdipus Ægyptiacus*, Volume I, 404)

Japoniorum Numen Triceps.   *Amida* Numen *Japoniorum.*

◄ **13.16** Amida and a three-headed idol in a temple. Amida is a Bodhisattva in Mahayana Buddhism, but Kircher does not know that name. (*China Illustrata*, 138)

◄▼ **13.17** Three-headed Japanese god: another figure ultimately derived from Buddhism but interpreted by Kircher according to a theory of his own. (*Œdipus Ægyptiacus*, Volume I, 410)

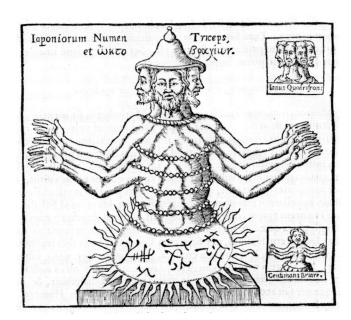

believes in the immortality of the soul, and worships an idol called Amida. It holds that nothing more is required for salvation than to repeat the phrase *Namu Amida Buth* (Blessed Amida, save us), and makes use, for this invocation, of a rosary similar to that of Christians. This other sect is evidently Pure Land Buddhism, a branch of the Mahayana whose devotees aspire to rebirth in the 'Western Paradise' or 'Pure Land'. Amida, who in various forms presides over this blissful state, is one of the chief Bodhisattvas (enlightened beings) in Mahayana Buddhism.

Kircher had already come across the manifestation of Amida as Avalokiteshvara, Bodhisattva of Compassion, who was pictured in Ludovicus Gusman's *Historia de Iaponia* with multiple heads and arms (**Ill. 13.17**). This suggested a comparison with the four-faced Janus of the Romans and the hundred-armed Briareus, a monster of Greek mythology. In conformity with the late classical theology that he had largely made his own, Kircher explains that these members signify the multiple effects of the sun. Gusman had gone farther, writing that the attributes of this statue symbolize the many perfections of God, and that a host of other statues surrounding it are divided into nine groups, like the Nine Orders of Angels. This was too much for Kircher, who retorts: 'Who cannot see here that the Devil has imitated the superstitions of the ancients mixed with Christian mysteries?'[37]

Another image of 'thousand-armed' Avalokiteshvara appears in *China Illustra*, faithfully copied from a Chinese original (**Ill. 13.18**) but given the outlandish name of Pussa. Like many Western interpreters, Kircher saw the smooth-faced image as that of a feminine deity,[38] and concluded that the sixteen arms represented the multiple powers of the great mother goddess. It followed that this must be the Chinese equivalent of the one known to the Greeks as Cybele and to the Egyptians as Isis. Kircher concedes that the educated Chinese agree in principle with his interpretation: 'Those Chinese sages who ridicule polytheism say that this representation of a goddess only describes the strength, power, and force of kindly Nature.'[39] As for the name of Pussa, I suspect that it was arrived at through the misunderstanding of a mantra. Many of the mantras addressed to the Bodhisattvas Amida and Avalokiteshvara, or their feminine version Kwan Yin or Kannon,[40] end with the word *pusa*, and Europeans hearing this repeatedly must have taken that for the name of the god or goddess.

One of the treasures of Kircher's museum was a Chinese painting donated by Father Grüber (**Ill. 13.19**).[41] This again was reproduced with a sincere effort to preserve its Oriental style. Looking at it, I wonder how this came about. Was the precious original loaned to Jansson in Amsterdam to be engraved, and if so, was it was safely returned? We shall never know. Kircher's information on the iconography was correct, up to a point: it shows the deified Emperor Fohi flanked by Confucius and Laotse, with divine attendants and elemental spirits. His interpretation, however, was characteristically facile: 'For what can the God Fe, with his attendants at B and C, signify except Jove with Apollo and Mercury? What could the middle order with swords and javelins be except Mars and Bacchus?'[42]

The confusion of divinities and of authentic with imaginary pictures of them reaches a low point in the often-reproduced illustrations of Amida/Pussa/Harpocrates. The woodcut in *Œdipus* (**Ill. 13.20**) is supposedly based on another picture in Kircher's collection, sent to him by the Portuguese envoy, but a good deal of imagination has entered into it. The engraver of *China* saw fit to improve it by placing it in a seascape, achieving a truly surreal emblem (**Ill. 13.21**). This Amida is no longer identified with Isis but with her son Harpocrates, the child-god of Alexandrian theology. The reasoning was simple: one of Harpocrates' forms is as a child seated on a lotus. Seeing that god-figures are found seated on lotuses or roses in Persia, India and the Far East, Kircher concluded that they all derive from this god.

Despite its title, *China Illustrata* contains much about India, and mingles it with Chinese and Japanese reports in a way that must have confused readers who were only just beginning to sort out the unfamiliar geography of the East. For example, just after describing the pagoda in southeast China, Kircher shows (twice!) a picture of 'Pagodes, a Divinity of the Indians'

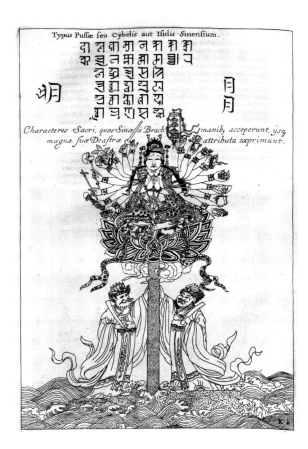

◄ **13.18** 'Pussa' or the Chinese Cybele, which Kircher interprets as female and would like to identify with Isis. (*China Illustrata*, opposite 141)

◄▼ **13.19** Chinese deities, a copy of a Chinese painting given to Kircher's museum by Father Grüber. (*China Illustrata*, fp. 136/137)

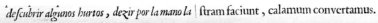

13.20, 13.21 Amida on the lotus, and Amida-Pussa on the sea, freely copied from Oriental originals, but only minimally understood by Kircher. (*Œdipus Ægyptiacus*, Volume I, 406, and *China Illustrata*, 140)

Idolum Pusse sub alia forma.

Pagodes *Indorum* Numen. Idolum *Menipe*.

Pagodes Indorum Numen.

◄ **13.22** Pagodes and the idol Menipe. A scene suggesting human sacrifice, based on mistaken nomenclatures. (*China Illustrata*, 131)

▲ **13.23** Pagodes, a divinity of the Indians. A Buddhist statue in Kircher's collection. (*Œdipus Ægyptiacus*, Volume I, 399)

(**Ill. 13.22**). This is another case of 'improvement'. for the statue was again in Kircher's museum, a gift from the Portuguese Jesuit envoy Nunnius Mascarenias, and had appeared in *Œdipus Ægyptiacus* (**Ill. 13.23**). There it was associated with the one god, called the King of Heaven, who is worshipped by the Chinese literati. For its appearance in *China* it is given a cloak adorned with the 'secret Brahmanic script' and a gloomy setting suggestive of human sacrifice.[43] The 'Menipe' who appears to share the temple with Pagodes is another imagined name based on the misunderstanding of a mantra. Here it is the common Sanskrit invocation of the Buddha, 'Om mani padme hum' which (in my limited experience) Tibetans pronounce as 'Om meni pemi hum'.

The empires of the East could never equal Egypt in Kircher's estimation. Egypt had been the site of a great civilization before the Flood, and the stage for some of the most dramatic subsequent events: the captivity of Joseph, the calling of Moses, the Exodus. Asia had no antediluvian monuments like the pyramids, no wise king like Hermes Trismegistus to recall it to the worship of the true god and inscribe his wisdom on the obelisks. The whole region had been populated by the straggling descendants of Cham, who had followed his deviations into idolatry, polytheism and the worship of demons. As far as writing was concerned, the Egyptian priests had developed the early hieroglyphs, with their naïve pictures of birds and animals, into a vehicle for mystical and spiritual meanings, but the Chinese hieroglyphs had never gone beyond the naturalistic phase.[44] There were, however, some encouraging signs. Kircher mentions one in his treatment of Amida-Harpocrates. According to sixteenth-century Portuguese sources, 'They say that he is an invisible substance, separate from all mixture of elements, existing before all creatures, the source of all things good'. Kircher comments approvingly on this, saying that wise men, instructed by the light of nature, believe very different things from the less intelligent.[45]

Having admitted that the Chinese literati shared his philosophical interpretation of polytheism, why could he go no further? Why was it that, in Dino Pastine's words:

> Kircher, having before him the best-known examples of Christian, Muslim and Jewish Neoplatonism, could find nothing better to say than that the Indians, supposing a final identification of the souls of the blessed with the essence of God, were falling into the same error as the Greeks and the Egyptians, who in their mythology often describe the process of *theomorphosis* or the divinization of man?[46]

Perhaps it was because *China Illustrata* was a popular work with an energetic message of propaganda for the Jesuit missions. An esoteric concordance of religions would have undermined the missionary effort, because if the same transcendent experience is at the heart of all religions, does it matter which path is taken?

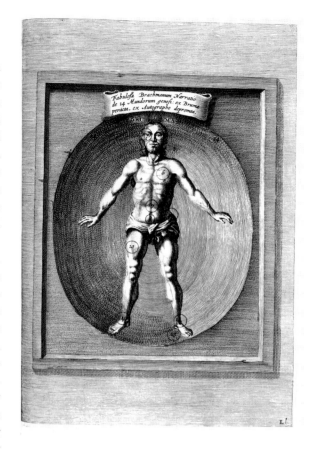

13.24 Brahma as universal man. Any connection between Brahma and the notion of universal man in the Jewish Kabbalah is left obscure by Kircher, since it would have amounted to heresy in the eyes of the Church. (*China Illustrata*, opposite 154)

13.25 Avatars of Vishnu. As with the Buddhist images, Kircher's illustrator has tried to preserve the indigenous style. (*China Illustrata*, 161)

I doubt that Kircher could have asked himself such a question, much less written it. No more does he attempt to correlate the image of Brahma as universal man (**Ill. 13.24**) with cognate notions in the Kabbalah, though this image, 'taken from the Autograph', resembles those of Robert Fludd's *History of the Microcosm* and indeed Kircher's own zodiacal men (see **Ill. 15.5**). Kircher scathingly recounts the Hindu myth that 'the whole universe was formed from one human body, each world in the universe corresponding to a part of the body', and the correlative belief that humans derive their dispositions from these worlds, and even mentions the seven worlds of the Kabbalah.[47] Had he not read the *Zohar*, with its far more grotesque analysis of the left eye, the beard and the genitals of Macroposopus? Surely he had; but the 'many worlds' hypothesis threatened the very tap root of Christian dogma: the unique incarnation of God on this earth. Proclaiming it had been Giordano Bruno's downfall.

Less attractive, but equally earnest in their attempted fidelity to the models, are the engravings of the ten incarnations or avatars of Vishnu, of which two are shown here (**Ill. 13.25**). Kircher's informant was another German Jesuit, Heinrich Roth, who had spent six years learning Sanskrit and Indian philosophy and mythology from a convert, 'so that we could more easily refute such absurdities by becoming familiar with them'.[48] This was the first appearance in Europe of these images and their associated doctrine, but in the wrong order, with omissions and interpolations, and in utterly garbled form.[49] One illustration is titled Krexno (i.e. Krishna), the eighth avatar, but instead of the divine cowherd, it shows the myth of the Churning of the Sea of Milk, with the Devas on the right, the Asuras on the left and Vishnu in his third incarnation as the tortoise Kurma supporting the whole contraption.

A similar mixture of fictitious and factual images fills the last section of *China Illustrata*, which treats the natural wonders of the Orient. Side by side are an example of mythic topography in the Dragon and Tiger Mountain of Ki'amsi (**Ill. 13.26**) in which the similarity of the mountain shapes to the two beasts is literalized, and one of relative naturalism in the Seven Peaks (**Ill. 13.27**) with their towers, mapping out on the ground the configuration of the Big Dipper or Great Bear constellation. (Is this perhaps the first occurrence in print of the idea, so fruitful in today's alternative literature, of ground formations replicating the sky?[50]) Somewhere in between the two styles is the mountain in the shape of the god Fe (**Ill. 13.28**). Kircher gives serious consideration to the question of whether is it a natural simulacrum, like Dragon and Tiger Mountain, or shaped by human agency. If it was the latter, he says, it so surpasses in scale the known wonders of the ancient world that it could hardly have gone unchronicled. In the course of the argument, he mentions a number of cases of natural formations that seem to represent human and other forms. At the end of this chapter on topographical prodigies, he makes a rare and tantalizing reference to his lost work on Tuscany: 'We have discussed this in our *Iter Hetruscum*, in the chapter on swimming islands.'[51]

The illustration of Lake Chin, known as the Starry Sea (**Ill. 13.29**), is likewise part topography and part mythology. It shows a credible present-day landscape and highlights the star-shaped waterlilies that give the lake its name. But the floating infant refers to the legend that where the lake is, there was once a city, 'destroyed by an earthquake because of the horrible crimes of its inhabitants'. The sole survivor of the inundation was a child floating on a piece of wood. Another illustration of ambiguous intent shows the flying turtles of Honan (**Ill. 13.30**). Only from the text does one discover that the turtles do *not* fly: Kircher has examined the report that they do, weighed it against reason and former experience of turtles, and found it wanting. In a way, these images are emblems, with the surreal quality typical of their kind. Using a naturalistic landscape as background, they picture an improbable event that invites a mythological or moralistic interpretation.

China Illustrata contains a number of realistic views of Chinese plants and animals. For want of space I omit the pineapple, the clematis, the two types of rhubarb, the hippopotamus, the cat-bat and the woolly chicken, as I regretfully omit the wonderful anecdotes he tells of these and other creatures, worthy of a medieval herbal and bestiary. They are all second-hand information except in two cases: the snake-stone and the plant called *Cha* or tea. The snake-stone has already been described (see page 35). As for tea, Kircher speaks with an enthusiasm redolent of another superhuman scribbler and tea addict, Dr. Samuel Johnson:

> It certainly is very strong. Unless I had learned to drink it at the frequent invitations by our fathers, I could hardly have been induced to believe it. It is a diuretic and marvellously opens the bladder. It frees the head from vapours. Nature has not given literary men a more noble and apt remedy for helping them do a great amount of work during long vigils. Although at first it is weak and bitter, after a while it becomes pleasant and one develops such an appetite that he can scarcely abstain from it. Although Turkish coffee and Mexican chocolate have the same effect, tea is better, for it is more temperate. Chocolate heats one up too much when the weather is warm, and coffee makes the bile ascend. Tea is always harmless and it is marvellously effective not once, but even a hundred times a day.[52]

Lastly, Kircher shows some of the technical achievements of the Chinese: a 'flying bridge' 440 cubits long, a bronze bell far outweighing Europe's largest bell (in Erfurt Cathedral), and part of the Great Wall. All of these bring exclamations of awe from Kircher's sources, completing the desired picture of a nation with a mastery of engineering, a philosophically minded elite, an Emperor who was *almost* a Christian, and the masses sunk in superstition and devil-worship: a fine field for evangelization!

It is instructive to compare Kircher's *China Illustrata* to an almost exactly contemporary work, Jan Nieuhoff's *An Embassy sent by the East India Company of the United Provinces to the Grand Tartar Cham or Emperor of China* (London, 1669).[53] Nieuhoff's travelogue brackets Kircher's, for it first appeared in Dutch and

► 13.26 Dragon and Tiger mountain, a wonder said to exist in the Orient. (*China Illustrata*, 171)

►▼ 13.27 Seven Peaks, another extraordinary landscape, in which the ground configuration reproduces the constellation of the Great Bear. (*China Illustrata*, 172)

► **13.28** Mountain of Fe, a Chinese god. Was the mountain a work of Nature or made by human hands? Kircher cannot decide. (*China Illustrata*, 173)

▼ **13.29** Lake Chin, part mythology and part landscape, said to be the site of a city 'destroyed by an earthquake because of the horrible crimes of its inhabitants'. The sole survivor was a child floating on a piece of wood. (*China Illustrata*, 176)

Latin in 1665, then when John Ogilby translated it into English he took advantage of Kircher's work of 1667. In fact, he added 106 pages of appendix which are a clever abbreviation of the latter, with Kircher's plates copied by no less an artist than Wenceslaus Hollar.[54] Nieuhoff was no missionary, but accompanied a diplomatic party. His drawings of the peoples of Asia make them look less sympathetic than those in *China Illustrata*, being ill-proportioned and even grotesque, but his account has the advantage of being the credible observations of one traveller, rather than a compilation of reports and rumours from many sources. What Nieuhoff and Ogilby do not conceal is the bitter rivalry between Protestant and Catholic missionaries, each denouncing the other side in their efforts to win the field for their brand of Christianity. One wonders what cultivated Chinese, Indians and Japanese thought of

13.30 Flying turtle. Kircher illustrated this wonder of nature, but did not believe it. (*China Illustrata*, 205)

KIRCHER IN RUSSIA

The researches of Robert Collis have revealed an unsuspected Kircherian influence at the very roots of modern Russia.[55] It concerns Archbishop Feofan Prokopovich (1681–1736), who 'was undoubtedly the most influential ecclesiastical figure in Petrine Russia, and is rightly regarded as the chief ideologist of Peter the Great's reforms of the Russian State'.[56] As a close friend of the Tsar and his chief ally in the Orthodox Church, Prokopovich was entrusted with the reorganization of the church hierarchy and the educational system. He also wrote official histories of Russia, philosophical justifications of Peter's absolutism, and works of theology and natural history.

Historians have generally considered him a progressive and 'enlightened' reformer. This may be so, but as Collis has shown, Prokopovich's enlightenment was of a rather particular nature. He shared without a qualm the Renaissance idea of a *prisca theologia*: that there had been an ancient wisdom, known to the pagans as well as to the Jews, which could be recaptured, and which had taught not only some of the truths of theology but the secrets of nature. The ancients knew that God's essence permeates the entire universe, and that it supports and preserves everything; that the macrocosm corresponds with the microcosm, and that both worlds are united by chains of sympathy.

This much Prokopovich would have learned from the classical authorities, especially Plato's *Timaeus* and the Neoplatonists, the *Corpus Hermeticum* and the works attributed to Dionysus the Areopagite. To these he added a magnificent library of modern authors, especially those of like bent such as Agrippa, Paracelsus, Cardan, Kircher and the alchemists, but not ignoring Galileo, Descartes, Kepler, Bacon, Hobbes and Locke.

In his theological writings, Prokopovich showed a deep knowledge of Hebrew sources, and a confidence that the conversion of the Jews will lead to the Millennium. The same wide-ranging view of sacred history led him to write on the condition of man before and after the Fall. He specified the location of Paradise in southern Mesopotamia, and calculated mathematically the possibility of including all known animals in Noah's Ark, except those spontaneously generated such as flies, mice, scorpions and bees.

In 1708, while he was Prefect of the Kiev Academy (a theological training college), Prokopovich instituted a new course in natural philosophy with himself as the lecturer. It was grounded in experimental science, for which he imported globes, telescopes, microscopes, compasses, astrolabes and other equipment, and on a strictly literal interpretation of the Bible. Consequently he rejected the Copernican

hypothesis and held to the cosmology of Tycho Brahe. He accepted that the heavenly bodies have an effect on the sublunary world. They affect the course of illnesses, the behaviour of animals like ants and oysters, and cause metals to grow underground. But, contrarily to the beliefs of astrology, they cannot override human free will.

In 1716, Prokopovich moved to St Petersburg, where he founded a literary-philosophical circle, the 'Brotherhood of Learning'. He regaled his colleagues with his views on monsters, apparently accepting Pliny's report of men with dogs' heads and those whose eyes are on their shoulders. Likewise, he credited the principle of animal hybrids: the leopard comes from the mating of a panther and a lion, the lynx from that of a wolf and a red deer, etc.

This sketch does not do justice to the breadth of Prokopovich's interests, the importance of his reforming work, or the other influences on him, such as German Pietism or the Pansophia of Comenius. But it surely qualifies him as the most dedicated Kircherian of his century. It also raises a question for future researchers of whether this sort of natural philosophy persisted in Russia after his time.

◄ **13.31** Chuennila, idol of the Mexicans, an amalgam of a Mexican book illustration in the Vatican Library and a description by Cortés. (*Œdipus Ægyptiacus*, Volume I, 424)

▲ **13.32** Mexican picture interpreted: a reproduction from one of the few Mesoamerican codices to escape destruction. Kircher realized it was related to the calendar. (*Œdipus Ægyptiacus*, Volume III, 32)

◄ **13.33** Temple of Horcholiuos, the god of the Americans, based on a description by Cortés. Kircher comments on the similarity to Egyptian architecture. (*Œdipus Ægyptiacus*, Volume I, 424)

this alien religion, when unconstrained by Oriental courtesy towards their visitors. In the case of Japan, at least, they had lost patience with it long before Kircher's book; the Tokugawa shogunate expelled the missionaries in 1614 as part of the general closing of Japan to foreign influences.

In Kircher's scheme of human migrations following the Universal Flood, as in present-day anthropology, the Asians were the ancestors of the Americans. He writes:

> Arias Montanus thinks that Jectan, with his sons Iobab and Sepher, were the ancestors of American Peru, an uncertain conjecture from the city *luctan* which is now found in that region. I think it more likely that they were first the ancestors of Tartary, China and Japan, and in the course of time travelled via the Tartarian isthmus, known as Aniam, by which access was given to North America, and afterwards colonized the said regions.[57]

Whatever religious depravities the missionaries found in Asia, they paled by comparison with what the Conquistadors reported from Mexico. A religion centred on human sacrifice was so obviously a service to the Devil as not to deserve much scholarly attention. There was no native elite in Mesoamerica to compare with the Confucian philosophers, no pantheon lending itself to parallels with the Old World, and to European eyes, the Aztec gods were extraordinarily hideous.[58] On the last page of his survey of the world's deities, Kircher offered his readers an image designed to disgust and horrify them (**Ill. 13.31**). He describes it thus:

> This loathsome and extremely deformed idol has a head like a basket, blazing eyes, ass's ears, teeth in its nose and mouth. In each hand it holds sacrificial vessels, and the rest of the idol is decorated with various animal heads, including some referring to the months and the zodiac. It has elephant feet, and the rest, for modesty's sake, I decline to describe.[59]

According to Jurgis Baltrušaitis, the artist combined elements from a Mexican book that had been in the Vatican Library since 1570 with Hernán Cortés's description of a Mexican idol.[60]

Even if they lacked real hieroglyphs, the Mexicans did have a sort of picture-writing, and this merited a walk-on part in the 'Hieroglyphic Theatre' of *Œdipus Ægyptiacus*. Here Kircher's artist reproduced in woodcut two pages from a Mexican codex (**Ill. 13.32**), copied from Samuel Purchas's *Hakluytus Posthumus* (1636).[61] This compendium of travelogues was Kircher's main source for what little he knew of Mexican religion and the Aztec calendar. It enabled him to describe the border as containing signs of the 51-year calendar cycle, and the whole picture as referring to the foundation of Mexico City. A to K are the first ten governors and founders of Mexico. L is the weapons used in taking Tanal; N the eagle which nested there. The lower compartment is the fortification made from clearing the marshes, and the St Andrew's cross represents the winds. 'From this it is evident that this writing of the ancient Mexicans is nothing but a sort of crude exhibition of deeds through their own images, containing no mystery, subtlety of mind or erudition.'[62]

Still more jejune in comparison with Kircher's banquets of Egyptian, Chinese and Latin topography is the one picture of a Mesoamerican temple (**Ill. 13.33**). It is again based on Cortés's description of the temple of the 'chief god of the great city of Mexico', called there Horcholiuos but in other places Chuennila or Quecadquaal (in which last we recognize Quetzalcoatl). Kircher comments:

> In some places in America, the sun and moon are also worshipped, in others the stars and the portents of meteors. In yet others, lions and similar wild beasts are worshipped, whose images and statues are kept in the temples. Thus their temples are not much different from those of the Egyptians, in which in place of the Gods every variety of monster was to be seen. From this chapter it is obvious who was the inventor of such a monstrous religion, namely the Devil, father of monsters.

He adds that devils are always thirsty for human blood, as we know from the cults of Moloch, Saturn, Mars and the Mithraic mysteries.[63]

If any visitor to Kircher's museum had doubted this, he could see for himself the Japanese executioner's sword, the cotton belt from Brazil hung with 68 human teeth[64] and an American stone club 'which had opened the gates of Heaven for some of our missionaries by breaking their necks, after having smashed their skulls'.[65] And they can still be seen. Alessandra Antinori writes with wonder of how the Brazilian missionaries took the trouble to collect the belt and a dozen other fragile artifacts, pack them up carefully and send them to Rome; and of how they survived the decline and dispersion of Kircher's museum to end up, still unspoiled, in the Museo Preistorico Etnografico Luigi Pigorini.[66]

Notes

1 See the article by Florence Hsia for insights into the political background and psychological consequences of Kircher's failure to go to China himself.

2 Illustrated in Lo Sardo, 77, 82–83, 94–95.

3 On the Sino-Syriac tablet (also called the Nestorian Monument and the Stele of X'ian or Sian-fu), see Mastroianni, 69–70; Pastine, 159–164. The tablet is accepted as genuine, but the translation has been refined since Kircher's time; see *China Illustrata*, Eng. ed., 1.

4 Pastine, 160.

5 Mastroianni, 72. For a more complete history, see Pastine 162–163.

6 The Nestorian heresy, in brief, holds that Christ had two separate natures, divine and human.

7 *China Illustrated*, 31.

8 On this and other broader issues, see Saussy, 108; Pastine, 164ff.

9 *China Illustrated*, 55.

10 *Œdipus Ægyptiacus*, III, 22.

11 *Œdipus Ægyptiacus*, III, 22–26.

12 See Wilding, 96; David, 32–38.

13 N. Trigault (1577–1628), *De Christiana Expeditione Apud Sinas Suscepta ab Societate Jesu* (Augsburg, 1615), followed by a French translation in 1616, cited in David, 32.

14 Chinese was still the main script of all these regions, according to Saussy, 111.

15 Quoted in David, 33.

16 On Leibniz's relations to Kircher and the *Polygraphia*, see David, 61–63.

17 *China Illustrated*, 217.

18 Saussy, 112.

19 *China Illustrated*, 64.

20 *China Illustrated*, 65–66. The last statement cannot be true, as the Dalai Lama was only the fifth of his line.

21 Mastroianni, 68; my translation.

22 *China Illustrated*, 71.

23 *China Illustrated*, 71.

24 *China Illustrated*, 100.

25 Rivosecchi, fig. 83.

26 *China Illustrated*, 100. David Porter gives an excellent background to the Jesuit missions in Porter, 78–132.

27 *China Illustrated*, 102.

28 Porter is equally informative on the beginnings and implications of Chinoiserie; see Porter 133–192.

29 *China Illustrated*, 140.

30 *China Illustrated*, 141–142. As Pastine explains, this 'sinful Brahman' is at the root of Kircher's grossest error: the identification of the historical Buddha with the Hindu epic hero Rama. See Pastine, 202–203.

31 *China Illustrated*, 125.

32 *China Illustrated*, 123.

33 *China Illustrated*, 142–143.

34 *China Illustrated*, 125.

35 *China Illustrated*, 125. The reference is to the Latin *Asclepius*, 24.

36 Baltrušaitis 1967, 208–213.

37 *Œdipus Ægyptiacus*, I, 411.

38 On this confusion, see Rivosecchi, fig. 95.

39 *China Illustrated*, 133.

40 This is not the place to enlarge on the relationships between these three Bodhisattvas. Suffice it to say that they all receive devotion in the Pure Land School of Buddhism.

41 Compare the copies of European pictures by Chinese converts reproduced in Rivosecchi, figs 17–31.

42 *China Illustrated*, 127.

43 Rivosecchi, fig. 90, makes the point that several images from *Œdipus Ægyptiacus* reappear in *China Illustrata* elaborated and placed in imaginary temples. There is nothing to distinguish these in the reader's mind from the authentic views of Oriental scenes.

44 Saussy, 111.

45 *Œdipus Ægyptiacus*, I, 407.

46 Pastine, 210.

47 *China Illustrated*, 144–145.

48 *China Illustrated*, 147. Roth's description is in APUG, Ms. 563, f.325–328 (cited after Pastine, 214).

49 See Pastine, 214–217.

50 See Hancock and Faiia, 126–128, for maps suggesting that the temples of Angkor in Cambodia are laid out according to the constellations.

51 *China Illustrated*, 168.

52 *China Illustrated*, 175.

53 Facsimile edition by Scolar Press, Menston, n.d.

54 Hollar's full-page engravings are true to the originals, while the woodcuts in the text, presumably done by less skilled artisans, reverse the originals left to right.

55 What follows is based on Robert Collis's paper (see Bibliography) and on extracts from his doctoral dissertation for the University of Turku, Finland, which he has kindly shared with me.

56 Collis, personal communication of extract from his dissertation.

57 *China Illustrata*, 228, my translation.

58 Some far superior copies from Mexican originals had been published in Cartari's and Pignoria's *Gli Immagini degli dei delli Antichi*, 2nd ed., Padua, 1626. This also contained a series of woodcuts of Japanese figurines. See reproductions in Rivosecchi, figs 7–9.

59 *Œdipus Ægyptiacus*, I, 423.

60 Baltrušaitis 1967, 249.

61 The original manuscript is in the Bodleian Library, Oxford, Ms. Selden A.1. The relevant page is illustrated opposite Kircher's version in Baltrušaitis 1967, 250–251. From the same source, 249, we learn that the manuscript was shipped from Mexico to Emperor Charles V, but intercepted by French warships. It came into the hands of the French Royal Geographer, who sold it to Richard Hakluyt, chaplain of the English embassy, who bequeathed it to Purchas.

62 *Œdipus Ægyptiacus*, III, 33. The second page is reproduced in Marrone, 80.

63 *Œdipus Ægyptiacus*, I, 422.

64 Illustrated and analysed in Lo Sardo, 92.

65 Catalogue of Kircher's museum, quoted in Antinori, 79.

66 Antinori, 80. Lo Sardo's book contains the most thorough treatment and illustration of the objects surviving from Kircher's museum. For the American objects, see Donatella Saviola's descriptions in Lo Sardo, 92–97.

Chapter 14   Images of the Gods

In *Obeliscus Pamphilius* and his other Egyptological works, Kircher made a pioneering attempt to contextualize Egyptian religion and, in the process, to survey all the religions of the pre-Christian world, including the recently discovered ones of Asia. In so doing, he virtually invented the discipline of comparative religion, identifying influences and commonalities on a global scale. Of course there were glaring omissions. It did not occur to him to investigate the pre-Christian religions of northern Europe, and for all his command of Arabic, his knowledge of Islam was almost nil.[1] His history of religions was part of a narrative bound inexorably to the biblical one, in which he tried to answer the question of what had gone wrong with the original, true religion of mankind. Nor was the question merely academic. Trained in a missionary order, he was painfully aware that myriads of Asians, Africans and Americans were sunk in a morass of polytheism and idolatry, and consequently heading for eternal damnation.

Yet behind polytheism, both ancient and modern, Kircher could discern the distorted shadow of a true doctrine. On good evidence from the Neoplatonists, he believed that some pagan myths contained metaphysical and cosmological truths, and that the images of the gods and goddesses were similar to hieroglyphs, veiling deeper meanings beneath their pictorial surfaces. He writes:

> There is no doubt that not only the Prophets, Apostles, and other holy men of God, but also the Gentile poets, priests, and prophets, moved by the inspiration of this divine *Numen*, prophesied many of the stupendous works of God and the deeds of the Eternal Word to be born in the flesh, though not without the most obscure veil of allegory.[2]

This had the advantage of acquitting the wise ancients from the crude idolatry and polytheism into which the common people inevitably fell. To such philosophers, the planetary divinities were not beings to be worshipped, but representations of the various ways in which the mind of God, as then known, influences things beneath it. Thus Saturn was an expression of the supreme mind as the light and provider of all things; Jupiter, the 'soul of the world' which keeps everything in order.

A second source of polytheism lay in the solar and lunar cults – already a falling away from the worship of the true God. The syncretic tendency in the later Roman Empire had led to the grouping of all feminine divinities under a single, 'lunar' type, and all masculine ones under a 'solar' type. Kircher follows the same principle in compiling his list of the names of Isis, which include such seemingly incompatible goddesses as Diana and Venus, Hecate and Juno. He interpreted not only Apollo, but also Mercury, Bacchus and Hercules as solar deities, and their attributes and legends as referring to the different properties and powers of the sun in the three worlds.

Thirdly, the gods and their myths might be allegories of physical processes badly understood, like the phenomena of weather or volcanoes. Lastly there was the euhemeristic view (named for Euhemerus, fl. 300 BC), which held that the so-called gods were originally human heroes who had become deified. We will find examples of all four explanations in the images of the gods and goddesses that follow, drawn for the most part from Kircher's Egyptological works, and explained as far as possible with translations or paraphrases of his own words.

Kircher initiated this series in *Obeliscus Pamphilius* with an impressive woodcut of the god Pan (**Ill. 14.1**). In the spirit of the late Renaissance mythographers (Cartari, Giraldi, Pignoria, etc.), he loaded the image with symbolic attributes that, to an audience trained in the Art of Memory, also served as memory-aids. These particular ones were collected from various classical sources by Boccaccio, the fourteenth-century novelist and author of *The Genealogy of the Gods*. Boccaccio had traced Pan's genealogy, but Kircher went much further, explaining it as a Neoplatonic chain of hypostases. First was Ouranos (Coelum, Heaven), who represents God or the One. In the Greek theogony, Ouranos begat Chronos (Saturn), who is the 'first mind'. Chronos begat Zeus (Jupiter), who is the 'world soul'. Zeus was the father of Pan (Greek for 'the All'), who is 'universal nature'.[3]

'Universal nature' includes the planets as well as the earth (assuming, contrarily to Aristotle, that the other planets are not essentially different from our own), and is all held together by a God-given scheme of sympathies and antipathies. The ancients symbolized this by the harmony of the spheres, and this is why Pan holds a syrinx or panpipe with seven pipes, aligned with the seven planetary orbits.

Kircher considered his image of Pan important enough to reproduce it twice more in *Œdipus Ægyptiacus*, and to include three more images in similar

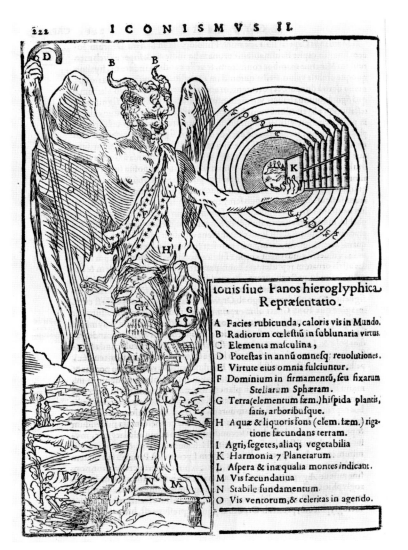

14.1 Pan, surrounded by symbolic attributes, drawn from the Renaissance mythographers. (*Obeliscus Pamphilius*, 222)

A. Ruddy face: the power of heat in the world
B. Power of the heavenly rays upon sublunary nature
C. Masculine elements
D. Power of the periodic return of the year and of all its revolutions
E. Everything is maintained by its virility
F. Power in the firmament, or the sphere of the fixed stars
G. Earth (a feminine element), growing plants and trees
H. Springs of water (feminine elements), fertilizing the earth by irrigation
I. Fields, crops and various forms of vegetable life
K. Harmony of the seven planets
L. Steep mountains
M. Power of fecundity
N. Firm foundation
O. Force of the winds and their speed when agitated

14.2 Isis, Great Mother of the Gods. Her many names are listed in the left-hand column. (*Œdipus Ægyptiacus*, Volume I, 189)

A. Denotes divinity, earth, the celestial spheres
BB. Winding path of the moon and the power of fertility
CC. Power of the moon in herbs and plants
D. Symbol of Ceres; for Isis discovered corn
E. Multicoloured garment of cotton, for the mottled face of the moon
F. Discovery of wheat
G. Dominion over all vegetation
H. Lunar rays
I. [sistrum] Genius of averting the evils of the Nile
K. Waxing and waning of the moon
L. Humidity, the power of the moon
M. [left foot] Victorious and divinatory power of the moon
N. Dominion over the humours and the sea
O. Symbol of the earth, and inventor of medicine
P. Fertility which follows irrigation of the soil
Q. Lady of the stars
R. Nurse of all
S,M. Lady of earth and sea

14.3 Serapis, a composite figure who baffled even Kircher's powers of explanation. (*Œdipus Ægyptiacus*, Volume I, 198)

A. Basket: the fertility of the Nile
B. Juvenile nakedness: the reflorescence after the inundation
C. Measure of the Nile's rising
D. Serapis the author of Time
E. Past time[4]
F. Present, represented by the fawning dog
G. Future, by the oblivious wolf
H. Succession of time
M. Sun's motion, shown by humidity

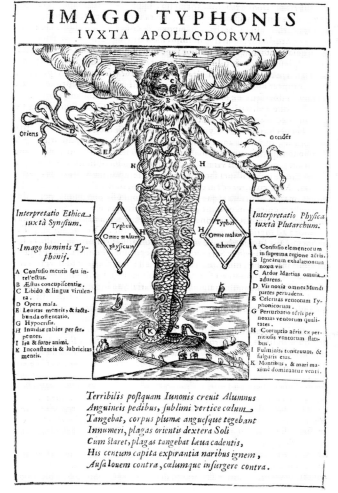

14.4 Typhon, who symbolizes all the evils of the world. (*Œdipus Ægyptiacus*, Volume I, 221)

Left:
A. Confusion of the mind or intellect
B. Fire of lust
C. Desire and virulent speech
D. Evil deeds
E. Frivolity and boasting
G. Hypocrisy
H. Madness of envy, shown by snakes
I. Anger and fury of the soul
K. Inconstancy and lubricity of the mind

Right:
A. Confusion of the elements in the highest region of air
B. Noxious force of fiery exhalations
C. All-consuming Martial heat
D. Noxious force pervading all parts of the world
E. Speed of Typhonic winds
G. Perturbation of the air through noxious qualities of the winds
H. Corruption of the air from the pernicious blowing of the winds
I. Lightning, thunders and destruction
K. Winds mostly prevailing on the mountains and sea

style: those of three Egyptian deities, Isis, Serapis and Typhon. For Isis (**Ill. 14.2**) he had the incomparable witness of Apuleius, fifth-century author of *Metamorphoses, or, The Golden Ass*. In its climactic pages, this novel describes the hero's vision of Isis and his initiation into her mysteries and those of Osiris. 'Every nation calls me by different names,' she tells him (they are listed in the left-hand column of the illustration). Kircher summarizes her in two Greek inscriptions: 'Isis, all-embracing and many-formed daimon; material nature called by a thousand names'; and, at the bottom, 'High mother of the gods, Isis of many names'.

If this made Kircher think of the Virgin Mary and the many names by which Catholics call on her (Queen of Heaven, Star of the Sea, Enclosed Garden, Mother of God, etc.[5]), it may have caused a momentary shudder. But it probably would not have occurred to him that 'Mary' might be just another of Isis's names. No: Isis was the moon! Her names meant nothing more nor less than the effects of the sun and moon upon the earth.

Kircher's exposition of the Egyptian gods was hampered by two great holes in his knowledge: he had no concept of their historical evolution, and he mistook the images of Horus and Osiris. When he came to Serapis (**Ill. 14.3**), he was unaware that this god was a latecomer to the Egyptian pantheon, unknown before the Alexandrian period. He admits that the definitions of the ancients are confusing and contradictory: Serapis is equated to 'subterranean Osiris', to Pluto, to Jupiter Ammon, to the Apis Bull, and even to Joseph, son of Jacob. The Egyptians, however, believed him to be the spirit or harmony of the worlds. Kircher remarks in the margin that these are the physical explanations of Serapis's attributes, but that anagogical, ethical, mystical and other analogies can also be drawn from them.

Osiris should rightly figure in this company, as the solar deity complementary to Isis, but he does not. Instead, Kircher presents his adversary Typhon (**Ill. 14.4**), the Greek version of the god Set who contrived Osiris's murder and dismemberment. If Osiris, in Kircher's scheme, symbolizes all the benefits that the sun brings, Typhon is the symbol of the evils in the world. Anticipating a theme of *Mundus Subterraneus*, Kircher writes of how Typhon represents the spiral winds (typhoons!) churning beneath the surface of the earth that cause earthquakes and erupt in flames and tempests. The ancients believed these to be the work of a subterranean giant or demon, and extended his meaning to cover all ills and evils. This image, based on the Greek mythographer Apollodorus, sets out in parallel the evils of human nature and those of outward nature.

Kircher's recipe for interpreting mythic images never failed him. As Dino Pastine says, 'He never admitted his own ignorance except before the sublimity of the divine essence'.[6] Anything to do with the workings of that essence found a ready explanation within his system. As explained in Chapter 2, this was founded on three worlds, descending in order from God: the Archetypal world, the Sidereal, and the Elementary. Sometimes, under the influence of Kabbalah, he counts not three but four worlds, dividing the upper one into

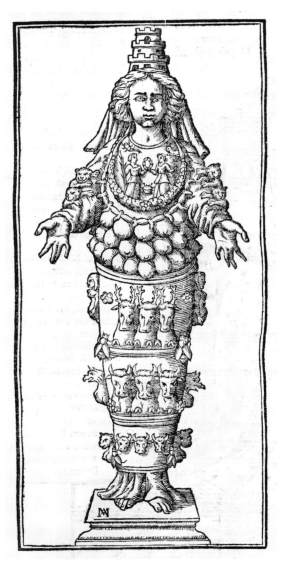

14.5 Many-breasted Isis. Kircher characteristically endows every attribute with cosmological meaning. (*Œdipus Ægyptiacus*, Volume I, 190)

the inaccessible idea of all the worlds in the mind of God (Atziluth) and the first expression of this idea in the angelic world (Briah, equivalent in paganism to the world of the Genii). This is the case when he comes to interpret the striking image generally known as 'Diana of Ephesus' (**Ill. 14.5**).

Kircher calls this a statue of 'Isis' or 'the Grecian Cybele'. He interprets it, broadly speaking, as the work of the Supreme Spirit that flows into the four worlds. The crowned head represents the Archetypal world; the pectoral, the world of Genii; the breasts, the Sidereal world ('whose stars are like breasts'); the skirt, the Elementary world with its three zones of animal, vegetable and mineral. He interprets its symbols or 'hieroglyphs' as manifold aspects of the universal feminine divinity. The threefold mural crown represents the three types of government that Isis introduced into the world. The pectoral bears the signs of the zodiac, through which influences flow into the world, notably Capricorn and Cancer, referring to the tropics and hence to the virtues of solar heat. The four lions on her arms amplify this theme of Isis as giver of strength; her many breasts signify the abundance and liberality with which she nourishes the lower worlds.

The cone-shaped skirt is divided into three zones to represent the three zones of the lower world. The three stags' heads refer to Diana, protector of plants and beasts. The bulls' heads refer to Isis's transformation into a cow, and the pair of bees to the legend that she taught agriculture and bee-keeping to mankind. As for the dragons' heads, these are the traditional guardians of trees and gardens, and signify Nature's unceasing care and prudence. Three further bulls' heads refer to the three parts of the year when the earth is tilled by oxen.[7]

This is a particularly full example of Kircher's cosmological intepretation, which always begins with the higher worlds and descends to the lower ones. Most of his readings of obelisk inscriptions follow this model. His other mode of approach is ethical, though as we have seen in the commentary to Typhon, the two approaches are not contrary but linked through analogy: every virtue and vice in man has its correspondence in the happy or unhappy effects of nature. Kircher's most elaborate ethical interpretation comes when he tackles the image of Harpocrates (**Ill. 14.6**), which he found in Herwart von Hohenberg's *Theatrum Hieroglyphicorum*. Harpocrates, supposedly the son of Isis and Serapis, was a hybrid Graeco-Egyptian deity, partly based on the image of Horus as a child holding his finger to his lips. This gesture easily lent itself to an interpretation in the spirit of the Mysteries,[8] and explains why Kircher put it on the closing page of *Obeliscus Pamphilius* with the inscription 'With this one I disclose secrets'. Here I translate part of what he writes about it, only commenting that nothing here is contrary to Christian asceticism:

14.6 Harpocrates, god of contemplation, the son of Isis and Serapis: 'With this one I disclose secrets.' (*Obeliscus Pamphilius*, 316)

Harpocrates is shown as a seated boy with snaky locks, pressing his finger to his lips to enjoin silence. His other hand holds a torch and three poppy heads. On the top of his head, emerging from a moon in its sextile phase, is an ear in which a leaf of the persea tree is inserted. Behind his back is a quiver with a bow, beside which is an owl also having an ear with a persea leaf emerging from its head. Then there is a cock, as shown in this illustration. The Hieromystae [priests of the Mysteries] indicated by this the idea of the wise man, illustrated by these symbols. Harpocrates is seated, because wisdom alone induces calm and tranquillity in the soul. He is young, because unfading wisdom always flourishes and grows. He holds his finger to his lips, because wisdom is learnt not amid noise and tumult but in silence, solitude, seclusion and contempt of all earthly things. The latter is indicated by the owl, a nocturnal and solitary bird. Harpocrates has a cock beside him, because he is wise in all his actions, and he must be vigilant lest he should unexpectedly transgress. He presses the throat of the cock with his left elbow [in the reversed illustration, his right], to show that the quiet and leisure of contemplation are not to be interrupted by the importunate actions of the daytime, of which the cock

is the herald and customarily awakens men to them with his voice. Thus, as Harpocrates presses his finger to his lips, so he forces the cock to be quiet by squeezing its throat; and now with a soft voice in its throat, it feels a silent and internal incitement. He has an ear on his head, with persea leaves inserted, because while Horapollo testifies that they resemble tongues, so the fruit expresses the figure of a heart; for wisdom must be listened to and teaches through the tongue and the wise master. He holds poppies with a lit torch, because the wise should be most attentive to death, signified by the poppy, and to meditation on higher things, and on the highest as signified by the lit torch. The quiver behind his back and the carelessly projected bow indicate that whoever wants to enter the penetralia of wisdom must first of all renounce all earthly things; and the corruption of obnoxious things, which are symbolized by the moon and the serpent of fleeting time, as Horapollo says, must be quite forgotten.[9]

In Herwart's collection, Kircher also found an image of Anubis, the Egyptian god with a jackal's or dog's head (**Ill. 14.7**). It was said to be from a stele originating in the temple of Isis, with symbols carved in relief. Taking the

14.7 Cynocephalic Mercury: in reality the Egyptian god Anubis. (*Obeliscus Pamphilius*, 294)

A. Dog-head of Anubis
B. Nudity, signifying truth
D. Caduceus, standing for quickness of mind and eloquence
E. He protects Egypt against Typhon (the crocodile)
G, K. Amon and Serapis, brother gods to Mercury, with baskets signifying the gifts of Anubis
F. Stars rising and setting, marking the Nile flood
L. Olive branch, denoting well-being
M. Palm leaf, denoting sterility[10]

euhemerist approach, he writes that Mercury (i.e. Hermes Trismegistus), the first lawgiver of Egypt, was called after his death 'Anubis', meaning 'dog', on account of that animal's skill in seeking and finding things. The dog in turn gave its name to the star Sirius, whose heliacal rising heralds the Nile flood and all the benefits that this brings to Egypt.

Kircher does not explain the other items here, but the image was of signal importance to his first hieroglyphic theories. In *Prodromus Coptus* he claims that the M in a triangle is an abbreviation of the name Amon, and an example of a phonetic sign (later taken over into the Greek and Latin alphabets) serving the symbolic purpose of a hieroglyph.[11] As for the crocodile, it stands for the ineffable nature of God because the animal has no tongue (or so says the Arabic authority Abenephi). A picture of a crocodile hiding in its den but showing its tail (says Valerianus) also refers to God, whose 'head' or substance is unknowable, but whose 'tail' can be known through his works. Then again, a crocodile in a boat bearing the sun indicates the sun's motion in humidity, causing generation. The crocodile symbolizes the sun itself through its prominent eyes, and through the fact that it is hatched from its egg by light, without any parental incubation. It can simply represent the land of Egypt, or the Nile, as on the coins of Augustus.[12] These are a sample of the lore that Kircher collects about all the creatures that appear in the hieroglyphs.

The last Egyptian deity that Kircher illustrates is Amon, whom he calls 'the Egyptian Jupiter' (**Ill. 14.8**). Lacking an original image, he invents his own on the basis of classical, Hebrew, Arabic and Ethiopian sources. He reports that travellers to Ethiopia still find idols and oracles of Amon in use there. The left-hand image comes from Pausanius, who writes that statues of Amon are found among the Arcadians, showing the god (A) with ram's horns, (B) mitred, (C) with the square base of a herm, and (D) draped with skin. Others represent Amon under the symbols of (E) an omphalos or navel, or (F) a ram. The right-hand image wears (G) a ram's hide, and (H) holds out his hand in the gesture of giving.

Kircher's treatment of Amon typifies the contradiction that runs through so much of his work. On the one hand there is his command of anything from twelve to thirty-five languages,[13] and his ability to pull the most recondite quotation off the shelf, or out of his memory. On the other hand, there is his carelessness in any matter of which he is ignorant, as for example the true nature of the Egyptian god Amon-Ra. This image only sows confusion in the reader's imagination by putting an Egyptian god into an Arcadian setting.

Another fictitious monument is called 'a Samaritan shrine' (**Ill. 14.9**). The enmity between these people and the Jews is proverbial. Kircher quotes rabbinic sources that trace it to the desecration of the Temple by a group of Samaritans. He also gives a long quotation in Samaritan characters from a Vatican Library manuscript, describing a schism between Jews and Samaritans under Alexander the Great. The Samaritans then serve as a type for all the idol-worshipping peoples adjacent to Israel. Kircher collects the names of their many deities, mostly from rabbinic writings, and tries to deduce what form

A Ammon
  arietinis
  cornibus.
B Mitratus.
C Tetrago-
  nus Her-
  mes.
D Pellis.
E Inſtar vm
  bilici pin-
  gebatur.
F Integrô
  ariete re-
  ferebatur
G Pelle ſeu
  exuuijs
  arietis .
H Et in ſta-
  tura ho-
  minis ex-
  tendentis
  manum
  ad dandú
  parati.

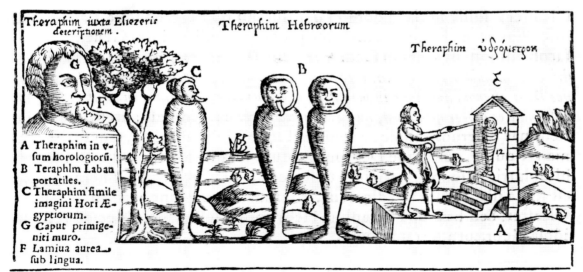

Theraphim iuxta Eliezeris
deſcriptionem .

Theraphim Hebræorum

Theraphim ὑδρόμετρον

A Theraphim in v-
  ſum horologiorū.
B Teraphlm Laban
  portatiles.
C Theraphim ſimile
  imagini Hori Æ-
  gyptiorum.
G Caput primige-
  niti muro.
F Lamiua aurea
  ſub lingua.

▸▴ 14.8 Amon, an image invented by
Kircher on the basis of classical, Arabic,
Hebrew and Egyptian sources. (Œdipus
Ægyptiacus, Volume I, 205)

▴ 14.9 A Samaritan shrine, a fictitious
monument invented by Kircher, who knew
of the enmity between Samaritans and
Jews. (Œdipus Ægyptiacus, Volume I, 367).

◂ 14.10 The theraphim of the Hebrews.
Kircher's curious reconstruction of idolatry
among the ancient Hebrews, with the
severed head of the first-born (G) placed on
a wall. (Œdipus Ægyptiacus, Volume I, 261)

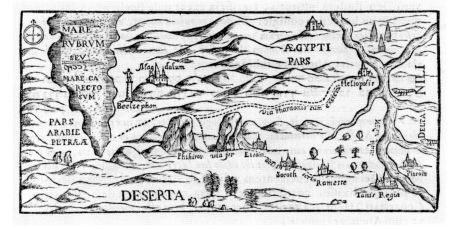

▲▲ **14.11** Moloch, a bloodthirsty god, to whom the Ammonites sacrificed their children. (*Œdipus Ægyptiacus*, Volume I, 334)

▲ **14.12** Beelzephon, a magical Egyptian image in the desert that prevented slaves from escaping. (*Œdipus Ægyptiacus*, Volume I, 279)

▶▲ **14.13** Derceto – a fish-like goddess mentioned by Ovid and identified by Kircher with a deity of the Syrians and the Philistines. (*Œdipus Ægyptiacus*, Volume I, 341)

▶ **14.14** Mithras and the bull. Mithras, according to Kircher, was the Persian name for Osiris and is a vegetation god, awakening life by the sun. (*Œdipus Ægyptiacus*, Volume I, 217)

their idols took. His object, as ever, is to trace each one to its roots in some perversion of the true theology, usually as an aspect of the sun or moon.

He then invents this seaside 'shrine', with curlicues like a Baroque altarpiece, and fills it up with images of outlandish deities. Some are familiar, e.g. (1) the ass-headed Typhon and (2) jackal-headed Anubis, holding Mercury's wand. Others are borrowed from the Graeco-Roman pantheon. Mercury is present as a herm (7); Pan, as a goat (8). Juno is symbolized by her peacock (10), Saturn by a star (6). Most curious is the presence of Noah's Ark (9), but Kircher's sources report that this, too, enjoyed the status of an 'idol' or object of worship among local peoples.

Kircher's rabbinic sources were at the origin of one of his oddest illustrations (**Ill. 14.10**) and one of his most disagreeable stories. This occurs in the course of a long dissertation on the 'Hebrew pantheon', or on polytheism and idolatry among the ancient Jews. First, the theraphim were house or family idols, as mentioned in Genesis 31:19 where Rachel steals the theraphim of Laban and hides them under her saddle. Second, according to Hebrew and Syriac commentators, they were the amputated heads of the first-born, preserved with salt and spices and placed on a wall (see G in the illustration). Inscribed gold leaves (F) were placed beneath their tongues, and they were then consulted and made to predict the future. A third use of the theraphim was in hydrometers or water-clocks, marked with the hours (A).

Kircher's explanation for these unseemly objects is that after Abraham came to the land of Canaan, his servants mingled with the Egyptians and caught the habit of idolatry from them. Even among Jacob's womenfolk and servants, it was still rife. The word 'theraphim' is simply a derivation from the Egyptian god Serapis, and Laban's idols were typical Egyptian idols (B and C). In case we wonder why these statuettes, so commonly offered by antique dealers, lack hands and feet, Kircher suggests that they were held in such reverence that it was better not to make them with parts that might break off.[14]

Another neighbour of the Hebrews was the tribe of the Ammonites, who sacrificed their sons and daughters to the idol of their god Moloch (**Ill. 14.11**). It stood in the valley of Tophet, and, according to rabbinic sources, had seven receptacles for burning the victims, each one marked with a different beast. The worshipper would choose a door and throw his or her child inside, while the music of drums and shouting would drown out the infant's shrieks.

Kircher sees the seven doors as a distorted image of the seven heavens, and the idol itself as a symbol of what the sun can cause when its influences are too strong: drought, sterility and famine. After the death of the Egyptian king known as Osiris, the land was thus afflicted, and the people started making human sacrifices in the hope of placating the god and bringing on the life-giving Nile flood. He points out that remnants of these customs are still visible in the Bible, when Abraham prepares to sacrifice Isaac, and in the Jewish custom of passing an infant harmlessly over the fire. Moreover, travellers and missionaries report that they are still going on, notably in a certain valley in Japan where 'innumerable victims are immolated every year in honour of Zaca and Amida'. The chapter closes with the well-known quotation from the Epicurean philosopher Lucretius on the many evils for which religion is responsible.

Few contemporaries could match Kircher's rabbinic lore, or contest his interpretations of it. Whoever had heard of Beelzephon (**Ill. 14.12**)? According to Rabbi Abenezra, the Egyptian magicians erected astrological images of brass in the desert, which they called by this name, and which put out an occult force that prevented any slave from fleeing Egypt. As we know, Kircher was reluctant to accept the occultist explanation until every other one had been exhausted. His studies of the machines of the ancients gave him the clue in this case. He knew how the pagan priests had used their knowledge of the hidden forces of nature, like steam, magnetism, acoustic and optical tricks, in order to fool the populace into believing in their gods. This was no different. The images of Beelzephon were made by *natural* magic in order to create the illusion of demons, and thus to scare any runaway slaves. He adds that the reader will see this principle applied throughout the work,[15] and indeed we have seen him propose using it for Christian purposes as well.

The goddess Derceto (**Ill. 14.13**) is mentioned by Ovid as a scaly-skinned figure haunting the Palestinian marshes.[16] Kircher identifies her as Atergatis, the Syrian goddess, and Dagon, the fish-god of the Philistines, and calls all of them 'none other than the maritime Venus'. Although in later life he would hearken to tales of mermaids, here he explains her form through the Egyptian custom of representing their gods and goddesses by wearing the skins and heads (and tails?) of animals. In the end, she is just another form of the universal moon-goddess, and her meaning is the lunar influence on growing things, especially those in water.

This woodcut draws on the legend recorded by Diodorus Siculus (2.4.2) that Derceto fell in love with a youth and killed herself on his account. Her mother, the goddess, saved her and placed her on a tower in the desert, where she was fed by doves, but overcome by shame, she threw herself into the marsh and turned into a fish. For this reason, the Syrians never eat fishes, and build their temples in marshy places. Another legend has Derceto as the mother of Queen Semiramis, to whom Kircher ascribes many of the grandest monuments of antiquity.[17]

The mystery religion of Mithras, so popular in the Roman Empire, especially among soldiers, seems to have passed Kircher by entirely. It is true that there are next to no classical sources concerning it, but that what is known comes from the Christian Fathers (naturally hostile) and from the monuments themselves. To Kircher, this was no problem when he was faced with a stele showing the most common Mithraic image, the Taurocthony or the god killing the bull (**Ill. 14.14**). Mithras, he says, is the same to the Persians as Osiris to the Egyptians. His name comes from Mythraim, who was the first king of both peoples and was paid divine honours as Zoroaster. One finds statues of this type in the Villas Ludovisi and Borghese, and in the walls of

SYNT. IV. PANTHEON HEBRÆORVM.   341

A   Signum Tauri in Aprili, seu Terra.
K   Mythras, Sol.
M   Vis Solis penetratiua eliciens genitalem humorem.
N   Terrestrium animalium nutrimentum.
O
Q   Vis confortatiua Solis.
R   Vis genitalis abscondita.
S   Sole in Scorpione constituto, vis genitalis frigore comprimitur.
T   Sole in Scorpione existente, calor minuitur, vnde corruptio.
X   Sole in Tauro, igneus
Y   calor inualescit ad
Z   generationem vegetabilium.

14.15 Leontocephalic Aion, a mysterious figure of Mithraism whom Kircher saw as the Egyptian god Momphta. (*Œdipus Ægyptiacus*, Volume III, 504)

in the private garden of the Duke of Muti, near Villa Ludovisi, and immediately fitted it into his Egyptian theology, identifying it as Momphta. This obscure god was one of his favourites, believed to symbolize the infusion of vital warmth into the universe, hence the universal principle of life and growth. The attributes of Aion fit the requirements: his keys show that he has jurisdiction over all the worlds, the serpent wrapped around his body represents vital warmth, and the globe beneath his feet is the earth.[18]

Although Kircher found the classical pantheon much less interesting than older or more exotic ones, he applied the same kind of interpretation to it. Three examples published in 1650 probably date from far earlier, for they concern objects known to Peiresc, and a book by Gafurio that any music theorist would have studied.

The first figure of a composite plate (**Ill. 14.16**) shows the Rape of Proserpine (Persephone) by Pluto, as figured in an antique bas-relief.[19] The second figure is a compound of solar symbols and attributes derived from the mythographers Phornutus, Fulgentius, Apollodorus and Macrobius. The third figure represents Mercury, who according to Kircher is 'nothing other than the sun's attractive energy'. Kircher extracted the image 'from the antiquities museum of the most excellent Lord Claudius Menedrius [or Manedrius], in which the symbols of almost all the gods occur: in the rays of the head, Apollo; in the horns, Ammon; in the ivy crown, Bacchus; in the lionskin, Hercules; in the serpents, Aesculapius; in the quiver and arrows, Diana; in the helmet, Pallas; lastly Mercury in the winged feet and shoulders'.[20]

The fourth figure is the solar deity of the 'Hieropolitani, who are a people of Assyria'. The most noteworthy elements here are the three figures rising from the ground (I, K, L): they represent Matter, Earth and Nature, and the serpent is the 'flexible path of the sun', i.e. its variation through the seasons.

The 'Symbolic scheme of the nine Muses and Apollo, after the idea of the mythologers, the Greeks and the Hebrews' (**Ill. 14.17**) imitates a woodcut illustration in Francesco Gafurio's *Practica Musica* (1496). The arcs should be imagined as continuing for 360 degrees, to make a diagram of the concentric spheres of the seven planets, the starry heaven and the Primum Mobile, all going round the earth in harmonious order.

The diagram, here as in Gafurio, illustrates the theory of correspondences, of which the idea of the harmony of the spheres is a well-known example. Its basis is the correspondence of the spheres of the cosmos (here marked with their planetary symbols, stars, etc.) with the notes of the scale (here given on the right, in Greek terminology). Gafurio also added the Muses (their names given in the centre, in capital letters), Apollo as ruler of the Primum Mobile, and the three-headed serpent Python as a link between all the worlds. Kircher contributes a Hebrew component: on the right, the first ten letters of the Hebrew alphabet, and on the left, the Hebrew names of the various ranks of angels (e.g. 'Seraphim' for the sixth sphere of Mars). In a bold syncretism, Apollo is thereby made equivalent to Metatron, the highest of the angelic hierarchy and first minister after God,

the Doge's Palace, among other places. The image refers to the sun's activity in Taurus (that is, in April), when it awakens vegetable life in the earth. The various elements are: (A, bull) Taurus; (K, Mithras) the sun; (M, sword) the sun's energy awakening generation; (N, blood, O, dog) the food of earthly creatures; (Q, lion) the sun's strengthening power; (R, testicles) the generative force removed; (S, scorpion) the sun in Scorpio, restricting the generative force; (T, scorpion) when the sun is in Scorpio, the heat lessens, causing corruption; (X, bull, Y, torch, Z, plant) when the sun is in Taurus, the heat increases and causes the generation of plants. So there is nothing more here than a symbol of the sun's effects between April and October.

In the underground temples of Mithras, one often comes across another image, that of the lion-headed god Aion (**Ill. 14.15**). Kircher found this statue

14.16 Ancient gods interpreted: a whole range of Roman gods and goddesses with their attributes and powers. The lower panels are fantastic representations of Mercury, Apollo and Osiris. (*Obeliscus Pamphilius*, 226) The top panel contains the following:

A. Ceres, the great mother of fruits, or the earth
B. Torches, the fiery heat of the sun through which the fruits are ripened
C. Furrow (or ploughing) of the fields, or the innate energy of the earth for producing fruits
D. Minerva, the moon's warmth
E. Diana, the moon's humid energy
F. Proserpine, cereals, herbs, plants
G. Pluto, the lower or wintry sun
HH. The four seasons of the year, or the four things with which it dominates the earth: earth, minerals, plants, fruits
I. Hercules [shows] the labour and industry in agriculture, or the same season
K. Jupiter, the seminal energy, i.e. what he sends from heaven
L. The vase turned over indicates the winter season, in which the flowers perish
M. The heavenly motion and the consequent season, essential for agriculture[21]

14.17 'Symbolic scheme of the nine Muses and Apollo, after the idea of the mythologers, the Greeks and the Hebrews.' Following Francesco Gafurio (1496), Kircher correlates the Muses with the spheres of the Cosmos, the letters of the Hebrew alphabet and the ranks of the angels. (*Obeliscus Pamphilius*, 244)

◄ **14.18** Mysteries of Apollo, an ancient marble tablet illustrating the power and responsibilities of Apollo, Bacchus, Hercules and Mercury. (*Œdipus Ægyptiacus*, Volume II, i, 206)

A. Apollo in juvenile form; sunrise
B. Sun's rays
C. Penetrative power in the quiver
D. Penetrative power, and throwing of rays
E. Costume of a physician or prophet, because of divination
F. Energy of vaticination
G. Energy in plants, flowers, fruits, trees
H. The sun's power in Hercules' lionskin
I. Hercules' clubs, the sun's solidifying energy
K. Bacchus's cup, the sun's humid and concoctive energy
L. Stability in action
M. Mercurial heaps, guardian of the fields
N. Harmony of the worlds, and effects of the sun
O. Life of the world, and domination in all things
P. Energy of the sun's rays in the reed stalk
Q. Consonance of the seven planets with the sun
R. The black part of the middle rod signifies night
S. The white part, day[24]

► **14.19** Tiburtine Sybil: she lived in the time of Augustus and predicted the coming of Christ. (*Latium*, 196)

that is, the spirit of rational life moved to communication, which is the angel Metatron, and is called the intellect of the sensible world supplying life to all lower things by the penetration of forms, flowing with its virtue into all that can move; and all this was anciently made known through Apollo, son of Jupiter, who we have said above is the soul of the world, and leader of the nine Muses represented by the eight celestial spheres and the Elemental world.[22]

This is an example of the first type of interpretation listed above, in which the pagan gods conceal true metaphysical mysteries.

The image that Kircher calls 'The Mysteries of Apollo, Bacchus, Hercules, and Mercury' (**Ill. 14.18**) looks home-made, but actually it depicts an ancient tablet of white marble, a foot and a half (half a metre) square, that was illustrated in Aleandro's book of 1616.[23] As Kircher later writes:

The ancients signified by Apollo, with his arrows and rays, nothing other than the sun, or the insensible and supramundane archetype that penetrates all sensible things and arranges them in a harmony. By Bacchus, they meant the ripening and digestive faculty in all things; by Hercules, the solidifying and invigorating of all things; and by Mercury, the sun's rapid energy working in all things. Thus they represented the one essence and nature of the supreme deity under four faculties.[25]

Crossing over from the pagan to the Christian world, we find as transitional figures the Twelve Sibyls. They were not goddesses, but legendary prophetesses revered in Roman lore: the Sybilline Books were a source of divination in ancient Roman history and religion. Towards the end of the pre-Christian era, new 'Sybilline' oracles were invented for propaganda on behalf of the Jews and not long after, further ones for the benefit of the Christians. The number of Sibyls was then established as twelve, each belonging to a different region, and their oracles, duly worked into Latin verse, were presented as prophetic of the coming of Christ. Kircher was particularly interested in the Tiburtine Sibyl (**Ill. 14.19**), whose residence was at one of his favourite places, Tivoli. She supposedly lived in the reign of the Emperor Augustus, and

SIBYLLA TIBURTINA *dicta* ALBUNEA

By applying the same theories of religious origins to Hinduism and Buddhism, Kircher made them appear as deviant as the ancient paganisms. They seemed to be uncouth, dinosauric remnants of superstitions that the Christian world had long since cast away. It only remained for the Enlightenment philosophers to do away with Christianity as well, and there was little motivation for further discovery or scholarship. It was a century before Sir William Jones and the Calcutta School began the concerted attempt to understand Eastern religions on their own terms: first Hinduism, then, after a considerable hiatus, Buddhism.[27]

Notes

1   This was not entirely Kircher's fault. Writing to Peiresc on 3 December 1636 of his difficulties studying Arabic works, he sighs 'if only the Koran were not so sternly prohibited here in Rome'. BNP, Fonds français No. 9538, f. 236–8, cited in Fletcher 2006, [369].

2   *Œdipus Ægyptiacus*, II, i, 191. The *Numen* is previously defined as the 'divine afflatus' that inspired the Hebrew prophets and the Sibyls to anticipate the birth of Christ.

3   *Œdipus Ægyptiacus*, II, i, 199.

4   Captions E–G are wrong, but corrected in the text: the all-devouring wolf should represent the past, the vigilant lion the present, and the fawning, hopeful dog the future.

5   According to Jeffrey Chipps Smith, the *Litany of Loreto*, with its string of over forty epithets of the Virgin, was promoted by the Jesuits as a popular form of devotion and approved for liturgical use in 1587 (Smith, 145).

6   Pastine, 86.

7   *Œdipus Ægyptiacus*, I, 190–192.

8   Rachewiltz and Partini, 76–77.

9   *Obeliscus Pamphilius*, 316–317.

10 *Obeliscus Pamphilius*, 295.

11 *Prodromus Coptus*, 233.

12 *Obeliscus Pamphilius*, 306–307.

13 'In this Roman College we speak thirty-five languages!' – Kircher to Queen Christina, 11 November, 1651 (APUG Ms. 561, f.50).

14 *Œdipus Ægyptiacus*, I, 254–261.

15 *Œdipus Ægyptiacus*, I, 278.

16 *Metamorphoses*, 4, 45–46.

17 *Œdipus Ægyptiacus*, I, 341.

18 *Œdipus Ægyptiacus*, III, 504–505.

19 From Girolamo Aleandro's *Expositio Sigillorum Zonae Veterum Statuam Marmoream Cingentes*. Published as an appendix to his *Antiquae Tabulae Marmoreae Solis Effigie* (Rome and Paris, 1616). For a reproduction, see [Peiresc], *Correspondance de Peiresc et Aleandro*, Volume I, pl. IV.

20 *Obeliscus Pamphilius*, 233.

21 *Obeliscus Pamphilius*, 225.

22 *Obeliscus Pamphilius*, 243.

23 For a reproduction, see [Peiresc], *Correspondance de Peiresc et Aleandro*, vol. I, pl. III.

24 *Obeliscus Pamphilius*, 235.

25 *Œdipus Ægyptiacus*, II, i, 205.

26 Especially Charles Dupuis, in *L'Origine de Tous les Cultes* (1794) and Sir William Drummond in the significantly titled *Oedipus Judaicus* (1811). On the fortunes of the solar theory after the Enlightenment, see Godwin 1994, 27–48. For evidence of its more ancient origins, see Fideler.

27 I have treated this process in Godwin 1994, 322–328.

foretold Jesus' annunciation in Nazareth and his birth in Bethlehem. In his late topographical study of Latium, Kircher writes that she was grafted onto Albunea, the original goddess of the region. His artist has adapted this image from a French book of 1586, *Sibyllarum Duodecim: Les Oracles des Douze Sibyls*. She holds a book in one hand, containing her prophecies, and in the other (for reasons I cannot explain) a whip.

Returning to the statement at the beginning of this chapter, we can see that Kircher's history of religions had its own integrity. He was primarily an adherent of the astral theory – that the gods and goddesses of polytheism originated in the worship of the heavenly bodies, especially the sun and moon. Human folly, given a slight push on the part of the Devil, had sufficed to divert our ancestors from the true faith, leaving only philosophers like Hermes, Zoroaster, Plato and his school in possession of the truth: that there is one God, and that the sun and moon are agents of his harmoniously designed universe. The solar theory of religious origins had a long life, and maybe still holds good in part. What Kircher could never have imagined is that one day freethinking antiquarians would apply it to Judaism and Christianity, too.[26]

Chapter 15   Didactic Images

Kircher the mathematics teacher knew how much can be drawn out of a simple geometrical diagram, if one only asks the right questions of it. The students' notes on his early lectures are already rich in figures and sketches, anticipating the use of graphics in his later books.[1] This final chapter addresses some of the illustrations that remain after the stories in the earlier chapters have essentially been told. They can be difficult to understand and not immediately attractive, but some readers will appreciate the deeper insights to which they give access, both into Kircher's mind and into the mentality of his era.

The simplest such diagram lies at the heart of Kircher's cosmology (**Ill. 15.1**). He ascribes its origin to ancient Egypt, though in fact he derived it from Robert Fludd, who had developed it as an illustration of a philosophical notion of Nicholas of Cusa. It is a shorthand sign for the Hermetic conception of a universe made from two contrary substances, or tendencies. One tendency, shown by the light pyramid, is spiritual and has its base or maximum (AB) in the perfection of God, its apex or minimum (C) on earth. The other, dark pyramid is material and the source of all suffering and evil; its base (DE) is on earth, and it gradually diminishes as it rises through the heavenly spheres until, on reaching God, it vanishes altogether (F). Kircher uses the image to explain the Egyptian love of building obelisks and pyramids. They buried their kings and heroes under huge pyramids 'to bear witness that once the body had dissolved and corrupted, the soul survives'. But they also believed that after the 'Hermetic cycle' of 36,500 years, the entire world is renewed, and the soul descends into another body.[2]

One development of the intersecting pyramids leads to the 'sphere of love', a diagram printed three times in *Œdipus Ægyptiacus* (**Ill. 15.2**).[3] Kircher says that it is found frequently among hieroglyphic inscriptions. Without a doubt, he invented it himself, for it derives from his idiosyncratic reading of the Bembine Table. Its source is the tiny tablet held by the scarab-man (see **Ill. 4.2**) which served as the starting point for a weighty symbolic structure, including his reconstruction of the Egyptian world system (see **Ill. 4.4**). He creates it by taking the four Coptic letters ΦVΛO that he alone perceived on the tablet, and combining them. Their geometrical forms provide a circle, a vertical line, and the light and dark intersecting pyramids. The circle is the spherical world, with its poles at A and B, its equator at C and D. The winged sphere is the threefold 'soul of the world', which enters the world and stirs

up its contents, filling them with love. Its penetrating influence is the light pyramid, with its base at C, while the dark pyramid based at D shows the dark, infernal and material mixtures rising upwards. When he includes this diagram among the Elogia preceding the text of *Œdipus Ægyptiacus*, Kircher adds as a title an adaptation of his favourite Virgilian phrase: *Sic agitat molem, et magno se corpore miscet* (Thus it shakes the heap, and mingles itself with the great body). He implies that this is what the 'Trismegistic' Ferdinand III does to his empire.

As already explained, Kircher's cosmology was based on four worlds, though he only presumed to speak of three. The first is the absolute unity of all things in God, which can only be called a 'world' by analogy with the others. The second is the Angelic world (in pagan language, the world of Genii; otherwise called the Archetypal world), which humans are able to know through their higher intellect. The third is the Celestial or Sidereal world of stars and planets, known through reason. The fourth is the Elemental world, known through the senses.

This diagram (**Ill. 15.3**), derived from Pico della Mirandola, represents the three lower worlds in two different ways.[4] On the vertical axis, we see the outer circle containing a stack of three circles, representing the three worlds: Angelic at the top, Celestial in the middle, Elemental at the bottom. Each world in turn serves as the containing circle for a stack of three smaller circles, called by Kircher 'choruses' or orders. These, furthermore, contain their own stacks of tiny circles. Perhaps the system goes on ad infinitum, like a fractal diagram.

The qualities of the three groups of tiny circles are expressed through numbers. The top group of each world is numbered 2, 3, 4, to which 1 must be added for the circle containing them, for a total of 10. The middle group is numbered 20, 30, 40, which plus 10 equals 100. The lowest group is numbered 200, 300, 400, which plus 100 equals 1,000. The progression from 10 to its square (100) and cube (1,000) is a mathematical analogy of the descent from the perfect unity of God into progressive solidification and complication.

The horizontal axis shows much the same scheme, only here the nine divisions of each world are named. The Angelic world contains the traditional Nine Orders of Angels: Seraphim, Cherubim, Thrones, Dominions, Virtues, Powers, Principalities, Archangels, Angels. The diagram is not quite correct

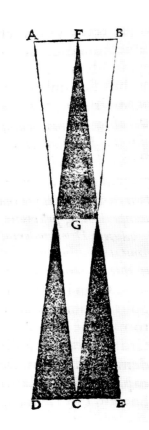

► **15.1** Light and dark pyramids: a diagram of Kircher's world-view. The light is the spiritual cosmos, the source of all good, the dark the material cosmos, the source of evil. (*Œdipus Ægyptiacus*, Volume II, ii, 212)

▼ **15.2** The 'sphere of love'. Kircher thought that the four Coptic letters of the Bembine Table yielded a complex system including the light and dark pyramids. (*Œdipus Ægyptiacus*, Volume II, ii, 112)

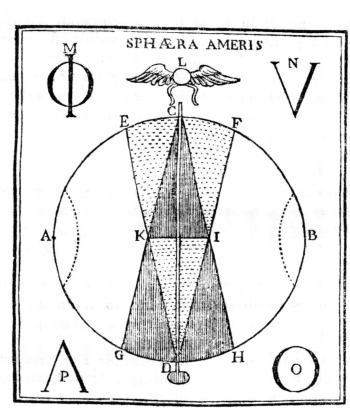

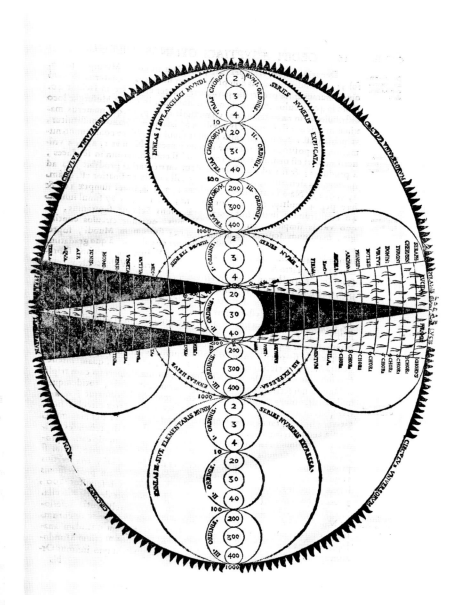

15.3 System of worlds, combining the light and dark pyramids with a mathematical allegory of the Angelic, Celestial and Elemental Worlds. (*Œdipus Ægyptiacus*, Volume II, ii, 15)

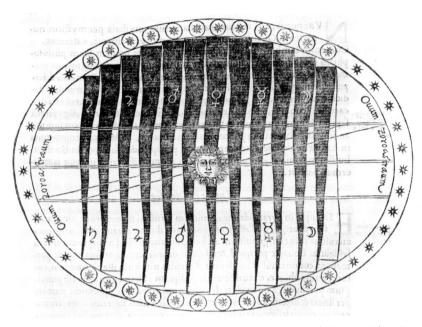

15.4 Zoroaster's egg. According to Plutarch, Oromazes put twenty-four good gods (white pyramids) to rule the cosmos, but Ahriman put twenty-four bad ones (black) in the same egg, which accounts for the mixture of good and evil in the world. The illustrator manages to show only twelve of each. (*Obeliscus Pamphilius*, 177)

in including in the Angelic world the Primum Mobile and the firmament. These belong, according to Kircher's text,[5] in the Sidereal world, which continues with the planets Saturn, Jupiter, Mars, the sun, Venus, Mercury and the moon, to make nine spheres. Nor do the divisions of the Elemental world correlate with the textual list of man, animal, zoophyte, tree, fruiting plant, herb, minerals, mixtures and elements. What is more significant is the pair of pyramids, one dark and one light. They illustrate the diminution of the divine light, at its maximum with the Seraphim and tapering off to a minimum at the bottom of the Elemental world.

The text explains, moreover, how each world corresponds to the whole, such that the highest orders of angels are concerned only with their own world, while the middle order is occupied with maintaining the harmony of the universe, and the lowest triad (Principalities, Archangels, Angels) with mankind.

The format of Kircher's page may have been responsible for compressing what should be a perfectly circular diagram into an elliptical shape. On the other hand, it might be a reference to Orphic theology, which gives the world the symbol and form of an egg.

In *Obeliscus Pamphilius* (**Ill. 15.4**), Kircher ingeniously adapts the symbol of intersecting pyramids to another ancient theology, the dualistic one of Persia, and simultaneously to astrology. According to Plutarch, Oromazes (the 'good god' of Persian theology) put twenty-four gods as stars into an egg, and charged them to rule the world. Thereupon Ahriman (the 'bad god') put

twenty-four opposite stars in the northern hemisphere, whose rays mingled with those of the good stars. The Egyptians likewise divided the heavens into forty-eight constellations: twenty-four good ones in the southern hemisphere, ruled by Osiris, twenty-four in the sinister north, which is the origin of darkness, famine, poison and the malignant realm of Typhon. Their superstitious religion required them to placate the evil genii and cultivate the good ones.[6]

In Kircher's diagram, he says that 'Here you see twenty-four stars in the north, twenty-four in the south, with as many obverse pyramids, twenty-four white and as many black, which are the roots of the genii of light and darkness.'[7] (In fact, only twelve of each type of pyramid are visible.) As the stellar influences pass through the spheres of the sun, moon and the other planets, they make various blends: of good stars with good planets, bad ones with bad, and every mixture in between. The earth is the recipient of these influences.

The Hermetic world-view holds that the macrocosm or megacosm (chiefly meaning the Sidereal world) is reflected in the microcosm of the human being. At the same time, in the web of sympathies and antipathies out of which the universe is woven, every star has its corresponding member in the animal, vegetable and mineral kingdoms. Since events in the macrocosm must affect the microcosm, this is the rationale for astrology and astrological medicine. To explain this, Kircher devised an elaborate 'Illustration of the sympathy of the microcosm with the megacosm' (**Ill. 15.5a, b**). It was made into a woodcut in *Musurgia Universalis* and reused in *Œdipus Ægyptiacus*, then recreated as a copper engraving for *Mundus Subterraneus*. The comparison of the two versions shows the improvement in quality that came with his decision to publish with Jansson van Waesberge in Amsterdam.

In *Musurgia*, the diagram refers to 'musica humana', the sympathetic connection of the human body and soul to the cosmos, but to judge by the far longer explanatory text that accompanies it in *Œdipus*, it was probably first conceived for that work. There it appears in a chapter on 'Hieroglyphic Medicine', which explains how the Egyptian physicians applied the astral or sidereal philosophy to the cure of diseases. The principle is that every plant is joined by sympathy to a sign of the zodiac and a planet, and so are the members and organs of the human body. By matching the appropriate plant to its organ, one activates its healing property.

The outer circle shows twenty groups of medicinal plants, each joined by a dotted line to the part of the body which it may heal. The diagram serves to illustrate the principle and serve as a memory image, but its information is cursory in comparison with the text. This explains the system exhaustively, listing many more plants under four grades for each of the twelve signs. Here is the herbal repertory for Aries:

Aries is a masculine, fiery, hot-dry sign, sympathetic to the head. The plants of the first hot-dry grade are:

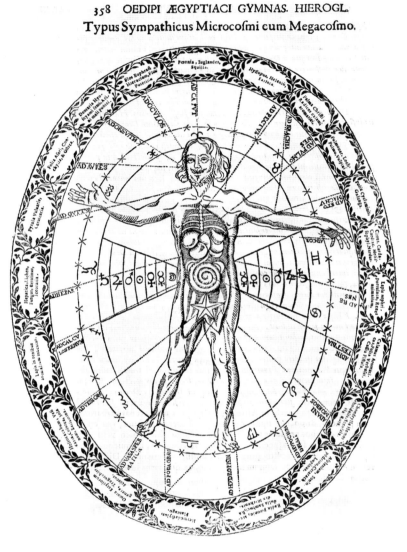

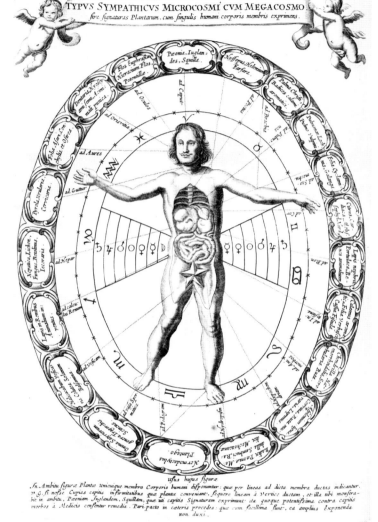

15.5a, b Zodiac man, showing how the macrocosm is reflected in the microcosm (man). The diagram exists in two versions, one a woodcut, the other a copper engraving (*Œdipus Ægyptiacus*, Volume II, ii, 358, and *Mundus Subterraneus*, Volume II, opposite 427)

Grade I: Artemisia rubra, Betonica, Cychorium, Consilida regalis, Ebulus, Mentha, Tussilago, Veronica. They are to be collected at the end of the Dog Days, after the full moon.

Grade II: Plants of the second hot-dry grade are: Asparagus, Hyparicum, Millefolium, Plantago, Poeonia. They are to be collected while the Sun and Moon are in Cancer.

Grade III: Agaricum, Cataputia, Chamaelea, Colocynthis, Farfara, Gentiana, Ligustrum, Ricinus, Sambucus. They are to be collected at the end of July and the beginning of August.

Grade IV: Abrotanum, Helleborus albus, Maiorana, Matrubium, Nasturcium sylvestre, Rosmarinus. They are to be collected partly in the month of April, partly in September.[8]

Another aspect of this kind of thinking emerges in the notion of universal harmony. The best known example is the harmony of the spheres, which is a way of expressing the intelligent design of the Sidereal world. Through the laws of correspondence, such design is reflected in the harmonious construction of the human body. Kircher writes: 'There is in the proportion of the

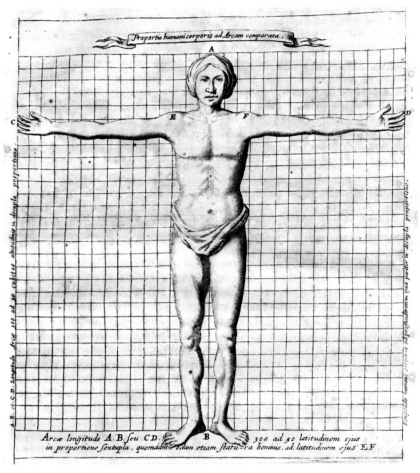

15.6 Human proportions in the Ark, a version of the familiar Renaissance diagram of the human body (Leonardo, Dürer) as measure of all things. (*Arca Noë*, 34)

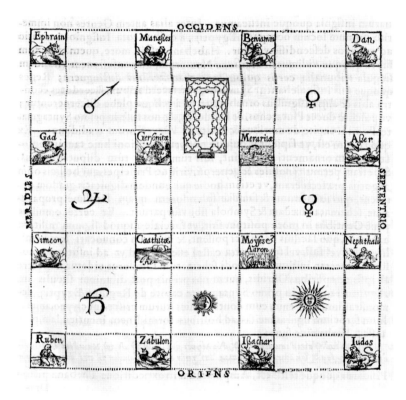

15.7 Emblems of the Twelve Tribes of Israel. Kircher equates the Twelve Tribes with the twelve signs of the zodiac. Also included are the seven planets and the four elements. (*Œdipus Ægyptiacus*, Volume II, i, 21)

human body something divine, constituted with such harmony and symmetry of all the members that there is not the slightest thing found in it that does not have the most precise laws of analogy to the others.'[9] Such principles, drawn from Plato, Hermetism and the Kabbalah, had to be reconcilable in Kircher's mind with the infallible authority of the Holy Scriptures. Genesis 1:26 states outright that man was created in God's image, so it stands to reason that the body should resemble the other designs that the Bible attributes to God: those of Noah's Ark, the Altar of Moses and Solomon's Temple, 'structures that were made to the symmetry of the human body, as though by a certain divine instinct imparted to the architects, so that man might be reconciled to God therein, or the very fabric might express man in a kind of mystical model'.[10]

Kircher illustrates this by comparing the human body to the God-given plan of the Ark (**Ill. 15.6**). The diagram shows an idealized male body against a grid, such as was used by the Renaissance theorists of propor-

tion (Leonardo da Vinci, Francesco Giorgi, Albrecht Dürer). Kircher follows the proportions given by St Augustine in his *City of God*, a dependable ally in this business. According to Augustine, man's height is six times the width of his chest, and ten times the depth from chest to back. These happen to be exactly the proportions of the Ark: 300 cubits long, 50 wide and 30 high.[11]

In a similar spirit, Kircher shows how the Children of Israel followed the principles of the Sidereal world, with its twelve zodiacal signs and seven planets, during their forty-year journey through the wilderness. In a plan of their camp (**Ill. 15.7**) based on Rabbi Abenezra, each of the twelve tribes marks its quarters with a banner displaying its emblem. There is no biblical evidence that these emblems were the twelve signs of the zodiac, but to adherents of the doctrine of correspondences, the conclusion is virtually irresistible. The next set of enclosures is dedicated to the seven planets, the empty space being occupied by the Tabernacle. The inner four squares, assigned to the

Gersonites, the Caathites, the Merarites, and to Moses and Aaron, correspond to the four elements. Each banner is of a different colour, corresponding to one of the twelve gemstones on the High Priest's breastplate. Thus, for example, the dominant tribe of Judah is symbolized by the noblest beast, the lion, and the zodiacal sign of Leo; he is placed at the eastern corner next to the sun, and his banner is green, the colour of emerald.

The Children of Israel were of course monotheists, except for their periodical backsliding, and the zodiac, rightly viewed, was nothing but a phenomenon of the Sidereal world. However, in the doctrine of correspondences this twelvefold order of the stars does have a powerful influence on things below, and it plays a crucial part in Kircher's history of religions. When people turned away from the worship of the one true God, they began worshipping the stars and planets, of whose effects they were well aware. With the wisdom of hindsight, Kircher can say: 'the multiple gods and goddesses shown by the mythologists are nothing but the multiple virtues of the one sun, or of the moon'.[12] His illustration of this principle (Ill. 5.8) shows the sun and moon sending out their various 'virtues' according to the twelve signs of the zodiac. In the corners are the four annual seasons, which are caused by the sun's tilted course, and the four monthly phases of the moon. For instance, the sun's ray at the eleven o'clock position is 'the energy concocted in liquors and wine', and it became deified as Bacchus, Dionysus and the Egyptian god Camos. The moon's ray at four o'clock is 'the energy in forests, lands, trees', and it became the goddesses Diana, Artemis and Astarte.

When it came to astrology, Kircher was ambivalent. As we have seen, his Hermetic principles required him to believe in stellar influences, both on man and on the elemental world. But astrologers dealt with two ideas that were anathema to him because they interfered with free will: first, that the position of the stars and planets at one's birth (the horoscope) dictated one's destiny; and second, that by calculating their future positions it was possible to foretell future events. The ancients, in his view, combined these fallacies with their worship of the heavenly bodies, in the hope that by paying due respect to the celestial gods, they could avert their evil effects. This is the explanation of the next diagram, in which Kircher reconstructs the constellations of north and south as the Egyptians supposedly imagined them (Ill. 15.9a, b). His basis was a description of the forty-eight images sent to him by his former amanuensis Michael Schatta (or Schaia), an Egyptian Copt, who had found them in the library of the monastery of St Mercurius. Although they were corrupt and incomplete, Kircher saw immediately that they agreed with the doctrine of the hieroglyphs, and was able to correct and amplify them by reference to Arabic sources.[13] The hemispheres centre not on the celestial poles (the 'polus mundi' is shown off-centre in the northern hemisphere), but on the poles of the zodiac. Kircher ascribed an Egyptian god to each of the familiar signs – for example, ram-horned Amon to Aries, the Apis Bull to Taurus, Canopus (shown as a jar spurting with water) to Aquarius. He 'Egyptianized' the other constellations on the basis of mythological paral-

15.8 Sun and moon as sources of all divinities. Kircher justified pagan polytheism as merely personifying the effects of the heavenly bodies. (*Obeliscus Pamphilius*, 252)

lels. But in his view the Egyptians, unlike the Greeks, did not envisage these symbolic figures as composed of stars, but as genii ruling certain areas of the sky. Each 'rhombus', house or twelfth part of the sphere is ruled by a different genius. The Egyptians and Chaldeans held the 'impious superstition' that the house ascending at the time of birth determined one's fate, and that the future could be predicted on the basis of the good or bad planets passing through the good or bad houses. The purpose of their sacrifices was to avert such evil influences.[14]

The reconstructions of the Egyptian celestial sphere were plausible, so long as one accepted Kircher's interpretations. Another Egyptian diagram is entirely his invention, and a good example of how he could give a memorable graphic expression to a difficult idea. This he calls 'The Wheel of Time as imagined by the Egyptians, by which the festivals of the months of the Egyptian gods, both fixed and variable, are shown, together with the Sothiac lustrum or lesser Canicular of 1,461 days, and the greater one of 1,461 years'

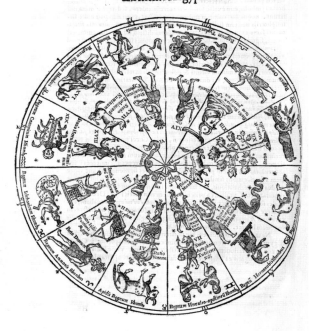

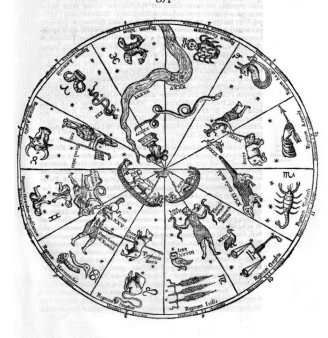

15.9a, b The Egyptian zodiac. With the
assistance of a Coptic colleague, Kircher is
able to reconcile the northern and southern
constellations with the Egyptian gods.
(*Œdipus Ægyptiacus*, Volume II, ii, 206, 207)

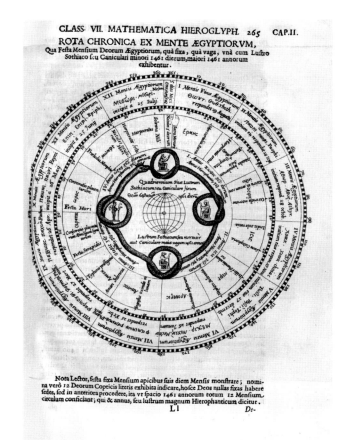

15.10 Wheel of Time, an exposition of the
Egyptian calendar correlated with festivals
of the gods. (*Œdipus Ægyptiacus*, Volume
II, ii, 265)

(**Ill. 15.10**). In plain language, the Egyptian year contained twelve months of thirty days each (shown here in the outer circle), plus five extra days (at the top) to make 365. The second circle shows the festivals of the gods, e.g. in the third month, the commemorations of 'Osiris enclosed in the ark' and 'Osiris's burial'. The five extra 'epagomenal' days commemorate the birth of the gods. However, since the solar year is actually 365¼ days long, a 365-day year gradually diverges from the solar year by one day every four years or 1,460 days. Nowadays we compensate for this by inserting an extra day in February every fourth (leap) year.

Kircher explains that the Egyptians had two calendars. The civil calendar, which the Greeks inherited, worked like ours, adding a 1,461st day every four years. The priestly calendar allowed the months to slip gradually behind, displacing all the festivals in relation to the seasons, until at the 1,461st year the slippage had amounted to an entire year and the calendar returned to its original position. This long period was regarded as a 'Great year', divided into four periods of 365 years.

The inner circle illustrates this. The Oroboros serpent eating its tail is the symbol of cyclical time or eternity. Each knot of his body contains a god figure: from the top, Sothis, Isis, Osiris and Horus. Following the principle of correspondence, each god rules both a 365-day year and a hierophantic period of 365 solar years.

Kircher had little regard for those modern philosophers (he mentions Cornelius Agrippa, Paracelsus, Robert Fludd and Guillaume Postel) who believed that future events can be read from the stars, as though the heavens were like a parchment, the stars letters, and the finger of God had inscribed the future on it. This notion, he says, comes from the Arabs, who saw the constellations not as images of animals or similar, but as forming letters that could, perhaps, be read. He reports that a French writer, Gaffarel, has concluded that the writing in question is not Arabic but Hebrew, and reproduces both hemispheres of Gaffarel's system in a pair of unusual white-on-black woodcuts (one shown here, **Ill. 15.11**). The white dots represent stars and form letters somewhat resembling those of Hebrew. Kircher demolishes Gaffarel's theory at some length, getting more and more angry about it until he exclaims: 'O asinine stupidity, deserving nothing but a walloping!'[15]

Another sort of asinine stupidity, as it seemed to Kircher on his rational days, was that of people who consulted the 'wheel of life and death' (**Ill. 15.12**), and he warns his reader that he only includes it in order to reveal the depths of human folly. He is astonished that this tool of divination appears even in the works of the Venerable Bede. It did in fact enjoy many centuries of popularity, sometimes as the 'Sphere of Biantis' or under the venerable cachet of the 'Sphere of Pythagoras'. Should you choose to consult 'Satan, arch-priest of the mysteries' about the truth or falsehood of something, this is how it works. You take the present hour, day and month, add them together, divide by thirty, and look for the remainder on the wheel. If you find it among the numbers above the diameter (which should be coloured red), it is true; if

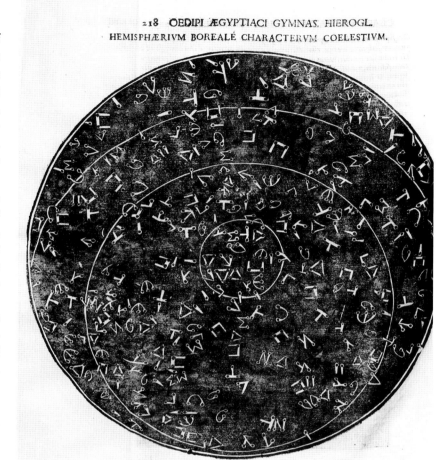

218 OEDIPI ÆGYPTIACI GYMNAS. HIEROGL.
HEMISPHÆRIVM BOREALÉ CHARACTERVM COELESTIVM.

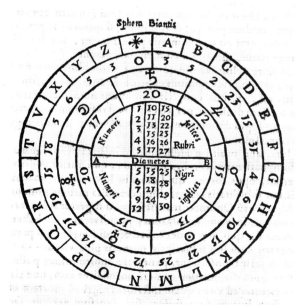

▲ **15.11** Stellar alphabet and the northern stars. Kircher brings evidence to disprove Gaffarel's theory that the stars form the same patterns as the letters of the Hebrew alphabet. (*Œdipus Ægyptiacus*, Volume II, ii, 210)

◄ **15.12** 'Wheel of life and death', a method of divination which Kircher firmly rejects. (*Œdipus Ægyptiacus*, Volume II, ii, 491)

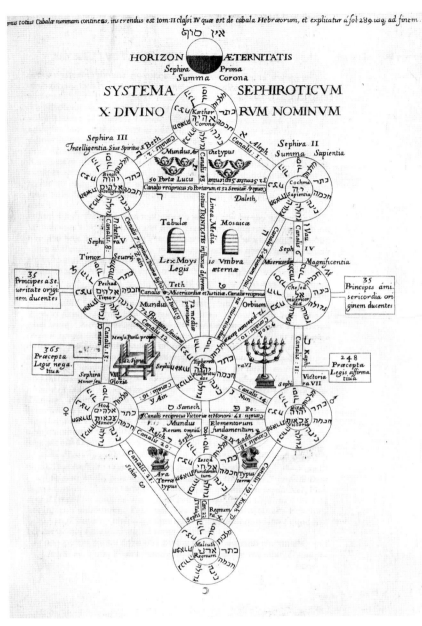

► **15.13** Tree of the Sephiroth. The fundamental diagram of Kabbalah, with its ten Sephiroth joined by twenty-two channels, and multiple correspondences. (*Œdipus Ægyptiacus*, Volume I, 288)

among the (black) numbers below, it is false. Also you may enquire if someone far away is alive or dead, by adding up the letters of their name (given in the outer circles), adding the month and the day, and proceeding likewise; only for true or false, read alive or dead.[16] Kircher does not remark on the fact that some numbers are absent or appear on both sides.

To the Renaissance magus, the system of correspondence par excellence was the Kabbalistic Tree of Life (**Ill. 15.13**) with its ten 'fruits,' called the Sephiroth. Working from rabbinic sources, Kircher devoted many pages to explaining the ten Sephiroth and the twenty-two 'channels' that join them, integrating other elements of his system into them and producing a diagram that has been reproduced again and again in modern esoteric texts. It associates the elements of the Tree to the ten Names of God (written in the centres of each Sephira), the three worlds (Archetypal, Sidereal – *mundus Orbium* – and Elemental), the twenty-two letters of the Hebrew alphabet (in the channels), the seven planets (in the seven lower Sephiroth), and the furnishings of Moses' Tabernacle (tablets of the Law, table of the shewbread, menorah, altars). Written around each Sephira in Hebrew letters are the names of all ten Sephiroth, signifying that every part contains or reflects the totality: another case of macrocosm–microcosm correspondence.

So far, so good; but Kircher fears and loathes the magic and superstition to which Kabbalah has also given rise. These, he says, are nothing less than demonic impositions introduced by the later rabbis.[17] Certainly Hebrew was the original language given to mankind, but it is misguided to try to read some profound mystery into every letter, accent and diacritical mark,[18] and still more so to think that Moses and the other Old Testament heroes performed their wonders by this means. How could anyone seriously suppose that the sun, the moon and the elements can be moved by simply hearing a man pronounce certain words?[19] Moreover, we read in the Scriptures that Moses parted the Red Sea; that Joshua ordered the sun to stand still; that Elijah and Elisha raised the dead and brought fire down from heaven; and that Daniel interpreted dreams. But nowhere in the whole of the Scriptures does it say that they did so by the use of Kabbalah. If this Kabbalistic magic is so powerful, why don't we see the rabbis performing similar miracles? If they could do so, the Christian world would never be safe! But all this Kabbalistic magic and angel conjuration is vain and impious, and rightly proscribed by the Church and the Holy Inquisition.[20]

One might think that he protests too much, but he had to be careful. As Dino Pastine remarks,

The Jesuits had aroused the suspicions of the Inquisition and of a part of public opinion through being the only Order that had not introduced into its statutes the necessity of the so-called proof of 'purity of blood' for admitting aspirants. For this reason, many thought that the Company was a receptacle for opportunistic Jews, superficially converted to Christianity.[21]

Apart from *Œdipus Ægyptiacus*, most Kabbalistic studies of the time came from the Protestant side.

In the Sephira of Tiphereth, at the centre of the Kabbalistic Tree, is the name we have seen repeatedly at the summit of Kircher's symbolic frontispieces: the name YHVH revealed to Moses from the Burning Bush (Exodus 3:14). Generally written in English as 'Yahweh', it has four letters (Yod, He, Vav, He), and is known in Christian Kabbalah by the Greek term Tetragrammaton (four-lettered). Kircher writes much about the power of this name, its adaptation by Pythagoras as the Tetraktys, and its connection with the name of Jesus, which consists of the same letters plus an inserted letter Shin.[22] That God's real name has four letters was plain to Kircher from the fact that every nation on earth instinctively writes or speaks it thus (**Ill. 15.14**). 'And this very fact indicates that everything in the world gets its subsistence from the force and efficacy of this name. Thus all peoples and nations of the world are obliged to agree under the cult of a single religion diffused throughout the universe with so many gifts of the divine goodness.'[23] This thought naturally called to mind the ambition of the Society of Jesus to evangelize the entire world. But another remarkable coincidence dawned on him. The Kabbalists generate from the Tetragrammaton 72 'paths' or three-letter combinations; and Kircher knew, or knew of, 72 languages in the world. Hence he designed this magnificent plate: 'Mirror of the mystic Cabala in which are contained all that the Hebrews have secretly related of the four-lettered name of God, and these are proved to refer to the name of Jesus the Messiah; and it teaches how all the nations of the world have mysteriously spoken the name of God with four letters.' The central image is 'The mystic tree planted in the middle of Paradise for the salvation of 72 nations, whose fruits are the 72 names of God'. Above it are its leaves, the 72 Kabbalistic 'paths' of three letters. To the left is the 'Mystic tree containing the seven planets, the members of the body, and the ruling angels'. To the right is the 'pomegranate tree containing the twelve signs of the zodiac, the twelve tribes of Israel, and the twelve anagrams of the name of God'.[24]

Kircher willingly accepted the rabbinic myth that Adam could read and write, and that the proto-Hebrew alphabet was revealed to him by angels. This is the starting point for all his alphabetic studies, encapsulated in his table (**Ill. 15.15**). The columns read, from left to right, 'Value of the letters', 'Double mystical character said to have been handed down by the Angels', 'Character of the time of crossing the river, author R[abbi] Abraham Balmis', 'Various forms of the old Samaritan characters extracted from coins and some authors', 'Florid character of the Samaritans extracted from Villalpando and coins', 'Mosaic character with which he wrote the law on the tables, taken from various monuments of the Rabbis', 'Syriac character', and 'True Hebrew or Assyrian character'. This meant that the Egyptian hieroglyphs, and the Coptic and Greek alphabets that he derived from them, belonged to a completely different line of evolution.

Kircher considered this an important enough discovery to publish his illustration of it three times: in *Obeliscus Pamphilius*, in *Œdipus Ægyptiacus*,

▲ **15.14** Seventy-two names of God. An illustration of the notion that the name of God in all languages is ultimately derived from the Hebrew Tetragrammaton YHVH ('Yahweh'). (*Œdipus Ægyptiacus*, Volume II, i, fp. 286/287)

TURRIS BABEL LIB. III. 157

TABULA COMBINATORIA

In qua ex probatissimis Authoribus primævorum Characterum formæ eorumque Omnium, qui ab ijs Originem duxerunt succesiva temporum propagatione exhibentur; Ex quibus luculenter deducitur Omnia linguarum Alphabeta, nonnulla in sepriscarum literarum vestigia tenere.

Valor Literarum.	Character duplex mysticus ab Angelis traditus dicitur.	Character temporum transsumptus flaminibus Authore R. Abrahamo Balmis.	Characterum veterum Samaritanorum formæ variæ ex nummis extractæ aliisque Authoribus.	Floridus Character Samaritanorum ex Vilalpando nummisque extractus.	Character Mosaicus, quo legem in tabulis scripsit ex varius Rabbinorum momentis depromptus.	Character Syriacus.	Character verus Hebraeus sive Assyrius.
A							
B							
C							
D							
H							
V							
Z							
Ch							
T							
I							
C							
L							
M							
N							
S							
Ayn							
P							
Ts							
QK							
R							
Sch							
Th							

15.15 Table of alphabets, illustrating the theory that all alphabets have a common origin in the proto-Hebrew, revealed by angels (second column). (*Turris Babel*, 157)

and twenty-five years later in *Turris Babel* (**Ill. 15.16a, b, c**). It is interesting to see the original woodcuts still used in the late work. The blocks had been trucked[25] from Rome to Amsterdam in the 1660s as part of Kircher's contract with Jansson, and stored there. Forgivably, the Dutch typographer inserted some of them upside-down.

This illustration of the 'primaeval Egyptian letters, instituted by Taut or Mercurius Trismegistus' is crucial to Kircher's interpretation of the Egyptian hieroglyphs. Having once deduced (rightly) that Coptic is a residue of the original Egyptian language, he concluded (wrongly) that its alphabet must mark the first stage of evolution from hieroglyphs to letters. The middle column here shows the Coptic alphabet. Whenever possible, he has found a Coptic word beginning with that letter that expresses some fundamental idea – for example, *agathos dæmon*, the good genius, which begins with A. It is represented by the sacred ibis with its beak between its legs, or else with a serpent wrapped around them. On the left is a hypothetical original hieroglyph expressing that idea, of which the letter is a shorthand version. On the right are the Greek letters that supposedly evolved from the Coptic ones. The meaning he gives them are Norm (Gamma), the Egyptian delta (Delta), Procession of lower to higher things (Upsilon), Mouth of the Lord (Omicron), Procession of higher to lower things (Lambda), Procession of the world-soul (Chi), Moon (Sigma, Omega), Vision (small Sigma), Fecundity (Beta), Life (Zeta), Thoth (Theta), Love (Phi), Water (Mu), Chain (Xi), Procession of elementary or vegetable things (Nu), Hook that brought Osiris's body out of the waters (Pi), Sun, moon again (Omicron, Sigma), Thoth or Taut (Tau).

The same kind of retrospective analysis led Kircher to interpret the 'Hieroglyphic Monad' of John Dee[26] as compounded from Egyptian hieroglyphs (**Ill. 15.17**). He had already noticed that the Bembine Table of Isis contained the sign of the cross, which led him to discourse on crosses and their symbolism in pre-Christian religions. In *Obeliscus Pamphilius* he also quotes at length from 'Deenus', giving the English magus's insights into the symbolism of the scarab as well as his explanation of how the monad contains the signs of all the planets, plus the sign of Aries.[27] He also quotes Cesare della Riviera's mysterious alchemical book *Il Mondo Magico de gli Heroi* (1603), which attributes the monad, in its original form, to Egypt. Lastly, he quotes Marsilio Ficino's *De Vita Coelitus Propaganda*[28] on the making of planetary talismans.

When Kircher introduced the diagram in *Œdipus Ægyptiacus*, it was with a much shorter text and without the quotations from these three suspiciously magical books. He now puts it in the context of the 'hieroglyphic mathematics' of the ancients, who knew that the number four is the key to the order of the universe. The Egyptians expressed it first by the symbol of a cross within a circle; later, by the *crux ansata* (handled cross, otherwise *ankh*), which shows all the quaternaries pervaded, ensouled and maintained by the *spiritus mundi*:

Since this world-spirit, the celestial Mercury, fills all things with numbers, proportions, and harmonies it certainly cannot be understood

Primæua literarum Ægyptiarum fabrica, & institutio facta à Tauto siue Mercurio Trismegisto.

	Character Zoographus.	Figura literarum Vulgaris.	Græcorum ad eas affinitas.
I.		Ⲁ ⲁⲅⲍⲃⲇⲥ ⲁⲉⲙⲟⲛ dicitur, id est, Bonus Dæmon.	A
II.		Γ ⲅⲓⲙⲉⲗ dicitur, id est, Norma.	Γ
III.		Ⲇ ⲇⲁⲗⲧⲁ dicitur, id est Bonus ager.	Δ
IV.		Ⲩ Processus inferiorum ad superiora. Symbolum est.	Υ
V.		Ⲟ ⲟⲫϯ dicitur, id est, Mundi Dominus.	O

ET FABRICA HIEROGLYPHICORVM.   131   CAP. VI.

VI.		Λ ⲗⲁⲃⲇⲁ dicitur Processus superiorum ad inferiora.	Λ
VII.		Χ Processus animæ mundi ⲁⲛⲱ ⲕⲁⲓ ⲕⲁⲧⲱ.	Χ
VIII. IX.		C Lunæ symbolum. Ⲱ O magnum.	Σ Ω
X.		Ⲥ ⲟⲣⲁⲁ dicitur, id est, Visio.	Ⲥ Σ
XI.		B ⲃⲁⲗⲉⲛ dicitur, id est, Fœcunditas.	B ⲃⲁⲩ
XII.		Ⲍ ⲍⲱⲧⲁ dicitur, id est, Vita.	Z
XIII.		Θ ⲑⲉⲧ dicitur, id est, Litera Thoth.	Θ Thita.
XIV.		Φ ⲫⲓⲗⲟ dicitur, id est, Amor.	Φ

R 2   XV.

CAP. VI.   132   LIBER II.   DE INSTITVTIONE

XV.		M ⲙⲟⲩ Aqua, Litera est. ⲕⲩⲣⲓⲟⲗⲟⲅⲓⲕⲏ ⲧⲟ ⲩⲇⲁⲧⲟⲥ.	M ⲙⲓ
XVI.		Ξ ⲝⲁⲛⲧⲁ dicitur, id est, Catena.	Ξ ⲝⲓ
XVII.		N Litera, idem est, ac processus rerum elementarium, ⲁⲛⲱ ⲕⲁⲓ ⲕⲁⲧⲱ, siuè vegetabilium processus.	N ⲛⲓ
XVIII.		P ⲕⲩⲣⲓⲟⲗⲟⲅⲓⲕⲏ ⲁⲣⲡⲁⲅⲟⲥ. Figura desumpta ex harpagone, quo Osiridis corpus ex vndis extractum.	P ⲣⲱ
XIX.		O Sol.	Ⲟ Σ
XX.		C Luna. Signa ⲕⲩⲣⲓⲟⲗⲟⲅⲓⲕⲁ.	
XXI.		T ⲧⲁⲫϯ Litera Thoth siuè Tauri Dei. Tau Hebræorum.	T

15.16a, b, c Coptic alphabet explained: hypothetical connections between Egyptian hieroglyphics and Coptic letters, which in turn lead to Greek. (*Obeliscus Pamphilius*, 130, 131, 132)

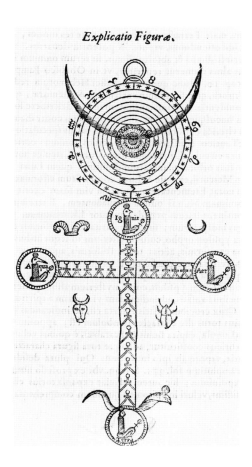

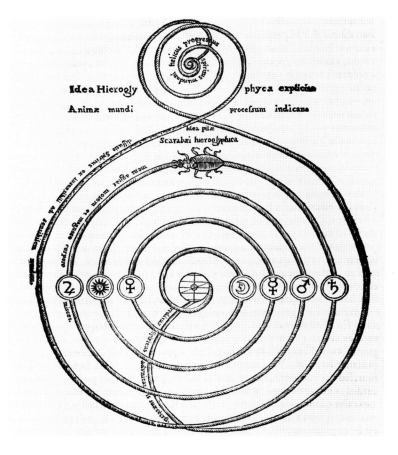

without numbers.... Hence it was not without reason that the ancients saw all the mysteries of number represented by his caduceus, or the character of Mercury. If you unfold it into its parts, namely into [circle, crescent, cross and Y], you will soon have that marvellous Pythagorean tektractys, which he called the source of perpetual nature, and the idea of all created things, and of the knowledge of things rationally operating in the divine mind.[29]

Kircher then applies Egyptian notions to it. The arms of the cross end with hieroglyphs of seated figures which he interpreted as the four 'presiding genii of the four elements'. The circle then represents the cosmos, with the four elements, the seven planets and the firmament of fixed stars. A serpent replaces the horns of Aries, which in the original Hieroglyphic Monad sprout from the bottom of the cross: it represents the divine energy permeating everything. The moon is the humid principle; this, and the warm principle of Aries, are the two principles of generation.

Kircher also drew on Dee for an alchemical interpretation of one of his favourite hieroglyphs, the scarab (**Ill. 15.18**). In *Œdipus Ægyptiacus* he writes that: 'The evolution and involution of the Hermetic Egg is beautifully explained hiero-glyphically by the operation of the scarab-beetle.' The scarab, he explains, represents the prime matter of the seven metals, agitated by the world spirit, which has the potential to take on all forms. The scarab's semen, enclosed in its ball of dung, represents the seed in the egg of the world waiting to come to life. This occurs through a cyclical process, as the world spirit descends in spirals through the seven planets (and their associated metals), ending at the earth (centre of the diagram) and then returning by a more direct route to its own sphere.[30] Once again, the quotation from Virgil seems the most apt motto.

From Kircher's retrospective reading of Dee's symbol, one can see how readily his cosmology found graphic expression. The same principles underlie a symbol of his own invention which he placed at the beginning of his late work on the Minervan obelisk, calling it 'Hieroglyphic scheme, exhibiting the idea of a book' (**Ill. 15.19**). The central figure had already appeared in *Œdipus Ægyptiacus*, and is explained in the commentary to **Ill. 5.10**. The winged globe and the two seals on the sides were first pictured in Kircher's earliest work of Egyptology, *Prodromus Coptus*.[31] He there describes the winged globe as a hieroglyph of subtle energy penetrating the world, or in other words the *anima mundi* or 'soul of the world'. The two seals on the left and right are copied from Pignoria.[32] The left one shows a recumbent human form in a boat, with a scarab above and two birds. Its meaning, Kircher later explains, is: 'The sun by its annual and diurnal motion is the cause of all things coming forth (or prospering) in the Elemental world.'[33] The one on the right translates as: 'The sun is the moderator of the seasons of the entire universe and the author of the whole cyclical conversion.'[34] The nine-pointed star containing a triangle occurred on the title-page of *Arithmologia* (see **Ill. 2.13**), where it represents the Trinity and the Nine Orders of Angels. It is not clear exactly how this adds up to the scheme of the book, but the five images together contain most of the presuppositions with which Kircher approached any Egyptian inscription.

In *Obeliscus Pamphilius* we first meet a cluster of small illustrations, done in woodcut, which recur in all of Kircher's Egyptological works (**Ill. 15.21**). The first of these is an image or hieroglyph of Horus. First found on the Bembine Table, it became fundamental to Kircher's understanding of Egyptian mythology, as can be seen from the number of times he reproduced it.

Kircher explains that Horus is a symbol of the sensible world. In another image (**Ill. 15.20**) he is wrapped in a net-like garment, symbolizing the 'unknown and hidden operations and effects of the world'.[35] His staff bears the head of the hoopoe, a bird whose crest has twenty-eight feathers, like the days of the lunar cycle, and four colours, like the seasons. It thus symbolizes the 'admirable variety of things' under the dominion of the Solar Numen.[36] He holds in his hands a lituus (curved Roman trumpet) and gnomon or masonic square, signifying respectively the highest harmony and the order of things. The triangle behind his neck and the globe attached to the staff refer to his being a product of the Egyptian Trinity of Osiris, Isis and Amun.[37] In sum, the hieroglyph states that God produces the world through his wisdom.

Those familiar with more recently discovered examples of Egyptian art, such as the sarcophagi of Tutankhamun, will realize that Kircher's 'lituus' and 'gnomon' are misreadings of the pharaonic attributes of the crook and the flail, and indeed that the figure is not Horus at all, but the god Ptah holding the staff known as the *was*.

The tiny triangle hanging from the back of Horus's neck was enough to persuade Kircher that the Egyptians knew about the Holy Trinity.[38] He illustrates what he thinks it means in a more abstract hieroglyph (top left of **Ill. 15.21**). It symbolizes the production of Horus from the Egyptian trinity of gods Hemepht, Ptah and Amun (otherwise Osiris, Isis and Amun). These correspond, says Kircher, to the upper three Sephiroth of the Kabbalistic Tree: Kether, Binah and Chokhmah. Thus both the esoteric systems, Egyptian and Jewish, preserved a vestige of the Trinitarian doctrine that, being Kircher's own belief, he was sure had been known to humanity ever since God taught it to Adam. As time went on, in pagan religions it became obscured by polytheism; in Judaism and Islam, by a too rigorous monotheism.

Another image of Horus, and this time an authentic one, was as an infant (bottom left of **Ill. 15.21**). We know already that Horus represents the world in

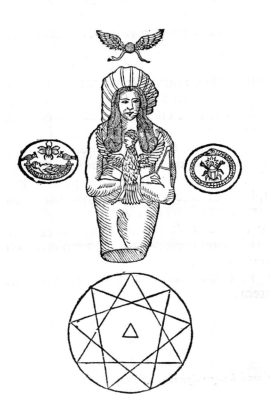

Schema hieroglyphicum Libri ideam exhibens .

◀ **15.19** Hieroglyphic scheme of a book: the winged globe as a symbol of energy, penetrating the world. (*Obeliscus Ægyptiacus*, +4ᵛ)

▼ **15.20** Symbol of Horus, representing the sensible world wrapped in the unknown. Kircher misinterpreted the pharaonic crook and flail for the curved Roman trumpet and masonic square. (*Œdipus Ægyptiacus*, 212)

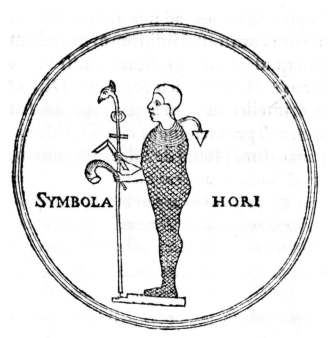

SYMBOLA HORI

15.21 A page from *Obeliscus Pamphilius*, with loosely related Egyptian images. Top left: Horus produced from the Egyptian Trinity, Kircher's attempt to impose the Christian Trinity upon Egyptian mythology. Centre left: Osiris as Archetypal intellect. In Kircher's Neoplatonic scheme, Intellect generates the entirety of Creation. Bottom left: Horus, the World. The cornucopia, says Kircher, equals abundance, the cube stability. His finger on his lips means ineffable mysteries. Bottom right: this is not an image of anything real but an assemblage of letters and fleurons in the shape of an obelisk. The Greek inscription, with Latin translation, is reported by Plutarch from the Temple of Isis in Sais. It says: 'I am Isis, all that will be, is, and was; and no mortal has ever lifted my veil.' (*Obeliscus Pamphilius*, 213)

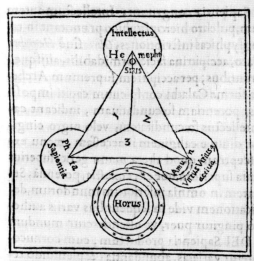

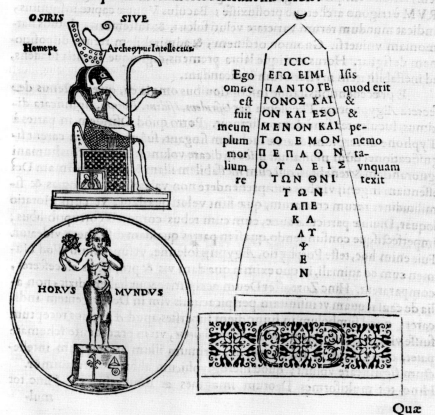

Kircher's Egyptian theology. He explains that this is because the world is like an infant produced by God's wisdom. Horus holds a cornucopia, denoting the variety and abundance of things in the world. He stands on a cube representing the world's solidity and stability, on which we see the symbols of triangle and globe, hoopoe-headed staff, lituus and gnomon. He presses his finger to his lips, enjoining silence and indicating ineffable mysteries.

Just as he assumed that Ptah, as represented on the Bembine Table, was Horus, so Kircher believed the hawk-headed Horus to be Osiris. He also did not know that the headdress in this image (centre left of **Ill. 15.21**) is the combined crowns of Upper and Lower Egypt. This opened the way to one of his more fantastic interpretations, in which the solar god Osiris is called by the name Hemept, also written Hemepht, Empht or Hemphta. In Neoplatonism, the visible sun (the one in the Sidereal world) is only a manifestation of the 'true' sun, and that is what Kircher thinks is represented by this form of Osiris: he is the first Intellect, the eternal sun and first producer of all things. He mates with Wisdom, personified as Isis, to produce Horus as the world. Kircher explains how he comes to this conclusion. The variegated throne represents Osiris's authority over the lower worlds. His black veil signifies that the divine nature is inaccessible. His extended left hand shows rule over all; the recurved sceptre, the influx of power into celestial things. His headdress, consisting of a flower with a 'Persaean fruit' (avocado pear?) inserted, represents his fecundating potency, placed on his head because he is the fecundating Intellect.[39]

The whole page is a virtuoso display of the book-designer's art, with its variety of framed and unframed figures and their integration with the text, titles and captions. The last image, at bottom right, is made from printer's lines and fleurons and resembles an obelisk. The Greek inscription comes from one of Kircher's favourite sources, Plutarch's book on Isis and Osiris, there attributed to the Temple of Athena ('who is the same as Isis') in the Delta city of Sais. It reads: 'I am Isis, all that will be, is, and was; and no mortal has ever lifted my veil' (*De Iside et Osiride*, ix). Surely Athanasius, bearer of a fatidically immortal name, smiled to himself as he quoted this, looking back over his own achievements in revealing the hidden wisdom of pagan antiquity, and in baring the secrets of universal Nature.

Such sentiments could be summed up in the 'Hieroglyphic Epigram' with which Kircher wryly concluded his first encyclopaedic work, Magnes (**Ill. 15.22**). It alludes to an anecdote about Christopher Columbus. When challenged by a group of Spanish grandees who doubted that he had really sailed to the New World, he challenged them in turn to stand an egg on its pointed end. After they had tried in vain and declared it impossible, he tapped the egg on the table, slightly crushing the end, and stood it upright. Columbus then pointed out that one cannot believe something until one knows it from experience, and then it is easy. Coming at the end of *Magnes* with the inscription 'And we shall have done this', the epigram defies anyone who doubts the extraordinary facts and experiments related in the book.

15.22 Hieroglyphic epigram: a witty anecdote showing how Christopher Columbus convinced those who doubted the truth of his discovery of the New World. (*Magnes*, last page of text)

In *The Eye of the Lynx*, a masterpiece of intellectual archaeology and relevant at many points to the study of Kircher, David Freedberg writes of him briefly but pungently:

> But what are we to make of his extraordinarily erudite works, with their spectacular and amazing illustrations? It would surely be hard to claim of them that they represent anything but the triumph of illustration. Indeed, they are just that; but as works of science (however we choose to understand that term) they are near to useless. It is no surprise that their appeal should now largely be confined to the bibliophile and the modern student of arcana.[40]

The last words are quite true, and the present book does little to alter the picture. But perhaps I don't understand 'science' in the same way. A former colleague of mine once opposed offering a course in the History of Science, saying 'You want to teach a course in Bad Science??' In his view, science has marched onward and upward to the pinnacle of the present. As a sceptical if not cynical observer, I fear that given time, much of his science will turn 'bad': it will be superseded by future discoveries and different ways of looking at things. This is still more true of humanistic studies which largely lack the stern discipline of experimental proof. They pass through a changing series of filters and fashions, of which the current one – define it as you please – will inevitably prove as bad in retrospect as, say, the Marxist filter does today. It is all part of an endless story, and I prefer not to theorize or moralize about it, but just to tell it. As far as I am concerned, Kircher was doing real science, pushing at the frontiers of knowledge whether of hieroglyphics, vulcanism or microscopy, but limited by the tools and restraints of his time and place, just as my colleague and I are limited by our own.[41] However, I have discovered that one way to transcend one's own limitations is through the temporary attunement of one's imagination to an alien world view: in this case, that of a convinced Christian Hermeticist very much more learned and gifted than myself. And that has been the adventure of this book.

Notes

1 For bibliographic details of these notebooks, see Chapter 3, note 1.
2 *Obeliscus Pamphilius*, 171.
3 A careless engraver titled it SPHÆRA AMERIS instead of AMORIS, an error corrected in most copies.
4 For a thorough analysis of this diagram and its sources, see Heninger, 92–98.
5 *Œdipus Ægyptiacus*, II, ii, 18.
6 *Obeliscus Pamphilius*, 176; *Œdipus Ægyptiacus*, II, ii, 195.
7 *Obeliscus Pamphilius*, 177.
8 *Œdipus Ægyptiacus*, II, ii, 359.
9 *Arca Noë*, 33.
10 *Arca Noë*, 33.
11 On the problem of the cubit, see Chapter 6, note 9.
12 *Obeliscus Pamphilius*, 253.
13 *Œdipus Ægyptiacus*, II, ii, 213.
14 *Œdipus Ægyptiacus*, II, ii, 205.
15 *Œdipus Ægyptiacus*, II, ii, 224.
16 *Œdipus Ægyptiacus*, II, ii, 421.
17 *Œdipus Ægyptiacus*, II, i, 358.
18 Kircher put this concisely in *China Illustrata*: 'I believe that the Chinese were taught by Hebrews and Moslems, who say that the letters in their Cabala reveal mysteries,

and who use these letters to create deeper roots of superstition for their doctrine in the minds of their followers.' Van Tuyl, 153.
19 *Œdipus Ægyptiacus*, II, i, 359.
20 *Œdipus Ægyptiacus*, II, i, 360.
21 Pastine, 24.
22 Thus yielding YHSVH, which transliterates approximately as the Hebrew name Jeshua or Joshua, Latinized as Jesu.
23 *Œdipus Ægyptiacus*, II, i, 287.
24 For a detailed analysis of the diagram and its unacknowledged sources, see Stolzenberg, 'Four Trees', 151–157. The plate refers to specific pages of *Œdipus Ægyptiacus* (e.g. in the central circle '*Explicatur in Cabala fol. 287*'), indicating that the second volume was already typeset when Pierre Miotte completed the engraving.
25 'Everyone here advises me to send the plates, etc., with the books by land, not by sea.' Kircher to Jansson, August 25, 1661, APUG Ms. 563, f.265.
26 John Dee, *Monas Hieroglyphica*, 1564.
27 *Obeliscus Pamphilius*, 373.
28 Kircher's Freudian slip for the correct title, *De Vita Coelitus Comparanda*.
29 *Œdipus Ægyptiacus*, II, ii, 27.
30 *Œdipus Ægyptiacus*, II, ii, 412.
31 *Prodromus Coptus*, 246, 248, 254.
32 Pignoria, 26, 31.
33 *Obeliscus Ægyptiacus*, 29.
34 *Obeliscus Ægyptiacus*, 27.
35 *Œdipus Ægyptiacus*, II, ii, 24.
36 *Obeliscus Ægyptiacus*, 39.
37 *Œdipus Ægyptiacus*, II, ii, 24.
38 *Œdipus Ægyptiacus*, II, ii, 24; I, 151–152.
39 *Obeliscus Ægyptiacus*, 213.
40 Freedberg, 400.
41 I find a similar sentiment in the wise words of the late Stephen Jay Gould, who treats Kircher in Gould 2002, 168, and elsewhere.

Athanasius Kircher's Writings
Bibliography of Works Cited
Sources of Illustrations · Index

Athanasius Kircher's Writings

This list gives shortened titles of works, in chronological order.

Ars Magnesia, Würzburg, 1631

Primitiae Gnomonicae Catoptricae, Avignon, 1635

Prodromus Coptus sive Ægyptiacus, Rome, 1636

[*Specula Melitensis Encyclica*, Naples, 1638, formerly attributed to Kircher but by Salvatore Imbroll]

Magnes sive De Arte Magnetica, Rome, 1641; Cologne, 1643; Rome, 1654

Lingua Ægyptiaca Restituta, Rome, 1643

Ars Magna Lucis et Umbrae, Rome, 1646; Amsterdam, 1671

Musurgia Universalis sive Ars Magna Consoni et Dissoni, 2 vols, Rome, 1650

Obeliscus Pamphilius, hoc est, Interpretatio Nova & hucusque Intentata Obelisci Hieroglyphici, Rome, 1650

Œdipus Ægyptiacus, 3 vols, Rome, 1652–1654

Itinerarium Exstaticum, Rome, 1656

Iter Extaticum II, qui & Mundi Subterranei Prodromus Dicitur, Rome, 1657

Scrutinium Physico-Medicum Contagiosae Luis, quae Pestis Dicitur, Rome, 1658; Leipzig, 1659, 1671

Iter Extaticum Coeleste...Hac Secundâ Editione Praelusionibus & Scholiis Illustratum... ipso Auctore Annuente, a P. Gaspare Schotto... Accessit ejusdem Auctoris Iter Exstaticum Terrestre, & Synopsis Mundi Subterranei, Würzburg, 1660, 1671

Diatribe de Prodigiosis Crucibus, Rome, 1661

Polygraphia Nova et Universalis ex Combinatoria Arte Detecta, Rome, 1663

Mundus Subterraneus, 2 vols, Amsterdam, 1664–1665, 1668, 1678

Historia Eustachio-Mariana, Rome, 1665

Arithmologia sive De Abditis Numerorum Mysteriis, Rome, 1665

Obelisci Ægyptiaci Nuper inter Isaei Romani Rudera Effossi Interpretatio Hieroglyphica, Rome, 1666 [*Obeliscus Ægyptiacus*]

China Monumentis qua Sacris qua Profanis, Nec non Variis Naturae & Artis Spectaculis, Aliarumque Rerum Memorabilium Argumentis Illustrata, Amsterdam, 1667 [*China Illustrata*]; trans. by Charles Van Tuyl as *China Illustrated with Sacred and Secular Monuments*, Muskogee, Okla.: Indiana University Press, 1987

Magneticum Naturae Regnum sive Disceptatio Physiologica, Rome, 1667

Ars Magna Sciendi, Amsterdam, 1669

Latium. Id est, Nova & Parallela Latii tum Veteris tum Novi Descriptio, Amsterdam, 1671

Principis Christiani Archetypon Politicum sive Sapientia Regnatrix, Amsterdam, 1672 [also titled *Splendor et Gloria Domus Joanniæ*]

Phonurgia Nova sive Conjugium Mechanico-physicum Artis & Naturae Paranympha Phonosophia Concinnatum, Kempten, 1673

Arca Noë, Amsterdam, 1675

Sphinx Mystagoga, sive Diatribe Hieroglyphica, Amsterdam, 1676

Turris Babel, sive Archontologia, Amsterdam, 1679

Tariffa Kircheriana id est Inventum Aucthoris Novum [vol. I], *Tariffa Kircheriana sive Mensa Pythagorica Expansa* [vol. II], Rome, 1679

Fasciculus Epistolarum Adm. R. P. Athanasii Kircheri, ed. Hieronymus Ambrosius Langenmantel, Augsburg, 1684

UNPUBLISHED WORKS

Mathematica Curiosa (Rome, Biblioteca Nazionale Vittorio Emanuele II, Ms. S. Fr. Paola 4)

Geocosmus (Rome, Biblioteca Nazionale Vittorio Emanuele II, Ms. Gesuiti 562)

Iter Hetruscum (lost)

Kircher's correspondence (Rome, Archivio della Pontificia Università Gregoriana [APUG], Mss. 555–568)

COMPILATIONS OF KIRCHER'S WRITINGS PUBLISHED IN HIS LIFETIME:

Kestler, Johann Stephan, *Physiologia Kircheriana Experimentalis*, Amsterdam: Jansson, 1680

Petrucci, Giosefo, *Prodromo Apologetico alli Studi Chircheriani*, Amsterdam: Jansson, 1677

Sepibus, Georgius de [Giorgio de Sepi], *Romanii Collegii Musaeum Celeberrimum cuius Magnae Antiquariae Rei...*, Amsterdam: Officina Janssonio-Waesbergiana, 1678.

Bibliography of Works Cited

Åkerman, Susanna, *Queen Christina of Sweden and Her Circle: The Transformation of a Seventeenth-Century Philosophical Libertine*, Leiden: Brill, 1991.

Aldrovandi, Ulisse, *Historia Serpentum et Draconum*, Bologna, 1640.

Allgemeines Künstlerlexikon: die bildenden Künstler aller Zeiten und Völker (new edn), Munich and Leipzig: K. G. Saur, 1992–. [*AKL*]

Antinori, Alessandra Cardelli, 'Oggetti stranieri provenienti da ogni regione del mondo', in Lo Sardo 2001, 79–85.

Arecco, Davide, *Il sogno di Minerva: La scienza fantastica di Athanasius Kircher (1602–1680)*, Padua: CLEUP Editrice, 2002.

Baldwin, Martha, 'Matters Medical', in Stolzenberg 2001, 85–92.

——, 'Reverie in Time of Plague: Athanasius Kircher and the Plague Epidemic of 1656', in Findlen 2004, 63–77.

——, 'The Snakestone Experiments', *Isis*, LXXXIII (1995), 394–418.

Baltrušaitis, Jurgis, *Aberrations: An Essay on the Legend of Forms*, trans. R. Miller, Cambridge, Mass.: MIT Press, 1989.

——, *Anamorphic Art*, trans. W. J. Strachan, New York: Harry N. Abrams, 1977.

——, *La Quête d'Isis: Essai sur la légende d'un mythe*, Paris: O. Perrin, 1967.

Barbieri, Patrizio, 'Michele Todini's Galleria Armonica: Its Hitherto Unknown History', *Early Music*, 30 (2002), 584–591.

Battini, Annalisa, 'Gli atlanti del Cinquecento: Mercatore e la cartografia moderna', in *Alla scoperta del mondo: L'arte della cartografia da Tolomeo a Mercatore*, Modena: Il Balino, 2001, 171–240.

Beck, Christoph, 'Einige Bemerkungen zur Kirchenmusik in der *Musurgia Universalis* des Athanasius Kircher', in Beinlich 2002b, 73–99.

Beinlich, Horst, 'Kircher und Ägypten: Information aus zweiter Hand: Tito Livio Burattini', in Beinlich 2002b, 57–72.

——, et al., eds, *Magie des Wissens. Athanasius Kircher 1602–1680. Universalgelehrter, Sammler, Visionär*, exhibition catalogue, Martin von Wagner Museum der Universität Würzburg, 1 Oct.–14 Dec. 2002, Dettelbach: J. H. Röll, 2002. [2002a]

——, ed., *Spurensuche: Wege zu Athanasius Kircher*, Dettelbach: J. H. Röll, 2002. [2002b]

——, et al., eds, *Magie des Wissens: Athanasius Kircher (1602–1680), Jesuit und Universalgelehrter*, exhibition catalogue, Fulda: Vonderau Museum, 17 Jan.–16 March 2003, Petersberg: Michael Imhof Verlag, 2003.

Bertini, Maria Augusta, ed., *Fra terra e cielo: I percorsi della geografia*, Urbino: Istituto di Geografia, 2003.

Briels, J. G. C. A., *Zuidnederlandse boekdrukken en boekverkopers, 1570–1630*, Nieuwkoop: B. de Graaf, 1974.

Capanna, Ernesto, 'Zoologia Kircheriana', in Lo Sardo 2001, 167–177.

The Chaldaean Oracles of Zoroaster as Set Down by Julianus the Theurgist..., ed. Sapere Aude [W. W. Westcott], Gillette, NJ: Heptangle Books, 1978.

Collis, Robert, 'Esotericism and the Russian Orthodox Church During the Reign of Peter the Great (1689–1725)', unpublished paper read at the Conference of the Association for the Study of Esotericism, University of California, Davis, 8–11 June 2006.

Corbett, Margery, and Ronald Lightbown, *The Comely Frontispiece: The Emblematic Title-Page in England, 1550–1660*, London: Routledge & Kegan Paul, 1979.

Curl, James Stevens, *Egyptomania. The Egyptian Revival: A Recurring Theme in the History of Taste*, Manchester: Manchester University Press, 1994.

David, Madeleine-V., *Le Débat sur les écritures et l'hiéroglyphe aux XVIIᵉ et XVIIIᵉ siècles et l'application de la notion de déchiffrement aux écritures mortes*, Paris: S.E.V.P.E.N., 1965.

Daxenmüller, Christoph, 'Ein Gang durch Zeit und Raum: Das Museum Kircherianum', in Beinlich 2002a, 49–66.

——, 'Die Welt als Einheit: Eine Annäherung an das Wissenschaftskonzept des Athanasius Kircher', in Beinlich 2002a, 26–48.

Desmond, Ray, *Great Natural History Books and their Creators*, London: British Library, 2003.

Dizionario biografico degli Italiani, Rome: Istituto della Enciclopedia Italiana, 1960.

Donadoni, Sergio, 'I geroglifici di Athanasius Kircher', in Lo Sardo 2001, 100–110.

Donelli, Simona Antellini, ed., *La fontana dell'organo nei giardini del Quirinale: Nascita, storia e trasformazioni*, Rome: Fratelli Palombi, 1995.

Eco, Umberto, *The Island of the Day Before*, trans. W. Weaver, New York: Harcourt, 1995.

——, 'Kircher tra steganografia e poligrafia', in Lo Sardo 2001, 209–213.

Fideler, David, *Jesus Christ, Sun of God: Ancient Cosmology and Early Christian*

Symbolism, Wheaton: Quest Books, 1993.

Findlen, Paula, ed., *Athanasius Kircher, the Last Man Who Knew Everything*, New York/London: Routledge, 2004.

——, 'A Jesuit's Books in the New World: Athanasius Kircher and His American Readers', in Findlen, 2004, 329–364.

Fletcher, John, 'Athanasius Kircher, a Man under Pressure', in Fletcher 1988, 1–15.

——, 'Athanasius Kircher and Duke August of Brunswick-Lüneburg: A chronicle of friendship', in Fletcher 1988, 99–138.

——, 'Athanasius Kircher, "Germanus Incredibilis": A Study of his Life and Works with a Report on his Unpublished Correspondence', M.A. thesis, University of London, 1966.

——, *Athanasius Kircher und seine Beziehungen zum gelehrten Europa seiner Zeit*, Wiesbaden: Otto Harrassowitz, 1988 (Wolfenbütteler Arbeiten zur Barockforschung, 17).

Fludd, Robert, *Tractatus Secundus, De Natura Simia seu Technica Microcosmi Historia*, Oppenheim: De Bry, 1618.

——, *Utriusque Cosmi Maioris Scilicet et Minoris Metaphysica, Physica Atque Technica Historia… Tomus Primus, De Macrocosmi Historia*, Oppenheim: De Bry, 1617.

Freedberg, David, *The Eye of the Lynx: Galileo, His Friends, and the Beginnings of Modern Natural History*, Chicago: University of Chicago Press, 2002.

Godwin, Joscelyn, *Athanasius Kircher: A Renaissance Man and the Quest for Lost Knowledge*, London: Thames & Hudson, 1979 (Art and Imagination). [1979b]

——, 'Instruments in Robert Fludd's *Utriusque Cosmi…Historia*', *Galpin Society Journal*, 26 (1973), 2–14.

——, 'Kircher and the Occult', in Fletcher 1988, 17–36.

——, *Music, Mysticism and Magic: A Sourcebook*, London: Routledge & Kegan Paul, 1986.

——, *Robert Fludd: Hermetic Philosopher and Surveyor of Two Worlds*, London: Thames & Hudson, 1979 (Art and Imagination). [1979a]

——, *The Pagan Dream of the Renaissance*, Grand Rapids: Phanes Press/London: Thames & Hudson, 2002.

——, *The Theosophical Enlightenment*, Albany: State University of New York Press, 1994.

Gómez de Liaño, Ignacio, *Athanasius Kircher: Itinerario del éxtasis o Las imágenes de un saber universal*, 2 vols, Madrid: Ediciones Siruela, 1985.

Gorman, Michael John, 'Between the Demonic and the Miraculous: Athanasius Kircher and the Baroque Culture of Machines', in Stolzenberg 2001, 59–70.

Gouk, Penelope, 'Making Music, Making Knowledge: The Harmonious Universe of Athanasius Kircher', in Stolzenberg 2001, 71–83.

Gould, Rupert T., *Enigmas: Another Book of Unexplained Facts*, New Hyde Park: University Books, 1965.

Gould, Stephen Jay, *I Have Landed: The End of a Beginning in Natural History*, New York: Harmony Books, 2002.

The [Grove] Dictionary of Art, ed. Jane Turner, London: Macmillan, 1996. [Grove]

Haakman, Anton, *Il Mondo sotterraneo di Athanasius Kircher*, trans. Fulvio Ferrari, n.p.: Garzanti Editore, 1995.

Hancock, Graham, and Santha Faiia, *Heaven's Mirror; Quest for the Lost Civilization*, New York: Three Rivers Press, 1998.

Hapgood, Charles, *Maps of the Ancient Sea Kings: Evidence of Advanced Civilizations in the Ice Ages*, New York: Chilton Books, 1966.

Hein, Olaf, and Rolf Mader, *Athanasius Kircher S.J. in Malta: Ein Beitrag zur Geschichte der Mittelmeer-Insel, zur Biographie Kirchers sowie zur Kultur- und Wissenschaftsgeschichte des 17. Jahrhunderts*, Berlin: Akademie Verlag, 1997 (Studia Kircheriana, Serien-Band VII).

——, *I modelli degli obelischi di Atanasio Kircher, S.J. nel Collegio romano*, Cologne: Böhlan Verlag, 1991 (Studia Kircheriana, I).

Heninger, S. K., Jr, *The Cosmographical Glass: Renaissance Diagrams of the Universe*, San Marino, Calif.: Huntington Library, 1977.

Hermetica: The Greek 'Corpus Hermeticum' and the Latin 'Asclepius' in a New English Translation, with Notes and Introduction, ed. and trans. Brian P. Copenhaver, Cambridge: Cambridge University Press, 1992. [*Corpus Hermeticum*].

Herwart von Hohenburg, Johann Georg, *Thesaurus Hieroglyphicorum*, n.p., n.d. [Munich or Augsburg, 1607–1610?]

Hine, William, 'Athanasius Kircher and Magnetism', in Fletcher 1988, 79–97.

Hsia, Florence, 'Athanasius Kircher's *China Illustrata* (1667): An Apologia Pro Vita Sua', in Findlen 2004, 383–404.

Jäger, Berthold, 'Athanasius Kircher, Geisa und Fulda: Zur Herkunft der Familie, zur Geschichte der Vaterstadt und zur politisch-religiösen Situation im Stift Fulda um die Wende vom 16. zum 17. Jahrhundert', in Beinlich 2002b, 9–40.

Janssen, Johannes, *Geschichte des deutschen Volkes*, vol. VII, 3. Bd., Freiburg im Breisgau, 1904.

Jatta, Barbara, *Lievin Cruyl e la sua opera grafica: Un artista fiammingo nell'Italia del Seicento*, Brussels/Rome: Institut Historique Belge de Rome, 1992.

Judson, J. Richard and Carl Van de Velde, *Corpus Rubenianum Ludwig Burchard, Part XXI: Book Illustrations and Title-Pages*, vol. II, London: Harvey Miller/Philadelphia: Heyden & Son, 1978.

Kelber, Klaus-Peter, and Martin Okrusch, 'Athanasius Kircher Retrospektiv: Pendelschläge geowissenschaftlicher Erkenntnis', in Beinlich 2002a, 137–162.

Klemp, Egon, *Africa in Maps Dating from the Twelfth to the Eighteenth Century*, Leipzig: Edition Leipzig, 1968.

Kuhnmünch, Jacques, 'Le Commerce de la gravure à Paris et à Rome au XVIIe siècle', *Nouvelles de l'Estampe*, 55 (1981), 6–17.

Langenmantel, Hieronymus Ambrosius, *Vita Admodum Reverendi P. Athanasii Kircheri S.J….in Fasciculus Epistolarum Adm. R.O. Athanasii Kircheri Soc. Jesu…*,

Augsburg, 1684.

Leibold, Michael, 'Kircher und China – Die *China Illustrata* als Dokument barocken Wissens', in Beinlich 2002a, 113–124.

Leinkauf, Thomas, *Mundus combinatus: Studien zur Struktur der barocken Universalwissenschaft am Beispiel Athanasius Kirchers SJ (1602–1680)*, Berlin: Akademie Verlag, 1993.

Leospo, Enrica, *La Mensa Isiaca di Torino*, Leiden: Brill, 1978 (Études préliminaires aux religions orientales dans l'empire romain, vol. 70).

Lo Sardo, Eugenio, ed., *Athanasius Kircher: Il Museo del Mondo*, exhibition catalogue, Rome, Palazzo di Venezia, 28 Feb.–22 April 2001, Rome: Edizioni de Luca, 2001.

Lucas, Thomas M., ed., *Saint, Site and Sacred Strategy: Ignatius, Rome and Jesuit Urbanism; Catalogue of the Exhibition*, Vatican City: Biblioteca Apostolica Vaticana, 1990.

McLemee, Scott, 'Athanasius Kircher, Dude of Wonders', *Chronicle of Higher Education*, 28 May 2002.

Marrone, Caterina, *I geroglifici fantastici di Athanasius Kircher*, Viterbo: Stampa Alternativa e Graffiti, 2002.

Marucchi, Orazio, *Gli obelischi egiziani di Roma*, Rome: Ermanno Loescher, 1898.

Mastroianni, Aldo, 'Kircher e l'Oriente nel Museo del Collegio Romano', in Lo Sardo 2001, 65–75.

Mayer-Deutsch, Angela, '"Quasi-Optical Palingenesis": The Circulation of Portraits and the Image of Kircher', in Findlen 2004, 105–129.

Merian, Matthäus, *Iconum Biblicarum*, Wenatchee, Wa.: AVB Press, n.d. [*Icones Biblicae*]

Merrill, Brian L., ed., *Athanasius Kircher (1602–1680), Jesuit Scholar: An Exhibition of His Works in the Harold B. Lee Library Collections at Brigham Young University*, Mansfield Centre, Conn.: Martino Publishing, 2003.

Mersenne, Marin, *Harmonie Universelle*, Paris: Ballard, 1636.

Miller, Peter N., 'Copts and Scholars: Athanasius Kircher in Peiresc's Republic of Letters', in Findlen 2004, 133–148.

Monaco, Giuseppe, 'Tra Tolomeo e Copernico', in Lo Sardo 2001, 145–158.

Morello, Nicoletta, 'Nel corpo della Terra: Il geocosmo di Athanasius Kircher', in Lo Sardo 2001, 179–196.

Das Museum Kircherianum: Die Welt besteht aus geheimen Verknüpfungen/ The Museum Kircherianum: The World is Bound with Secret Knots, exhibition catalogue, The Museum of Jurassic Technology and the Karl Ernst Osthaus-Museum, Hagen, Hagen: Neuer Folkwang Verlag, 2002.

Ndalianis, Angela, *Neo-Baroque Aesthetics and Contemporary Entertainment*, Cambridge, Mass.: MIT Press, 2004.

Olivieri, Luciana Cassanelli, 'Athanasius Kircher: Singolare presenza al Quirinale', in Donelli, 67–77.

Partini, Anna Maria, *Athanasius Kircher e l'alchimia*, Rome: Edizioni Mediterranee, 2004.

Pastine, Dino, *La nascita dell'idolatria: L'Oriente religioso di Athanasius Kircher*, Florence: La Nuova Italia Editrice, 1978 (Pubblicazioni del 'Centro di studi del pensiero filosofico del Cinquecento e del Seicento in relazione ai problemi della scienza', del Consiglio nazionale delle ricerche, no. 13).

[Peiresc, Nicolas-Claude Fabri de], *Correspondance de Peiresc et Aleandro*, 2 vols, ed. and commentary by Jean-François Lhote and Danielle Joyal, Clermont-Ferrand: Éditions Adosa, 1995.

——, *Lettres à Cassiano dal Pozzo*, ed. and commentary by Jean-François Lhote and Danielle Joyal, Clermont-Ferrand: Éditions Adosa, 1989.

Pignoria, Lorenzo, *Vetustissimæ Tabulæ Æneæ Sacris Ægyptiorum simulachris cœlatæ accurata explicatio, in qua antiquissimarum superstitionum origines, progressiones, ritus ad barbaram, Græcam, Romanamque historiam illustrandam enarrantur, & multa scriptorum veterum loca qua explanantur, qua emendantur*, Venice, 1605.

Porter, David, *Ideographia: The Chinese Cipher in Early Modern Europe*, Stanford: Stanford University Press, 2001.

Rachewiltz, Boris de, and Anna Maria Partini, *Roma Egizia: Culti, templi e divinità egizie nella Roma imperiale*, Rome: Edizioni Mediterranee, 1999.

Radelet de Grave, Patricia, 'Le Magnétisme et la localisation en mer', in Marcel Watelet, ed., *Gérard Mercator cosmographe*, Antwerp: Fonds Mercator, 1994, 209–219.

Rak, Michele, *Immagine e scrittura: sei studi sulla teoria e la storia dell'immagine nella cultura del Barocco in Napoli*, Naples: Liguori Editore, 2003.

Rhodes, Neil, and Jonathan Sawday, *The Renaissance Computer: Knowledge Technology in the First Age of Print*, London: Routledge, 2000.

Rivosecchi, Valerio, *Esotismo in Roma Barocca: Studi sul Padre Kircher*, Rome: Bulzoni, 1982 (Biblioteca di Storia dell'Arte).

Ronan, Steven, 'Hekate's Iynx: An Ancient Theurgical Tool', *Alexandria*, 1 (1991), 321–335.

Rowland, Ingrid, *The Ecstatic Journey: Athanasius Kircher in Baroque Rome*, exhibition catalogue, University of Chicago Library, 1 Feb.–7 April 2000, Chicago: University of Chicago Press, 2000.

Rubens and the Book: Title Pages by Peter Paul Rubens; Prepared by Students in the Williams College Graduate Program in the History of Art, exhibition catalogue, Williams College, 2–31 May 1977, Williamstown, Mass.: Chapin Library, 1977.

Saussy, Haun, '*China Illustrata*: The Universe in a Cup of Tea', in Stolzenberg 2001, 105–114.

Scharlau, Ulf, 'Athanasius Kircher und die Musik um 1650: Versuch einer Annäherung an Kirchers Musikbegriff', in Fletcher 1988, 53–67.

——, *Athanasius Kircher (1601–1680) als Musikschriftsteller: Ein Beitrag zur Musikanschauung des Barock*, Marburg: Görich & Weiershäuser, 1969 (Studien zur hessischen Musikgeschichte, 2).

Schilder, Günter, *Monumenta cartographica Neerlandica*, IV, Alphen aan den Rijn: Uitgeverij Canaletto, 1993.

Schneider, Marius, *La danza de espadas y la tarantela; ensayo musicológico*, *etnográfico y arqueológico sobre los ritos medicinales,* Barcelona: Instituto Español de Musicología, 1948.

Schott, Gaspar [Kaspar], *Mechanica Hydraulicopneumatica,* Frankfurt am Main, 1658.

——, *La 'Technica curiosa' di Kaspar Schott,* annotated Italian translation by Maurizio Sonnino, Introduction [Italian and English] by Michael John Gorman and Nick Wilding, Florence: Edizioni dell'Elefante, 2000.

Schürmann, Maike, 'Athanasius Kircher und Latium', in Beinlich 2002a, 125–130.

Selim, Abdel-Kader, *Les Obélisques égyptiens: Histoire et archéologie,* Cairo: Organisme général des Imprimeries gouvernementales, 1991.

Shirley, Rodney W., *The Mapping of the World: Early Printed World Maps 1472–1700,* London: Holland Press, 1984.

Siebert, Harald, 'Kircher and His Critics: Censorial Practice and Pragmatic Disregard in the Society of Jesus', in Findlen 2004, 79–104.

——, 'Kircher und die Astronomie', in Beinlich 2002a, 183–190.

——, 'Vom römischen *Itinerarium* zum Würzburger *Iter*: Kircher, Schott und die Chronologie der Ereignisse', in Beinlich 2002b, 163–188.

Sigurdsson, Haraldur, *Melting the Earth: The History of Ideas on Volcanic Eruptions,* New York: Oxford University Press, 1999.

Smith, Jeffrey Chipps, *Sensuous Worship: Jesuits and the Art of the Early Catholic Reformation in Germany,* Princeton: Princeton University Press, 2002.

Stolzenberg, Daniel, 'The Connoisseur of Magic', in Stolzenberg 2001, 49–57.

——, 'Four Trees, Some Amulets, and the Seventy-two Names of God: Kircher Reveals the Kabbalah', in Findlen 2004, 149–169.

——, 'Kircher Among the Ruins: Esoteric Knowledge and Universal History', in Stolzenberg 2001, 127–139.

——, 'Kircher's Egypt', in Stolzenberg 2001, 115–125.

——, ed., *The Great Art of Knowing: The Baroque Encyclopedia of Athanasius Kircher,* exhibition catalogue, Stanford University Library, April–July 2001, Stanford: Stanford University Libraries, 2001.

Strasser, Gerhard F., 'Science and Pseudoscience: Athanasius Kircher's *Mundus Subterraneus* and His *Scrutinium...Pestis*', in Gerhild Scholz Williams and Stephan K. Schindler, eds, *Knowledge, Science, and Literature in Early Modern Germany,* Chapel Hill: University of North Carolina Press, 1996, 219–240.

——, '*Spectaculum Vesuvii*: Zu zwei neuentdeckten Handschriften von Athanasius Kircher mit seinen Illustrationsvorlagen', in Richard Brinkmann et al., eds, *Theatrum Europaeum: Festschrift für Elida Maria Szarota,* Munich: Wilhelm Fink Verlag, 1982, 363–384.

Taylor, René, 'Hermetism and Mystical Architecture in the Society of Jesus', in Rudolf Wittkower and Irma B. Jaffe, eds, *Baroque Art: The Jesuit Contribution,* New York: Fordham University Press, 1972, 63–97.

Thieme, Ulrich, and Felix Becker, eds, *Allgemeines Lexikon der bildenden Künstler von der Antike bis zur Gegenwart,* Leipzig: W. Engelmann, 1907–1950; Leipzig: Hans Vollmer, 1919–1950. [Thieme-Becker]

Thomsen, Marie-Louise, 'Athanasius Kircher – *Arca Noë* und *Turris Babel*', in Beinlich 2002b, 99–112.

Tooley's Dictionary of Mapmakers, rev. edn, Riverside, Conn.: Early World Press, 2001.

Vehse, Eduard, *Geschichte der Höfe der Häuser Baiern, Würtemberg, Baden und Hessen,* 1. Theil, Hamburg, 1853 (Geschichte der deutschen Höfe, 23).

Verwey, H. de La Fontaine, *Drukkers, liefhebbers en piraten in de zeventiende eeuw,* Amsterdam: N. Israël, 1976.

Vollrath, Hans-Joachim, 'Das Organum mathematicum: Athanasius Kirchers Lehrmaschine', in Beinlich 2002b, 101–136.

——, 'Das Pantometrum Kircherianum: Athanasius Kirchers Messtisch', in Beinlich 2002b, 119–136.

Walker, D. P., *Spiritual and Demonic Magic from Ficino to Campanella,* Notre Dame, Ind.: Notre Dame University Press, 1975.

Wechsler, Lawrence, *Mr Wilson's Cabinet of Wonder,* New York: Vintage Books, 1995.

Wilding, Nick, '"If You Have a Secret, Either Keep It, or Reveal It": Cryptography and Universal Language', in Stolzenberg 2001, 93–103.

Zarpellon, Roberto, 'La musica degli affetti', in Lo Sardo 2001, 261–273.

Sources of Illustrations

With few exceptions, all the illustrations were provided by the Division of Rare and Manuscript Collections, Carl A. Kroch Library, Cornell University, USA, to which the author and publisher are deeply indebted, both for its technical expertise and the friendly cooperation of its staff.

The exceptions are pictures from manuscripts and from books not held by Cornell:

Biblioteca Nazionale Vittorio Emanuele II, Rome: 3.2–3.12, 5.12
Pontificia Università Gregoriana, Rome: 4.5, 4.15
The Butler Library, New York: 2.3, 2.13, 2.17, 2.18, 2.20, 2.21, 2.22, 2.23, 2.24, 2.28, 5.34, 5.36, 5.37, 7.38
The Wellcome Library, London: 7.9
The Bodleian Library, Oxford: 3.1
Author's photographs: 3.13, 3.14, 3.15

Index